Changing International Law
to Meet New Challenges:
Interpretation, Modification
and the Use of Force

To Aida

Andreas Laursen

Changing International Law to Meet New Challenges: Interpretation, Modification and the Use of Force

DJØF Publishing
2006

Changing International Law to Meet New Challenges:
Interpretation, Modification and the Use of Force
1. edition

© 2006 by Jurist- og Økonomforbundets Forlag
DJØF Publishing, Copenhagen

Printed in Denmark 2006
ISBN 87-574-1529-2

Published with support from
»Jurist- og Økonomforbundets legat til støtte af videnskabelig litteratur«

DJØF Publishing
17, Lyngbyvej
P.O.B 2702
DK 2300 Copenhagen
Phone: +45 3913 5500
Fax: +45 3913 5555
e-mail: forlag@djoef.dk
www.djoef-forlag.dk

Cover: Sandro Botticelli (1445-1510): *Pallade e il Centauro*. The painting depicts a woman – who is most often identified as the goddess Pallas Athena but also sometimes as the Amazon Camilla – who is seizing the Centaur by his hair. The painting is generally seen as representing wisdom/reason overcoming or controlling instinct/force. Painted around 1482, it was possibly part of a trilogy with the more well-know paintings the Primavera and the Birth of Venus. All three are now found in the Galleria degli Uffizi in Florence, Italy.

Acknowledgments

This book is my doctoral dissertation, which I defended at the Department of Law at the European University Institute in Florence, Italy. I would like to thank the Danish Rectors' Conference, which sponsored my three years at the European University Institute. I would also like to express my great appreciation to the members of my committee: Dr. Christine Gray from Cambridge University, Professor Francesco Francioni from the European University Institute and Professor Natalino Ronzitti from LUISS University. My special thanks goes to my supervisor, Professor Philip Alston from New York University.

Chapter 9 has appeared in 'The Use of Force and (the State of) Necessity', 37 Vanderbilt Journal of Transnational Law, no. 2, 2004, 485-526.

I would like to thank chief editor Vivi Antonsen at DJØF Publishing for her assistance.

Most of all, I would like to thank my wonderful wife, Aida, who has been present throughout; always patient and providing support and love to me and our children, Annika and Benedict.

Table of Content

Chapter 4: Terrorism in the Work of the United Nations

Part II: The Use of Force Against Terrorists

Chapter 5: Self-defence and Terrorism

Chapter 6: Self-Defence and Terrorism: Cases from the 1980s and 1990s

Chapter 7: Self-defence and Terrorism: Afghanistan 2001

Chapter 8: Self-defence and Terrorism: Three further post-9/11 Cases

Chapter 9: The Use of Force and (the State of) Necessity

Conclusion

Chapter 10: Analyses and Conclusions

PART I

Changing International Law

Chapter 1

Thinking About Change:
Developing the Law of the Charter

1.I. Introduction

Many believe that September 11, 2001 constitutes a watershed in international relations and international law; that 9/11 changed the world.[1] Indeed, it is hardly possible to overestimate the importance of the fateful event on the sunny autumn day in 2001 in contemporary history. I remember how I listened to the news on the radio at 9 am and heard of a plane hitting one of the World Trade Centre towers. I turned on the television only to see the second plane impacting in real time a few minutes later.

Vice President Cheney made one of numerous statements on the security implications, as perceived by the US Administration:

> September 11th, 2001 changed everything for this country. We came
> to recognize our vulnerability to the treats of a new era. If terrorists
> ever do acquire that capability [chemical, biological and nuclear
> weapons], on their own or with help from a terror regime, they will
> use it without the slightest constraint of reason or morality. The
> strategy of deterrence ... will no longer do. Our terrorist enemy has
> no country to defend, no assets to destroy in order to discourage an
> attack. Strategies of containment will not assure our security either.
> There's no containing a terrorist who will commit suicide for the
> purposes of mass slaughter. There's also no containing a terrorist
> state that secretly passes along deadly weapons to a terrorist

---

[1] Slaughter and Burke-White spoke about 'an international constitutional moment' and the need for new rules to respond adequately to the need threats and challenges brought on by September 11 in particular and terrorism in general, Anne-Marie Slaughter and William Burk-White 'An International Constitutional Moment' 43 *Harvard International Law Journal* 2002, 1-21 at 2. Cassese spoke about the September 11 attacks having 'shattering consequences for international law' Antinio Cassese 'Terrorism is also Disrupting Some Crucial Legal Categories of International Law' 12 *European Journal of International Law* 2001 993 at 997. Müllerson, too, speculated that the September 11 attacks 'may have shocked the world enough to open the way to radical reappraisal through customary process of some basic principles of *jus ad bellum,* Rein Müllerson '*Jus ad bellum* and International Terrorism' 32 *Israel Yearbook of International Law* 2003, 1-52 at 9-10.

network. There is only one way to protect ourselves against catastrophic terrorist violence, and that is to destroy the terrorists before they can launch further attacks against the United States.[2]

Here, the concept of pre-emptive use of force is articulated. The enunciation of this concept was very much connected to the events that took place on September 11 as is clear from numerous statements by US administrations officials from the President and down.[3] Still, once time passes by and the events are put into perspective, one may realize that – although momentous – individual events rarely reverse current developments and break completely new ground. They are better seen as catalysts that accentuate and further consolidate a trend that is already present but that may have been difficult to identify without the significant event acting as a kind of signpost.

Hence, the idea of pre-emptive use of force is not new within the American administration: In a 1984 speech, the Secretary of State George Shultz stated that the US could not allow itself to 'become the Hamlet of nations, worrying endlessly over whether and how to respond'. Rather, the Secretary of State called for 'active prevention, preemption, and retaliation'.[4] At the time, Shultz 'was disowned and dismissed by official Washington and on leading editorial pages'.[5] Still, today 'preemption with military force is an operative idea, with wide support', according to Shultz.[6] In the context of Mr. Shultz's reminition, Charles Hill reminds us that 'the war against terrorism that began on September 11, 2001 is the second such campaign that the

---

[2] Remarks by the Vice President to the Heritage Foundation, October 10, 2003. www.heritage.org/Research/MiddleEast/hl800.cfm?renderforprint=1, visited January 7, 2004. See also the Secretary of Defense who made the following reflection concerning the word 'defensive': 'If a terrorist can attack at any time, in any place, and using any technique and it's physically impossible to defend in every place, at every time against every technique, then one needs to calibrate the definition of "defensive". Because literally, the only way to defend against individuals or groups or organizations or countries that have weapons of mass destruction and are bent on using then against you …then the only defense is to take the effort to find those global networks and to deal with them as the United States did in Afghanistan', Secretary Rumsfeld Press Conference at NATO Headquarters, Brussels Belgium, June 6, 2002, available at www.defenselink.mil/news/Jun2002/t06062002_t0606sd.html, visited June 7, 2002.
[3] 'In this new kind of war, America is following is following a new strategy. We are not waiting for further attacks. We are striking our enemies before they can strike us again', President Bush Discusses the Economy and the War on Terror, October 16, 2003, available at www.whitehouse.gov/news/release/2003/10/print/20031016-3.html, visited October 21, 2003.
[4] George P. Shultz 'The Work of Diplomacy', speech given by former Secretary of State George P. Shultz on the occasion of the dedication ceremony for the The George P. Shultz National Foreign Affairs Training Center, on May 29, 2002, in Arlington, Virginia, available at http://www.fpri.org/enotes/diplomacy.20020611.shultz.workofdiplomacy.html, visited October 23, 2004.
[5] Ibid.
[6] Ibid.

U.S. has waged. The first began in the 1970s and continued through most of the 80s. Many have forgotten that we even fought that war – and that we won'.[7]

One may further consider the initiatives by the United Nations bodies immediately following the attacks on September 11. These included the establishment by the Security Council of the Counter-Terrorism Committee (CTC) and are rightly perceived by many as groundbreaking. However, as will be documented in the present thesis, the real change in overall UN attitude to the issue of terrorism took place some years before 2001, during the mid-1990s. Without these earlier changes, the Security Council might not have been able to act so resolutely.

The question of how and when to use force against terrorists is, of course, intimately connected to the more general question of using force in international relations. Here, too, certain single incidents are characterized as ground breaking. The 1999 NATO campaign over Kosovo is seen as a watershed in the potential development of the right to humanitarian intervention. Here again 'the current debate about intervention for human protection purposes also takes place in a historical, political and legal context of evolving international standards of conduct for states and individuals, including the development of new and stronger norms and mechanisms for the protection of human rights'.[8] And it is interesting to observe that the states that were actually involved in the 1999 intervention were reluctant to vindicate the operation under a general doctrine of humanitarian intervention.[9]

Although debates about the use of force in general and for avowed humanitarian purposes in particular increasingly had taken place during the 1990s,[10] it was – more than anything else – the 1999 NATO intervention over Kosovo which really ignited fierce debate. Among the countless analyses of the conflict, that of the Independent International Commission on Kosovo stands out. The Commission found the intervention 'legitimate, but not legal, given existing international law'.[11] The UN

---

[7] Charles Hill 'A Herculean Task: The Myth and Reality of Arab Terrorism' in Strobe Talbott and Nayan Chanda (ed.): *The Age of Terrorism: American and the World after September 11* Perseus Press 2001, 84.

[8] International Commission on Intervention and State Sovereignty *The Responsibility to Protect: Report of the International Commission on Intervention and State Sovereignty* December 2001, page 6, paragraph 1.25, available at: www.idrc.ca, visited November 3, 2003.

[9] See, in particular, Bruno Simma 'NATO, the UN and the use of force: legal aspects' 10 European Journal of International Law (1999) 1-22. See also Antonio Cassese '*Ex iniuria ius oritur*: are we moving towards international legitimation of forcible humanitarian countermeasures in the world community?' 10 European Journal of International Law (1999) 23-30; Antonio Cassese 'A follow-up: forcible humanitarian countermeasures and *opinio necessitatis*' 10 European Journal of International Law (1999) 791-799.

[10] See for example Fernando R. Teson: *Humanitarian Intervention: An Inquiry into Law and Morality*, Transnational Pub; 2nd edition, 1997.

[11] The Independent International Commission on Kosovo: *The Kosovo Report: Conflict, International Response, Lessons Learned* Oxford University Press 2000, 289. See also 186.

Secretary-General Kofi Annan has attempted focus the international community on the task of debate and consensus building. Speaking in the autumn of 1999, Annan stated:

> In response to this turbulent era of crises and interventions, there are those who have suggested that the Charter itself – with its roots in the aftermath of global inter-State war – is ill-suited to guide us in a world of ethnic wars and intra-State violence. I believe they are wrong. The Charter is a living document, whose high principles still define the aspirations of peoples everywhere for lives of peace, dignity and development. Nothing in the Charter precludes a recognition that there are rights beyond borders. Indeed, its very letter and spirit are the affirmation of those fundamental human rights. In short, it is not the deficiencies of the Charter which have brought us to this juncture, but our difficulties in applying its principles to a new era; an era when strictly traditional notions of sovereignty can no longer do justice to the aspirations of peoples everywhere to attain their fundamental freedoms.[12]

Subsequently, the International Commission on Intervention and State Sovereignty produced a report aimed at providing precise guidance for states faced with human protection claims in other states and proposing a principle based on the 'responsibility to protect'. The Commission emphasized how issues and preoccupations of the 21st century present new and often fundamentally different types of challenges from those that faced the world in 1945, when the United Nations was founded. As new realities and challenges have emerged, so too have new expectations for action and new standards of conduct in national and international affairs: 'the conditions under which sovereignty is exercised – and intervention is practiced – have changed dramatically since 1945[13] ... By signing the Charter, states accept the responsibilities of membership flowing from that signature. There is no transfer or dilution of state sovereignty. But there is a necessary re-characterization involved: from *sovereignty as control* to *sovereignty as responsibility* in both internal functions and external duties[14] ... This has to be coupled

---

[12] Secretary-General Presents his Annual Report to General Assembly, 20 September 1999, Press Release, SG/SM/7136, GA/9596, available at http://www.un.org/News/Press/docs/1999/19990920.sgsm7136.html, visited December 28, 2004.
[13] International Commission on Intervention and State Sovereignty *The Responsibility to Protect: Report of the International Commission on Intervention and State Sovereignty* December 2001, page 7, paragraph 1.33, available at: www.idrc.ca, visited November 3, 2003.
[14] Ibid., page 13, paragraph 2.14, emphasis in original.

with the idea that if a state is unwilling or unable to assume said responsibility, 'that responsibility must be borne by the broader community of states'.[15]

During the 2004 UN General Assembly, the Canadian Prime Minister Paul Martin further elaborated on the Commissions findings: 'Put simply, there is still no explicit provision in international law for intervention on humanitarian grounds. The "responsibility to protect" is intended to fill this gap. It says that we should have the legal right to intervene in a country on the grounds of humanitarian emergency alone when the government of that country is unwilling or unable to protect their people from extreme harm as a result of internal war, repression or state failure. ... Thus customary international law is evolving to provide a solid basis in the building of a normative framework for collective humanitarian intervention. To speed it along, member-states should now adopt a General Assembly Resolution recognising the evolution of sovereignty to encompass the international responsibility to people'.[16]

Slaughter and Feinstein have recently elaborated on the ideas initially presented by the International Commission on Intervention and State Sovereignty by proposing a corollary principle to the 'responsibility to protect', related to the field of global security, i.e. a collective 'duty to prevent' nations run by rulers without internal checks on their power from acquiring or using weapons of mass destruction.[17] The duty to prevent stems from the premise that the rules now governing the use of force, found in the UN Charter are inadequate and that new threats require a proactive rather than a reactive stance.[18] Similarly, the authors argued that the concept of sovereignty is developing and ought now to imply responsibilities as well as rights. This latter idea is, in fact, not as much of a challenge to the traditional understanding of sovereignty as the authors suggest. Hence, the close connection between rights and duties has traditional been central to international law. As Eagleton wrote in 1928: 'International law is not concerned with the form of organization, which the political entity recognized might care to adopt. The community of nations asks only that its members shall have machinery capable of discharging effectively its obligations under international law'.[19] The International Court of Justice, too, has stressed obligations: In 1948, the Court held that among the conditions for admission to the United Nations were acceptance of the obligations of the

---

[15] Ibid., Foreword, page viii.

[16] Statement by the right honourable Paul Martin Prime Minister of Canada to the fifty-ninth session of the United Nations General Assembly, New York, 22 September 2004, www.un.int/canada/s-22Sep2004Martin.htm, visited October 4, 2004.

[17] Lee Feinstein and Anne-Marie Slaughter 'A Duty to Prevent' *Foreign Affairs* January-February 2004, 136.

[18] Lee Feinstein and Anne-Marie Slaughter 'A Duty to Prevent' *Foreign Affairs* January-February 2004, 137.

[19] Clyde Eagleton *The Responsibility of States in International Law* New York University Press 1928, 26

Charter, ability to carry out these obligations and the willingness to do so.[20] In 1950, the ICJ found with regard to South Africa that 'to retain the rights derived from the Mandate and to deny the obligations there under could not be justified'.[21]

Finally, in December 2004, a High-Level Panel, organized by Kofi Annan in response to the 2003 Iraq war, submitted its report; a report that put forward a new vision of collective security, addressing all of the major threats to international peace and security felt around the world.[22] Among other things, the Panel found that

> the attacks of 11 September 2001 revealed that States, as well as collective security institutions, have failed to keep pace with changes in the nature of threats. ... Smaller and smaller numbers of people are able to inflict greater and greater amounts of damage, without the support of any State. ... Technologies designed to improve daily life can be transformed into instruments of aggression. We have yet to fully understand the impact of these changes, but they herald a fundamentally different security climate — one whose unique opportunities for cooperation are matched by an unprecedented scope for destruction.[23]

Echoing the above-mentioned International Commission on Intervention and State Sovereignty, the Panel asserted that

> In signing the Charter of the United Nations, States not only benefit from the privileges of sovereignty but also accept its responsibilities. Whatever perceptions may have prevailed when the Westphalian system first gave rise to the notion of State sovereignty, today it clearly carries with it the obligation of a State

---

[20] 1948 ICJ 62.

[21] 1950 ICJ 133. Certain states have also often made reference to rights come with obligations and duties. Thus, in 1981, the Israeli representative admonished Iraq that 'a State cannot invoke in its favour benefits deriving from certain provisions of international law without being prepared at the same time to abide by the duties flowing from international law', S/PV.2280, June 12, 1981, page 46.

[22] A More Secure World: Our Shared Responsibility Report of the High-level Panel on Threats, Challenges and Change, A/59/565, December 2, 2004, available at www.un.org/secureworld, visited December 4, 2004, page 6. See Marco Odello 'Commentary on The United Nations' High-Level Panel on Threats, Challenges and Change' 10 *Journal of Conflict & Security Law* (2005) 231-262.

[23] A More Secure World: Our Shared Responsibility Report of the High-level Panel on Threats, Challenges and Change, A/59/565, December 2, 2004, available at www.un.org/secureworld, visited December 4, 2004, page 19.

to protect the welfare of its own peoples and meet its obligations to the wider international community.[24]

Among the challenges dealt with by the Panel was the issue of the use of force.[25] Addressing some of the concerns articulated by the US administration, the Panel asked: 'what happens if peaceful prevention fails? If none of the preventive measures so far described stop the descent into war and chaos? If distant threats do become imminent? Or if imminent threats become actual? Or if a non-imminent threat nonetheless becomes very real and measures short of the use of military force seem powerless to stop it'?[26] Considering Article 51 of the Charter, the Panel went on to endorse anticipatory self-defence in response to an imminent threat.[27] When it came to a non-imminent or non-proximate threat, the Panel found that the obvious answer is to put the matter before the Security Council. 'For those impatient with such a response, the answer must be that, in a world full of perceived potential threats, the risk to the global order and the norm of non - intervention on which it continues to be based is simply too great for the legality of unilateral preventive action, as distinct from collectively endorsed action, to be accepted. Allowing one to so act is to allow all'.[28] In conclusion regarding self-defence, the Panel did 'not favour the rewriting or reinterpretation of Article 51'.[29]

1.II. How does Law Change?

As should be clear from preceding overview, a very fervent debate is currently taking place as to how and when to use force in international relations.[30] Even if the UN

---

[24] A More Secure World: Our Shared Responsibility Report of the High-level Panel on Threats, Challenges and Change, A/59/565, December 2, 2004, available at www.un.org/secureworld, visited December 4, 2004, pages 21-22

[25] A More Secure World: Our Shared Responsibility Report of the High-level Panel on Threats, Challenges and Change, A/59/565, December 2, 2004, available at www.un.org/secureworld, visited December 4, 2004, pages 45-49.

[26] A More Secure World: Our Shared Responsibility Report of the High-level Panel on Threats, Challenges and Change, A/59/565, December 2, 2004, available at www.un.org/secureworld, visited December 4, 2004, page 53.

[27] A More Secure World: Our Shared Responsibility Report of the High-level Panel on Threats, Challenges and Change, A/59/565, December 2, 2004, available at www.un.org/secureworld, visited December 4, 2004, page 54.

[28] A More Secure World: Our Shared Responsibility Report of the High-level Panel on Threats, Challenges and Change, A/59/565, December 2, 2004, available at www.un.org/secureworld, visited December 4, 2004, page 55.

[29] Ibid.

[30] On a more personal note, writer Michael Walzer wrote in 2004 that he had not 'dropped the presumption against intervention' that he defended in his book *Just and Unjust Wars*; he had, however, 'found it easier and easier to override the presumption' and has become more willing to call for

Secretary-General's High-level Panel found that 'the Charter of the United Nations, properly understood and applied, is equal to the task' of regulating the use of force,[31] others have found that the rules governing the use of force are in 'serious disarray, their application erratic and their interpretation contested'.[32] The Kosovo Commission, for its part, cautioned that 'allowing this gap between legality and legitimacy to persist is not healthy' thereby encouraging further debate about the issue.[33] These debates about the changing circumstances under which it is right to fight, naturally raised question about how international law adjusts to new threats and challenges. Thus, one may ask how (international) law adapts and changes when this becomes necessary.[34] Or, as Kohen put it: Since the resort to force is more prevalent today than a decade ago, it is legitimate – and, one may add, highly interesting and pertinent – to inquire whether international law has undergone change in this important sphere.[35]

The question just posed implicitly accepts as axiomatic that law in fact does change: 'It is well accepted that one of the most important features of an effective legal system is its capacity to reflect the changing needs and demands of a society in which it operates. In view of this basic requirement, it is clear that a viable legal system presupposes continuous law-making activity'.[36] As an aside, one may ask where the impetus for legal change comes from. The straightforward answer is that changing circumstances generate political demands for change in the law.[37] Or, as Thirlway put it:

---

military intervention in the face of human rights horrors, Michael Walzer *Arguing about War* Yale University Press, 2004 xiii.

[31] A More Secure World: Our Shared Responsibility Report of the High-level Panel on Threats, Challenges and Change, A/59/565, December 2, 2004, available at www.un.org/secureworld, visited December 4, 2004, page 53.

[32] Gareth Evans 'When is it Right to Fight?' 46 *Survival* 2004, 59-82 at 59.

[33] The Independent International Commission on Kosovo: *The Kosovo Report: Conflict, International Response, Lessons Learned* Oxford University Press 2000, 186.

[34] For a recent essay on this issue with regard to the United Nations Convention on the Law of the Sea (UNCLOS), see Alan Boyle 'Further Development of the Law of the Sea Convention: Mechanisms for Change' 54 *International and Comparative Law Quarterly* 2005, 563-584.

[35] Marcelo Kohen 'The use of force by the United States after the end of the Cold War and its impact on international law' in Michael Byers og Georg Nolte (ed.) *United States Hegemony and the Foundations of International Law,* Cambridge University Press, 2003, 197-223 at 197.

[36] Danilenko: *Law-Making in the International Community*, Dordrecht: Nijhoff, 1993, 1.

[37] One recent example of an articulation of perceived changing needs and demands with relevance for international law is the following statement by the United States National Security Advisor: 'The United States has made very clear that we believe it's time to move on to a new era. The 1972 ABM [Anti-Ballistic Missile] Treaty belonged to another era. It belonged to a relationship of implacable hostility between the United States and the Soviet Union and so it's time to move on. ... We think of this [the move away from the ABM treaty] as really proposing a new strategic architecture that is more in line with the threats of today. It cannot be a treaty that was born in 1972, when the United States and the Soviet Union were implacably hostile enemies, when the Soviet Union was sitting with its troops in Poland, where we just were seeing the NATO flag flying, that that world [the Cold War world], somehow enshrined in the ABM Treaty, can possible be the cornerstone of strategic stability for 2001.

'Law does not develop of its own motion, but only as development is required by the development of relationships in the society in which it operates'.[38] This dynamic is well recognized[39] and uncontroversial and has found its most simple expression in Henkin's 'Law is politics'.[40] International law, as a legal system, is subjected to the imperative of being able to accommodate change. Yet, international law is, on occasion, criticized for being static and out of touch with reality.

On a philosophical level, such perceptions of international law as being static may be directed at the theoretical foundations of the discipline: If a legal system is perceived as being the union of primary and secondary rules, the absence of for example a secondary 'rules of change' may imbue the primary rules with a static character because the 'only mode of change in the rules known to such a society will be the slow process of growth, whereby courses of conduct once thought optional become first habitual or usual, and then obligatory' or vise versa where prohibitions 'once severely dealt with, are first tolerated and then pass unnoticed'.[41] Leaving aside the question of international law's qualities as law properly so-called or designation as a primitive or simple legal system, it has been argued that international law, in form, 'resembles such a regime of primary rules' and lacks, *inter alia*, 'the secondary rules of change'.[42] In other words, 'international law has always been a legal system which largely lacked strict formal requirements regarding law-making'.[43]

At a jurisprudential level, individual members of the International Court of Justice have, on occasion, also expressed concerns over the obstacle of past or traditional doctrine, while at the same time endorsing and emphasizing international law's dynamism: 'Law is a living deed, not a brilliant honours-list of past writers whose work

---

It makes no sense'. National Security Advisor, Ms C. Rise, on 'Meet the Press', June 17, 2001, available at http://www.msnbc.com/news/588007.asp, visited June 25, 2001.

[38] H. W. A. Thirlway *International Customary Law and Codification: An Examination of the Continuing Role of Custom in the Present Period of Codification of International Law* A. W. Sijthoff, 1972, 33-34.

[39] 'Legitimate interest may be the *inspiration*, motive power or force behind certain practices of States leading to the evolution of a customary rule of general international law. But of course the *source* of the eventual rule is the custom or practice: the interests involved are only the reason for it', Gerald Fitzmaurice: *The Law and Procedure of the International Court of Justice*, Cambridge, Cambridge University Press, 1995, Vol. I, 199-200. Quoted in Hugh Thirlway: 'The Law and Procedure of the International Court of Justice, 1960-1989, 61 *British Yearbook of International Law*, 1990, 15.

[40] 'Law is made by political actors, through political procedures, for political ends' Louis Henkin *International Law: Politics and Values* Kluwer Law International (1995) 4.

[41] H. L. A. Hart *The Concept of Law* 2nd ed. 1994, Oxford University Press, 92 and 227.

[42] H. L. A. Hart *The Concept of Law* 2nd ed. 1994, Oxford University Press, 214 and 227.

[43] Danilenko: *Law-Making in the International Community*, Dordrecht: Nijhoff, 1993, xiv. The author, however, appear to contradict this assertion when he writes that 'international law, like other systems of law, also contains a number of rules defining the means of making and changing substantive legal prescriptions'. Ibid., 11 and 14.

of course compels respect but who cannot, except for a few great minds, be thought to have had such a vision of the future that they could always see beyond their own times. Everything goes to show how difficult it is to free ourselves from the servitudes of the past through which we have ourselves lived and from traditions we have always respected'.[44] One may also quote Judge Jessup from his dissenting opinion in the 1966 *South West Africa Case*: 'The law can never be oblivious to the changes in life, circumstance and community standards in which it functions. Treaties – especially multipartite treaties of a constitutional or legislative character – cannot have an absolute immutable character'.[45] The Court as such has explicitly accepted and expressed the dynamic nature of international law: 'Throughout its history, the development of international law has been influenced by the requirements of international life'.[46] Elsewhere the Court emphasized that 'in seeking to determine the law applicable to this case, the Court has to bear in mind the continuous evolution of international law'.[47] In the 1974 *Fisheries Jurisdiction Case*, the Court made clear that 'the possibility of the law changing is ever present'.[48]

---

[44] Legal Consequences for States of the Continued Presence of South Africa in Namibia (South West Africa) Notwithstanding Security Council Resolution 276 (1970), Separate Opinion by Judge Ammoun, ICJ Reports, 1971, 75. Writing about the right of self-determination and the UN Charter and UN resolutions

[45] 1966 ICJ 6 at 439. Jessup also makes reference to the Nuremberg Tribunal's Judgment of October 1, 1946, in which it held: 'The law is not static but by continual adaptation follows the needs of a changing world', 1966 ICJ 440, text of Nuremberg Judgment is found in 41 *American Journal of International Law* (1947) 172. Similarly, individual judges at the Court who possessed a vision for a new international law were eager to embrace the need for change: 'international life is in a state of constant evolution, and ...international law must always be a reflection of that life', The *Corfu Channel Case*, Individual Opinion by Judge Alvarez, ICJ Reports, 1949, 41 (For an, arguably unkind, review of the legal thinking of Judge Alvarez, see William Smore 'The New International Law of Alejandron Alvarez' 52 *American Journal of International Law* (1958) 41). Elsewhere Judge Alvarez stated: 'Indeed, since that time the international life of peoples and, consequently, the law of nations have consistently undergone profound changes and have assumed new directions and tendencies which must be taken into consideration. The Court must, therefore, declare what is the new international law which is based upon the present requirements and conditions of the life of peoples: otherwise, it would be applying a law which is obsolete in many respects, and would disregard these requirements and conditions as well as the spirit of the Charter which is the principal source of the new international law', *Interpretation of Peace Treaties with Bulgaria, Hungary and Romania*, Dissenting Opinion of Judge Alvarez, ICJ Reports, 1950, 177.

[46] 1949 ICJ 174 at 178.

[47] Case Concerning Barcelona Traction, Light and Power Company, Limited, ICJ Reports, 1970, p. 34, paragraph 37.

[48] ICJ Reports 1974, p. 20, paragraph 40. The evolutionary nature of law is also implicit in the statement that 'the Court, as a court of law, cannot render judgment *sub specie legis ferendae*, or anticipate the law before the legislator has laid it down', Ibid. Paragraph 24-25, 53. One might add the statements of the Court from the Case Concerning Military and Paramilitary Activities in and against Nicaragua: 'It has to be considered whether there might be indications of a practice illustrative of belief in a kind of general right for States to intervene, directly or indirectly, with or without armed force, in

1.III. Doctrinal Disputes

At a doctrinal level, the question of how international law developed or stood up under the fire of various international crises has always engaged scholars.[49] A well-known example is Franck's famed 1970 article on the changing norms governing the use of force.[50] Although Franck's dire analysis did draw an immediate reaction,[51] the debating climate in public international law may seem somewhat more ferocious today. This impression may, of course, be due to the proximity in time of the current debate. Even taking this into account, however, the views of legal scholars have elicited strong reactions in recent years. One example is Francis Boyle's call for a boycott of Franck and Glennon's book on Foreign Relations and National Security in response to an op-ed by Glennon in the New York Times in November of 2001.[52] Glennon received a more traditional response to a subsequent article in *Foreign Affairs* in which he again proclaimed the 'Death of a law'.[53] While scuffles between colleagues in academe may be commonplace, it is surprising when a judge at the International Court of Justice (ICJ)

---

support of an internal opposition in another State, whose cause appeared particularly worthy by reason of the political and moral values with which it was identified. For such a general right to come into existence would involve a fundamental modification of the customary principle of non-intervention.' (ICJ Reports 1986, p. 108, paragraph 206) and 'Reliance by a State on a novel right or an unprecedented exception to the principle [of non-intervention] might, if shared in principle by other States, tend towards a modification of customary international law. ' (Case Concerning Military and Paramilitary Activities in and against Nicaragua, ICJ Reports 1986, p. 109, paragraph 207)

[49] This is so even if international law scholarship – like most other things – passes through phases and have certain topics that are more in vogue than others at certain times. Hence, in 1986, the distinguished British professor Brownlie lamented that 'the use of force is a subject younger lawyers tend to avoid these days', Ian Brownlie 'The United Nations Charter and the Use of Force, 1945-1985' in A. Cassese (ed.) *The Current Legal Regulation of the Use of Force* Martinus Nijhoff 1986, 491. Brownlie found that in the 1980s human rights and the protection of the environment attracted greater attention in spite of the fact that, according to Brownlie, the main threats to human rights and the environment came *inter alia* from the use of force by states. At the beginning of the 21st century, debates about international law and the use of force have gained new momentum. Spurred on by the end of the Cold War as well as the armed conflicts over Kosovo (1999), Afghanistan (2001) and Iraq (2003), in addition to the publication of the two recent security strategies by the US administration, international legal scholarship has seen nothing if not an overwhelming resurgence of the interest in the regulation of the use of force.

[50] Thomas M. Franck 'Who Killed Article 2(4)? Or: Changing Norms Governing the Use of Force by States' 64 *American Journal of International Law* (1970) 809-837.

[51] Louis Henkin 'The Reports of the Death of Article 2(4) Are Greatly Exaggerated' 65 *American Journal of International Law* (1971) 544-548.

[52] See http://legalminds.lp.findlaw.com/list/forintlaw/msg00899.htlm, visited August 24, 2004.

[53] Michael J. Glennon 'Why the Security Council Failed' *Foreign Affairs* May 2003 - June 2003. See the responses: Edward C. Luck 'Stayin' Alive: The Rumors of the UN's Death Have Been Exaggerated', Anne-Marie Slaughter 'Misreading the Record', and Ian Hurd 'Too Legit to Quit' all in *Foreign Affairs* July 2003 - August 2003.

alerts the Court to authors who reject the international legal regulation of the use of force found in the UN Charter:

> Everybody will be aware of the current crisis of the United Nations system of maintenance of peace and security, of which Articles 2 (4) and 51 are cornerstones. We currently find ourselves at the outset of an extremely controversial debate on the further viability of the limits on unilateral military force established by the United Nations Charter. ... What we cannot but see outside the courtroom is that, more and more, legal justification of the use of force within the system of the United Nations Charter is discarded even as a fig leaf, *while an increasing number of writers appear to prepare for the outright funeral of international legal limitations on the use of force.* If such voices are an indication of the direction in which legal-political discourse on use of force not authorized by the Charter might move, do we need more to realize that for the Court to speak up as clearly and comprehensively as possible on that issue is never more urgent than today?[54]

While Judge Simma avoided naming names, Judge *ad hoc* Rigaux, who was appointed by Iran in the same case, juxtaposed the late Oscar Schachter and Thomas Franck, 'ces deux éminents juristes', with John Bolton, the former US Under Secretary of State for Arms Control and International Security and current recess-appointed US ambassador to the United Nations, and in particular his article entitled 'Is There Really "Law" in International Affairs?'[55] In this article, John Bolton *inter alia* made the following assertions and conclusions: International law is used to constrain the US and its accumulating force 'will even more dramatically impede us [the US] in the future';[56] the UN Charter basically represents a 'political deal' rather than a 'legal obligation';[57] and 'international law is not law; it is a series of political and moral arrangements that stand or fall on their own merits, and anything else is simply theology and superstition masquerading as law'.[58]

---

[54] The Oilplatforms Case, Separate Opinion of Judge Simma, page 3-4, paragraph 6 (emphasis added)(footnotes omitted).

[55] The Oilplatforms Case, Opinion Individuelle de M. le Juge Rigaux, page 20, paragraph 31, available at www.icj-cij.org, visited December 4, 2003.

[56] John R. Bolton 'Is There Really "Law" in International Affairs?' 10 *Transnational Law and Contemporary Problems* (2000) 1- 48 at 8.

[57] John R. Bolton 'Is There Really "Law" in International Affairs?' 10 *Transnational Law and Contemporary Problems* (2000) 1- 48 at 9.

[58] John R. Bolton 'Is There Really "Law" in International Affairs?' 10 *Transnational Law and Contemporary Problems* (2000) 1- 48 at 48.

Similarly reacting to an author's reflection on international law,[59] the President of the American Society of International Law issued a rallying cry for supporters of international law to 'fight back'.[60] Although Slaughter also mentions John Bolton, her immediate concern was Jeb Rubenfeld who wrote that the Kosovo conflict 'illustrates how Americans do not quite recognize the UN Charter as law', primarily because of the lack of enforceability, which is perceived as necessary in order for law to possess a claim to meaning.[61]

Considering these debates, one may intuitively agree with one side or the other – assuming that it is possible to speak of only two 'sides'. Ignoring the opposite side can, however, only be done at one's own peril because the academic debate matters – as can be seen from the fact that judges at the ICJ care enough to express concern – and opinions and conclusions may have an impact. Hence, as pointed out by Gray, there are signs that states are adopting some of the arguments proposed by authors.[62] Byers and Chesterman, too, find that a 'novel conception of international law [] is being constructed and reinforced by a limited group of Anglo-American international lawyers'.[63]

One of the 'Anglo-American international lawyers' they may have had in mind – and certainly someone who has not shied away from controversy – is the already mentioned Michael Glennon.[64] He has made it clear on various occasions that he

---

[59] Jeb Rubenfeld 'The Two World Orders' 27 *The Wilson Quarterly* (2003) 22-36.

[60] Anne-Marie Slaughter 'A Rallying Cry' *ASIL Newsletter* November/December 2003, 1 and 6. Mention may also be had of Brad R. Roth who devoted a chapter to scholarly discourse and ended up opining that 'juridical scholarship should ... contribute to the preservation and strengthening of the legal order by resisting conclusions that undermine its practical and moral relevance' Brad R. Roth 'Bending the Law, Breaking it, or Developing it? The United States and its Humanitarian Use of Force in the Post-Cold War Era' in Michael Byers and Georg Nolte (ed.) *United States Hegemony and the Foundations of International Law,* Cambridge University Press, 2003, 232-263 at 261.

[61] Jeb Rubenfeld 'The Two World Orders' 27 *The Wilson Quarterly* (2003) 22-36 at 29.

[62] Christine Gray *International Law and the Use of Force* 2nd ed. Oxford University Press, 2004, 22-23.

[63] Michael Byers and Simon Chsterman 'Changing the Rukes about Rules? Unilateral Humanitarian Intervention and the Future of International Law' in J. L. Holzgrefe and Robert O. Keohane (ed.) *Humanitarian Intervention: Ethical, Legal and Political Dilemmas* Cambridge University Press, 2003, 190.

[64] One could mention a number of other authors who have similarly been critical of the role of international law when it comes to the use of force, such as Mark Weisburd and Anthony Arend. In 1997, Weisburd concluded that 'state practice simply does not support the proposition that the rules of the UN Charter can be said to be a rule of customary international law', see A. Mark Weisburd *Use of Force: The Practice of States since World War II* Penn State Press, 1997, 315. Weisburd reached his conclusion based on the conception of (international) law where rules of international law are those that states either obey generally or that are the basis for sanctions against states in the event of disobedience, 10 and 21. International conduct must therefore by measured against 'international sanctions' that 'have the effect of reversing the conduct of the acting state and of leading that state to make good any harm it has done. If states other than the actor react to the conduct with behavior clearly not capable of reversing the conduct, they in effect indicate that they are willing to live with the

believes that 'there is, today, no coherent international law concerning intervention by states'[65] and 'the regime governing the use of force, that has been established by the UN Charter, has collapsed'.[66]

---

conduct in question. That, in turn, suggests that those states do not regard the conduct as unlawful, since labelling behavior "unlawful" in a customary system is simply another way of saying that the participants in the system have concluded that they *cannot* live with the behavior and will take steps to see that it does not occur'. Thus, 'condemnations standing alone, then, cannot reasonably be expected to affect state behavior and therefore are not "sanctions"', 316-317. More recently, he has – agreeing with Michael Glennon – reiterated that 'the inconsistency between state practice and the Charter is so great that the Charter can be said to state international law only by distorting the concept of international law beyond recognition', see A. Mark Weisburd 'The War in Iraq and the Dilemma of Controlling the International Use of Force' 39 *Texas International Law Journal* (2004) 521-560 at 539. In 1993, Anthony Arend and Robert Beck. Here the authors found that 'based on what states have been saying and what they have been doing, there simply does not seem to be a *legal* prohibition on the use of force against the political independence and territorial integrity of states as provided in even a modified version of Article 2(4) [of the UN Charter]. The rule craeting process, authoritative state practice, has rejected that norm', Anthony Clark Arend and Robert J. Beck *International Law and the Use of Force: Beyond the UN Charter Paradigm*, Routledge 1993, 185. This book was preceded by Arend's article 'International Law and the Recourse to Force: A Shift in Paradigms' 27 *Stanford Journal of International Law* 1990, 1. The legal approach that Arend and Beck employed in order to reach said conclusion, has been elaborated upon in Arend's *Legal Rules and International Society*, Oxford University Press, 1999. Here, Arend takes a swing at traditional positivism when he posits that 'many positivists would assert that the mere existence of the U.N. Charter provision is sufficient to demonstrate that Article 2(4) is reflective of a legal rule. This claim, I believe, denies the right of states to withdraw their consent through custom and thus denies the dynamic nature of international law', 75. In order to determine the existence of a rule of international law, Arend proposes what he terms the 'authority-control' test: a putative rule of international law can be regarded as 'law' if it possesses authority and control, 87. A purported rule is authoritative if it is perceived by decision-making elites as law. In addition, the rule must be controlling: it must be reflected in the actual practice of states. If, however, there are substantial indications that a treaty provision generally lacks authority or is no longer controlling of behaviour, it is no longer law. Under this test, the UN Charter prohibition in Article 2, paragraph 4, fails: 'states have chosen to reject this strict proscription in favor of a more permissive norm...', Anthony Clark Arend and Robert J. Beck *International Law and the Use of Force: Beyond the UN Charter Paradigm*, Routledge 1993.

[65] Michael J. Glennon *Limits of Law, Prerogatives of Power: Interventionism after Kosovo* Palgrave, 2001, 2. In this, his main work, Glennon, in the words of one reviewer 'scoffs at what the structure of Charter-based use-of-force law has become, labelling it as a fifty-year doctrinal experiment that no longer works, and taking a sharp logical axe to the many attempts at propping up that venerable structure'. Charles Tiefer 'Recent Books on International Law: Book Review: Limits of Law, Prerogatives of Power: Intervention after Kosovo. By Michael J. Glennon' 96 *American Journal Of International Law* (2002) 489-493 at 489. In a separate chapter, Glennon addresses Security Council practice. Glennon argues for a fundamental difference between practice of states and practice of the Security Council and finds that the VCLT 'seems simplistic' when it fails to differentiate between the effect of subsequent practice under a bilateral and multilateral treaty respectively: 'There is, in sum, a powerful reason to treat states differently from the Security Council in applying the doctrine of desuetude'. This reason being that 'states are the creators; the Security Council is a creature', Michael J. Glennon *Limits of Law, Prerogatives of Power: Interventionism after Kosovo* Palgrave, 2201, Chapter 4 at 126. Such a statement is entirely dependent upon the specifics of the situation at hand.

1.IV. Secondary Rules of Recognition and Change

In order to properly argue about the conclusion of a scholar like Glennon, however, it is necessary to go behind the fact and ask *how* the person making the claim reached his conclusion because the root causes of disagreement between international lawyers are often their sometimes starkly divergent views on foundational aspects of international law.[67] This brings us back to the philosophical level and the question of choice of approach: In 1999, Slaughter and Ratner arranged a Symposium on method in international law. The aim was to bring different theories together in one place and to contrast the workings of the various approaches. In their conclusion, they found that the choice of method was often highly personal and informed by 'differing understandings and beliefs about how each individual lawyer can best advance his or her normative commitments'.[68] Implicit in the reference to 'normative commitments' is the understanding that the choice of method may be dictated by the aims pursued and, furthermore, as a logical conclusion and as pointed out by Farer, 'one's preferred conception of the nature of law [i.e. method] can affect one's conclusions about its [the law's] contents'.[69] Based on these observations, the final recommendation from the symposium organizers made good sense: International lawyers 'should be as self-conscious as possible' about their choice of method.[70] Here, one could reasonably add

---

Even if a certain body is created by states, these may have delegated a number of powers to the new body, as is prominently the case with the European Union. Hence, the modes of operation and authority of the Security Council have to be established concretely and cannot be determined by the fact that it is a creature of states.

[66] Michael J. Glennon 'Seventeenth Waldemar A. Soft Lecture in International Law' 181 *Military Law Review* (2004) 143.

[67] Michael Byers 'The Shifting Foundations of International Law: A decade of Forceful Measures against Iraq' 13 *European Journal of International Law* 2002, 21-41 at 22-23.

[68] Anne-Marie Slaughter and Steven R. Ratner 'Symposium on Method in International Law: The Method is the Message' 93 *American Journal of International Law* (1999) 410-423 at 422. See a similar effort in the German Yearbook of International Law: Anne Peters 'There is Nothing More Practical than a Good Theory: An Overview of Contemporary Approaches to International Law' 44 *German Yearbook of International Law* 2001, 25-38. See generally: 'Focus Section: International Theory' 44 *German Yearbook of International Law* 2001, 25-200.

[69] Tom J. Farer 'Human Rights in Law's Empire: The Jurisprudence War' 85 *American Journal of International Law* 1991, 117-127 at 117.

[70] Anne-Marie Slaughter and Steven R. Ratner 'Symposium on Method in International Law: The Method is the Message' 93 *American Journal of International Law* (1999) 410-423 at 423. The conclusions do not seem far from what Richard Falk advised in 1988: 'What I am trying to say is that one of the least appreciated ideological battles concerns the degree to which a traditional view of the law-making process continues to be attributed validity by international jurists. My argument is that this is inevitably a political choice. There is no technical solution to this choice, and we must have the integrity not to hide behind professional arguments, but to confront the implications directly and honestly', Richard Falk 'To what Extent are International Law and International Lawyers Ideological Neutral?, Presentation' in Antonio Cassese and Joseph H. H. Weiler (ed.) *Change and Stability in*

then Professor Higgins' caution and observation about the essential relationship between law and policy and the desirability that the policy factors are dealt with systematically and openly, including allowing public scrutiny and discussion about choices made.[71] Similarly, professor Simma agreed with the 'call for self-consciousness of one's own political, economic, religious, ethical, male or other bias'.[72]

Turning to Glennon, he has provided an outline of the sociological reasons behind the demise of the Charter rules in various publications; the main one being 'an unbridgeable attitudinal chasm among the peoples of the world'.[73] Among other reasons, Glennon has listed 'the existence of great disparities in power among states;[74] a cultural fault line that divided nations of the North and West from nations of the South and East on the most fundamental of issues: when use of force is appropriate;[75] and differences in attitude over the need to comply with the UN use of force rules.[76] Even if these reasons are accepted as correctly identified, they do not address legal mechanisms. In a footnote, Glennon explains that much of his book is directed at assessing the soundness of international law's meta-rules or structural rules that shape substantive rules regulating intervention.[77] As pointed out above, these are the rules designated as 'secondary' by Hart. Glennon further states that he will critique international law on its own terms, addressing, for example, the illogical way in which customary international norms are created. He does indeed provide a stinging, albeit familiar, appraisal of the formation and identification of customary norms.[78] In general, Glennon has scant regard for what is described as traditional international law, at various times describing it in derogative

---

International Law-Making Walter de Gruyter 1988, 139. See also Koskenniemi: who argued that traditional international legal concepts 'thinly hides from sight political choices which are inevitable in the solution of practical disputes but provides no criteria on which such choices can be made'. Martti Koskenniemi *From Apology to Utopia: The Structure of International Legal Argument* Lakimiesliiton Kustannus 1989, 483.

[71] Rosalyn Higgins *Problems and Process: International Law and How We Use It*, Oxford University Press, 1994, 5.

[72] Bruno Simma and Andreas L. Paulus 'The Responsibility of Individuals for Human Rights Abuses in Internal Conflict: A Positivist View' 93 *American Journal of International Law* (1999) 302-316 at 307.

[73] Michael J. Glennon *Limits of Law, Prerogatives of Power: Interventionism after Kosovo* Palgrave, 2001, 7.

[74] Michael J. Glennon 'The UN Security Council in a Unipolar World' 44 *Virginia Journal of International Law* (2003) 91-112 at 94.

[75] Michael J. Glennon 'The UN Security Council in a Unipolar World' 44 *Virginia Journal of International Law* (2003) 91-112 at 96.

[76] Michael J. Glennon 'The UN Security Council in a Unipolar World' 44 *Virginia Journal of International Law* (2003) 91-112 at 98.

[77] Michael J. Glennon *Limits of Law, Prerogatives of Power: Interventionism after Kosovo* Palgrave, 2001, footnote '†', pages 7-8 and page 9.

[78] Michael J. Glennon *Limits of Law, Prerogatives of Power: Interventionism after Kosovo* Palgrave, 2001, 9 and 49-60.

terms as 'disembodied, acontextual rules of law',[79] 'overly schematised and scholastic',[80] and as 'legalist catechism'.[81] Considering this, it may come as a surprise that Glennon often relies on scholars like Schachter, Brownlie and Akehurst who may reasonably be described as belonging to mainstream 'traditional' international law.[82] Similarly, it is surprising that he ultimately appears to rely on the traditional modes of change and development of international law. He dissects international law but without providing a theoretical approach that is different to the 'traditional' he so dislikes:[83] even if one accepts the scholastic tenets of international law doctrine,

> massive violation of a treaty by numerous states over a prolonged period can be seen as casting that treaty into desuetude, as transforming its provisions to paper rules that are no longer binding. Or those violations can be regarded as subsequent custom that creates new law supplanting the old treaty norms and permitting conduct that was once a violation. Or state practice can be considered to have created a non liquet, to have thrown the law into a state of confusion where legal rules are not clear and where no authoritative answer is possible. It makes no practical difference as to which analytical framework is applied. The "default position" of international law has long been that when no restriction can be authoritatively established, a state is seen as being free to act.[84]

Glennon's basic argument is that the law of the Charter has 'collapsed' due to repeated violations. Do the alleged violations necessarily lead to the collapse of these provisions of international law? Or: are Glennon's dire conclusions correct? Again, any attempt at

---

[79] Michael J. Glennon *Limits of Law, Prerogatives of Power: Interventionism after Kosovo* Palgrave, 2001, 2.

[80] Michael J. Glennon *Limits of Law, Prerogatives of Power: Interventionism after Kosovo* Palgrave, 2001, 5.

[81] Michael J. Glennon *Limits of Law, Prerogatives of Power: Interventionism after Kosovo* Palgrave, 2001, 6.

[82] Michael J. Glennon *Limits of Law, Prerogatives of Power: Interventionism after Kosovo* Palgrave, 2001, Chapter One, pages 13-35.

[83] As remarked by Farer, 'Glennon raises, but hardly resolves law's most profound epistemological issue, namely the effect of deviance on the authority of norms', Tom J. Farer 'The Prosepect for International Law and Order in the Wake of Iraq' 97 *American Journal of International Law* 2003, 621-628 at 621.

[84] Michael J. Glennon 'The UN Security Council in a Unipolar World' 44 *Virginia Journal of International Law* (2003) 91-112 at 98. See also Michael J. Glennon *Limits of Law, Prerogatives of Power: Interventionism after Kosovo* Palgrave, 2001, Chapter 4 and Michael J. Glennon 'Why the Security Council Failed' *Foreign Affairs* May 2003 - June 2003: 'This conclusion [the death of a law] can be expressed a number of different ways under traditional international legal doctrine'.

answering these questions requires insight into Glennon's analysis and method. Whereas he does refer to classical legal categories as 'desuetude' and 'subsequent custom that creates new law' and falls back on 'traditional' international law mechanisms,[85] it is difficult to precisely identify legal framework at the foundation of his conclusions, i.e. his conception of the secondary rules of change. His general lack of precision is this regard is exemplified by the assertion that the choice of analytical framework makes no practical difference.

1.V. The Present Thesis

The very importance of the analytical framework is central to the present thesis, in which I propose to analyse how the rules of international law that govern the use of force have met the challenge that is posed by terrorist violence and state responses. Addressing this issue has, for obvious reasons, become somewhat of a cottage industry in post-September 11 legal circles.[86] In an approach that is more comprehensive than most other contributions, however, I will set out in some detail the secondary rules of change that address how a primary rule is influenced by and responds or adapts to challenging acts of states – i.e. state practice – that are unprecedented, outside the perceived rule or even contrary to that rule. In order to discover these secondary rules, I propose to examine and analyse a significant number of cases that have been before international tribunals where the acts and/or claims of one side in some fashion challenged or contravened the wording of the underlying treaty. As described in more detail in chapters 2 and 3, this challenge to the treaty may be determined to constitute a new interpretation or a modification of the treaty depending upon a number of conditions and upon whether the new reading of the treaty is within or beyond the normative range of the relevant treaty provision. At the centre is state consent and states' freedom to conclude agreements – whether tacit or explicit – with very few limitations. This will help indicate my own

---

[85] By contrast, applying simple labels, Weisburd may be termed an Austinian with his emphasis on sanction, whereas Arend's approach recalls McDougal and Lasswell save for the 'human dignity' component. Arguably, both find their points of departure in a certain philosophical conception of (international) law.

[86] See, for example, Steven R. Ratnet '*Jus ad bellum* and *jus in bello* after September 11' 96 *American Journal of International Law* (2002), 905-921; Rein Müllerson '*Jus ad bellum* and International Terrorism' 32 *Israel Yearbook of International Law* 2003, 1-52 at 36; Michael N. Schmitt 'Counter-Terrorism and the Use of Force in International Law' in 32 *Israel Yearbook on Human Rights* 2003, 53-116; Rüdiger Wolfrum 'The Attack of September 11, 2001, the Wars Against the Taliban and Iraq: Is There a Need to Reconsider International Law on the Recourse to Force and the Rules in Armed Conflict?' in 7 *Max Planck Yearbook of United Nations Law* 2003, 1-78. See also Chapter 6 in Christine Gray *International Law and the Use of Force* 2nd ed. Oxford University Press, 2004: 'The Use of Force against Terrorism: a New War for a New Century'.

methodological biases: As per Slaughter *et al*, 'disclosure is the name of the game',[87] I can state that of the 'schools' presented at the 1999 ASIL Symposium, I identify primarily with that of positivism as presented by Simma and Paulus. Yet, this does not necessarily reveal much. Weisburd's point of departure is in many ways a positivist one. However, where Weisburd's basis for his secondary rule is found in philosophy of (international) law, this thesis will identify the secondary rule based on the practice of international tribunals.

The overall thesis is that international law has changed and developed substantially when it comes to addressing the challenge of terrorism. This has happened somewhat reluctantly and slowly at first but has taken on a new urgency during the past decade.

Of course, this approach is not beyond reproach. Some of the cases that are examined are decades old. Particularly at present, when there is much talk about 'changing the rules about rules'[88] the risk exists that the secondary rules identified in the following two chapters are actually not current. This is a reasonable concern but it is probably too early to identify 'changing rules about rules' on the basis of only a decade or so of practice. The approach chosen here, on the other hand, is attractive because a large amount of empirical data is available.

There are several reasons for focusing on state practice: Firstly, a main objection of critics like Glennon[89] is what they perceive as a detachment between traditional doctrine and the practice of states. Even if one feels that the critics are too bombastic in their condemnation of 'traditional' approaches, one may still agree with Fitzmaurice when he observes that there is a 'great preponderance of the written word in the international field'.[90] Hence, they all place great emphasis on state practice and their approaches, although different in the details, may all be characterised as inductive: 'Actual state practice should be the starting point, not an afterthought, in legal analysis...'.[91] In other words, these critics object to traditional international law doctrine being out of touch

---

[87] Thomas Franck 'Comments on Chapters 7 and 8' in Michael Byers and Georg Nolte (ed.) *United States Hegemony and the Foundations of International Law* Cambridge University Press, 2002, 264.

[88] Michael Byers and Simon Chsterman 'Changing the Rules about Rules? Unilateral Humanitarian Intervention and the Future of International Law' in J.L. Holzgrefe and Robert O. Keohane (ed.) *Humanitarian Intervention: Ethical, Legaland Political Dilemmas* Cambridge University Press, 2003, 177-203.

[89] And also, for example, Weisburd and Arend.

[90] Fitzmaurice, Gerald: *The Law and Procedure of the International Court of Justice*, I, Cambridge University Press, 1995, 386.

[91] Michael J. Glennon *Limits of Law, Prerogatives of Power: Interventionism after Kosovo* Palgrave, 2001, 65. Arend's approach may be said to be semi-deductive: 'a treaty creates a presumption of the existence of a legal rule' but it must remain authoritative and controlling; otherwise it is not law, Anthony Clark Arend *Legal Rules and International Society*, Oxford University Press, 1999, 90. See also an outline of the debate in Anthea Elizabeth Roberts 'Traditional and Modern Approaches to Customary International Law: A Reconciliation' 95 *American Journal of International Law* (2001) 757-791.

with reality and inadaptable to change and – as a natural consequence of this – states will invariably violate international law. I intend to show how – even under what may be described as a traditional approach – state practice subsequent to the promulgation of a treaty may interpret, revise and modify that convention in order for it to be current with present-day conditions and demands. This dynamic is equally if not more important when it comes to what can be termed constitutional treaties, such as the UN Charter and its regulation of the use of force in international relations

Secondly, whereas subsequent practice is a well recognized element in the interpretation of treaties, it has received relatively little attention in its own right and its exact workings and characteristics have been described as disputed and largely unresolved.[92] In this regard, the present work attempts to clarify some of the controversial issues including the 'blurred' distinction between subsequent practice, which helps interpret a treaty, and subsequent practice, which might modify or amend a treaty.

A third reason is rather obvious, that if the evolution of the law is the research topic, the focus should be on a dynamic aspect of interpretation. The extent to which an interpretation can be described as dynamic largely depends upon the interpretative approach adopted. Or, vice versa, the approach adopted depends on whether the interpreter seeks a dynamic interpretation.

Finally, as will be discussed in more detail below, some authors argued the interpretation of the Charter call for an approach different from the one set out in the VCLT because of the alleged constitutional character of the Charter. While these modified approaches vary somewhat from author to author, they, more often than not, include subsequent practice, of states and institutional organs, as a key element. Hence, in addition to being a recognized element in the interpretation of a normal treaty, cf. Article 31 of the VCLT, practice is also perceived as a key element, even in a modified constitutional approach. Thus, after determining that constitutive instruments of international organizations are 'particularly susceptible to the changing circumstances wrought by a dynamic international society'[93] Zacklin went on to find that 'it is the nature of such instruments that they develop and change as a result of the practice of the parties'.[94]

---

[92] Giovanni Distefano 'La Pratique Subséquente des États Parties à un Traité' 60 *Annuaire Français de Droit International* (1994) 41 at 42.

[93] Ralph Zacklin *The Amendment of the Constitutive Instruments of the United Nations and Specialized Agencies* Sijthoff (1968) 172.

[94] Ibid. Zacklin builds on the work of Engel (Salo Engel 'The Changing Charter' 7 *Year Book of World Affairs* (1953) 71) which distinguishes between interpretation, non-application and the conclusion of supplementary agreements, Ralph Zacklin *The Amendment of the Constitutive Instruments of the United Nations and Specialized Agencies* Sijthoff (1968) 173. See similarly Leland M. Goodrich *The United Nations* Thomas Y. Crowell Company (1959) 70-74.

1.VI. A Note on the Terminology

Glennon employs the term 'desuetude' as relevant in the current context. One could also mention '*rebus sic stantibus*', i.e. fundamental change of circumstances. Each of these concepts or doctrines is applicable under very specific legal conditions and have detailed consequences. Desuetude concerns the discontinuety of the use of a treaty and its implied termination by consent.[95] Mere old age or lack of invocation of a treaty is, however, not enough: 'To prove the extinction by desuetude of a previously existing treaty is no simpler than proving the formation of a new treaty' or customary rule.[96] It is debatable whether the concept of desuetude is relevant in the present context. In the view of the current author, it is not. It is, however, not of great importance considering the just stated fact that desuetude requires a normative development. The present project does indeed consider the possibility of normative changes and this approach can include the issue of desuetude if deemed necessary. Fundamental change of circumstances is now regulated in the Vienna Convention on the law of Treaties, Article 62, and addresses the possibility of terminating or withdrawing from a treaty. This issue has, however, never been an option considered in the case of the UN Charter and will not be pursued further.

When the ILC drew up the draft provisions concerning treaty change, the Commission deliberately differentiated between treaty amendment and treaty modification. The former was employed with regard to general changes of a treaty whereas the latter was reserved for *inter se* modifications, see Articles 40 and 41 of the Vienna Convention on the Law of Treaties. It seems clear that *inter se* modifications are not considered appropriate or possible in the context of the law of the UN Charter. During the discussion of the possibility of modifying treaties through subsequent practice, Israel, in its observations to draft Article 68(b) of the 1964 ILC draft Law of Treaties, objected to the distinction between interpretation and modification and found that modification by subsequent practice is indistinguishable 'in its practical effect' from interpretation by subsequent practice.[97] The Special Rapporteur Waldock partly agreed that in the case of a bilateral treaty, the practical effects may in essence be identical whether the process is depicted as interpretation or modification.[98] With regard to multilateral treaties, however, the Special Rapporteur submitted that the distinction be maintained because many multilateral treaties operate bilaterally and special bilateral arrangements under a multilateral treaty, which only bind the two parties, are more

---

[95] Athanassios Vamvoukos *Termination of Treaties in International Law: The Doctrines of* Rebus Sic Stantibus *and Desuetude* Clarendon Press, 1985, 219.
[96] Athanassios Vamvoukos *Termination of Treaties in International Law: The Doctrines of* Rebus Sic Stantibus *and Desuetude* Clarendon Press, 1985, 261.
[97] *Yearbook of the International Law Commission, 1966*, II, 86 and 300.
[98] *Yearbook of the International Law Commission, 1966*, II, 89.

correctly described as modifications of the treaty than as interpretations.[99] He did, however, further stress that in the case of certain multinational treaties, bilateral or group arrangements to modify particular provisions may be irreconcilable with the treaty. As an example, he mentioned that an application of the Vienna Convention on Diplomatic Relations which differentiates between one party and another may *ipso facto* constitute a violation of the treaty.[100] In the latter case, since bilateral arrangements are ruled out, the distinction between interpretation and modification would presumably be without object. This conclusion, i.e. that *inter se* modifications are ruled out with regard to certain treaties, is also valid with regard to the UN Charter, 'because this [*inter se* modification] would lead to conflicting schemes within the organization'.[101] Since *inter se* modification is out of the question with regard to the Charter, the original ILC differentiation between amendment and modification does not serve a purpose in the present context and the words amendment and modification will be used interchangeably. In addition, the word 'revision' will be applied in the same sense as amendment or modification although the ILC, due to, it seems, more historical-political considerations, chose not to use it at all.[102] Finally, the word 'variation' has been employed by Schermers and Blokker. They point out that some international organizations grant organs the power to vary provisions of the constitution of the organization: 'Variation should be distinguished from amendment: if a variation occurs, no change is made to the text of the constitution, although the actual result of the variation may prove identical to amendment'.[103] The term 'variation' will not be used here.

---

[99] *Yearbook of the International Law Commission, 1966*, II, 90.

[100] *Yearbook of the International Law Commission, 1966*, II, 90.

[101] Karl/Mutzelburg, Ress in Bruno Simma (ed.) *The Charter of the United Nations: A Commentary*, Oxford University Press (1994) p.1164). The Commentary further finds that from the start, there is very little room for variation, owing to the constitutional character of the Charter, ibid. p. 1166, paragraph 9. See similarly Schermers and Blokke: What would in effect amount to *inter se* amendments would in practice be unsuitable for constitutional amendments since it would lead to members being subject to different provisions, which, particularly in respect of institutional articles, would be unacceptable (Henry Schermers and Nield Blokker *International Institutional Law: Unity within Diversity* Martinus Nijhoff, 3rd edition (1995) 726, paragraph 1169 and 735, paragraph 1188) and Ralph Zacklin *The Amendment of the Constitutive Instruments of the United Nations and Specialized Agencies* Sijthoff (1968): 'the very nature of these [constitutive] instruments, their function and purpose, require that they be based on a uniformity of rights and obligations of the member states' ... 'the procedure of amendment by a new agreement which does not involve the complete identity of the parties is ... quite unsuitable ... [because] ... in practice it would lead to the disintegration of the original constitutive instrument' (12) ... 'Inter se modifications to constitutive instruments 'is totally inapposite, if not impossible' (17).

[102] See Year Book of the International Law Commission, 1966, Vol. II, 232.

[103] Henry Schermers and Nield Blokker *International Institutional Law: Unity within Diversity* Martinus Nijhoff, 3rd edition (1995) 721-722, paragraph 1162. Engel mentions an example from the UN Charter: According to Article 18, paragraph 3, the General Assembly may add, by a mere majority

1.VII. Outline of What is to Follow

The following presentation falls in two main parts: Part I will encompass this and the following three chapters. Chapter 2 addresses various aspects related to subsequent practice as an interpretative aid. Initially, based on Article 31, paragraph 3(b) of the Vienna Convention on the Law of Treaties (VCLT), the Chapter will elaborate on the elements that make up this provision and will summarize what is required for subsequent practice to play a determining role in the interpretation of a legal text. Secondly, the chapter will address some objections to the present focus on subsequent practice. In closing, some remarks are made about the difference between the interpretation and modification of a treaty through subsequent practice. Chapter 3 examines how subsequent practice may operate to modify a treaty. The chapter firstly establishes that this proposition may be seen as somewhat controversial but, based on an extensive examination of the case-law, it can be determined that the process nonetheless takes place and is recognized. It remains, however, to justify this process legally. Finally, the chapter deals with some aspects of customary international law as it relates to the thesis. Part I concludes with Chapter 4 examining how the international community, through the United Nations, has chosen to handle terrorism. The chapter documents a marked change in perception from the mid-1990s and onward. More fundamentally for the present purposes, the chapter illustrates how international mores and norms have come to view terrorism as completely unacceptable, which has important normative implications for the development of customary international law. Chapters 5 through 9 combine to make up Part II and concentrate on the use of force regulation. As will be clear from Chapter 5, the use of force in self-defence against terrorists has been plagued by legal problems throughout the 1980s and 1990s. A fact that is observable when analysing five cases from the two decades, as is done in Chapter 6. Chapter 7 deals in depth with the US attack on Afghanistan in October of 2001 whereas Chapter 8 completes the examination of post September 11 cases with the 2002 Israeli incursion into the West Bank, the 2002 Russian bombing of Georgia and the 2003 Israeli bombing of Syria. Chapter 9 considers the not very well appreciated justification in international law of necessity and whether it may serve as an excuse when using force against terrorists. The findings are analysed and conclusions are then drawn in Chapter 10.

---

vote, new categories of important questions to those listed in paragraph 2 of the same Article. Salo Engel 'The Changing Charter of the United Nations' 7 *The Yearbook of World Affirs* 1953, 71. Kelsen: 'The procedure of this amendment ... constitutes an exception to the provisions of Chapter XVIII regulating the amendment procedure', Hans Kelsen *The Law of the United Nations, with Supplement* Praegerm 1950, 183.

Chapter 2

Subsequent Practice: Interpretation

2.I. Introduction

Every text has a number of possible interpretations. Each of these may be quite different from one another while at the same time being reasonable reflections of the text. When looking at legal texts, this means that a legal injunction may change according to the prevailing interpretation even if the base text remains the same. It is argued that the practice of state parties to a treaty and the reaction of other states and international organs to such practice may 'be bellwethers of evolution in Charter interpretation'.[1] The crucial and often unanswered question remains: How exactly does subsequent practice influence the interpretation of a treaty?

The present chapter constitutes the first part of our investigation into the dynamics of subsequent practice in relations to a treaty text. Below, I set out how subsequent practice may help the interpretation of a treaty provision. Various elements of this process are identified and finally summarised in order create a working formula to be applied when analysing specific state practice later in the thesis. The chapter leads to the second and last part of the examination of subsequent practice under a treaty, i.e. how such practice may modify a treaty. Before moving on to this question, however, some of the objections to the proposed approach will be addressed and a short review is provided of what differentiates subsequent practice in regard to interpretation and modification respectively.

2.II. Subsequent Practice as an Element in Interpretation

The importance of subsequent practice in the application of a treaty as an element of interpretation is 'obvious' and 'well established'.[2] Subsequent practice has been referred to as an element in the interpretation of a treaty on several occasions by the Permanent Court of International Justice, on numerous occasions by the International Court of Justice[3] and other international tribunals[4] and was codified in the Vienna Convention on the Law of Treaties, Art, 31, paragraph 3(b):

---

[1] Thomas Franck 'Interpretation and Change in the Law of Humanitarian Intervention' in Michael Byers and Georg Nolte (ed.) *United States Hegemony and the Foundations of International Law* Cambridge University Press, 2002, 216.

[2] Report of the International Law Commission, YBILC, Vol. II, 1964, 203 and YBILC, II, 1966, 221-222.

[3] See for example the *Corfu Channel Case,* 1949 ICJ 4; the *Rights of Nationals of the United States of America in Morocco Case*, 1952 ICJ 176; the *King of Spain Award Case*, 1960 ICJ 192; the *IMCO*

3. There shall be taken into account, together with the context:

...

(b) any subsequent practice in the application of the treaty which establishes the agreement of the parties regarding its interpretation;

The International Court of Justice has further emphasized that 'Article 31, paragraph 3, of the 1969 Vienna Convention on the Law of Treaties ... reflects customary law'.[5] Recently, the ICJ rendered the following example dealing with the interpretation of Article 12 of the UN Charter:[6]

> As regards the practice of the United Nations, both the General Assembly and the Security Council initially interpreted and applied Article 12 to the effect that the Assembly could not make a recommendation on a question concerning the maintenance of international peace and security while the matter remained on the Council's agenda. ... However, this interpretation of Article 12 has evolved subsequently. Thus the General Assembly deemed itself entitled in 1961 to adopt recommendations in the matter of the Congo (resolutions 1955 (XV) and 1600 (XVI)) and in 1963 in respect of the Portuguese colonies (resolution 1913 (XVIII)) while those cases still appeared on the Council's agenda, without the Council having adopted any recent resolution concerning them. In

---

Case, 1960 ICJ 150; the *Certain Expenses Case*, 1962 ICJ 151; the *Nicaragua Case (Jurisdiction)*, 1984 ICJ 392; the *Border and Transborder Armed Actions Case*, 1988 ICJ 71; the *Territorial Dispute Case*, 1994 ICJ 6; the *Kasikili/Sedudu Case*, 39 ILM (2000) 310.

[4] See for example *Italy-United States Air Transport Arbitration*, Arbitral Tribunal, Advisory Opinion of July 17, 1965. The Tribunal was composed by Otto Riese, Standley D. Metzger and Riccardo Monaco. Reproduced in 45 *International Law Reports*, 1972, 393; *Beagle Channel Arbitration* (Argentina v. Chile), Court of Arbitration composed of H. Dillard, A. Gros, C. Onyeama and S. Petren. Decision delivered on February 18, 1977. Reproduced in 52 *International Law Reports* 93. Reproduced in part in 17 *International Legal Materials* 632; Arbitral Tribunal for the Agreement on *German External Debts*, composed of Castren, Arndt, Robinson, Maier, Monguilan and Kewenig, 59 *International Law Reports*, 1980, 494. See, finally, the recent observation of the Yugoslav Tribunal (ICTY) concerning the interpretation of the phrase 'threat to the peace' in Article 39 of the UN Charter: 'It can thus be said that there is a common understanding, manifested by the "subsequent practice" of the membership of the United Nations at large, that the "threat to the peace" of Article 39 may include, as one of its species, internal armed conflicts', *Prosecutor v. Dusko Tadic*, Decision on the Defence Motion for Interlocutory Appeal on Jurisdiction, October 2, 1995, paragraph 30.

[5] See the *Kasikili/Sedudu Case*, 39 ILM (2000) 310 at 330, paragraph 48. See also *Sovereignty over Pulau Ligitan and Pulau Sipadan* (Indonesia v. Malaysia) Judgment, Merits, December 17, 2002, paragraphs 37-38.

[6] Article 12, paragraph 1 provides: 'While the Security Council is exercising in respect of any dispute or situation the functions assigned to it in the present Charter, the General Assembly shall not make any recommendation with regard to that dispute or situation unless the Security Council so requests.'

response to a question posed by Peru during the Twenty-third session of the General Assembly, the Legal Counsel of the United Nations confirmed that the Assembly interpreted the words "is exercising the functions" in Article 12 of the Charter as meaning "is exercising the functions at this moment" (Twenty-third General Assembly, Third Committee, 1637th meeting, A/C.3/SR.1637, para. 9). Indeed, the Court notes that there has been an increasing tendency over time for the General Assembly and the Security Council to deal concurrently with the same matter concerning the maintenance of international peace and security (see, for example, the matters involving Cyprus, South Africa, Angola, Southern Rhodesia and more recently Bosnia and Herzegovina and Somalia). It is often the case that, while the Security Council has tended to focus on the aspects of such matters related to international peace and security, the General Assembly has taken a broader view, considering also their humanitarian, social and economic aspects. … The Court considers that the accepted practice of the General Assembly, as it has evolved, is consistent with Article 12, paragraph 1, of the Charter.[7]

Subsequent practice as an integral element of treaty interpretation has, finally, been reviewed in the literature[8] and received broad support.[9]

---

[7] Legal Consequences of the Construction of a Wall in the Occupied Palestinian Territory, Judgment 9 July 2004, paragraphs 27-28, available at www.icj.org, visited August 2, 2004.

[8] In addition to the obligatory mention in general works on international law (see, for instance, Oppenheim's International Law and Brownlie), subsequent practice has been dealt with in works on the law of treaties: Lord McNair *The Law of Treaties* Oxford University Press (1961) Chapter XXIV, 424-431; Ian Sinclair *The Vienna Convention on the Law of Treaties* Manchester University Press (1984) 136-138 ; Elias; Paul Reuter *Introduction to the Law of Treaties* Kegan Paul International (1995) 96-97, paragraph 144. Francis G. Jacobs 'Varieties of approaches to Treaty Interpretation: with Special Reference to the draft Convention on the Law of Treaties before the Vienna Diplomatic Conference' 18 *International and Comparative Law Quarterly*(1969) 318 at 327-329. In addition, a number of articles examine the issue: Jean-Pierre Cot 'La Conduite Subséquente des Parties a un Traité' 70 *Revue Générale de Droit International Public* (1966) 632-666 ; Salo Engel '''Living'' International Constitutions and the World Court (The Subsequent Practice of International Organs under their Constituent Instruments) 16 *International and Comparative Law Quarterly* (1967) 865-910; Ferald P. McGinley 'Practice as a Guide to Treaty Interpretation' 9 *The Fletcher Forum* (1985) 211-230; Giovanni Distefano 'La Pratique Subséquente des États Parties à un Traité' 60 *Annuaire Français de Droit International* (1994) 41-71.

[9] The subsequent practice of the parties is one of Fitzmaurice's five (later six) 'major principles of interpretation' and recourse to this practice, in interpreting a text, is 'not only permissible but desirable': 'the way in which the treaty has actually been interpreted in practice is evidence (sometimes the best evidence) of what its correct interpretation is' Gerald Fitzmaurice: *The Law and Procedure of the International Court of Justice*, I, Cambridge University Press, 1995, 50 and 345. Elsewhere Fitzmaurice writes that subsequent practice 'is good presumptive (and may in certain cases be virtually

The rule in the VCLT, however, leaves a number of questions unanswered: What form must the practice take in order to be an aid in the interpretation? Must the practice have taken place over a substantial period of time? What is meant by 'establishes an agreement'? Is there a 'subjective element' to the practice and, if so, what is it?

2.III. The Form of the Subsequent Practice

A major controversy between different theories of customary international law concerns the form that the 'general practice accepted as law' has to take. A strong promoter of only accepting actual acts, Professor D'amato, holds 'a claim is not an act' and 'although it may articulate a legal norm [it] cannot constitute the material component of custom'.[10]

Among legal scholars, some appear to espouse a similar view with regard to the form of subsequent practice used to aid in the interpretation of a legal text. Fitzmaurice writes: 'Conduct usually forms a more reliable guide to intention and purpose than anything to be found for instance in the preparatory work of the treaty, simply because it has taken concrete and active, and not merely verbal or paper, form'.[11]

It is, however, somewhat unclear from the context whether Fitzmaurice was excluding for example government statements from subsequent practice or whether his reference to concrete and active forms was meant as a reference to a party to a treaty making concrete decision regarding actual issues that arise under a treaty. In the latter case, one could argue that such concrete decisions made in response to actual issues and expressed in verbal form could still be valuable as evidence of that party's understanding and interpretation of the treaty. Elsewhere, in his separate opinion in the *Temple Case*, Fitzmaurice referred to 'a party's attitude, state of mind or intentions at a later date' and, hence, not to material acts.[12]

---

conclusive) evidence of what the correct legal interpretation is', 62 ICJ 201. Similarly, McDougal finds that a major purpose of examining subsequent practice is that of 'canvassing an exceptionally reliable source for determining their [the parties] genuine shared expectations'. Myres S. McDougal, Harold D. Lasswell and James C. Miller: *The Interpretation of Agreements and World Public Order: Principles of Content and Procedure* Yale University Press (1967) 134. See also Karl: 'Die Völkerrechtslehre und –judikatur sieht sich einig in der Anerkennung dieser Funktion [as a factor in the interpretation] der späteren Praxis' Wolfram Karl: *Vertrag und spätere Praxis im Völkerrecht: zum Einfluß der Praxis auf Inhalt und Bestand völkerrechtlicher Verträge* Springer, 1983, 123 See also comment that, since the conclusion of the VCLT there is no doubt that subsequent practice can function as an authentic interpretation aid, ibid., 206.

[10] Anthony D'amato *The Concept of Custom in International Law* Cornell University Press, 1971, 88.

[11] Gerald Fitzmaurice: *The Law and Procedure of the International Court of Justice*, I, Cambridge University Press, 1995, 357.

[12] 1962 ICJ 61. Fitzmaurice also points out that rules of procedure 'may afford evidence of the *view* of the [constitutive] instrument taken by those who frame the rules … Such rules may therefore by illustrative of a common practice on the part of the parties to an international instrument, which may be evidence as to its correct meaning' Gerald Fitzmaurice: *The Law and Procedure of the International Court of Justice*, I, Cambridge University Press, 1995, 63.

As pointed out by Lauterpacht, 'the courts have never attempted to provide an answer to this question [the form of practice] in general terms'.[13] Yet, the jurisprudence of the International Court quite clearly indicates that subsequent practice does not have to be material practice in order to assists in the interpretation of a disputed text or term.[14] Throughout, both the Permanent Court and the International Court have recognized very diverse acts, such as discussions in an international organization,[15] rules of procedure for organs of international organizations,[16] acts of domestic administrative agents,[17] statements from a president, a foreign minister and from the

---

[13] Elihu Lauterpacht 'The Development of the Law of International Organizations by the Decisions of International Tribunals' *Recueil des Cours – Collected Courses,* The Hague Academy of International Law, 1976, IV, Tome 152, 454.

[14] Similarly, see Lauterpacht: 'it is apparent that practice may not only take the form of an act ... but also of a statement', Elihu Lauterpacht 'The Development of the Law of International Organizations by the Decisions of International Tribunals' *Recueil des Cours – Collected Courses,* The Hague Academy of International Law, 1976, IV, Tome 152, 456. Lauterpacht divides his examination of what may constitute practice, i.e. form, according to whether the words under interpretation create powers, constitute substantive obligations or simply establish procedures although he is uncertain as to whether the form actually varies according to this division, Ibid. 454. McDougal states that 'any behavior ... which appears to be relevant or useful in determining the continuing consensus of the parties' is to be included in subsequent conduct, Myres S. McDougal, Harold D. Lasswell and James C. Miller: *The Interpretation of Agreements and World Public Order: Principles of Content and Procedure* Yale University Press (1967) 133. See also Bernhardt who makes the following reflections with regard to the requirement of an 'agreement': 'One will probably have to depart from the fact that neither art. 27, section 3 [later Article 31, paragraph 3(b)] nor art. 38 envisages a formal treaty' and 'art. 27 and art. 38 can only mean concludent agreements and a practice, which have not found expression in a formal treaty', Rudolf Bernhardt 'Interpretation and Implied (Tacit) Modification of Treaties' 27 *Zeitschrift für Ausländisches Öffentliches Recht und Völkerrecht* (1967) 491 at 499.

[15] In the Advisory Opinion concerning the *Competence of the International Labour Organization* (ILO), the Permanent Court of International Justice (PCIJ) had to determine whether the ILO was 'competent to deal with questions of agricultural labour', Advisory Opinion No. 2, August 12, 1922, reproduced in Manley O. Hudson (ed.): *World Court Reports, Vol. I, 1922-1926,* Carnegie Endowment for International Peace, 1934, 124-135. The examined several aspects of Part XIII of the Versailles Treaty, which related to Labour. The PCIJ found that if Part XIII was read as a whole there could be no doubt that agricultural labour was included. The Court went on to say that if there had been any ambiguity, recourse could be had to 'the action which has been taken under the Treaty'. The Court pointed out that the subject of agriculture 'had repeatedly been discussed and had been dealt with in one form or another' during the period from June 1919, when the Treaty was signed, and October 1921, when reservations were raised concerning the competence of the ILO to deal with agriculture.

[16] In the second admissions case, for example, the Court found that the General Assembly, in its Rules of Procedure, had indicated a certain interpretation of Article 4 of the Charter, 1950 ICJ 4 at 9. See also: Advisory Opinion no. 14 (Jurisdiction of the European Commission of the Danube) finding that Regulations drawn up by the majority of the European Commission were of interest to the Court as showing the intention of the signatories to the Treaty of London.

[17] In the *Rights of Nationals of the United States of American in Morocco Case* from 1952, the Court *inter alia* had to interpret Article 95 of the 1906 General Act of Algeciras, 1952 ICJ 176. To assist in this interpretation, the Court, among other aspects, examined 'the practice of the customs authorities since 1906', 1952 ICJ 208. The Court, however, did not get much help from this source. It found that those responsible for the administration of the customs had 'made use of all the various elements of

national legislative assembly,[18] elections in an international organization,[19] mention in official publications[20] and reports and resolutions from an international organization[21] as helpful when it comes to determining how the parties might interpret a word in an agreement between them.

Even the absence of practice or negative practice may constitute 'subsequent practice': In the *Corfu Channel Case*, one question was whether the Court had jurisdiction, under the Special Agreement concluded by the United Kingdom and

---

valuation available to them, though perhaps not always in a consistent manner', 1952 ICJ 211. Dissenting Judges Hackworth, Badawi, Levi Carneiro and Sir Benegal Rau, however, found that the practice subsequent to 1906 was 'in favour of the interpretation put forward by the United States', 1952 ICJ 231.

[18] In the *King of Spain Award*, Nicaragua challenged the validity and binding character of an arbitral award by the King of Spain regarding a section of the border between Honduras and Nicaragua, 1960 ICJ 192. Among the questions addressed by the Court was the whether the King had been designated in conformity with the formal provisions agreed to by Honduras and Nicaragua and the treaty containing these provisions had terminated before the King of Spain accepted to act as arbitrator. With regard to the former, the two national arbitrators agreed to designate the King and, thus, interpreted the treaty to allow this. Furthermore, five days after the designation, the President of Nicaragua replied to the Spanish Minister, that Nicaragua would be satisfied and honored if the King would accept the role as arbitrator, 1960 ICJ 206. With regard to the latter, i.e. the possible termination of the treaty, the record showed that Nicaragua had made a number of statements, subsequent to the date on which Nicaragua argued the treaty had lapsed, which indicated that Nicaragua did not regard the treaty as having lapsed on that date, 1960 ICJ 208-209. Nicaragua further argued that the award was a nullity but again, statements made by Nicaraguan officials indicated that Nicaragua had previously accepted the award, 1960 ICJ 210-213.

[19] In the 1960 *IMCO Case*, the Court had to determine whether the phrase 'the largest ship-owning nations' referred to the tonnage beneficially owned by the nationals of a State or referred to the registered tonnage of a flag State, 1960 ICJ 150 at 167. In addition to other elements, the Court examined the actual practice of the Organization Assembly under the Convention [for Establishment of the Inter-Governmental Maritime Consultative Organization]. The Court found that the Assembly, at least twice, had acted on the basis that registered tonnage was the determining criteria1960 ICJ 168-169. The two situations involved election of members where a main criteria was the seizure of the merchant fleet.

[20] In 1984, the Court had to determine whether Nicaragua, through a 1929 Declaration, had accepted the compulsory jurisdiction of the Court (*Case Concerning Military and Paramilitary Activities in and Against Nicaragua*, Nicaragua v. United States of America, 1984 ICJ 392). The Court *inter alia* examined the conduct of States and international organizations. The Court found that a number of official publications had 'regularly' placed Nicaragua on the list of States that have recognized the compulsory jurisdiction of the Court (1984 ICJ 408, paragraph 36). The Court found that this inclusion 'attest a certain interpretation … and the rejection of an opposite rejection' (1984 ICJ 409, paragraph 38). The Court found that for nearly 40 years States had 'every opportunity of accepting or rejecting' the assertion implicit in the publications and that they had 'never challenged the interpretation to which the publications of the United Nations bear witness' (1984 ICJ 409-410, paragraphs 38-40).

[21] In 1996, in the *Advisory Opinion on the Legality of the use by a State of Nuclear Weapons in Armed Conflict (Request of the World Heath Organization)*, the Court considered whether the issue of the legality of nuclear weapons was within the scope of the activities of the World Health Organization, 1996 ICJ 75 at paragraph 27.

Albania, to assess the amount of compensation.[22] The subsequent attitude of Albania included submissions to the Court which failed to contest the Court's competence to address the amount of compensation and which implied acceptance of the Court jurisdiction to do so.[23]

More recently, in the *Oil Platforms Case (Preliminary Objections)*, the Court found that neither Iran nor the United States had relied upon Article I of the Treaty of Amity in previous cases before the Court.[24] The Court found that this absence of practice confirmed its interpretation of Article I. It should, however, be noted that Judge Rigaux, in his separate opinion, found that it is 'hardly appropriate to draw conclusions from the absence of a practice in order to confer one interpretation rather than another on a treaty. The practice would have been relevant if it had shown that the parties or one of them had interpreted Article I in the same way as the Court had or, at the very least, had, if only implicitly, discarded the opposite interpretation'.[25]

In the *Sovereignty over Pulau Ligitan and Pulau Sipadan* case between Indonesia and Malaysia, the Court had to interpret a provision from an 1891 treaty. The primary question was whether the treaty had designated two disputed islands as either British or Dutch. Based on the objective and purpose of the treaty, the Court found that the treaty did not intend to deal with the allocation of the islands. It found that this interpretation was confirmed by the subsequent practice of the parties.[26] Amongst other items, the Court examined a map, which was annexed to a 1915 agreement. The map was one of

---

[22] 1949 ICJ 4, 23.

[23] 1949 ICJ 25. Both parties had, furthermore, repeatedly declared that they accepted UN Security Council Resolution 22 of April 9, 1947, which recommended that the parties submit their dispute to the Court. The Court found that this resolution 'without doubt' aimed at a final adjustment of the entire dispute, i.e. including questions of compensation 1949 ICJ 24. Similarly, in the 1994 *Territorial Dispute Case* between Libya and Chad, the Court had to interpret the relevant provisions of a 1955 Treaty between France and Libya to determine whether or not the Treaty resulted in a boundary between the territories of the parties *(Case Concerning Territorial Dispute*, Libyan Arab Jamahiriya v. Chad, 1994 ICJ 6). The Court first investigated agreements entered into subsequent to the entry into force of the 1955 Treaty. The Court found that the lack of reference to a possible dispute over the frontier indicated that the 1955 Treaty delimitation had been accepted and acted upon by the parties: 'If a serious dispute had indeed existed regarding frontiers … one would expect it to have been reflected in the [subsequent] 1966 Treaty' (1994 ICJ 34-35, paragraph 66). The Court then looked at the 'attitudes of the parties' when issues pertinent to the frontiers arose in international fora (1994 ICJ 36, paragraph 68). This practice showed a consistency in Chad's conduct and an absence of Libyan reaction (1994 ICJ 36-37, paragraphs 68-71).

[24] 1996 ICJ 803 at 815, paragraph 30.

[25] 1996 ICJ 865. Reference may also be had to the 1988 decision on the question of jurisdiction of the Court in the *Border and Transborder Armed Actions Case* (Nicaragua c. Honduras), 1988 ICJ 71. Here the Court also found negative practice, or lack of practice, to support its favored reading of Article XXXI of the Pact of Bogota. The practice of the parties to the Pact showed that they had 'not, at any time, linked together Article XXXI and the declaration of acceptance of compulsory jurisdiction made under Article 36, paragraphs 2 and 4, of the Statute [of the ICJ]'(1988 ICJ 87).

[26] *Sovereignty over Pulau Ligitan and Pulau Sipadan* (Indonesia v. Malaysia) Judgment, Merits, December 17, 2002, paragraphs 59-80, at 80.

only two, which had been agreed upon by the parties to the 1891 treaty.[27] On the map, there was no line indicating the boundary in the relevant area. In other words, the subsequent practice, in this case a subsequent map, confirmed that the parties to the treaty had not intended to address the issue of the two islands in the context of the 1891 treaty.

This does not mean, of course, that material acts cannot constitute subsequent practice in interpretation of a treaty as in the 1977 *Beagle Channel Arbitration*. On the whole, material acts will probably carry greater probative value. Again, however, it must be recalled that the aim is: 'not to deduce a legal standard from the practice followed but merely to reveal the interpretation the parties gave to the provision in dispute'.[28] Almost any relevant act which helps to show what the parties considered the terms of their agreement to mean may be considered when interpreting the agreement. Whether an act reveals their attitude and understanding depends not so much on the form of the practice but on the specific circumstances of the situation.

2.IV. The Duration of the Subsequent Practice

Similar to the question of the form of the practice, the issue concerning the duration of the practice appears to have been influenced by conceptions connected to the establishment of customary international law.[29] In its Report to the General Assembly, the ILC used the same characterization of the practice used to aid interpretation as the practice required to modify a treaty, applying the term 'consistent'.[30] Indeed, several writers, for example Fitzmaurice[31] and Amerasinghe,[32] apply the term 'consistent'. Mr.

---

[27] *Sovereignty over Pulau Ligitan and Pulau Sipadan* (Indonesia v. Malaysia) Judgment, Merits, December 17, 2002, paragraph 72.

[28] *Italy-United States Air Transport Arbitration*, Arbitral Tribunal, Advisory Opinion of July 17, 1965. The Tribunal was composed by Otto Riese, Standley D. Metzger and Riccardo Monaco. Reproduced in 45 *International Law Reports*, 1972, 393 at 419. The Tribunal went on to find that continuity could not be denied even though the actual operations only extended over some six years because the practice was followed 'without exception', ibid. 420.

[29] In its Memorial in the *Kasikili/Sedudu Island Case*, Namibia spoke of 'a uniform course of conduct extending over a long period' as constituting subsequent conduct within Article 31. Namibia, Memorial of the Republic of Namibia, paragraph 167, (available at www.icj-cij.org, visited April 2, 2002). As Lauterpacht puts it: 'It might have been expected that the courts would have been reluctant to rely upon practice as an element in interpretation unless it were sufficiently often repeated to justify the view that it was pursued out of a sense of conformity with the law', 457.

[30] YBILC, 1966, Vol. II, 236. The question of practice modifying a treaty is fundamentally one of law-creation or law-change, and is dealt with below.

[31] 'a *consistent* practice must come very near to being conclusive as to how the treaty should be interpreted'. Gerald Fitzmaurice: *The Law and Procedure of the International Court of Justice*, I, Cambridge University Press, 1995, 357 (emphasis in original). Fitzmaurice elsewhere considers that 'the practice must be well settled', Gerald Fitzmaurice: *The Law and Procedure of the International Court of Justice*, II, Cambridge University Press, 1995, 796.

Ruda of Argentina emphasized that the practice 'should be established, and should not just be any action arbitrarily taken by the parties'.[33]

In the 1965 *Italy-United States Air Transport Arbitration,*[34] however, the Arbitral Tribunal explicitly differentiated between the practice required to establish a rule of customary international law and the practice required to assist the interpretation of an already established rule and pointed out, that when considering subsequent practice for the purpose of interpretation, the issue was:

> Not to deduce a legal standard from the practice followed but merely to reveal the interpretation the parties gave to the provision in dispute, which can serve as additional evidence in ascertaining the intentions of the parties and illustrate their intent as of the time the Agreement was concluded. For this purpose a shorter period of continuity is sufficient.[35]

In this regard, the World Court has accepted even quite brief practice[36] and practice consisting of a very limited number of acts[37] as aiding in the interpretation.

---

[32] Amerasinghe writes that it would seem that the practice 'must be repeated and consistent', C.F. Amerasinghe *Principles of the Institutional Law of International Organizations* Cambridge University Press 1996, 50.

[33] 33rd meeting, April 22, 1968, 180, paragraph 23

[34] *Italy-United States Air Transport Arbitration*, Arbitral Tribunal, Advisory Opinion of July 17, 1965. The Tribunal was composed by Otto Riese, Standley D. Metzger and Riccardo Monaco. Reproduced in 45 *International Law Reports*, 1972, 393. The Arbitral Tribunal investigated the subsequent conduct of the parties to adduce additional evidence as regards the question whether the Transport Agreement granted a right for all-cargo flights. From the actual practice, the Tribunal found that it appeared that both parties acted from 1948 up to mid-1963 on the basis that their agreement did cover all-cargo services (45 ILR (1972) 419). The Tribunal found that Italy only objected in 1963 because the US carriers in 1963 began contemplating using jet equipment which the Italians did not possess (45 ILR (1972) 420). Both parties conducted all-cargo services without applying for special permissions. Among objections presented by Italy was that the all-cargo operations lacked continuity. The Tribunal took this as a reference to the requirements associated with practice necessary in order to create a rule of customary international law.

[35] Ibid. 419. The Tribunal went on to find that continuity could not be denied even though the actual operations only extended over some six years because the practice was followed 'without exception', Ibid. 420.

[36] In the Advisory Opinion concerning the *Competence of the International Labour Organization* (ILO), the Permanent Court of International Justice (PCIJ) pointed out that the subject of agriculture 'had repeatedly been discussed and had been dealt with in one form or another' during the period from June 1919, when the Treaty was signed, and October 1921, when reservations were raised concerning the competence of the ILO to deal with agriculture.

[37] In the 1951 *Anglo-Iranian oil Co. Case*, the Court found its interpretation of an Iranian Declaration 'confirmed by an Iranian law' passed a few months after the Declaration and approving it, 1951 ICJ 93 at 106-107.

It would be fair to assert, all other things being equal, that the longer a certain practice has been followed the more reliable it would be as an aid in the interpretation. It would, however, seem doubtful that a minimum period of time can be stipulated. The duration of practice required depends on the number of parties to the treaty and on the specific circumstances. Obviously, it is easier to establish and determine a practice in an interaction between two parties. Yet, it must be recalled that what is being sought is evidence of a certain attitude and even when it comes to multilateral treaties there would appear to be nothing to rule out practice followed for a short time.[38]

Hence, the decisive question is not to set a certain time limit during which the practice must have taken place but rather whether evidence can be established that the parties understand a provision in the treaty in a specific manner, even if this evidence is gathered from a very short practice. If, for example, all the parties to a multilateral treaty meet for the first time one year after the entry into force of the treaty and, through the declarations of the attendees, state that they understand Article 1 to mean X then all these statements would count as practice under the VCLT, Article 31, paragraph 3(b) and would assist in the interpretation of Article 1 even if these statements were the only practice carried out under the treaty. Thus, it is not the amount of time but whether the practice is usable as evidence of how the parties interpret Article 1. The scenario just outlined is unlikely to occur in the suggested form but from a theoretical point of view there is no reason to preclude even very short practice.

2.V. The Number of Participants in Subsequent Practice

A central question is whether all the parties have to participate in the practice. Even the practice of one party to a treaty may have relevance for interpretation when the said practice 'relates to the performance of an obligation which particularly concerns that State'.[39] As regards bilateral treaties, however, the practice will normally involve both parties either actively or by one party accepting the other party's actions, possibly through acquiescence: 'The failure of one party to a treaty to protest against acts of the other party in which a particular interpretation of the terms of the treaty is clearly asserted affords cogent evidence of the understanding of the parties of their respective rights and obligations under the treaty'.[40]

When it comes to multilateral treaties, it has to be determined whether all the parties have to participate in or accept the practice or whether a certain interpretation

---

[38] Lauterpacht finds that 'it is impossible to extract from them [court decisions] either any statement of principle or any consistent method from which one might imply a principle', Elihu Lauterpacht 'The Development of the Law of International Organizations by the Decisions of International Tribunals' *Recueil des Cours – Collected Courses,* The Hague Academy of International Law, 1976, IV, Tome 152, 457.

[39] Report of the International Law Commission, YBILC, Vol. II, 1964, 204, paragraph 13. The ILC based this on a *dictum* from the ICJ in the *Status of South West Africa Opinion* 1950 ICJ 135-136.

[40] I. C. MacGibbon 'The Scope of Acquiescence in International Law' 31 *British Year Book of International Law* 1954, 143-186 at 146.

can be sustained even if faced with some opposition. The 1964 Draft Article 69 demanded that the practice establish 'the understanding of *all* the parties regarding its interpretation'.[41] In the subsequent 1966 Draft Article 27, the word 'all' was deleted. The reason was not, however, to loosen the requirements: 'By omitting the word 'all' the Commission did not intend to change the rule. It considered that the phrase 'the understanding of the parties' necessarily meant 'the parties as a whole'. It omitted the word 'all' merely to avoid any possible misconception that every party must individually have engaged in the practice where it suffices that it should have accepted the practice'.[42]

The question as to whether active participation is necessary in order to establish a practice under Article 31, paragraph 3(b) was also implicated in the choice between the words 'understanding' and 'agreement'. Initially, 'the word 'understanding' was chosen by the Commission instead of 'agreement' expressly in order to indicate that the assent of a party to the interpretation may be inferred from its reaction or absence of reaction to the practice'.[43] The wording was, however, changed back to 'agreement' by the drafting committee at the UN Conference on the Law of Treaties.[44] As pointed out by Namibia in the *Kasikili/Sedudu Island Case*, the change does not, however, appear to have been motivated by a wish to rule out inferences from inaction but was rather due to an effort at aligning the English language version with the French and Spanish versions.[45]

---

[41] Report of the International Law Commission, YBILC, Vol. II, 1964, 199 (emphasis added) and 204, paragraph 13..

[42] YBILC, II, 1966, 222, paragraph 15. See the previous comment by the United States that the reference to 'the understanding of all the parties' might be open to the construction that some affirmative action was required of each and every party., YBILC, II, 1966, 93. See also the observation of the United States that the reference to 'all the parties' might 'be open to the construction that some affirmative action is required of each and every party. In its [the United States'] view, a course of action by one party not objected to by others may be substantial guide to interpretation', YBILC, Vol. II, 1966, 93. See also the Special Rapporteur, Waldock's comments at YBILC, Vol. I, 1966, 876th meeting, 222, paragraph 55.

[43] YBILC, II, 1966, 99, paragraph 18.

[44] 1968, Seventy-fourth Meeting, 442. Elias emphasizes the requirement of an agreement, 'not merely the understanding of the parties' but goes on to state that 'it is not necessary that every one of the parties to the treaty should have engaged in the particular practice'. It is sufficient that every party has accepted the practice, even by tacit consent or acquiescence. T.O. Elias *The Modern Law of Treaties* A.W. Sijthoff (1974) 76.

[45] Ibid. and Namibia also the general elaboration on what constitutes an 'agreement' by Professor Faundez during the oral arguments: 'the agreement of the parties may be established through joint or parallel activity of the parties or through the activity of one party which is assented to or not objected to by the other. In other words the agreement of the parties regarding the interpretation of the treaty may be based on the activity of one of the parties and the silence or failure to respond by the other party when the circumstances call for some reaction. The affirmative conduct of both parties is not an essential requirement', Oral Arguments, February 17, 1999, paragraph 12, (available at www.icj-cij.org, visited April 2, 2002)

The conclusion that the word 'agreement' does not indicate a requirement for an active reaction on the part of all the parties finds support in the *Beagle Channel Arbitration*. In front of the Court of Arbitration, Argentina challenged that the Chilean action, and Argentinean inaction, could aid in the interpretation because no 'agreement', as stipulated in VCLT, Article 31, paragraph 3(b), could be said to have been reached.[46] The Court of Arbitration held that it could not 'accept the contention that no subsequent conduct, including acts of jurisdiction, can have probative value as a subsidiary method of interpretation unless representing a formally stated or acknowledged 'agreement' between the parties'.[47] The Court further found that the VCLT did not specify the ways in which an 'agreement' might manifest itself.[48]

In the *Kasikili/Sedudu Island Case*, Namibia claimed that various forms of control and jurisdiction which had been exercised over the island were known to the Bechuanaland authorities [Botswana] and that they 'made no objection or protest'.[49] This, according to Namibia, constituted subsequent practice to confirm the interpretation of the 1890 Treaty whereby the island was attributed to Namibia.[50] Botswana, in its Counter-Memorial, stressed that the 'Court should be cautious in face of this suggestion that the text of Article 30(3)(b) [sic], which, in its final form, requires practice which 'establishes the agreement of the parties', should be watered down'.[51] The Court did not find that the practice – the peaceful and public use of the island – had been linked to territorial claims and, thus, not linked to the 1890 Treaty. Similarly, the toleration of the presence on and use of the island was also unconnected to the Treaty. Hence, the Court did not make any ruling as to whether an 'agreement' under Article 31, paragraph 3(b) may result from inaction in response to a certain practice.[52]

Scholars, too, accept that parties do not have to actively participate but may concur and that not all have to concur even if a substantial majority have to: 'the practice must be well settled, and not itself the subject of controversy amongst the parties to the

---

[46] 52 *International Law Reports*, 223, paragraph 168.

[47] 52 *International Law Reports*, 223, paragraph 169.

[48] Ibid.

[49] 39 ILM (2000) 310 at 342, paragraph 71

[50] Ibid.

[51] Botswana, Counter-Memorial of the Republic of Botswana, paragraph 238, (available at www.icj-cij.org, visited April2, 2002). Botswana's arguments in this regard are not particularly convincing and at no time is it actually argued that an 'agreement' cannot be determined to exist through inaction.

[52] See, however, Vice-President Weeramantry's Dissenting Opinion in which he maintains that the Court, in its Judgment, gives its support to the view that the parties' understanding of the Treaty is the basis for the importance of subsequent practice' and, hence, includes silence and inaction, 386, paragraph 23. Vice-President Weeramantry, in his own capacity, finds that the term 'agreement' in Article 31, paragraph 3(b) can 'include an understanding manifested by conduct' (386, paragraph 24) and 'embraces a consensus or common understanding, as shown by conduct, regarding its [the treaty's] interpretation or application' (386, paragraph 26). Judge Parra-Aranguren, in his Dissenting opinion, too, find that an 'agreement' may be 'expressed through their [the parties'] joint or parallel positive activity, but it may also be ascertained from the activity of only one of the parties, where there is assent or lack of objection by the other party' (423, paragraph 17).

convention – which is to say that it must be participated or concurred in by at least the great majority of them, including all those which stand on any special relationship to the convention by reason of the functions they have to perform, or as beneficiaries under it, or otherwise'.[53]

2.VI. The Subjective Element Underlying Subsequent Practice

In order for state practice to contribute to the formation of customary international law it is traditionally required that the practice is perceived as obligatory. In this sense, one may ask whether practice, which assists the interpretation of a treaty, has to be carried out with some sort of subjective conviction.

Whereas the Court rarely elaborated on the issue, at least two central cases have explicated that the practice has to be carried out in the belief that it is legal under the treaty. In the 1977 *Beagle Channel Arbitration*, the Court of Arbitration had to interpret the 1881 Boundary Treaty between Argentina and Chile.[54] Among the acts considered as 'confirmatory or corroborative' of a certain interpretation were acts of jurisdiction exercised by Chile with regard to three islands. The Court of Arbitration found that the Chilean acts of jurisdiction 'tended to confirm the correctness of the Chilean interpretation of the Islands clause of the Treaty'.[55] The Chilean acts consisted of a 'series of administrative activities' over a number of years beginning in 1892 including the granting of concessions and the establishment of a postal service and, during the ensuring years, provision of medical services and education and the exercise of civil and criminal jurisdiction.[56] It was further established that Argentina had failed to object or protest the Chilean acts. The Court of Arbitration went on to state:

> In the context of the present case the acts of jurisdiction were not intended to establish a source of title independent of the terms of the Treaty; nor could they be considered as being in contradiction of those terms as understood by Chile. The evidence supports the

---

[53] Gerald Fitzmaurice: *The Law and Procedure of the International Court of Justice*, II, Cambridge University Press, 1995, 796. See also: 'It is, of course, axiomatic that the conduct in question must have been that of both or all – or, in the case of general multilateral conventions, of the great majority of the parties', Gerald Fitzmaurice: *The Law and Procedure of the International Court of Justice*, I, Cambridge University Press, 1995, 357. See also Georg Ress 'Die Bedeutung der nachfolgenden Praxis für die Vertragsinterpretation nach der Wiener Vertragsrechtskonvention (WVRK)' in Roland Bieder and Georg Ress (ed.) *Die Dynamik des Europäischen Gemeinschaftsrechts/The Dynamics of EC-Law* Nomos (1987) 49 at 55-56.

[54] *Beagle Channel Arbitration* (Argentina v. Chile), Court of Arbitration composed of H. Dillard, G. Fitzmaurice, A. Gros, C. Onyeama and S. Petren. Decision delivered on February 18, 1977. Reproduced in 52 *International Law Reports* 93. Reproduced in part in 17 *International Legal Materials* 632.

[55] 52 *International Law Reports* 221, paragraph 165.

[56] 52 *International Law Reports* 221-222, paragraph 166.

view that they could only derive from the Treaty. Under these circumstances the silence of Argentina permits the inference that the acts tended to confirm an interpretation of the meaning of the Treaty independent of the acts of jurisdiction themselves.[57]

In the recent *Kasikili/Sedudu Island Case*, the Court examined 'abundant references to the subsequent practice of the parties to the 1890 Treaty … as an element in the interpretation of that Treaty.[58] Namibia, for its part, relied on subsequent practice akin to the practice claimed by Chile in the *Beagle Channel Arbitration*: 'the control and use of Kasiskili Island by the Masubia of Caprivi, the exercise of jurisdiction over the Island by the Namibian governing authorities, and the silence by Botswana and its predecessors persisting for almost a century with full knowledge of the facts'.[59] The Court set out two criteria, which, as a minimum, had to be satisfied in order to establish a practice that constituted subsequent practice in the sense of Article 31, paragraph 3(b):

> the occupation of the Island by the Masubia was linked to a belief on the part of the Caprivi authorities [i.e. Namibia and predecessors] that the boundary laid down by the 1890 Treaty followed the southern channel of the Chobe; and, second, that the Bechuanaland authorities [i.e. Botswana and predecessors] were fully aware of and accepted this as a confirmation of the Treaty boundary.[60]

---

[57] 52 *International Law Reports* 224, paragraph 169.

[58] 39 *International Legal Materials*, 2000, 310 at 329, paragraph 47. The Court had to determine whether the reference to 'the main channel' Chobe River in an 1890 treaty between Great Britain and Germany respecting the spheres of influence of the two countries in Africa was to the northern/western channel or the southern channel in a bifurcated stretch of the river. Botswana principally relied on three sets of documents in support of its interpretation that the 'main channel' was the northern. The first document, the Eason Report, was an internal British document which had never been made known to Germany and could therefore not be 'regarded as representing "subsequent practice in the application of the treaty" of 1890' (39 *International Legal Materials*, 2000, 331, paragraph 55). The second document was an arrangement arrived at by authorities on both sides of the border with regard to the operation of a transport business on the Chobe River. The Court, however, found that this episode 'demonstrated the absence of agreement' and that the arrangement, therefore, was unable to aid in the interpretation (39 *International Legal Materials*, 2000, 338, paragraph 63). The last document relied upon by Botswana was a joint survey conducted by South Africa and Botswana in 1984/85. Again, however, the Court found that there was no agreement 'regarding the application of the 1980 Treaty' (39 *International Legal Materials*, 2000, 340, paragraph 69).

[59] 39 *International Legal Materials*, 2000, 342, paragraph 71.

[60] 39 *International Legal Materials*, 2000, 342-343, paragraph 74. Concretely, the ICJ did not find these criteria to be present: The Court did not find that the presence of Masubia tribespeople was 'linked to territorial claims by the Caprivi authorities' (39 *International Legal Materials*, 2000, 343, paragraph 74) Furthermore, 'the intermittent presence of the Masubia on the Island did not trouble anyone and was tolerated, not least because it did not appear to be connected with interpretation of the

These, in effect if not *ad verbatim*, are the criteria laid down by the Court of Arbitration in the *Beagle Channel Arbitration*: The practice must be:

- Related to the treaty which is being interpreted,
- Conducted in a belief that it is in accordance with the treaty or, in the words of the *Beagle Channel Arbitration*, not in contradiction of the Treaty, and
- Known by the other party and accepted by the other party as practice under the treaty.

This conclusion is further supported by the literature. Fitzmaurice finds that subsequent practice may indicate what the correct legal interpretation is 'because it is possible and reasonable in the circumstance to infer from the behaviour of the parties that they have regarded the interpretation they have given to the instrument in question as the legally correct one, and have tacitly recognized that, in consequence, certain behaviour was legally incumbent upon them'.[61] Amerasinghe makes a similar observation when he finds that the subjective element of an organ of an international organization is 'the belief that it was acting lawfully under the constitutive instrument. The *opinion juris* in this case is usually not a sense of obligation but a sense that the practice or conduct is lawful or not unlawful'.[62]

2.VII. Summary of the Findings

Concluding on the analysis set out above, it is possible to outline the following elements as necessary in order to identify subsequent practice in the application of the treaty that establishes an agreement of the parties regarding its interpretation: As just mentioned, the practice has to be related to the treaty and has to be conducted with a conviction that it is in accordance with the treaty proscriptions. The practice need take no particular form, i.e. it may consist of statements or acts, and no specific time span can be set; the central issue is whether the practice evidences a certain understanding, i.e. an agreement. Finally, parties can be seen to have accepted such an agreement if they do not object, i.e. by acquiescence. Still, a number of objections may be put forward and it is to those that we now turn.

---

terms of the 1890 Treaty' (Ibid.). Consequently, the practice did constitutes 'subsequent practice in the application of the 1890 Treaty and could, thus, not aid in its interpretation' (Ibid. paragraph 75).
[61] In the specific context of the *Certain Expenses Case* Fitzmaurice, however, that 'it [was] hardly possible to infer from the mere fact that Member States pay, that they necessarily admit in all cases a positive legal obligation to do so' and, hence, a certain interpretation of the Charter, 1962 ICJ 201.
[62] C.F. Amerasinghe *Principles of the Institutional Law of International Organizations* Cambridge University Press 1996, 50. See also Bernhardt who concludes that the conduct should be 'expressly limited to cases where the practice is consistent with the text of the treaty' Rudolf Bernhardt 'Interpretation and Implied (Tacit) Modification of Treaties' 27 *Zeitschrift fürAusländisches Öffentliches Recht und Völkerrecht* (1967) 491 at 501.

2.VIII. Objections to the Proposed Approach

An initial objection to the proposed approach based on subsequent practice might be the principled objection to a decidedly dynamic approach. Some may emphasize the original intent of the framers and point out that, if subsequent practice has a role to play it can only be to elucidate the original intentions of the framers (objection A). Some may further object to the proposed prominence of subsequent practice because they only consider it a subsidiary aid in the interpretation of a treaty (objection B). Furthermore, even if considered on par with other interpretative elements, it is but one among several interpretative tools that an interpreter ought to apply (objection C). Moreover, some may argue that the practice of an organ of the United Nations cannot be a supporting element of an interpretation (objection D). Each of these four objections will here be addressed in turn.

2.VIII.A. The Centrality of the Original Intent

As pointed out by several scholars, various approaches exist to interpretation. The predominant three are often listed as the 'subjective', the 'objective' and the 'teleological'.[63] Although all three approaches have a long history, the 'intentions' approach is the 'traditional'.[64] The entire process of interpretation of a provision or a term has often been seen as an attempt at determining the meaning of the term according to the intention of the parties at the time when they entered into the agreement.[65] There are plenty of statements, both past and present, to the effect that the task of the interpreter, and hence the assisting role to be played by interpretative criteria such as subsequent practice, is to establish the original intentions of the parties: In Advisory Opinion No. 12, the PCIJ found that the 'facts subsequent to the conclusion of the Treaty of Lausanne can only concern the Court in so far as they are calculated to

---

[63] See, for example, Ian Sinclair *The Vienna Convention on the Law of Treaties* 2nd ed. Manchester University Press (1984) 115. Fitzmaurice lists the same approaches as the 'intention of the parties' or founding fathers' school, the 'textual' or 'ordinary meaning of the word' school, and the 'teleological' or 'aims and objects' school, Gerald Fitzmaurice: *The Law and Procedure of the International Court of Justice*, I, Cambridge University Press, 1995, 42. Jacobs mentions the 'subjective approach', the 'textual approach' and the 'teleological approach', Francis G. Jacobs 'Varieties of approaches to Treaty Interpretation: with Special Reference to the draft Convention on the Law of Treaties before the Vienna Diplomatic Conference' 18 *International and Comparative Law Quarterly* (1969) 318 at 319.

[64] Gerald Fitzmaurice: *The Law and Procedure of the International Court of Justice*, I, Cambridge University Press, 1995, 44.

[65] Thirlway, Hugh 'The Law and Procedure of the International Court of Justice 1960-1989, Part Three, 62 *British Yearbook of International Law*, 1991, 51. See also, for example, Bowett, D.W.: 'Estoppel Before International Tribunals and its Relation to Acquiescence' in 33 *British Yearbook of International Law*, 1957, 176 at 178.

throw light on the intention of the Parties at the time of the conclusion of the Treaty'.[66] In the *Certain Expenses Case*, Judge Spender, in his separate opinion, held that 'it is of course a general principle of international law that the subsequent conduct of the parties to a bilateral – or multilateral – instrument may throw light on the intentions of the parties *at the time the instrument was entered into* and thus may provide a legitimate criterion of interpretation'.[67] More recently, Vice-President Weeramantry, in his Dissenting Opinion in the *Kasikili/Sedudu Island Case*, pointed out that action taken many years after the conclusion of the treaty (in this case 60 years after) 'can scarcely be used to help in showing how the Parties understood the Treaty', where understood (past tense) must refer to 'original intentions'.[68]

The 'intentions approach' entails a number of difficulties or drawbacks, especially if applied as the sole approach: As Karl, among others, points out when a controversy over a treaty term arises, it is often impossible to refer back to an original, common treaty understanding. The idea of an original intention between the parties may often be denied by the fact that they never considered the specific issue in detail. Even if they considered it, they may not have agreed in detail and, for this very reason, left the provision in question rather vague.[69] Moreover, the further removed in time an

---

[66] PCIJ, Series B, No. 12, 24. See also the 1935 Harvard Draft: In interpreting a treaty, the conduct or action of the parties thereto cannot be ignored. If all the parties to a treaty execute it, or permit its execution, in a particular manner, that fact may reasonably be taken into account as indicative of the real intention of the parties or of the purpose which the instrument was designed to serve. 1935 Harvard Research in International Law, Draft Convention on the Law of Treaties, With Comments, 966 and Wolfram Karl: *Vertrag und spätere Praxis im Völkerrecht: zum Einfluß der Praxis auf Inhalt und Bestand völkerrechtlicher Verträge* Springer, 1983, 127.

[67] 62 ICJ 189 (emphasis added). See similarly the 1956 *Italy-United States Air Transport Arbitration*, where the Arbitral Tribunal held that practice 'can serve as additional evidence in ascertaining the intentions of the parties and illustrate their intent as of the time the Agreement was concluded' 45 *International Law Reports*, 1972, 393 at 419. In its written statement in the *Namibia Case*, South Africa asserted that subsequent practice could be relevant 'only to the ascertainment of that common intent [of the parties] as it existed when the treaty was concluded' and interpretation cannot have a result of giving the treaty a meaning different from that which it bore at its inception'. 1971 ICJ Vol 1. 390.

[68] The *Kasikili/Sedudu Case*, 39 ILM (2000).389, paragraph 39. In the Eritrea-Ethiopia Boundary Decision, the Commission made reference to Lord McNair's *dictum* in the *Palena Award* in which he indicated that the role of the interpreter was to establish what the parties actually intended or their "common will". 21, 3.4. In his monograph on the Law of Treaties, Lord McNair also wrote about subsequent practice as having 'high probative value as to the intentions of the parties at the time of its [the treaty's] conclusion', Lord McNair, *The Law of Treaties*, 1961, 424. It may be asserted that the 'original intentions' approach, combined with the *uti possidetis juris* principle, may be quite suitable when interpreting border treaties, as in the *Kasikili/Sedudu* and *Eritrea/Ethiopia* cases.

[69] Wolfram Karl: *Vertrag und spätere Praxis im Völkerrecht : zum Einfluß der Praxis auf Inhalt und Bestand völkerrechtlicher Verträge* Springer, 1983, 139. See also, for example, Gerald Fitzmaurice: *The Law and Procedure of the International Court of Justice*, I, Cambridge University Press, 1995, 43, note 1 and 44-45 and Francis G. Jacobs 'Varieties of approaches to Treaty Interpretation: with Special Reference to the draft Convention on the Law of Treaties before the Vienna Diplomatic Conference' 18 *International and Comparative Law Quarterly* (1969) 318 at 338-339. See also McGinley who finds

interpretation is from the conclusion of the treaty, the more difficult it may become to pretend to project an interpretation based on subsequent practice back to the parties' original intentions.[70]

The 'original intentions' approach, while it may have been the traditional, has, however, lost ground during the course of the past 50 years. Thus, in 1957, Fitzmaurice could write that, by then, 'the textual approach is the one [method] on the whole favoured by the Court [over the 'intentions' approach]'.[71] This development was codified, so to speak, by Article 31 of the VCLT from 1969, which adopted the textual approach.[72]

Furthermore, the developments in the conception of inter-temporal law exhibit similar trends. The doctrine of inter-temporal law found its classical expression in Judge Huber's *dictum* in the Island of Palmas Case: 'A judicial fact must be appreciated in the light of the law contemporary with it, and not of the law in force at the time when a dispute in regard to it arises or falls to be settles'.[73] In other words, a treaty must be interpreted in light of the rules of international law as they existed at the time of the conclusion of the treaty and 'it is not permissible to import into the legal evaluation ... of an old treaty, doctrines of modern law that did not exist or were not accepted at the time, and only resulted from the subsequent development or evolution of international law'.[74] This seemingly straightforward doctrine has, however, undergone modification and qualification.[75]

---

that the 'original intentions' approach 'seems artificial and unduly restrictive', Ferald P. McGinley 'Practice as a Guide to Treaty Interpretation' 9 *The Fletcher Forum* (1985) 211-230 at 221.

[70] Blum, who also subscribes to the original intent approach, appears to support the idea that only practice from the period immediately following the conclusion of a treaty can be taken into account. One might call it 'original subsequent practice' Yehuda Z. Blum *Eroding the United Nations Charter* Martinus Nijhoff (1993) 248-249. The case in which the parties' intention was to let terms and provisions change with time is discussed below in the context of inter-temporal law.

[71] Gerald Fitzmaurice: *The Law and Procedure of the International Court of Justice*, I, Cambridge University Press, 1995, 338.

[72] See, in general, Jacobs 'It seems, that the Draft Convention [the later VCLT], in placing subsequent practice among the principle ... means of interpretation, represents a considerable from the practice of the Court.' Francis G. Jacobs 'Varieties of approaches to Treaty Interpretation: with Special Reference to the draft Convention on the Law of Treaties before the Vienna Diplomatic Conference' 18 *International and Comparative Law Quarterly* (1969) 318 at 329. See also Amerasinghe, 55: 'The Vienna Convention on the Law of Treaties gives a subsidiary place to the ascertainment of intentions as a means of interpretation'.

[73] *United Nations Reports of International Arbitrary Awards*, II, 1949, 845. The second part of the inter-temporal doctrine elaborated by Huber concerned the continued existence of a right acquired sometime in the past. This part of the doctrine, which does not concern us here, stipulates that the right, in order to be deemed to continue to exist, must have been maintained in accordance with the changing requirements according to the evolution of the law.

[74] Gerald Fitzmaurice: *The Law and Procedure of the International Court of Justice*, I, Cambridge University Press, 1995, 135. Fitzmaurice also states this notion as the 'principle of contemporaneity': 'The terms of a treaty must be interpreted according to the meaning which they possessed, or which would have been attributed to them, and in the light of current linguistic usage, at the time when the

The inter-temporal aspect has played a role in a number of cases.[76] Two cases are of particular interest for the present purposes.[77] In the 1971 Namibia Case, the Court began by stating the main principle of the inter-temporal doctrine: 'Mindful as it [the Court] is of the primary necessity of interpreting an instrument in accordance with the intention of the parties at the time of its conclusion…'.[78] The Court, however, then found that it 'is bound to take into account the fact that the concepts embodied in Article 22 of the Covenant [of the League of Nations] – "the strenuous conditions of the modern world" and "the well-being and development" of the peoples concerned – were not static, but were by definition evolutionary, as also, therefore, was the concept "sacred trust". The parties to the Covenant must consequently be deemed to have accepted them as such'.[79] It follows that the Court:

---

treaty was originally concluded', Fitzmaurice, Gerald: *The Law and Procedure of the International Court of Justice*, I, Cambridge University Press, 1995, 346. See also Ibid. 359-61.

[75] In spite of the fact that the issue was discussed in the International Law Commission, the Vienna Convention on the Law of Treaties does not refer to inter-temporal law. The reference to 'relevant rules of international law' in Article 31(3c) may, however, be read as a 'hint' to inter-temporal law, Higgins, Rosalyn: 'Some Observations on the Inter-Temporal Rule in International Law' in Makrczyk, Jerzy (ed.) *Theory of International Law at the Threshold of the 21st Century*, The Hague, Kluwer Law International, 1997, 181. In the context of the work of the International Law Commission on the Law of Treaties, some confusion involving the doctrine of inter-temporal law appear to have arisen during the consideration of draft Article 68(c): 'The operation of a treaty may also be modified by the subsequent emergence of a new rule of customary law relating to matters dealt with in the treaty and binding upon all the parties', *Yearbook of the International Law Commission*, 1964, Vol. II, 198. Some governments, in their comments, found that this provision expressed, in the words of Israel, 'the second leg' of the inter-temporal law doctrine as enunciated by Judge Huber, *Yearbook of the International Law Commission, 1966*, II, 87. The Special Rapporteur Waldock agreed that it was somewhat unclear whether draft Article 68(c) was to be understood either as dealing with inter-temporal law or as dealing with the relationship between treaty and custom, *Yearbook of the International Law Commission, 1966*, II, 90. The provision was subsequently dropped.

[76] See for example the Morocco Case, ICJ Reports 1952, 176; the Minquiers Case, ICJ Reports 1953, 47; and the Indian Passage Case, ICJ Reports, 1960, 6.

[77] Mention may also be had of the early case from the Permanent Court concerning the Nationality Decrees. Here the Court found that 'the words "solely within the domestic jurisdiction" seem rather to contemplate certain matters which, though they may very closely concern the interests of more than one State, are not, in principle, regulated by international law. As regards such matters, each State is sole judge. The question whether a certain matter is or is not solely within the jurisdiction of a State is an essentially relative question; it depends upon the development of international relations. Thus in the present state of international law, questions of nationality are, in the opinion of the Court, in principle within this reserved domain', Nationality Decrees in Tunis and Morocco (French Zone) on November 8, 1921, Advisory Opinion No. 4, Permanent Court of International Justice. Reproduced in Hudson, Manley O. (ed.): *World Court Reports: A Collection of Judgments, Orders and Opinions of the Permanent Court of International Justice*, Washington, Carnegie Endowment for International Peace, Vol. I (1922-1926), 1934, 156.

[78] Legal Consequences for States of the Continued Presence of South Africa in Namibia (South West Africa) Notwithstanding Security Council Resolution 276 (1971), ICJ, Advisory Opinion, 31, 53.

[79] Legal Consequences for States of the Continued Presence of South Africa in Namibia (South West Africa) Notwithstanding Security Council Resolution 276 (1971), ICJ, Advisory Opinion, 31, 53.

must take into consideration the changes which have occurred in the supervening half-century, and its interpretation cannot remain unaffected by the subsequent development of law, through the Charter of the United Nations and by the way of customary law. Moreover, an international instrument has to be interpreted and applied within the framework of the entire legal system prevailing at the time of the interpretation. In the domain to which the present proceedings relate, the last fifty years, as indicated above, have brought important developments.[80]

This is indeed a *dictum* with potentially far reaching consequences. Although the Court implicitly invokes the intention of the parties – they must be deemed to have accepted the words and concepts as dynamic – it does not provide any statements to support this contention.[81] In the 1978 Aegean Sea Continental Shelf Case, the Court again had to address the question of how to deal with decades old instruments:[82]

Once it is established that the expression "the territorial status of Greece" was used in Greece's instrument of accession as a generic term denoting any matters comprised within the concept of territorial status under general international law, the presumption necessarily arises that its meaning was intended to follow the evolution of the law and to correspond with the meaning attached to the expression by the law in force at any given time. The presumption, in view of the Court, is even more compelling when it is recalled that the 1928 Act was a convention for the pacific settlement of disputes designed to be of the most general kind and of continuing duration, for it hardly seems conceivable that in such a convention terms like "domestic jurisdiction" and "territorial status" were intended to have a fixed content regardless of the subsequent evolution of international law.[83]

---

[80] Legal Consequences for States of the Continued Presence of South Africa in Namibia (South West Africa) Notwithstanding Security Council Resolution 276 (1971), ICJ, Advisory Opinion, 31, 53.

[81] As Thirlway observes: 'The doubts prompted by this line of argument do not relate to the legal logic, but to the basic finding, as to the intentions of the States concerned in 1919, upon which it is built'. Hugh Thirlway 'The Law and Procedure of the International Court of Justice 1960-1989, Part One, 60 *British Yearbook of International Law*, 1989, 136.

[82]See also the Guinea-Bissau/Senegal Arbitration, mentioned by Kontou, where it was found that the parties intended terms such as 'territorial sea' and 'continental shelf' to be interpreted in accordance with their customary law meaning at the time of the award, Kontou, Nancy *The Termination and Revision of Treaties in the Light of New Customary International Law*, Oxford University Press, 1994, 133.

[83] Aegean Sea Continental Shelf Case, ICJ Reports, 1978, 32, para. 77. Greece in some sense caused to the Court to take this line of reasoning by invoking a dynamic interpretation of the word 'rights' as a ground for the Court's jurisdiction: 'The Greek Government invokes as a basis for the Court's

In addition to the reference to 'a generic term',[84] it is interesting to observe that the Court found its conclusion supported by the fact that the 1928 Act 'was a convention for the pacific settlement of disputes designed to be of the most general kind and of continuing duration' indicating that central concepts in the treaty could not have been 'intended to have a fixed content regardless of the subsequent evolution of international law'. These attributes are also characteristic of the UN Charter.

The modified version of the inter-temporal doctrine can thus, in the words of Thrilway, be stated as: 'Provided that, where it can be established that it was the intention of the parties that the meaning or scope of a term or expression used in the treaty should follow the development of the law, the treaty must be interpreted so as to give effect to that intention'.[85] Based on this, as well as on the Court's references to generic terms, it may reasonably be argued that terms such as 'territorial integrity' and 'political independence', found in Article 2(4) of the UN Charter and 'armed attack', found in Article 51 of the same treaty, were intended by the parties to develop along international law in general over time or are inherently or 'by definition' evolutionary.

---

jurisdiction in the present case Article 17 of the General Act under which parties agreed to submit to judicial settlement all disputes with regard to which they "are in conflict as to their respective rights". Yet the rights that are the subject of the claim upon which Greece requests the Court in the application to exercise its jurisdiction under Article 17 are the very rights over the continental shelf of which, as Greece insists, the authors of the General Act could have had no idea whatever in 1928. If the Greek government is correct, as it undoubtedly is, in assuming that the meaning of the generic term "rights" in Article 17 follows the evolution of the law, so as to be capable of embracing rights over the continental shelf, it is not clear why the similar term "territorial status" should not likewise be liable to evolve in meaning in accordance with "the development of international relations"', ICJ Reports, 1978, 33, para. 78. In addition, part of Greece's claim concerned an area, which Greece had been ceded by Italy in 1947. In a territorial context, Greece had thus evolved and this 'clearly had some bearing on the interpretation of the Greek reservation as to "territorial status"', Sinclair, Ian: *The Vienna Convention on the Law of Treaties*, Manchester, Manchester University Press, 1984, 126. The Court found that 'it would be a little surprising if the meaning of Greece's reservation of disputes relating to its "*territorial status*" was not also to evolve in light of the change in the territorial extent of the Greek State brought about by "development of international relations"', ICJ Reports 1978, 33, para. 78 (emphasis in original). 'Greece could not, therefore, eat its cake and have it, too', Elias, T.O.: 'The Doctrine of Intertemporal Law' in 74 *American Journal of International Law*, 1980, 285 at 301.

[84] When examining the criteria of interpretation, Schachter employs a category he terms 'standards', which include 'highly generalized prescriptions which emphasize the necessity of evaluating the individual features of events'. As examples he mentions 'due care', 'good faith' and 'peace-loving'. When interpreting such standards, one need necessarily consider the basic aims of the Charter and the 'felt necessities of time and place', Oscar Schachter 'Interpretation of the Charter in the Political Organs of the United Nations' Salo Engel (ed.) *Law, State and International Legal Order: Essays in Honor of Hans Kelsen*, The University of Tennessee Press, 1964, 276-277.

[85] Hugh Thirlway 'The Law and Procedure of the International Court of Justice 1960-1989, Part Three, 62 *British Yearbook of International Law*, 1991, 57. Sinclair comes to a similar but slightly different conclusion: There is scope for the narrow and limited proposition that the evolution and development of the law can be taken into account when interpreting terms that by their nature lend themselves to an evolutionary interpretation. Such an approach must, however, not conflict with the intentions of the parties, see Sinclair, Ian: *The Vienna Convention on the Law of Treaties*, Manchester, Manchester University Press, 1984, 140.

Consequently, while the 'original intentions' approach today is less influential, it makes a lot of sense to maintain an emphasis on the 'contemporary' or 'current intentions' of the parties: Imagine a treaty article for which three different interpretations (a, b and c) are compatible with the wording. It would not be impossible to imagine that at the conclusion of the treaty, say 30 years ago, the parties believed interpretation 'a' to be the correct. 15 years later, their practice under the treaty, however, indicates that option 'b' was at that point the agreed interpretation. More recently, however, changing circumstances in general have caused the parties to change their practice so that they now are in harmony with alternative 'c'.

Whereas the outlined developments are perfectly conceivable, it would appear conceptually strained to legitimize the changing interpretations by referring back to the intention of the parties at the time of the conclusion of the treaty. Yet, the process as described is legitimate. Thrilway, for instance, finds such a scenario, where a working relationship has been established under the treaty [i.e. subsequent practice] which was not contemplated by the parties when they prepared the treaty, 'equally conceivable' [and legitimate] as the more orthodox version where the practice is taken as indicative of the intention of the parties at the time of the conclusion of the treaty.[86] A comparable sentiment is expressed by McDougal: 'In our recommended goals, evidence of the parties' expectations at the time of the commitment should of course be given an initial presumption which would hold in the absence of persuasive indices that such expectations had been altered by subsequent explicit communications or implicit acts of collaboration. If such evidence is produced, however, the parties' contemporary expectations should be respected'.[87]

While the idea that the subsequent practice of the parties may be utilized to throw light on their original intentions was often clearly expressed,[88] it arguably attained some appearance of an illusion the older the treaty became. If, on the other hand, the parties' intentions are taken to mean their current intentions, their subsequent practice may play an obvious role in clarifying these: As noted by Ress, subsequent practice 'regularly illustrates not the historical intentions of the [then] new treaty but ... a dynamic consensus of interpretation based on the organizational purpose'.[89] Franck examined the

---

[86] Thirlway, Hugh 'The Law and Procedure of the International Court of Justice 1960-1989, Part Three, 62 *British Yearbook of International Law*, 1991, 51-52. See also Fitzmaurice: 'If, whatever its exact wording and the precise intentions its framers may have had, a convention has in practice been understood and applied in a certain way, this will be a factor that may legitimately be taken account of in any dispute as to its correct interpretation and application', Gerald Fitzmaurice: *The Law and Procedure of the International Court of Justice*, II, Cambridge University Press, 1995, 796.

[87] Myres S. McDougal, Harold D. Lasswell and James C. Miller: *The Interpretation of Agreements and World Public Order: Principles of Content and Procedure* Yale University Press (1967) 143-144. For a further, similar, attitude reference may be had to Reuter who finds it essential 'to give precedence to its [the parties' intention] most immediate manifestation'. Paul Reuter *Introduction to the Law of Treaties* Kegan Paul International (1995) 96, paragraph 143.

[88] PCIJ, Series B, No. 12, 24.

[89] Ress in Bruno Simma (ed.) *The Charter of the United Nations: A Commentary*, Oxford University Press (1994) 39, paragraph 27. Fitzmaurice notes that 'the way in which the treaty has actually been

Appeals Chamber decision in *Tadic* concerning the constitutionality under the Charter of the ICTY[90] and found that the decision marked 'recognition of the role of practice in interpreting the Charter, sometimes in radical departure from original intent'.[91] Jacobs found that such a shift, from original to current intentions, took place with the VCLT: 'It is arguable that the main significance of subsequent practice in the Convention is not in clarifying the original intentions of the parties, but in enabling effect to be given to their subsequent intentions, at least within the framework of the original text'.[92]

2.VIII.B. The General Role of Subsequent Practice

Fitzmaurice wrote that 'the principle of subsequent practice ... must ... be regarded as being, in general, subordinate to the principle of the textual and natural meaning'[93] and 'not intended to introduce any conclusive or determinative element into the matter [of interpretation], but merely one which, along with others, has evidential value, though perhaps one of a high degree of certainly and reliability'.[94] More recently, Reuter has expressed a related view that the various elements in Article 31 are 'carefully and subtly graduated' and he perceives some elements, such as the subsequent practice of the parties, as carrying 'less weight'.[95]

These observations are, by now, at odds with the general rule laid down in Article 31 of the VCLT. Article 31 contains and is entitled the 'General Rule of Interpretation'. The International Law Commission emphasized that the heading was chosen in the singular specifically to convey the message that the elements enumerated in the article

---

interpreted in practice is evidence (sometimes the best evidence) of what its correct interpretation is'. And he continues: 'It is probably implicit in this view that while it may often be uncertainty about the original intentions of the framers ... there is usually neither as regards the way in which the parties have subsequently operated the treaty', Gerald Fitzmaurice: *The Law and Procedure of the International Court of Justice*, I, Cambridge University Press, 1995, 50 and 50, note 1.

[90] The Appeals Chamber found that 'it can thus be said that there is a common understanding, manifested by the "subsequent practice" of the membership of the United Nations at large, that the "threat to the Peace" of Article 39 [of the UN Charter] may include, as one of its species, internal armed conflicts', *Tadic* Decision on the Defence Motion for Interlocutory Appeal on Jurisdiction, IT-94-1-AR 72, ICTY Appeals Chamber, October 2, 1995, para. 30.

[91] Thomas M. Franck *Recourse to Force: Sate Action Against threats and Armed Attacks* Cambridge University Press (2002) 43.

[92] Francis G. Jacobs 'Varieties of approaches to Treaty Interpretation: with Special Reference to the draft Convention on the Law of Treaties before the Vienna Diplomatic Conference' 18 *International and Comparative Law Quarterly* (1969) 318 at 329.

[93] Gerald Fitzmaurice: *The Law and Procedure of the International Court of Justice*, I, Cambridge University Press, 1995, 358.

[94] Gerald Fitzmaurice: *The Law and Procedure of the International Court of Justice*, II, Cambridge University Press, 1995, 796.

[95] Paul Reuter, *Introduction to the Law of Treaties*, 2nd Ed., Kegan Paul International, 1995, 96, paragraph 144. See also Professor Reuter's comments as a member of the International Law Commission about proceeding 'from the simple to the complex, from the immediate to the remote', YBILC, I, part II, 1966, 188, paragraph 40.

were not in any hierarchical order.[96] The various elements are to be applied in 'a single combined operation'.[97]

Related to the question of the place of subsequent practice in the interpretation process is the question of when doubt exists regarding a text. This is because, if subsequent practice is relegated to a second tier and regarded merely as a subsidiary or extraneous means of interpretation it will only have a role to play if the primary interpretation yields an ambiguous or absurd result.

On the face of it, one might think that, obviously, no interpretation is needed if no doubt exists regarding the meaning of a term: The Spanish jurist Vattel held that 'it is not permissible to interpret that which has no need of interpretation'.[98] This conclusion has been drawn by the PCIJ,[99] by the ICJ,[100] by individual judges, for example Spender[101] and Weeramantry[102], and authors, such as Bowett.[103] Yet, one may query as to which elements are to be relied upon to achieve the clear meaning. One may, as a matter of theory, agree or disagree with these reflections. McDougal, for one, disagreed. Speaking as the delegate of the United States at the Conference, he found that: 'In reality, words [have] no fixed or natural meaning which the parties to an agreement [cannot] alter. The "plain and ordinary" meanings of words [are] multiple and ambiguous and [can] be made particular and clear only by reference to the factual circumstances of their use'.[104] Judge Spender, too, found that 'the ordinary and natural

---

[96] 'The words 'together with' indicated that the stipulations that follow are to be taken as incorporated in the basic statement of the rule, and not as norms of an inferior character', Robert Jennings and Arthur Watts, *Oppenheim's International Law*, 9th Ed., 1992, 1274, note 17.

[97] *Yearbook of the International Law Commission, 1966*, II, 87, 219-220. See, for example, the European Court of Human Rights' judgment in the Golder Case, Paragraph 30.

[98] E. de Vattel *The Law of Nations or the Principles of Natural Law: Applied to the Conduct and to the Affairs of Nations and of Sovereigns* Vol III, Oceana (1964) Chapter XVII, 199. Quoted by McDougal at the Vienna Conference, 31st meeting, April 19, 1968, 167, see United Nations Conference on the Law of Treaties: official records: summary records of the plenary meetings and of the meetings of the Committee of the Whole, 1968/1969, Vienna, Austria.

[99] See, for example, the *Brazilian Loans Case* where the Court found that subsequent conduct might help ascertain the intention of the Parties, but only where the contract 'is ambiguous', PCIJ Ser. A, No. 21 (1929) 118-120.

[100] 'If the relevant words in their natural and ordinary meaning make sense in their context, that is the end of the matter'. Competence of the General Assembly, 1950 ICJ 8.

[101] In any case subsequent conduct may only provide a criterion of interpretation when the text is obscure, Spender 1962 ICJ 189 see also 185-186 and 191.

[102] Vice-President Weeramantry's Dissenting Opinion: 'I stress, of course, that resort to subsequent practice, as showing contemporaneous understanding of the treaty, can only be had when the ordinary meaning of the words used in the Treaty is not sufficiently clear'. 39 ILM 387, paragraph 28.

[103] Derek Bowett "Estoppel Before International Tribunals and its Relation to Acquiescence 33 *British Yearbook of International Law* (1957) 177.

[104] 31st meeting, 167, 44, see United Nations Conference on the Law of Treaties: official records: summary records of the plenary meetings and of the meetings of the Committee of the Whole, 1968/1969, Vienna, Austria.

sense of words may at times be a matter of considerable difficulty to determine. What is their ordinary and natural sense to one may not be so to another'.[105]

Be that as it may, subsequent to the coming into force of the VCLT, and the finding by the ICJ that the provisions on interpretation reflect customary international law, one may reasonably assert that there is no 'ordinary meaning' in the sense of Article 31 of the VCLT without subsequent practice: 'subsequent practice may be taken into account when establishing such [ordinary] meaning'.[106] The Court would seem, in the *Kasikili/Sedudu Case,* to have confirmed that the determination of the 'ordinary meaning' of a word is a cumulative exercise involving the elements of Article 31: 'determin[ing] the ordinary meaning of the words "main channel" by reference to the most commonly used criteria in international law and practice'.[107]

2.VIII.C. The Primary Role of Subsequent Practice

When the Court interprets a treaty, it often applies the 'belt and suspenders' approach which entails an initial indication of how the Court understands the ordinary meaning of a certain term to be followed by a confirmation of this finding based on various elements of interpretation, including the subsequent practice of the parties. In this process, the Court often follows the order found in Article 31 of the VCLT. (As pointed out, this order is not an 'order of importance' or a hierarchy but merely a kind of chronological order.) This again means that an element such as subsequent practice rarely serves as a determining element in its own right.

One may, however, consider whether this broad observation is equally valid when the Court deals with the interpretation of constituent instruments. The general question concerning the interpretation of constituent instruments is somewhat controversial and a thorough study of this question would require its own thesis.[108] When considering the UN Charter and its interpretation, most authors start out establishing the fact that the Charter, like other constituent instruments, is a multilateral treaty.[109] Similar

---

[105] 62 ICJ 184.

[106] C.F. Amerasinghe *Principles of the Institutional Law of International Organizations* Cambridge University Press 1996, 48.

[107] 39 ILM 310 at 323, paragraph 27. In this case the reference to 'criteria' must be to criteria of interpretation, since one may reasonably assert that international law does not carry general criteria for what is meant by 'main channel'.

[108] For a recent example, see Tetsuo Sato *Evolving Constitutions of International Organizations* Kluwer Law International (1996). One controversial issue is whether constituent instruments of international organizations require their own, entirely separate interpretative framework, as Sato argues, or as proposed by E. Lauterpacht, there is an overlap between the general rules found in the VCLT and the rules of constitutional interpretation and that the latter have their foundation in the former, Elihu Lauterpacht 'The Development of the Law of International Organizations by the Decisions of International Tribunals' *Recueil des Cours – Collected Courses,* The Hague Academy of International Law, 1976, IV, Tome 152, 416.

[109] Blaine Sloan 'The United Nations Charter as a Constitution' 1 *Pace Yearbook of International Law* (1989) 61: 'To state the obvious, the Charter of the United Nations is a multilateral convention to

observations have been made by the International Court of Justice.[110] As pointed out by the Court, this would indicate the application of the general rules of interpretation:[111] 'On the previous occasions when the Court has had to interpret the Charter of the United Nations, it has followed the principles and rules applicable in general to the interpretation of treaties, since it has recognized that the Charter is a multilateral treaty, albeit a treaty having certain special characteristics'.[112] These general rules are now found in the Vienna Convention on the Law of Treaties (VCLT).[113] The rules on interpretation found in the VCLT have, furthermore, been determined by the ICJ to reflect customary international law.[114]

---

which all the members of the Organization are parties'. Benedetto Conforti *The Law and Practice of the United Nations* Kluwer Law International (1996) 10: 'The Charter ... is an international treaty'. Bardo Fassbender 'The United Nations Charter as Constitution of the International Community' 36 *Columbia Journal of Transnational Law* (1998) 529 at 531: 'The Charter of the United Nations was brought into existence in the form of an international treaty'.

[110] See, for example, the first admissions case (in response to a claim that the Court could not deal with interpretations of the Charter): 'Nowhere is any provision to be found forbidding the Court ... to exercise in regard to Article 4 of the Charter, *a multilateral treaty*, an interpretative function which falls within the normal exercise of its judicial powers' (emphasis added), 1948 ICJ 61 (repeated in the second admissions case: 1950 ICJ 4 at 6). Recently, the Court held that 'from a formal standpoint, the constituent instruments of international organizations are multilateral treaties, to which the well-established rules of treaty interpretation apply', the *Legality of the Use by a State of Nuclear Weapons in Armed Conflict – WHO Request*, 1996 ICJ 75, paragraph 19.

[111] Verdross and Simma, *Universelles Völkerrecht*, 1984, 165, paragraph 270.

[112] 1962 ICJ 151 at 157.

[113] This also represents the formal standpoint of the VCLT itself, which in Article 5 stipulates that the Convention applies to conventions, which are constituent instruments of an international organization. See also Ress who points out that the VCLT does not distinguish between different types of treaties, Georg Ress 'Die Bedeutung der nachfolgenden Praxis für die Vertragsinterpretation nach der Wiener Vertragsrechtskonvention (WVRK)' in Roland Bieder and Georg Ress (ed.) *Die Dynamik des Europäischen Gemeinschaftsrechts/The Dynamics of EC-Law* Nomos (1987) 49 at 52.

[114] 'The Court would recall that, in accordance with customary international law, reflected in Article 31 of the 1969 VCLT', 1994 ICJ 6 at 21-22, paragraph 41. This indicates that Article 4 of the VCLT which stipulates that the Convention only applies to treaties 'which are concluded by States after the entry into force' of the VCLT does not prevent the Court from interpreting earlier treaties, see the *Kasikili/Sedudu Case* 39 ILM 310 at 320, paragraph 18.

This having been said, many authors[115] and the Court[116] emphasize the special or constitutional character of the Charter and the need for a modification of the VCLT approach when interpreting the Charter. It is suggested that one such modification to the VCLT framework would be a stronger focus on subsequent practice: When the Court has dealt with constituent treaties there is some evidence to indicate that subsequent practice, whether by member states or by organs, has played a more prominent role than in the case of a normal treaty. In the *Reparations Case*, for example, the Court, initially, had to decide whether 'the [UN] Organization [had] such a nature as involves the capacity to bring an international claim? ... in other words, does the Organization possess international personality?'[117] The Court found that the Charter did not explicitly settle this issue. However, the Court further found that the Charter had equipped the Organization with organs with special tasks and instituted obligations for the Member States *vis-à-vis* the Organization.[118] Moreover, the Court found that 'practice – in particular the conclusion of conventions to which the Organization is a party – has

---

[115] See, for example, E. Lautherpacht who writes that 'it is a fact ... that the existing rules of treaty interpretation have not always proved fully or adequately applicable to the interpretation of constitutions. The Court has therefore developed an approach to interpretation marked by several elements, which have a relevance only to constitutional problems', Elihu Lauterpacht 'The Development of the Law of International Organizations by the Decisions of International Tribunals' *Recueil des Cours – Collected Courses,* The Hague Academy of International Law, 1976, IV, Tome 152, 416. See, furthermore, Ress who asserts that 'different rules of interpretation must be applied ... to the normative part' of the Charter (27, paragraph 1) and that 'specific organizational peculiarities must be considered when interpreting the Charter' Ress in Bruno Simma (ed.) *The Charter of the United Nations: A Commentary*, Oxford University Press (1994) 30, paragraph 9. See also Blaine Sloan 'The United Nations Charter as a Constitution' 1 *Pace Yearbook of International Law* (1989) 61: 'But the Charter is also a constitution'. Benedetto Conforti *The Law and Practice of the United Nations* Kluwer Law International (1996) 10: 'In so far as it [the Charter] gives rise to a set of organs that are designed to carry out basic functions within the international community ... it is usually considered also as a kind of Constitution'. Amerasinghe: 'Constitutional texts are treaties or conventions and must be interpreted as treaties or conventions, though there may be special considerations which are relevant and they may have special characteristics' C.F. Amerasinghe *Principles of the Institutional Law of International Organizations* Cambridge University Press 1996, 23. *Contra*, see Macdonald's review in 'The United Natiosn Charter: Constitution or Contract?' in R. St. J. Macdonald and Douglas M. Johnston (ed.) *The Structure and Process of International Law: Essays in Legal Philosophy, Doctrine and Theory* Martinus Nijhoff (1993) 889-912.

[116] See, for example, the *Legality of the Use by a State of Nuclear Weapons in Armed Conflict – WHO Request* where the Court maintained that 'the constituent instruments of international organizations are also [in addition to being multilateral treaties] treaties of a particular type', 1996 ICJ 75, paragraph 19. Among the individual judges of the Court, Alvarez was, early on, very conscious and explicit about the unique aspects of an international constitution such as the Charter: The institution, established by the Charter, 'acquires a life of its own ... and it must develop ... in accordance with the requirements of international life' (1948 ICJ 68). Two years later, he continued: Interpretation to-day (1950) 'must be made in such a way as to ensure that institutions and rules of law shall continue to be in harmony with the new conditions in the life of the peoples' (1950 ICJ 16).

[117] 1949 ICJ 178.

[118] 1949 ICJ 178.

confirmed this character [of having international personality] of the Organization'.[119] The importance of practice was further accentuated when the Court held that 'whereas a State possesses the totality of international rights and duties recognized by international law, the rights and duties of an entity such as the [UN] Organization must depend upon its purposes and functions as specified or implied in its constituent documents and *developed in practice*.[120] Reading the Court's argument, it is, as openly acknowledged by the Court, very much based on the establishment of powers implied by the function and purpose of the Organization.[121] The primary traditional element of interpretation claimed by the Court was the practice, which confirmed that the UN in certain respects occupies a detached position from its Members.

Chronologically, one may, at this point, add the observation of Judge Lauterpacht, in the 1955 *Voting Procedure* case, according to which 'a proper interpretation of a constitutive instrument must take into account not only the formal letter of the original instrument but also *its operation in actual practice* and in the light of the *revealed tendencies in the life* of the organization'.[122]

In the 1962 *Certain Expenses Advisory Opinion*, the Court was asked whether expenditures authorized in a number of General Assembly resolutions constituted 'expenses of the Organization' within the meaning of Article 17, paragraph 2 of the UN Charter.[123] In the course of answering the question, the Court made reference to the practice of the Organization, and in particular the General Assembly, on several occasions. The Court's extensive reliance on the subsequent practice of the organs prompted serious criticism voiced in a separate opinion by Judge Spender.[124]

The developments which took place with regard to Article 27, paragraph 3 of the UN Charter and which were dealt with in the 1971 *Namibia* decision can, as will be discussed in the next chapter, be viewed either as the result of interpretation or the result of modification. The Court found that the proceedings of the Security Council 'extending over a long period supply abundant evidence' that the members of the Council, including the permanent members, 'have consistently and uniformly interpreted the practice of voluntary abstention by a permanent member as not constituting a bar to the adoption of resolutions'.[125] At least two of the authors who

---

[119] 1949 ICJ 179.

[120] 1949 ICJ 174 at 180 (emphasis added).

[121] The forward looking and evolutionary nature of the decision may be confirmed by Judge Alvarez's approval of the decision as being 'in accordance with the general principles of the new international law', Separate Opinion by Judge Alvarez, 1949 ICJ 190.

[122] Lauterpacht, 1955 ICJ 67 (emphases added).

[123] 1962 ICJ 151.

[124] Spender found that he was unable 'to regard any usage or practice followed by any organ of the United Nations which has been determined by a majority therein against the will of a minority as having any legal relevance or probative value', Judge Spender, Separate Opinion, 1962 ICJ 197. Rather Judge Spender proposed looking at the words in their ordinary and natural sense, in their context and illuminated by the purpose of the Charter.

[125] Legal Consequences for States of the Continued Presence of South Africa in Namibia (South West Africa) Notwithstanding Security Council Resolution 276 (1971), Advisory Opinion, 22, paragraph 22.

view the process as best described as one of interpretation, point out that the ICJ did 'not stress that the result gained from scrutinizing the practice could have been achieved just the same by other means of interpretation'[126] and that 'the Court used the practice of the Security Council and the General Assembly directly to give meaning to provisions of the Charter, where, it would appear, there were gaps in the language'.[127]

Recently, in the *Legality of the Use by a State of Nuclear Weapons in Armed Conflict – WHO Request*, the Court stressed 'the imperatives associated with the effective performance of its functions, as well as its *own practice*, are all elements which may deserve special attention when the time comes to interpret these constituent treaties'.[128] The Court then proceeded to draw out the pertinent elements of interpretation to be the following: 'a treaty must be interpreted "in its context and in light if its object and purpose" and there shall be

> "taken into account, together with the context:
>
> ....
>
> (b) any subsequent practice in the application of the treaty which
> establishes the agreement of the parties regarding its
> interpretation"'.[129]

Hence, in addition to emphasizing the 'own practice' of the organization, the Court went out of its way to quote the VCLT provision on subsequent practice *ad verbatim*.

The central importance of subsequent practice in Charter interpretation is confirmed by several authors. Sloan, for example, finds that the special features which distinguish constituent treaties, such as the Charter, from other treaties 'preeminently warrant' the application of the following points when interpreting the text: evolutionary development, subsequent practice, structural interpretation and effectiveness.[130] Reuter notes that it has often been said that constituent instruments of an international organization should be interpreted in a 'constructive' fashion.[131] He, however, finds that the ICJ 'always relies on practice' and that the real question is whether this practice includes the practice of the member states in addition to the practice of the organization. Hence, Reuter appears to reverse the more common question concerning the admittance of the practice of the organs of an organization. By way of conclusion he states that 'established practice' is a practice which 'member states have not objected to'.[132] Sato,

---

[126] Mark E. Villiger, *Customary International Law and Treaties*, The Hague, Kluwer Law International, 1997, 41, paragraph 33.

[127] C.F. Amerasinghe *Principles of the Institutional Law of International Organizations* Cambridge University Press 1996, 49.

[128] 1996 ICJ 75, Paragraph 19 (emphasis added).

[129] 1996 ICJ 75, Paragraph 19

[130] Blaine Sloan 'The United Nations Charter as a Constitution' 1 *Pace Yearbook of International Law* (1989) 61 at 117.

[131] Paul Reuter *Introduction to the Law of Treaties* Kegan Paul International (1995) 149, note 142.

[132] Paul Reuter *Introduction to the Law of Treaties* Kegan Paul International (1995) 149, note 142.

in his new doctrine of constituent instruments as constitutions of an international organization, finds that the interpretative framework differs from general treaties in two respect, one of which (the qualitative) emphasizes the importance of subsequent practice of the organs of the organization.[133]

All in all, the developments just sketched out, i.e. the movement away from the original intentions of the parties and the elevation of the subsequent practice to the status of a primary element in the process of interpretation in addition to the importance of subsequent practice of organs (to be discussed immediately below), may be seen as part of an overall trend with a movement away from the historical approach as a 'symptom of the general trend towards treating at least major normative multilateral conventions as having a life of their own'.[134] E. Lauterpacht notes 'the diminished importance of the intention of the parties as an element in the interpretation of international constitutions is matched by, and reflected in, the growing value attached to the actual practice of organizations as an element in the interpretative process'.[135] Finally, Ress, in his Charter Commentary stressed that 'whereas the static interpretation ... was undisputed in the past, the dynamic-evolutionary method prevailed under the influence of the development of the law of treaties'.[136] He further finds that 'an evolutionary interpretation [of the Charter] was already envisaged during the San Francisco Conference'[137] and concludes that 'quasi-authentic interpretation by way of an almost uniform practice on the part of the organs and its explanation as an interpretational agreement among the member states ... will be of increasing importance'.[138]

---

[133] Tetsuo Sato *Evolving Constitutions of International Organizations* Kluwer Law International (1996) 12 and 232-242.

[134] Hugh Thirlway 'The Law and Procedure of the International Court of Justice 1960-1989, Part Three, 62 *British Yearbook of International Law*, 1991, 56.

[135] Elihu Lauterpacht 'The Development of the Law of International Organizations by the Decisions of International Tribunals' *Recueil des Cours – Collected Courses,* The Hague Academy of International Law, 1976, IV, Tome 152, 447. Karl, too, traces a development from an emphasis on the original intention of the parties towards a more dynamic use of subsequent practice, Wolfram Karl: *Vertrag und spätere Praxis im Völkerrecht: zum Einfluß der Praxis auf Inhalt und Bestand völkerrechtlicher Verträge* Springer, 1983, 139 et seq.

[136] Ress in Bruno Simma (ed.) *The Charter of the United Nations: A Commentary*, Oxford University Press (1994) 35, paragraph 20.

[137] Ress in Bruno Simma (ed.) *The Charter of the United Nations: A Commentary*, Oxford University Press (1994) 36, paragraph 21.

[138] Ress in Bruno Simma (ed.) *The Charter of the United Nations: A Commentary*, Oxford University Press (1994) 43-44, paragraph 44. See also Amerasinghe: 'The principles of effectiveness and subsequent practice have become forceful elements in constitutional interpretation in particular, because constitutions are regarded as organic instruments that have to be developed through interpretation'. C.F. Amerasinghe, *Principles of the International Law of International Institutions*, Cambridge, Cambridge University Press, 1996, 60.

2.VIII.D. Practice of an International Organ

An important question concerns the relationship between practice of the member states under the Charter and practice of organs of the UN and whether and to what extent practice by organs, such as the UN Security Council and General Assembly, can be of assistance in the interpretation of the Charter. There is no doubt that the UN organs interpret the Charter on a daily basis. This was explicitly acknowledged at the San Francisco Conference: 'In the course of the operation from day to day of the various organs of the Organization, it is inevitable that each organ will interpret such parts of the Charter as are applicable to its particular functions'.[139] The question is, however, whether and to what extent these interpretations will have effect outside the organ itself. The oft-quoted sceptical voice in this regard belonged to Judge Spender who stated that 'it is not I think permissible to move the principle of subsequent conduct of parties to a bilateral or multilateral treaty into another field and seek to apply it, not to the parties to the treaty, but to an organ established under the treaty'.[140] The dissimilarities, both in practice and theory, between the conduct of states and conduct of organs and the text of Article 31, paragraph 3(b) would indicate that the practice of the organs cannot be formally taken into consideration under the VCLT.[141] Hence, the question is whether the role in interpretation of organ practice can be found to rest on some independent legal basis.[142] As was previously pointed out, many regard the Charter as possessing a constitutional quality: Thomas Franck based this on the legal primacy found in Article 103: 'Clearly, it illustrates that the drafters intended to create a special treaty different from all others. This difference becomes relevant when we consider the instrument's capacity for adaption through the interpretative practice of its organs and members' and 'the extent to which the Charter establishes political and executory machinery for implementing its purposes, principles and norms distinguishes it from ordinary treaties and invests it with a potential for adaption through *organic practice* ... the Charter will be subjected to continuous interpretation and adaption through the member states' individual and *collective practice*: Their actions, voting and rhetoric.[143]

---

[139] Statement of Committee IV/2 of the San Francisco Conference, UNCIO, Vol. 13, 709. Quoted in Thomas M. Franck 'Interpretation and Change in the Law of Humanitarian Intervention' in J.L. Holzgrefe and Robert O. Keohane (ed.) *Humanitarian Intervention: Ethical, Legal and Political Dilemmas,* Cambridge University Press, 2003, 204-231 at 205-206.

[140] 1962 ICJ 192.

[141] In his review of the draft VCLT, Bernhardt suggested that the provision in the VCLT should explicitly provide for the inclusion of the practice of international organizations 'in so far as it is approved by the member States', see Rudolf Bernhardt 'Interpretation and Implied (Tacit) Modification of Treaties' 27 *Zeitschrift für Ausländisches Öffentliches Recht und Völkerrecht* (1967) 491 at 501.

[142] Elihu Lauterpacht 'The Development of the Law of International Organizations by the Decisions of International Tribunals' *Recueil des Cours – Collected Courses,* The Hague Academy of International Law, 1976, IV, Tome 152, 464.

[143] Thomas M. Franck *Recourse to Force: State Action Against threats and Armed Attacks* Cambridge University Press (2002) 5 and 7, emphases added, footnotes omitted.

In 1962, Judge Spender investigated the judicial precedents proposed in favor of the authority of the probative value of practice of organization organs. He found these precedents sadly lacking, either because their references were *obiter dicta* or 'quite irrelevant'.[144]

Even if the Court in the *Namibia* decision made mention of the practice of the members of the Security Council and, thus, not to the practice of the Council as such, the Court has, on several occasions, invoked the practice of UN organs as an aid in interpretation. The prime example is still the *Certain Expenses Case* where the Court made numerous references to the practice of, for example, the General Assembly. Recently, the Court found that an international organization's 'own practice, are [among the] elements which may deserve special attention' when interpreting the constituent instrument of the organization.[145] In July 2004, the Court explicitly referred to the 'practice of the United Nations, both the General Assembly and the Security Council...'.[146]

Even if it is accepted that the practice of organs, in principle, may have probative value, questions remain concerning for example Assembly resolutions passed by a majority but opposed by a, small or large, minority. Ciobanu, for example finds that 'one can, of course, ascertain the existence of a general political interest to restate the content of the Charter provisions by the subsequent practice of the United Nations political organs. However, this can be done only in those cases in which the resolutions adopted by political organs have received general acceptance [as opposed to, for example, two thirds majority] from the members of the organ concerned, and, generally speaking, from the membership of the United Nations as a whole'.[147] Amerasinghe considers three possibilities: unanimous practice, practice supported by a large majority and practice supported by a simple majority. He finds only the latter category to cause potential problems and concludes that 'the mere fact of a majority vote ... cannot be sufficient to establish a practice'.[148] Ciobanu's reference to 'general acceptance' is based on the San Francisco Conference's understanding that 'if an interpretation made by any organ of the Organization ... is not generally acceptable it will be without binding force'.[149] The 1994 Charter Commentary further emphasizes the need for member state approval: Derived form subsequent practice of the member or from the practice of the Organization, which *they have approved*'.[150] In conclusion, it is difficult

---

[144] 1962 ICJ 192-195.

[145] 1996 ICJ 75, paragraph 19.

[146] Legal Consequences of the Construction of a Wall in the Occupied Palestinian Territory, Judgment 9 July 2004, paragraph 27, available at www.icj.org, visited August 2, 2004.

[147] Dan Ciobanu 'The Impact of the Characteristics of the Charter upon its Interpretation' in Antonio Cassese (ed.) *Current Problems of International Law* Multa Paucis (1975) 3 at 50-51.

[148] C.F. Amerasinghe *Principles of the Institutional Law of International Organizations* Cambridge University Press 1996, 51-52.

[149] UNCIO, Vol. 13, 710.

[150] Simma/Brunner in Bruno Simma (ed.) *The Charter of the United Nations: A Commentary*, Oxford University Press (1994) 'Commentary to Article 27', 447, paragraph 47. 'This teleological

to determine exactly how large the majority will have to be in order for a practice to have received 'general acceptance'. While the phase does allow for a few states opposing the measure without invalidating it for interpretative purposes, it will not take very many negative votes to hamper or cancel its probative value.

2.IX. Subsequent Practice: Interpretation versus Modification

At what point does a treaty interpretation in fact become a treaty modification? The ILC Special Rapporteur and the ILC in its reports to the General Assembly made the point on several occassions that 'Although the line may sometimes be blurred between interpretation and amendment of a treaty through subsequent practice, legally the processes are distinct'.[151] Scholars, such as Akehurst,[152] Bernhardt,[153] Brownlie,[154] Glennon,[155] Karl,[156] and Villiger[157] have made similar assertions.[158]

---

interpretation, adopted by the SC as a UN organ, was *accepted by the member states,* and is therefore binding as consent interpreting the Charter'. Simma/Brunner 'Commentary to Article 27', 449, paragraph 51 (emphasis added).

[151] International Law Commission: Report of the Commission to the General Assembly, *Yearbook of the International Law Commission*, 1964, Vol. II, 198 and 1966, Vol. II, 236.

[152] Akehurst, Michael: 'Hierarchy of Sources in International Law', *British Yearbook of International Law*, 1974/75, 277: 'amendment merges into termination at one extreme and into interpretation at the other extreme'.

[153] 'It is true and generally known that the limits between both an authentic interpretation and modification of a treaty are fluid'. Rudolf Bernhardt 'Interpretation and Implied (Tacit) Modification of Treaties' 27 *Zeitschrift für Ausländisches Öffentliches Recht und Völkerrecht* (1967) 491 at 499.

[154] Describing the distinction as 'rather fine', Ian Brownlie *Principles of Public International Law* Oxford University Press, 1998, 631.

[155] Glennon found that 'sorting out one [form of practice] from the other often depends upon contextual factors not easily quantified or even identified' and 'in most instances, it is virtually impossible to determine for which of the two purposes state practice is pertinent', Michael J. Glennon *Limits of Law, Prerogatives of Power: Interventionism after Kosovo* Palgrave, 2001, 48.

[156] Like Bernhardt, Karl describes the dividing line between interpretation and modification as fluid (fließend), Wolfram Karl: *Vertrag und spätere Praxis im Völkerrecht: zum Einfluß der Praxis auf Inhalt und Bestand völkerrechtlicher Verträge* Springer, 1983, 204.

[157] Asserting that 'there is no fine line of demarcation between interpretation and modification', Mark E. Villiger, *Customary International Law and Treaties*, The Hague, Kluwer Law International, 1997, 213, paragraph 335

[158] Karl further asserts that treaty interpretation through subsequent practice and treaty modification through subsequent practice cannot be separated and that the content of the treaty be changed even within the ambit of normal treaty interpretation will, Wolfram Karl: *Vertrag und spätere Praxis im Völkerrecht: zum Einfluß der Praxis auf Inhalt und Bestand völkerrechtlicher Verträge* Springer, 1983, 45-46. Similarly, see Engel: 'It is also clear that the adoption of one interpretation to the exclusion of others which are equally possible, leaves the text of the Charter intact while it changes its contents' Salo Engel 'The Changing Charter of the United Nations' 7 *The Year Book of the World Affairs* (1953) 71 at 75-76. See, in addition, Salo Engel 'De Facto Revision of the Charter of the United Nations' 14 *Journal of Politics* (1952) 132 at 134.

These observations, however, do little to draw a line between interpretation and modification. Even if such a line may be tenuous or illusory it may still be of use for schematic purposes. The core of the matter is whether a normative change occurs.[159] As Hexner presents it, it belongs to 'the essence of a normative text that its interpretative radius, the range of the possible meanings attributable to it, be limited'.[160] Correspondingly, Bernhardt stresses that the action must be 'compatible with the treaty text' in order to be characterized as an interpretation. If the practice violates the text, it may involve a modification.[161] Similarly, in the context of the work on the VCLT, Yasseen noted that some delegates at the Vienna Conference believed that subsequent practice was adequately covered by Draft Article 27, paragraph 3(b) [31, paragraph 3(b) of the VCLT], Yasseen pointed out that subsequent practice in the context of interpretation was 'quite distinct' from modification: it was a difference 'in kind between a declaratory act and a constituent document'.[162] Karl determines the common denominator in cases of modification to be open or overt deviation from the treaty.[163] Mention may also be made of Cassese's investigation of the possible erosion of the UN

---

[159] 'Interpretation and modification differ in that the results of the former are (still) compatible with the written framework'. Mark E. Villiger, *Customary International Law and Treaties*, The Hague, Kluwer Law International, 1997, 213, paragraph 334.

[160] Ervin Hexner 'Teleological Interpretation of Basic Instruments of Public International Organizations' Salo Engel (ed.) *Law, State, and International Legal Order – Essays in Honor of Hans Kelsen*, The University of Tennessee Press, 1964, 123. Hexner continues: 'The authority of an organ to interpret the text of an constituent instrument extends to the selection of one (authentic) alternative meaning among a number of possible alternatives *within* the interpretative range', Ibid. (emphasis in original). The authority of an organ to interpret 'does *not* include the authority to *exceed* the interpretative radius', Ibid. 124 (emphasis in original). 'An action by which a meaning outside the interpretative range is attributed to an instrument ... involves a *modification* of the instrument in contrast to its interpretation', Ibid. (emphasis in original). Racklin differentiates between 'interpretation *sub lege*' and 'interpretation *contra legem*', Ralph Zacklin *The Amendment of the Constitutive Instruments of the United Nations and Specialized Agencies* A.W. Sijthoff (1968) 174 *et seq.* See also Schermers and Blokker who refer to Racklin, 734, paragraph 1185. Similarly, Ress emphasizes that the 'ordinary meaning of a term is a boundary that protects against arbitrary interpretation', in Bruno Simma (ed.) *The Charter of the United Nations: A Commentary*, Oxford University Press (1994) 37, paragraph 22.

[161] Rudolf Bernhardt 'Interpretation and Implied (Tacit) Modification of Treaties' 27 *Zeitschrift fürAusländisches Öffentliches Recht und Völkerrecht* (1967) 491 at 499.

[162] 38th meeting, 211, paragraph 11, see United Nations Conference on the Law of Treaties: official records: summary records of the plenary meetings and of the meetings of the Committee of the Whole, 1968/1969, Vienna, Austria.

[163] Wolfram Karl: *Vertrag und spätere Praxis im Völkerrecht: zum Einfluß der Praxis auf Inhalt und Bestand völkerrechtlicher Verträge* Springer, 1983, 214, (offene Abweichung). See also Ress, who finds that the guiding principle (Leitbild) of treaty interpretation is the identity (Identität) of the treaty whereas aim of the treaty amendment is the conscious alteration (Umgestaltung) of the rights and obligations contained in the treaty. Georg Ress 'Die Bedeutung der nachfolgenden Praxis für die Vertragsinterpretation nach der Wiener Vertragsrechtskonvention (WVRK)' in Roland Bieder and Georg Ress (ed.) *Die Dynamik des Europäischen Gemeinschaftsrechts/The Dynamics of EC-Law* Nomos (1987) 49 at 62.

Charter system regarding the use of force. His examination revealed that 'attempts at deviating from the Charter occur *at the interpretative level*, not at the normative one'.[164]

The foregoing theoretical reflections may be illustrated by two of Namibia's claims to the Kasikili/Sedudu Island and Botswana's reply thereto. Namibia claimed that subsequent conduct was relevant to the question in three distinct ways, two of which will be considered here.[165] Firstly, Namibia argued that the subsequent conduct was relevant for the interpretation of the treaty, as has been dealt with above.[166] Secondly, the subsequent conduct, according to Namibia, gave 'rise to a second and entirely independent basis for Namibia's claim under the doctrine concerning acquisition of territory by prescription, acquiescence and recognition'.[167] Botswana objected strongly to the utilization of the same conduct for two different legal purposes, i.e. firstly to support the interpretation of a treaty and secondly as a basis for acquisition of territory by prescription. Thus, Botswana maintained that subsequent conduct, relating to an existing treaty, 'is opposed to prescription, the purpose of which is to destroy and to supplant a pre-existing title'.[168]

Similarly, when the question of prescription was investigated by the Court, Botswana objected that this issue was outside the scope of the question submitted to the Court. Botswana argued that the Special Agreement[169] that was the basis for the case, and which authorized the Court to determine the boundary 'on the basis of the Anglo-German Treaty of the 1 July 1890 and principles of international law ', precluded the consideration of prescription because this 'involved adopting a totally different basis [than the 1890 Treaty] for determining the boundary'.[170] Namibia, however, continued to argue that 'either the subsequent conduct operates as a 'practice ... which establishes the agreement of the parties regarding the interpretation' of the Treaty; or it stands as an independent root of title based on the doctrine of prescription and/or acquiescence'.[171]

---

[164] Antonio Cassese 'Return to Westphalia? Considerations on the gradual Erosion of the Charter System' in Antonio Cassese (ed.) *The Current Legal Regulation of the Use of Force* Martinus Nijhoff, 1986, 514 (emphasis in original).

[165] See the *Kasikili/Sedudu Case*, 39 ILM (2000) 341, paragraph 71.

[166] The practice in question was the continued presence of Masubia tribespersons on the island. As set out above, the International Court of Justice did not find that the presence of the tribespersons constituted subsequent practice in the VCLT sense, the *Kasikili/Sedudu Case*, 39 ILM (2000) 343, 75.

[167] Ibid. In its submissions to the Court, Namibia set out four conditions, which it believed had to be fulfilled in order to enable possession by a State to mature into a prescriptive title: The possession must be (1) exercised *a titre de souverain*, (2) peaceful and uninterrupted, (3) public and (4) endure for a certain length of time, the *Kasikili/Sedudu Case*, 39 ILM (2000) 348, paragraph 94. Botswana accepted these criteria (Ibid. 349, paragraph 95), whereas the Court did not reveal its opinion. It merely found that Namibia had not fulfilled its own conditions (Ibid. 350, paragraph 97).

[168] *Kasikili/Sedudu Case*, 39 ILM (2000) 342, Paragraph 72.

[169] The *Kasikili/Sedudu Case*, 39 ILM (2000) 318, paragraph 11.

[170] Ibid. 347, paragraph 91. The Court, however, found that the wording 'shows that the Parties had intention of confining the rules and principles of law applicable in this case solely to the rules and principles of international law relating to treaty interpretation' and the it was not precluded from 'examining arguments relating to prescription', Ibid. 348, paragraph 93.

[171] Ibid. 348, paragraph 92.

The claims by Namibia in the *Kasikili/Sedudu Case* raise a number of questions. Firstly, one may ask whether the same acts can be legally relevant as both subsequent practice in regard to treaty interpretation and the foundation of title by prescription. Botswana emphatically denied this whereas Namibia defended its argument on the basis of a right to argue in the alternative.[172] On the face of it, there would seem to be nothing to logically prevent identical, actual material acts, in this case primarily the presence of the tribespersons on the island, to be the basis of either treaty interpretation or prescription.[173] If, for example, a practice is consistent, uniform, wide spread etc. enough to create the basis for a customary rule, then *a fortiori*, the same practice will *mutatis mutandis* complete the requirements for a practice to aid in interpretation.

A second issue would, however, appear to arise when one considers the belief behind the acts. Specifically with regard to the *Kasikili/Sedudu Case*, the Court found that, in regard to interpretation, the practice had to be 'linked to a belief' that the practice was in accordance with the Treaty.[174] In the case of prescription, the practice (or possession) must be exercised *a titre de souverain* in order to, in this case, establish a title independent of, rather in contravention of, the underlying treaty.[175] More generally, the difference is one between interpretation of a treaty (or governing law) and title creation (or law creation or change).[176]

---

[172] Ibid. 341-342, paragraph 71.

[173] Still, the issue of the probative value of, in this case, Namibia's argument remains. Whereas the same acts on the ground may be claimed for either interpretation or prescription, a difficulty appears when the subjective or qualitative element enters the equation. See, however, Vice-President Weeramantry's Dissenting Opinion in which he argues that 'factors throwing light on the contemporaneous understanding of the Treaty can be considered quite apart from their weight as supporting acquisitive prescription, Ibid. 390, paragraph 40.

[174] Ibid. 342-343, paragraph 74.

[175] See also, for example: 'Prescription is not so much now a singular mode of acquisition, or loss, of territorial sovereignty, as a convenient term for one group of elements which go together to *make or break* a title', Robert Jennings and Arthur Watts *Oppenheim's International Law*, 9th edition, Longman Publishers, 1992, 708 (emphasis added).

[176] Judge Kooijmans, in his Separate Opinion, touches upon the relationship between interpretation and prescription. He points out that the alternative claim of prescription rests on virtually the same grounds as the claim based on the Treaty, 378, paragraph 16. He goes on the query: 'If Namibia had been able to prove that the requirements for acquisitive prescription ... had been fulfilled, would that not have constituted subsequent practice as well?' Ibid. 378, paragraph 19. His line of argument was a critique of the fact that the Court entertained Namibia's claim of prescription. In this regard, he found that the Special Agreement clashed with the Court's handling of the case. At a more general level, however, it might be maintain that, whereas the actual acts in question may, as pointed out, be identical, the psychological element is one of following the treaty in the case of interpretation and one of changing/making law in the case of prescription/modification. Vice-President Weeramantry, in his Dissenting Opinion, also makes a distinction when he says: 'I stress particularly that this is not material on the basis of which the terms of the Treaty can be altered. It is only a basis on which the terms to the treaty can be interpreted and better understood' Ibid. 392, paragraph 51. He does, however, not elaborate upon the difference.

Having thus attempted to explicate the rather fine line between interpretation and modification based on subsequent practice, we now turn to the controversial question of whether subsequent practice may indeed operate to modify a treaty.

Chapter 3

Subsequent Practice: Modification

3.I. Introduction

As we have seen, subsequent practice under a treaty may be a central aid in the interpretation of that treaty. Practice ensuing the conclusion of a treaty may, however, as will be argued presently, work to modify the normative content of a treaty.

The possibility of developing a treaty informally is particularly pertinent when the treaty is the UN Charter: contrast the need for dynamism and change caused by international development with the rather rigid formal amendment rules. Most will probably agree with Judge Spender when, in 1962, he stated of the framers of the Charter, that the 'wisest of them could never have anticipated the tremendous changes which politically, militarily, and otherwise have occurred in the comparatively few years which have elapsed since 1945'.[1] At the time Judge Spender was writing, the all-encompassing concern was 'a world in thraldom to atomic weapons'.[2] Although the framers of the Charter knew of terrorism, it is safe to assert that few would have perceived terrorism as a threat to the security of even the greatest power(s) in 1945. If it is accepted that the framers of the Charter did not have terrorism in mind when they drew up the provisions relating to the use of force, one may ask whether it is incapable of dealing with this issue or whether Charter is capable of adapting and developing responses to new challenges.

The initial advice to someone who might complain that the current state of the law is unsatisfactory would be to look for options for changing and developing the treaty. In the case of the UN Charter, Articles 108 and 109 stipulate the conditions required for changing the Charter. Both articles outline the conditions under which amendments to

---

[1] 1962 ICJ 186. See also Goodrich who finds that the provisions of the Charter 'require interpretation, adaptation and even change to meet new situations as they arise', Leland M. Goodrich *The United Nations* Thomas Y. Crowell Company (1959) 68. See, finally, Gross: 'Flexibility is the life blood that sustains and perpetuates constitutions. Concepts as to the nature of the foundations of peace and freedom change. This underlies the advisability of letting the United Nations Charter evolve, little by little, case by case' Ernest A. Gross 'Revising the Charter: is it Possible? Is it wise?' 32 *Foreign Affairs* (1952), 203 at 216. See also Glennon: 'The most farsighted among the Charter's framers saw their handiwork not as a finished and final product (as it is portrayed today as its more zealous defenders) but only as a tentative and initial effort, the first sketch of what inevitably would be a work-in-progress, Michael J. Glennon *Limits of Law, Prerogatives of Power: Interventionism after Kosovo* Palgrave, 2001, 138.

[2] 1962 ICJ 186.

the UN Charter may come into force.[3] No detailed analysis of these two provisions will be conducted here.[4] The ease or otherwise of accomplishing formal change of the Charter through the procedures in Articles 108 and 109 is much debated. The fact is that Article 108 has been successfully applied in three cases so far.[5] This has prompted Schwarzenberger to call the revision process 'a complicated and protracted affair ... yet, whenever the necessary consensus exists, the feat can, and has been, accomplished'.[6] Still, in spite of the three actual amendments, the majority of commentators appear to agree that, in the words of Kelsen: 'amendments to the Charter are practically impossible'.[7] Based on this evidence, one may conclude that formal Charter changes are impractical; and, it might be added, this is particularly true for amendments in sensitive areas, such as the regulation of the use of force.

In spite of the fact that the Charter has been subjected to only minor formal changes, numerous authors maintain that 'the Charter [has] undergone great changes,

---

[3] Kelsen notes that there is hardly any essential difference between the procedure of Article 108 and that of Article 109. Hans Kelsen *The Law of the United Nations, With Supplement* Praeger (1950) 817.

[4] Reference in this regard may be made to Karl and Mützelburg's commentary to Article 108 (pp. 1163-1178) and Article 109 (pp. 1179-1189) in Bruno Simma (ed.) *The Charter of the United Nations: A Commentary*, Oxford University Press (1994).

[5] Karl and Mützelburg's commentary to Article 108, in Bruno Simma (ed.) *The Charter of the United Nations: A Commentary*, Oxford University Press (1994) p. 1176. See also Egon Schwelb 'Amendments to Articles 23, 27 and 61 of the Charter of the United Nations' 59 *American Journal of International Law* (1965) 834.

[6] Georg Schwarzenberger *The Dynamics of International Law* 1976, 10.Similarly, Zacklin observes that the actual formal amendments have shown 'that important modifications of the Charter may be achieved effectively through the application of Article 108', Ralph Zacklin *The Amendment of the Constitutive Instruments of the United Nations and Specialized Agencies* A.W. Sijthoff (1968) 129.

[7] Hans Kelsen *The Law of the United Nations, With Supplement* Praeger (1950) 911. Zacklin writes that the requirement of great power unanimity 'is a major obstacle to amendment of the Charter through formal processes', Ralph Zacklin *The Amendment of the Constitutive Instruments of the United Nations and Specialized Agencies* A.W. Sijthoff (1968) 171. Goodrich concluded that 'the amendment procedure finally agreed upon did not give assurance that change would be easy and often, as it was of a highly complicated nature', Leland M. Goodrich 'The Changing United Nations' in Transnational Law in a Changing Society: Essays in Honor of Philip C. Jessup, Columbia University Press, 1972, 260. Hexner found that the formal amendment procedure 'proved to be somewhat unworkable' and 'virtually unworkable'. Ervin Hexner, 'Teleological Interpretation of Basic Instruments of Public International Organizations' Salo Engel (ed.) *Law, State and International Legal Order: Essays in Honor of Hans Kelsen,* The University of Tennessee Press, 1964, 122 and 134. Wolfke makes the general point that 'the history of international organizations has already shown that the introduction of necessary amendments to their constitutions often meets with serious obstacles'. From this he concludes that 'of necessity, therefore, the statues are adjusted and supplemented by practice itself' Karol Wolfke *Custom in Present International Law*, Martinus Nijhoff, 1993, 79. Karl and Mützelburg find that, while the Charter appeared from its original conception to be relatively flexible, it 'has proved to be rather rigid under the given circumstances', Commentary to Article 108, in Bruno Simma (ed.) *The Charter of the United Nations: A Commentary*, Oxford University Press (1994) 1165.

without any formal acts directed towards this purpose'.[8] Even authors who express some disquiet concerning the formless development of constituent instruments, such as Blum, acknowledges that modifications of the Charter, often presented as interpretations, are an 'undeniable fact'.[9] Several authors have attempted to identify the provisions of the Charter that have been amended informally.[10]

Therefore, if it is correct that subsequent practice of the parties can develop and change a treaty either by interpreting it or by modifying it,[11] this would aleviate some of the allegations that the law of the Charter is rigid and static. Yet, as will be seen shortly, such a proposition is controversial[12] and draft Article 38 of the VCLT, which in part dealt with this issue was the only provision of the ILC draft articles to be voted down in

---

[8] Jacob Robinson 'Metamorphosis of the United Nations' 94 *Recueil des Cours* (1958-II) 558. Similarly, Engel maintains that 'in the daily practice of the Members and organs, the Charter has undergone far-reaching changes even without the adoption of formal amendments' Salo Engel 'Procedures for the *de facto* revision of the Charter' 59 *Proceedings of the American Society of International Law* (1965) 108 at 108. Zacklin finds that as a result of practice, the Charter 'has undergone a transformation of impressive proportions', Ralph Zacklin *The Amendment of the Constitutive Instruments of the United Nations and Specialized Agencies* Sijthoff (1968) 129. See, finally, Sohn who concludes that 'the Charter of the United Nations, like the Constitution of the United States, is almost immutable as far as its text is concerned, but over less than fifty years its interpretations changed as much as those of the Constitution of the United States in two hundred years', Louis B. Sohn 'Interpreting the Law' in Oscar Schachter and Christopher Joyner (ed.) *United Nations Legal Order* Vol. I Cambridge University Press (1995) 169 at 227.

[9] Blum finds that the difficulties inherent in the notion of treaty modification through subsequent practice 'tend to explain the widespread tendency to present even the most far-reaching departure from the plain meaning of the provision ... as interpretation (rather than modification) through subsequent practice,' Yehuda Z. Blum *Eroding the United Nations Charter* Martinus Nijhoff (1993) 243-244 and 250. Ciobanu finds that the 'liberal (or dynamic) interpretation school' has prevailed with regard to the interpretation of the Charter, Dan Ciobanu 'The Impact of the Characteristics of the Charter upon its Interpretation' in Antonio Cassese (ed.) *Current Problems of International Law* Multa Paucis (1975) 3 at 49-50.

[10] See, for example, Hans Kelsen *The Law of the United Nations, With Supplement* Praeger (1950) 911-990; Jacob Robinson 'Metamorphosis of the United Nations' 94 *Recueil des Cours* (1958-II) 550-555; Ralph Zacklin *The Amendment of the Constitutive Instruments of the United Nations and Specialized Agencies* Sijthoff (1968) 171-197.

[11] The practice of the UN organs as well as that of the members states within the framework of the UN is not only an important element for specifying and developing the material understanding of the respective Charter provisions, but also constitutes a mixture of 'interpretation' and 'adaptation', if this subsequent development meets the different needs and intentions of nearly all the members states, in particular also those member states concerned, and can thus be considered to reflect the global balance of political interests'. Ress in Bruno Simma (ed.) *The Charter of the United Nations: A Commentary*, Oxford University Press (1994) 29, paragraph 5.

[12] Pauwelyn writes that it is 'much more controversial' that a pre-existing treaty may be terminated or revised by means of the establishment of new customary law than vice versa, Joost Pauwelyn *Conflict of Norms in Public International Law: How WTO Law Relates to other Rules of International Law* Cambridge University Press, 2003, 137-138.

its entirety. Due to this controversial nature, an extensive review of central cases will be conducted following evaluation of the debates in the ILC.

3.II. Debates in the International Law Commission and the Literature

The 1964 Draft Law of Treaties from the International Law Commission included Draft Article 68 entitled 'Modification of a treaty by subsequent treaty, by subsequent practice or by customary law'.[13] The possible modification of a treaty by subsequent practice is the present focus.[14] In its Report to the General Assembly, the ILC found that 'a consistent practice, embracing all the parties and establishing their common consent to the application of the treaty in a manner different from that laid down in certain of its provisions, may have the effect of modifying the treaty'.[15]

Among the members of ILC there appear to have been some confusion and difference of opinion about exactly how subsequent practice might operate to modify a treaty. Some, it seems, regarded the issue as one of customary international law.[16] Others found that Draft Article 68(b) was already dealt with in the rule on interpretation, Draft Article 69, paragraph 3(b). Briggs, for example, found that the difference was 'one of degree' and that any change was arrived at through 'stretching' the meaning of a term rather than modifying it.[17] Others again found that since 'something new' was introduced into the text, it could not be considered an interpretation.[18] The Special Rapporteur, too, did not perceive the issue as one of stretching the meaning of the text by subsequent practice.[19] On the other hand, he agreed that 'there was a similarity between the formation of custom and the implied agreement contemplated in [draft] article 68'.[20]

---

[13] YBILC, Vol. II, 1964, 198.

[14] Indeed, the references to modification by treaty and by a customary rule were later dropped by the Drafting Committee, YBILC, 1966, Vol. I, 220, paragraph 12.

[15] Ibid.

[16] See for example Tunkin's comments, YBILC 1966, Vol. I, 866th meeting, 164-165, paragraphs 15-20, and 876th meeting 220, paragraph 24 and 221, paragraph 35.

[17] YBILC, 1966, Vol. I, 866th meeting, 165, paragraph 25 and 876th meeting, 221, paragraph 31. See also subsequent comments by Elias, who finds that Article 31, paragraph 3(b) 'already covers the situation sought to be dealt with in draft Article 38 on the modification of treaties by subsequent practice. The Convention [the VCLT], therefore, contains no separate provision on this point'. T.O. Elias *The Modern Law of Treaties* A.W. Sijthoff (1974) 100. This conclusion, however, seems at odds with two facts: Firstly, one may wonder why the ILC endorsed draft Article 38 if the process was really covered by Article 31, paragraph 3(b); and secondly, the states participating in the Vienna Conference did not repudiate draft Article 38 because they thought it already covered. As will be dealt with shortly, they had a number of other reservations.

[18] Yasseen, YBILC, 1966, Vol. I, 866th meeting, 166, paragraph 36.

[19] YBILC, 1966, Vol. I, 876th meeting 220, paragraph 18.

[20] YBILC, 1966, Vol. I, 876th meeting 221, paragraph 44. The relationship with other means of normative change is emphasized by the original Draft Article 68 which, in addition to modification by subsequent practice, also allowed for modification of the operation of a treaty by a subsequent treaty

At the United Nations Conference on the Law of Treaties (the Vienna Conference), Draft Article 38 received a cool reception. Some of the delegates did not find that the proposed article reflected international law.[21] Other comments bear out what comes across as a fear that Draft Article 38, if included, could undermine the international legal system.[22] There was, moreover, domestic constitutional concerns over what some saw as the risk of minor officials changing treaties through their practice.[23] On the other hand, several delegates found that the proposed article did in fact reflect the realities of international legal relations.[24]

As was the case in the ILC, divergent opinions existed as to how Draft Article 38 operated legally. France, for instance, gave the impression of perceiving the practice under Article 38 as identical to the practice that may assist treaty interpretation.[25] The Iraqi delegate, Yasseen would appear to provide a good description of the workings of Draft Article 38:

---

relating to the same subject matter and the by the emergence of a new rule of customary law relating to the treaty matter, see text in YBILC, Vol. II, 1964, 198.

[21] See for example the representative of Turkey who 'did not think that the article stated an existing rule of international law', (38th meeting, 212, paragraph 27) and the representative from Tanzania who did not believe the rule existed 'and even if it did, it would be a bad rule' (38th meeting, 212, paragraph 38), for all references, see United Nations Conference on the Law of Treaties: official records: summary records of the plenary meetings and of the meetings of the Committee of the Whole, 1968/1969, Vienna, Austria.

[22] See for example comments by Venezuela (37th meeting, 208, paragraph 59-60), Guinea (38th meeting, 212, paragraph 30-32), and Cuba ('The retention of article 38 would weaken the *pacta sunt servanda* rule', 38th meeting, 213, paragraph 40). Chile made similar comments, (37th meeting, 210, paragraph 75). For all references, see United Nations Conference on the Law of Treaties: official records: summary records of the plenary meetings and of the meetings of the Committee of the Whole, 1968/1969, Vienna, Austria.

[23] See, for example, Spain's comments, 37th meeting, 209, paragraph 67, see United Nations Conference on the Law of Treaties: official records: summary records of the plenary meetings and of the meetings of the Committee of the Whole, 1968/1969, Vienna, Austria.

[24] See for example comments from Italy ('Article 38 reflected a legal fact which had always existed', 38th meeting, 211, paragraph 22) and Austria (recognizing the existence of the rule and emphasizing that 'it was a principle of international law', 38th meeting, 212, paragraph 33). For all references, see United Nations Conference on the Law of Treaties: official records: summary records of the plenary meetings and of the meetings of the Committee of the Whole, 1968/1969, Vienna, Austria.

[25] 'Although the idea of recourse to State practice in the application of a treaty as a means of interpretation [is] unexceptionable, it is quite a different matter to lay down a rule whereby that practice could *in itself* alter the substance of treaty obligations', 37th meeting, 208, paragraph 63 (emphasis added). See, similarly, the comments of Chile: The Chilean delegation considered that subsequent practice might be a useful element in the interpretation of a treaty ... but it could not agree that *such* practice in the application of the treaty *in itself* sufficed to modify the treaty without an express consent of the parties', 37th meeting, 210, paragraph 75 (emphases added). For all references, see United Nations Conference on the Law of Treaties: official records: summary records of the plenary meetings and of the meetings of the Committee of the Whole, 1968/1969, Vienna, Austria.

Formalism was certainly not an established principle of international law and sovereign States were not subject to the requirements of the *"acte contraire"* theory, which was not accepted in international law ... The agreement of the parties sufficed to terminate and modify a treaty. The agreement need not be in the form of a treaty. ... Article 38 did not depart from those principles. It provided that agreement to modify a treaty was established by practice, that was to say by a series of acts: not just any practice, but one which could be attributed to States.[26]

In the end, an amendment deleting Draft Article 38 was adopted by 53 votes to 15, with 26 abstentions.[27] On the basis of this rejection, one may question the possibility of informal modification of treaties. Scholarly views on this issue are divided. The debates within the Institute of International Law in 1994 and 1995 as outlined by Pauwelyn, attest to this.[28]

Referring to the defeat of draft Article 38 at the Vienna Conference, Zoller finds that 'a treaty may not be modified by subsequent practice in applying the treaty, even if that practice should establish the agreement of the parties to modify the provisions of the treaty'.[29] Blum observes that the legislative developments at the Vienna Conference 'clearly indicated the unwillingness of States to accept subsequent practice as a legitimate method for the modification of treaties'.[30] South Africa, in its submissions to the ICJ in the *Namibia Case*, emphasized the reluctance of governments to accept Draft Article 38 and found that 'events at the [Vienna] Conference cast doubt on the ambit and indeed on the existence of such a principle'.[31] Similarly, Bederman maintains that

---

[26] 38th meeting, 211, paragraph 9. Zacklin describes the concept of *acte contraire* as the idea that 'a legal act could only be modified by the same process with which it was formulated initially' Ralph Zacklin *The Amendment of the Constitutive Instruments of the United Nations and Specialized Agencies* A.W. Sijthoff (1968) 10. See also the description in the 1966 ILC Report to the General Assembly: 'A consistent practice, establishing the common consent of the parties to the application of the treaty in a manner different from that laid down In certain provisions', YBILC, 1966, Vol. II, 236.

[27] United Nations Conference on the Law of Treaties: official records: summary records of the plenary meetings and of the meetings of the Committee of the Whole, 1968/1969, Vienna, Austria, 215, paragraph 60.

[28] Joost Pauwelyn *Conflict of Norms in Public International Law: How WTO Law Relates to other Rules of International Law* Cambridge University Press, 2003, 138-139.

[29] Elisabeth Zoller 'The "Corporate Will" of the United Nations and the Rights of the Minority' 81 *American Journal of International Law* (1987) 610 at 616.

[30] Yehuda Z. Blum *Eroding the United Nations Charter* Martinus Nijhoff (1993) 243.

[31] Written Statement of South Africa, Legal Consequences for States of the Continued Presence of South Africa in Namibia (South West Africa) Notwithstanding Security Council Resolution 276 (1970), Vol. I, 393-395 and Oral Statement by Mr. Grosskopf, Legal Consequences for States of the

'the Vienna Convention [VCLT], by its very silence [i.e. by the non-inclusion of draft Article 38], has eschewed the notion of subsequent modification of treaty terms by later interpretation'.[32] Also, Thomas observers that 'the doctrine that treaties can be modified by subsequent practice is ... of questionable validity'.[33] On the other hand, Karl finds that treaty modification through subsequent practice cannot be considered to have been ruled out by events at the Conference.[34] This, in turn, means that customary international law, which he finds endorses informal modification, governs the issue.[35] Reuter maintains that the idea that a treaty may be modified by a treaty based on oral or tacit consent is 'sound': 'another solution would hardly be conceivable since there are no requirements in international law as to the form of treaties'.[36] Handl notes that the deletion of draft Article 38 'does not necessarily imply a rejection of tacit or informal treaty modification through subsequent practice as a generally valid concept of international law'.[37]

A number of individual judges have touched upon the issue. Judge Spender, for one, found that subsequent conduct may 'provide evidence from which to infer a new agreement with new rights and obligations between the parties, in effect superimposed or based upon the text of the treaty and amending the same'.[38] Similarly, President Winiarski held that if a practice is introduced without opposition in the relations between the contracting parties, this 'may bring about, at the end of a certain period, a modification of a treaty rule'.[39] Judge Fitzmaurice, in his Dissenting Opinion in the 1971 *Namibia Case*, cautiously stated that 'without in any absolute sense denying that, through a sufficiently steady and longcontinued course of conduct, a new tacit agreement may arise having a modificatory effect, the presumption is against it, especially in the case of an organization whose constituent instrument provides for its own amendment, and prescribes with some particularity what the means of effecting

---

Continued Presence of South Africa in Namibia (South West Africa) Notwithstanding Security Council Resolution 276 (1970), Vol. II, 203.

[32] Davis Bederman 'Revivalist Canons and Treaty Interpretation' 41 *UCLA Law Review* (1994) 954 at 974.

[33] M.A. Thomas 'When the Guests move in: Permanent Observers to the United Nations gain the Right to Establish Permanent Missions in the United States' 78 *California Law Review* (1990) 197 at 203.

[34] Wolfram Karl: *Vertrag und spätere Praxis im Völkerrecht: zum Einfluß der Praxis auf Inhalt und Bestand völkerrechtlicher Verträge* Springer, 1983, 373 'nicht als grundsätzlich ausgeschlossen angesehen werden kann'.

[35] Ibid. 376.

[36] Paul Reuter *Introduction to the Law of Treaties* Kegan Paul International (1995) 137, paragraph 211.

[37] Gunther Handl 'The Legal Mandate of Multilateral Development Banks as Agents for Change towards Sustainable Development' 92 *American Journal of International Law* (1998) 642 at 657, note 116.

[38] 62 ICJ 191.

[39] Dissenting Opinion of President Winiarski, 62 ICJ 230.

this are to be'.[40] Finally, Judge Parra-Aranguren, in his Dissenting opinion, in the *Kasikili/Sedudu Island Case*, makes, seemingly with approval, reference to the deliberations of the ILC concerning Draft Article 38.[41]

As will be clear from the debates about the VCLT and in the literature, the proposition that practice might modify a treaty is somewhat controversial. This fact justifies the following thorough but non-exhaustive review of a number of cases in which the issue has been raised.

3.III. Cases Accepting Modification Through Practice

3.III.A. Case Concerning Sovereignty over Certain Frontier Land

In 1959, the Netherlands and Belgium concluded a Special Agreement requesting the Court to determine whether sovereignty over two plots of land belonged to the Netherlands or to Belgium.[42] In its final contention, the Netherlands argued that, if sovereignty was vested in Belgium by virtue of the 1843 Boundary Convention (following the separation of Belgium from the Netherlands in 1839), acts of sovereignty exercised by the Netherlands since then had established sovereignty in the Netherlands.[43] As the Court put it: 'This is a claim to sovereignty in derogation of title established by treaty'.[44] It went on to state that 'the question for the Court is whether Belgium has lost its sovereignty, by non-assertion of its rights and by acquiescence in acts of sovereignty alleged to have been exercised by the Netherlands'.[45] The Court proceeded to examine the facts and found that they were insufficient to displace Belgian sovereignty, which thus had not been extinguished.[46]

3.III.B. The Temple of Preah Vihear Case

In justifying the draft Article 38 [similar to Article 68 in the 1964 draft] rule that subsequent practice may modify a treaty, the ILC made reference to two, then recent, cases, the first of which was the 1962 *Temple of Preah Vihear Case*: 'the boundary line acted on in practice was not reconciliable with the ordinary meaning of the terms of the

---

[40] 1971 ICJ 16 at 282.
[41] the *Kasikili/Sedudu Case*, 39 ILM (2000) 423, paragraph 16.
[42] 1959 ICJ 209.
[43] 1959 ICJ 227.
[44] Ibid.
[45] Ibid.
[46] 1959 ICJ 228-230.

treaty, and the effect of the subsequent practice was to amend the treaty'.[47] As the ILC Special Rapporteur pointed out, instances could be imagined 'when it was really impossible to regard the practice as not amounting to a modification of the treaty'.[48] He found the *Temple of Preah Vihear Case* to be such as case: 'In that case the treaty had laid down a perfectly clear criterion for a boundary, namely the line of the watershed, intended to apply not in one place alone but throughout the length of the boundary. In a given area there had been an unquestionable deviation from that criterion and if that was not an instance of 'modification' rather than 'interpretation', the words would no longer have their true meaning'.[49]

Rosenne, however, objected to the reference to the *Temple of Preah Vihear Case* in the commentary to Draft Article 68.[50] In spite of the Special Rapporteur's previous adamant statements, he agreed to the deletion of the reference and, although he still considered it to be correct, he admitted that the 'implications of the Court's reasoning were complex and by no means easy to analyse'.[51]

Indeed, the reasoning of the Court is difficult to pin down. The basis for the Court's decision was a boundary treaty from 1904. Article 1 stipulated that the frontier between Siam (Thailand) and Cambodia at a certain stretch 'follows the watershed' between the basins of two rivers.[52] Article 3 further specified that the actual delimitation of the frontiers should be carried out by a Mixed Commission.[53] In 1908/09 maps were drawn up and the one dealing with the Temple area showed the whole Preah Vihear as being on the Cambodian side. This position of the border was, however, at variance with the requirement in Article 1 of the 1904 treaty, i.e. that the border was to follow the watershed.

The Court found that Thailand had accepted the map in 1908/09.[54] Hence, the question arose as to how the discrepancy between the text of Article 1 and the map

---

[47] *Case Concerning the Temple of Preah Vihear*, 1962 ICJ 6. See YBILC, 1964, Vol. II, 198, paragraph 2. see also, for eample, de Arechaga's comments in YBILC, 1966, Vol. II, 866th meeting, 164, paragraph 8.

[48] YBILC, 1966, Vol. II, 866th meeting, 168, paragraph 63.

[49] Ibid. This reading of the case is echoed by Thirlway: 'At first sight, this looks more like an agreed modification of the treaty than an agreed interpretation: it surely cannot be possible to read the word 'watershed' as meaning 'a line which the surveyors thought was the watershed but which wasn't'. Hugh Thirlway 'The Law and Procedure of the International Court of Justice 1960-1989, Part Three, 62 *British Yearbook of International Law*, 1991, 54.

[50] YBILC, 1966, Vol. I, 894th meeting, 336, paragraph 12. Rosenne indicated that the case had primary importance in connection with the article on error.

[51] YBILC, 1966, Vol. I, 894th meeting, 336, paragraph 16. In fact, the reference was not included in the 1966 Report of the ILC to the General Assembly, YBILC, 1966, Vol. II, 236 (now Draft Article 38).

[52] 1962 ICJ 16.

[53] Ibid.

[54] 1962 ICJ 32. Even if this had not been the case, the Court found that Thailand had subsequently been precluded from objecting to the map, Ibid.

would be resolved. The Court found that when the parties accepted the map they 'adopted an interpretation of the treaty settlement which caused the map line, in so far as it may have departed from the line of the watershed, to prevail over the relevant clause of the treaty'.[55] This statement from the Court appears to indicate a process akin to modification of the treaty by subsequent practice, as maintained by Waldock: The acceptance of the map by the parties constituted the subsequent practice which allowed the 'inconsistent' map to prevail, i.e. modify, the treaty.

There does, however, seem to be a simpler explanation, indeed one more explicitly espoused by the Court. The Court found that the acceptance of the map caused it to become an integral part of the treaty settlement. One could add that the map, i.e. delimitation, was plainly authorized, in the words of the Court 'required', by Article 3. The Court further maintained that this integration could not be said to 'involve a departure from, or even a violation of, the terms of the Treaty'. In effect, the Court was holding that even if the map departed from the watershed this did not mean that the map departed from or violated the Treaty. This may be explained by the relationship between Articles 1 and 3. This relationship is implicitly characterized by the Court as one of *lex generalis* and *lex specialis.* The Court found that Article 1 set out 'the general character of the frontier', whereas Article 3 referred to 'the exact course of the frontier'.[56] The Court continued: 'although this delimitation [according to Article 3] had, prima facie, to be carried out by reference to the criterion indicated in Article 1, the purpose of it was to establish the actual line of the frontier. In consequence, the line of the frontier would, to all intents and purposes, be the line resulting from the work of delimitation, unless the delimitation was shown to be invalid'.[57] These *dicta* would seem to indicate that Article 3, as *lex specialis,* prevailed over Article 1, being *lex generalis.* This reading of the judgment is further confirmed when the Court considered which analysis an 'ordinary treaty interpretation' would result in: Giving particular weight to the object of frontier settlements, the Court found that finality and precision were paramount object.[58] It moreover found that the parties regarded the reference to the 'watershed' as insufficient and no more than a way of describing the frontier in a general way. The parties, according to the Court, did not attached special significance to the watershed line as compared to a precise and final delimitated line. In conclusion, the judgment may either be explained as treaty interpretation or, as done by Waldock, by reference to a tacit agreement based on the practice of the parties.

---

[55] 1962 ICJ 34.
[56] 1962 ICJ 17.
[57] Ibid.
[58] 1962 ICJ 34.

3.III.C. The Air Transport Services Agreement Arbitration

The second of two cases mention by the ILC was the 1963 *Air Transport Services Agreement Arbitration*.[59] The Tribunal found that, as a result of the attitude adopted by the French authorities, the right to serve certain cities in the Middle East could no longer be contested, save in exceptional circumstances. This finding was not based on the original agreement 'but rather [reached] by virtue of an agreement that implicitly came into force at a later date'.[60] In reaching this conclusion, the Tribunal had established that the conduct of the parties may 'be taken into account not merely as a means useful for interpreting the Agreement, but also as something more: that is, as a possible source of subsequent modification, arising out of certain actions or certain attitudes, having a bearing on the judicial situation of the Parties and on the rights that each of them could properly claim'.[61]

3.III.D. The Namibia Advisory Opinion

In 1971, the Court found itself having to rule on a longstanding practice of the UN Security Council which, on the face of it, was at variance with the wording of Article 27, paragraph 3 of the UN Charter: 'Decisions of the Security Council on all other [than procedural] matters shall be made by an affirmative vote of nine members including the concurring votes of the permanent members'. Contrary to the requirement of 'concurring votes', the Council had, almost from the very beginning, adopted a practice according to which an abstention by a permanent member of the Council was not considered a negative vote. On the first such occasion, on April 29, 1946, the Soviet Union abstained without this being interpreted by the Security Council as a veto, and up until the end of 1966 this practice had been followed at least 264 times.[62] Franck found the number to be 319 as of 2001.[63] In the spring of 2005, the latest example was the decision by the Security Council to refer the situation in Dafur since July 1, 2002 to the Prosecutor of the International Criminal Court.[64]

---

[59] Decision of the Arbitration Tribunal Established Pursuant to the Arbitration Agreement Signed at Paris on January 22, 1963, Between the United States of American and France, Decided at Geneva on December 22, 1963, reproduced in 3 *International Legal Materials* (1964) 668. The tribunal was composed of Ago,

[60] 3 *International Legal Materials* 1964, 668 at 716.

[61] 3 *International Legal Materials* 1964, 668 at 713.

[62] Constantin Stavropoulos, 'The Practice of Voluntary Abstentions by Permanent Members of the Security Council under Article 27, Paragraph 3, of the Charter of the United Nations', 61 *American Journal of International Law*, 1967, 738 and 743.

[63] Thomas M. Franck *Recourse to Force: State Action Against threats and Armed Attacks* Cambridge University Press (2002) 8.

[64] Resolution 1593, China and the United states abstaining.

Various writers commented upon the practice and members of the Court made reference to it.[65] Interestingly, in an early case, the Court phrased the situation as follows: 'the recommendation was not adopted because it failed to obtain the requisite majority or *because of the negative vote of a permanent member*'.[66] Although the situation just referred to was hypothetical, it may seem somewhat surprising that the Court, which could not be unaware of the controversy which existed already then, applied a formulation that was inconsistent with the wording of Article 27, paragraph 3 but consistent with the emerging practice.

In the *Certain Expenses Case*, Judge Bustamante described the practice as 'an unwritten amendment' in his dissenting opinion.[67] Judge Bustamante, however, went on to state that 'no doubt this type of amendment may be legally repudiated in a given case by invoking the text of the Charter ... since no permanent member has undertaken to apply it without reservation'.[68] Judge Dillard, in his separate opinion in the same case,

---

[65] It is interesting to observe how most writers were unsure of how to analyze the developing practice which, on the one hand, from a strict point of view was incompatible with the wording of Article 27, paragraph 3 but, on the other hand, appeared very useful. For an early review, see Yuen-Li Liang 'The Settlement of Disputes in the Security Council: The Yalta Voting Formula' 24 *British Yearbook of International Law* (1947) 330 at 357-359, noting that 'it is not certain that voluntary abstention by one of the permanent members is compatible with the literal language of Article 27, paragraph 3' at 358. Liang, however, found that the practice might develop as a 'means to mitigate the rigours of the 'veto'', at 359. See furthermore Norman Padelford 'The Use of the Veto' 2 *International Organization* (1948) 227 who worried about the uncertainties connected to the early practice and found that 'abstention by great powers can be viewed as concurrence only in a backhanded sort of way', at 245. He further found the practice as a way of getting around the veto but called for some agreement 'upon which reliance could be more certainly placed', at 245. See also Yuen-Li Liang 'Notes on Legal Questions Concerning the United Nations', 44 *American Journal of International Law* (1950) 694. Liang found, already after four years of practice, that 'the practice of the Security Council in not treating it [the voluntary abstention of a permanent member] as a negative vote seems to have been established and generally recognized', Ibid. at 707. Kelsen considered the issue at some length in his 1950 monograph on the law of the UN: He found that the absence of the word 'all' before 'permanent members' in the sentence 'the concurring votes of the permanent members', if compared to Articles 108 and 109, which do require the votes of 'all the permanent members' allowed for an interpretation according to which the abstention from voting by a permanent member (and maybe up to four permanent members) would not prevent the passage of a non-procedural resolution. He further found that the most satisfactory solution would be for the permanent member abstaining to indicate whether the abstention was to be considered as a veto or not, Hans Kelsen *The Law of the United Nations*, Praeger (1950) 239-244. In addition, see, for example, Engel referring to the practice as 'a significant interpretation' of Article 27. He also stated that an abstention could 'hardly be considered as an *affirmative* concurring vote but, also, that the practice 'complied with the literal meaning of the term veto which is to say 'no''. As for the latter, the problem is that the term veto does not appear in the Charter even if that was what was meant, Salo Engel 'The Changing Charter of the United Nations' 7 *The Year Book of the World Affairs* (1953) 71 at 84.

[66] 1950 ICJ 4 at 7.

[67] 1962 ICJ 151 at 291.

[68] Ibid.

appears to deny that the wording of Article 27, paragraph 3 contains such a 'precise prescription' as to rule out that 'subsequent conduct of the parties is a clearly a legitimate method of giving meaning to the Article in accordance with the expectations of the parties, including, in particular, the permanent members'.[69]

In 1971, the Court had to consider the issue in a specific case. In the *Namibia Advisory Opinion*, South Africa contended that Security Council Resolution 284, which was the basis for the Advisory Opinion, was invalid because two permanent members of the Security Council (the United Kingdom and the Soviet Union) abstained.[70] The Court found that the proceedings of the Security Council 'extending over a long period supply abundant evidence' that the members of the Council, including the permanent members, 'have consistently and uniformly interpreted the practice of voluntary abstention by a permanent member as not constituting a bar to the adoption of resolutions'.[71]

While no dispute remains about the correct reading of Article 27, paragraph 3, i.e. that an abstention is no veto, disagreement persist with regard to the justification for the change.[72] One objection to the Court's *dictum* may be that the employment of the word 'interpreted' is dubious. It is hard to accept that the word 'concurring' can be interpreted to include abstentions. Amerasinghe, however, argues that 'the practice of treating an abstention as not giving rise to the absence of an affirmative vote in regard to the votes of the permanent members of the SC [Security Council] is not a contradiction amounting to an amendment of Article 27(3). ... The practice in fact adopted resulted in giving the meaning 'not negative' to the term 'affirmative' which is less removed and may be construed as development rather than amendment'.[73] The representative of the UN Secretary-General, Mr. Stavropulos, submitted to the Court that 'the constant practice ... is ... customary law, and was the valid customary law of

---

[69] 1971 ICJ 153-154.

[70] Legal Consequences for States of the Continued Presence of South Africa in Namibia (South West Africa) Notwithstanding Security Council Resolution 276 (1971), Advisory Opinion, 22, paragraph 21.

[71] Legal Consequences for States of the Continued Presence of South Africa in Namibia (South West Africa) Notwithstanding Security Council Resolution 276 (1971), Advisory Opinion, 22, paragraph 22.

[72] For a somewhat similar example, one may point to the abandonment by the IMF of the system of fixed exchange rates in 1971. Berrisch terms this the development of internal customary international law, see Georg M. Berrisch 'The Establishment of New Law through the Subsequent Practice in GATT' 16 *North Carolina Journal of International Law and Commercial Regulation* (1991) 497 at 509.

[73] C.F. Amerasinghe *Principles of the Institutional Law of International Organizations* Cambridge University Press 1996, 54. In a more general perspective, there appears to be a substantial difference between 'not negative' and 'affirmative'. One need only consider the difference between the Security Council 'affirming' (or, rather authorizing) a certain, maybe coercive, action and the same Council. See, for example, the exchange in the ILC, where de Arechaga characterized the process as one of sutomary law, while the Chairman (Mr. Yasseen) found that it related to an interpretation rather than a modification, YBILC, 1966, Vol. I, 876th meeting, 221, paragraphs 50-51.

the United Nations long before the Security Council resolutions' regarding Namibia.[74] Some authors, for example Wolfke, similarly categorize the process which took place with regard to Article 27(3) as the development or emergence of a new rule of international custom: '… it is a definite and no doubt very important addition to Article 27 of the Charter by means of subsequent practice of the Organization, accepted as law by all of its member-states, hence by means of an international custom'.[75] In this context, it may be pointed out, as does E. Lauterpacht, that although the Court accepted the 'interpretation' of the Security Council, it identified and qualified the subsequent practice as a practice that had extended over a 'long period' and had been followed 'consistently and uniformly'.[76] Still others merely assign the process concerning Article 27(3) to either 'practice departing from the terms of a treaty so as to amount to an agreed modification of it' or 'practice … giving rise to new customary rights, independent of the treaty'.[77]

---

[74] Oral Statement by Mr. Stavropoulos, ICJ Pleadings, Legal Consequences for States of the Continued Presence of South Africa in Namibia (South West Africa) Notwithstanding Security Council Resolution 276 (1970), Vol. II, 39.

[75] Wolfke. Elsewhere Wolfke writes: 'It should be added yet that this practice, being clearly at variance with the text of Article 27(3), cannot be considered merely as its interpretation but also is its amendment by accepted custom, that is, custom' Wolfke, Karol: 'Some Reflections on Kinds of Rules and International Law-Making by Practice' in Makarczyk, Jerzy (ed.): *Theory of International Law at the Threshold of the 21st Century*, The Hague, Kluwer Law International, 1996, 590. Danilenko, too, appears to adopt the customary rule explanation, G.M. Danilenko *Law-Making in the International Community*, Martinus Nijhoff, 1993, 167. In addition, Villiger characterizes the process as one of custom. He applies the term, borrowed from Müller, 'coutume constitutionelle internationale', see Mark E. Villiger, *Customary International Law and Treaties*, The Hague, Kluwer Law International, 1997, 201, paragraph 314.

[76] Elihu Lauterpacht 'The Development of the Law of International Organizations by the Decisions of International Tribunals' *Recueil des Cours – Collected Courses,* The Hague Academy of International Law, 1976, IV, Tome 152, 457. Judge Dillard, in his separate opinion, termed the practice 'undeviating', 1971 ICJ 154. These qualities of the practice are reminiscent of the requirements for the formations of a rule of customary international law.

[77] Thirlway, Hugh 'The Law and Procedure of the International Court of Justice 1960-1989, Part Three, 62 *British Yearbook of International Law*, 1991, 48-49. See also 'The Law and Procedure of the International Court of Justice 1960-1989, Part Two, 61 *British Yearbook of International Law*, 1990, 77-78. Similarly, in his 1967 article, Mr. Stavropoulos writes that whether the practice taking place with regard to Article 27, paragraph 3 'is considered as a case of interpretation or a case of modification through subsequent practice' it shows that a voluntary abstention by a permanent member is not tantamount to a veto, Constantin Stavropoulos, 'The Practice of Voluntary Abstentions by Permanent Members of the Security Council under Article 27, Paragraph 3, of the Charter of the United Nations', 61 *American Journal of International Law*, 1967, 741-742.

3.III.E. The Arbitration on the Delimitation of the Continental Shelf

The law of the sea has undergone rapid development during the past fifty years. This has meant that, in spite of a series of major treaties in, for example 1958, the law quickly appeared to overtake the codification efforts. Hence, in his Hague Lectures in 1967, Jennings wondered how states could claim a fishery zone beyond their territorial sea when the 1958 Geneva Convention on the High Sea stipulated that the high sea is 'all parts of the sea that are not included in the territorial sea or in the internal waters of a State' (Article 1) and that all states have freedom of fishing on the high seas (Article 2).[78] Jennings found that the practice of declaring fishery zones was too well established to be shrugged off as mere irregularity and was 'a gloss on the convention established by practice'.[79]

In the 1977 *Arbitration on the Delimitation of the Continental Shelf* between France and the United Kingdom, the Court of Arbitration was faced with a submission by France, that 1958 Continental Shelf Convention had 'been rendered obsolete by the recent evolution of customary law'.[80] The United Kingdom argued that these developments, primarily in the context of the Third United Nations Conference on the Law of the Sea, which eventually led to the 1982 United Nations Convention on the Law of the Sea, had not yet become law.[81] The Court agreed with the British position but it did emphasize that 'the Court recognizes both the importance of the evolution of the law of the sea which is now in progress and the possibility that the development in customary law may, under certain conditions, evidence the assent of the States concerned with the modification, or even termination, of previously existing treaty rights and obligations'.[82]

---

[78] R.Y. Jennings 'General Course on the Principles of International Law' *Recueil des Cours – Collected Courses,* The Hague Academy of International Law, 1967, II, Tome 121, 380-381.

[79] Ibid. 381.

[80] 18 *International Legal Materials* (1979) 397 at 416, paragraph 45. The Court of Arbitration was composed of Mr. Erik Carsten, Mr. Herbert Briggs, M. Andre Gros, Mr. Endre Ustor and Sir Humphery Waldock.

[81] 18 *International Legal Materials* (1979) 397 at 416, paragraph 46.

[82] 18 *International Legal Materials* (1979) 397 at 417, paragraph 47. Mention may also be had of Judge Shahabuddeen's Separate Opinion in the *Jan Mayen Case.* Shahabuddeen finds that the literature is heavy with the view that the interpretation given to Article 6 of the 1958 Continental Shelf Convention 'varies from the terms of the provision'. He goes on to ask, how this has come to pass and proposes, *inter alia,* modification. Examining Article 1 of the 1958 Convention, he considers that the limit prescribed there 'falls to be regarded as having been modified by Article 76 of the 1982 Convention [on the Law of the Sea] applying as customary international law. Hence, Judge Shahabuddeen recognizes that a legal rule, whether customary or conventional in nature, may be modified or superceded by subsequent custom.

3.III.F. The Award in Boundary Dispute Concerning the Taba Area

Following the 1979 peace treaty between Egypt and Israel an area around Taba remained in dispute. In 1988, the Egypt-Israel Arbitration Tribunal handed down its *Award in Boundary Dispute Concerning the Taba Area*.[83] The basis for the Award was a 1906 Agreement between the Ottoman Empire and the British administration in Egypt. Article 3 of the Agreement provided that boundary pillars were to be erected 'at intervisible points'.[84] With regard to Boundary Pillar 91, Israel argued, *inter alia*, that the location suggested by Egypt violated the requirement of intervisibility.[85] When it examined this question, the Tribunal confirmed that 'the Agreement does not provide for any exceptions to intervisibility'.[86] The Tribunal proceeded to consider practical reasons as to why the requirement of intervisibility might in practice have been dispensed with. As for legal considerations, the Tribunal held that since the locations of the boundary pillars in question 'were recognized by the States concerned as forming part of the boundary line during the critical period, lack of intervisibility cannot affect this finding since the boundary line, in spite of non-intervisibility, was accepted by the parties concerned'.[87] With regard to the recognition by the parties, the Tribunal had, in the immediately preceding section, emphasized that 'where the States concerned have, over a period of more than fifty years, identified a marker as a boundary pillar and acted upon that basis, it is no longer open to one of the parties or to third States to challenge that longheld assumption on the basis of an alleged error [as was one of Israel's arguments]'.[88] In effect, the Tribunal held that the subsequent practice of the parties had suspended or modified the requirement in the Agreement of intervisibility.

3.III.G. The Eritrea-Ethiopia Boundary Decision

Mention may further be had of the recent decision in the *Eritrea-Ethiopia Boundary Decision* where the possibility of subsequent conduct changing the treaty relationship between the parties is subjected to extensive investigation.[89] In its initial comments

---

[83] Spetember 29, 1988. The Tribunal was composed of Gunnar Lagergren, Pierre Bellet, Dietrich Schindler, Hamed Sultan and Ruth Lapidoth (dissenting). The Award is reproduced in 27 *International Legal Materials* (1988) 1421.

[84] 27 *International Legal Materials* (1988) 1442, paragraph 50.

[85] 27 *International Legal Materials* (1988) 1484, paragraph 218.

[86] 27 *International Legal Materials* (1988) 1490, paragraph 236.

[87] 27 *International Legal Materials* (1988) 1491, paragraph 237.

[88] 27 *International Legal Materials* (1988) 1489-1490, paragraph 235. In this context, the Tribunal referred to the *Temple of Preah Vihear Case*.

[89] Eritrea-Ethiopia Boundary Commission, Decision Regarding Delimitation of the Border between the State of Eritrea and the Federal Democratic Republic of Ethiopia (hereinafter the Eritrea-Ethiopia Decision), made public April 15, 2002. The Commission was composed of Professor Elihu

about the law, the Commission's reference to subsequent practice is primarily related to the role of such practice in affecting the legal relations between the parties and not the function of subsequent practice in the interpretation of treaties, although this latter role is acknowledged:[90]

> Thus, the effect of subsequent conduct may be so clear in relation to matters that appear to be the subject of a given treaty that the application of an otherwise pertinent treaty provision may be varied, or even cease to control the situation, regardless of its original meaning.[91]

The approach may be illustrated by the Commission's opening remark concerning the 1900 Treaty covering the Central Sector:

> The Commission will begin its consideration of the sector of the border covered by the 1900 treaty by interpreting the Treaty itself and the annexed Treaty map. The outcome of this interpretation will determine the border in this sector, *subject only* to two important qualifications flowing from the *subsequent conduct* of the parties and an admission made by one Party during the proceedings.[92]

The Commission paid particular interest to three categories of subsequent conduct that all might 'constitute assertions of sovereignty, or acquiescence in or opposition to such assertions': maps, activities on the ground and diplomatic and other similar exchanges.[93]

Lauterpacht, Prince Bola Adesumbo Ajibola, Professor W. Michael Reisman, Judge Stephen M. Schwebel and Sir Arthur Watts. The decision is available at the website of the Permanent Court of Arbitration: www.pca-cpa.org, visited April 18, 2002.

[90] The Eritrea-Ethiopia Decision, 22, 3.6.
[91] The Eritrea-Ethiopia Decision, 22, 3.8.
[92] The Eritrea-Ethiopia Decision, 31, 4.1 (emphasis added).
[93] The Eritrea-Ethiopia Decision, 25, 3.16.

3.III.H. The Land and Maritime Boundary Between Cameroon and Nigeria[94]

In 1994, Cameroon filed an application with the ICJ, asking it to address a number of issues relating to the land and maritime border between Cameroon and Nigeria. For the present study, the question concerning the land territory is of particular interest. Addressing the area near Lake Chad, an initial question before the Court was whether the border between Cameroon and Nigeria in this area had already been delimited. The Court found this to be the case and, thus, that Cameroon held legal title to the contested area. Nigeria, however, claimed sovereignty based on '(1) long occupation by Nigeria and by Nigerian nationals constituting an historical consolidation of title; (2) effective administration by Nigeria, acting as sovereign and an absence of protest; and (3) manifestations of sovereignty by Nigeria together with the acquiescence by Cameroon in Nigerian sovereignty over Darak and the associated Lake Chad villages'.[95]

In evaluating the Nigerian claim, the Court initially noted that, since the frontier had been delimited, 'it necessarily follows that any Nigerian *effectivités* are indeed to be evaluated for their legal consequences as acts *contra legem*'.[96] The Court made relatively short shift of the argument based on historical consolidation, finding that the theory is 'highly controversial' and observing that 'nothing in the *Fisheries* Judgment [*Fisheries* Case, United Kingdom v. Norway, I.C.J. Reports 1951, 130] suggests that the "historical consolidation" referred to, in connection with the external boundaries of the territorial sea, allows land occupation to prevail over an established treaty title'.[97]

With regard to Nigeria's claims (2) and (3), the Court noted that since Cameroon held a pre-existing title, 'the pertinent legal test is whether there was thus evidenced acquiescence by Cameroon in the passing of title from itself to Nigeria'.[98] Such a prospect 'cannot be wholly precluded as a possibility in law'.[99] Here, the Court made reference to the *Land, Island and Maritime Frontier Dispute case* where the Chamber explained that the principle of *uti possidetis juris* in Spanish America should not be considered to freeze for all time the provincial boundaries, the Chamber went on to hold that 'it was obviously open to those States to vary the boundaries between them by

---

[94] Land and Maritime Boundary Between Cameroon and Nigeria (Cameroon v. Nigeria, Equatorial Guinea Intervening), Judgment, Merits, October 10, 2002. About the case, see J. G. Merrills 'Land and Maritime Boundary Between Cameroon and Nigeria (Cameroon v. Nigeria, Equatorial Guinea Intervening), Merits, Judgment of October 10, 2002' 52 *International and Comparative Law Quarterly* (2003) 788-797 and Pieter H. F. Bekker 'International Decision: Land and Maritime Boundary Between Cameroon and Nigeria (Cameroon v. Nigeria, Equatorial Guinea Intervening), 97 *American Journal of International Law* (2003) 387-398.
[95] See the Court quoting the Nigerian submissions, paragraph 62.
[96] Ibid., paragraph 64.
[97] Ibid., paragraph 65.
[98] Ibid., paragraph 67.
[99] Ibid., paragraph 68.

agreement; and some forms of activity, or inactivity, might amount to acquiescence in a boundary other than that of 1821. ... The situation was susceptible of modification by acquiescence in the lengthy intervening period'.[100]

However, even if the transfer of a legal title was possible by acquiescence, preference should be given to the holder of the title where the alleged *effectivités* do not correspond to the law that is where the territory, which is the subject of the dispute, is effectively administered by a State other than the one possessing legal title.[101]

The conclusion of the Court's deliberations must thus be said to be that, whereas a legal title is highly resistant to challenges, a scenario where such a title is eroded and displaced through acts *contra legem* on the one side and acquiescence on the other, 'cannot be wholly precluded as a possibility in law'.[102]

3.III.I. Husserl v. Swiss Air Transport Co., Ltd. and Day v. Trans World Airlines

Reference may finally be made to the USA where at least two domestic decisions have been identified as accepting the proposition that subsequent practice may modify a treaty.[103] The two cases, *Husserl* v. *Swiss Air Transport Co., Ltd.*[104] and *Day* v. *Trans World Airlines,*[105] both concerned the relationship between the 1929 Warsaw Convention and the 1966 Montreal Agreement and the question whether hijacking was within the ambit of the word 'accident'. [106] The Courts found that the Montreal Agreement did not constitute a treaty but rather should be viewed as 'subsequent action

---

[100] Land, Island and Maritime Frontier Dispute, El Salvador v. Honduras, Nicaragua intervening, I.C.J. Reports 1992, 408, paragraph 80.

[101] Here the Court quoted from the *Frontier Dispute Case*, I.C.J. Reports, 1986, 587, see *Land and Maritime Boundary Between Cameroon and Nigeria* (Cameroon v. Nigeria, Equatorial Guinea Intervening), paragraph 68.

[102] Similar considerations were presented with regard to the area of the Bakassi Peninsular, paragraphs 218-224. Merrills concludes 'that once a treaty boundary is in place, a heavy burden lies on the party seeking to argue for its displacement', J.G. Merrills 'Land and Maritime Boundary Between Cameroon and Nigeria (Cameroon v. Nigeria, Equatorial Guinea Intervening), Merits, Judgment of October 10, 2002' 52 *International and Comparative Law Quarterly* (2003) 788-797 at 796.

[103] Maria Frankowska 'The Vienna Convention on the Law of Treaties before United states Courts' 21 *Virginia Journal of International Law* (1988) 281 at 343.

[104] *Husserl* v. *Swiss Air Transport Co., Ltd.*, 351 F. Supp 702 (1972), affirmed 485 F.2d 1240 (2d Cir. 1973).

[105] *Day* v. *Trans World Airlines,* 528 F.2d 31 (2d Cir. 1975).

[106] Convention for the Unification of Certain Rules Relating to International Transportation by Air, concluded in Warsaw, Poland October 12, 1929. The Montreal agreement consisted of an interim agreement among airlines, a tariff, a 'Note to Passengers' and an order from the Civil Aeronautics Board, see *Husserl* v. *Swiss Air Transport Co., Ltd.*, 351 F. Supp 702 at 703, note 1 and Maria Frankowska 'The Vienna Convention on the Law of Treaties before United states Courts' 21 *Virginia Journal of International Law* (1988) 281 at 344.

of the parties' and that the Montreal Agreement was intended to modify the contractual relationship between the parties within the Warsaw Convention system.[107]

3.IV. Cases not Accepting Modification Through Practice

In all fairness, it is necessary to point to a number of cases in which international courts have explicitly rejected the idea that a treaty may be modified solely through subsequent conduct. The cases are from the European Court of Justice and the European Court of Human Rights. The former has, on occasion, referred to the possibility of modifying a treaty through practice but has generally been reluctant to accept such a process.

In *French Republic* v. *Commission of the European Communities*, the Court of Justice faced a question concerning the Commission's power to negotiate and conclude a treaty. The Commission argued that the wording of the relevant provision showed that that the Commission 'may derive its powers from sources other that the Treaty, such as the practices followed by the institutions'.[108] The Commission had, in fact, built up a practice of concluding a variety of agreements.[109] Based on this, the Advocate General asked:

> Does this support the inference that, as a result of an interpretation of Article 228 which has gained ground in practice, the Commission has been vested with an autonomous power to conclude international agreements, in that the Council and the Member States have not so far called into question the agreements which it has nevertheless concluded?[110]

This question precisely asks whether practice by the Commission, not objected to by the Council and Member States, may modify a provision of the EEC Treaty. The Advocate General found that a question existed regarding the extent of actual knowledge on the part of the Council and Member States about this practice. One may somehow doubt

---

[107] *Husserl* v. *Swiss Air Transport Co., Ltd.*, 351 F. Supp 702 at 707-708. In note 6 on page 707, the Court made reference to VCLT, Article 31(3)(6) [sic, should be 31(3)(b)]. In *Day* v. *Trans World Airlines*, the Court found that the Montreal Agreement 'did not alter' the language of the Warsaw Convention but provided 'decisive evidence of the goals and expectations currently shared by the parties' to the Convention, 528 F.2d 31 at 36. Bederman notes that 'it seems that article 31(3)(b) ... was been erroneously cited in some cases [*Day* and *Husserl*] ... as a basis for amending the terms of the Warsaw Convention', Davis Bederman 'Revivalist Canons and Treaty Interpretation' 41 *UCLA Law Review* (1994) 954 at 974-975.

[108] Case C-327/91, August 9, 1994, paragraph 31.

[109] Case C-327/91, Opinion of Mr. Advocate General Tesauro, December 16, 1993, paragraph 28.

[110] Ibid.

that the Member States were unaware of the agreements concluded by the Commission. Be that as it may, the Advocate General found the idea that 'an infringement of the rules of the Treaty acquires legitimacy only because it is repeated!' to be untenable.[111] Similarly, the Court of Justice, somewhat parsimoniously, found that, in any event, 'a mere practice cannot override the provisions of the Treaty'.[112]

In *The Queen* v. *Minister for Agriculture ex parte S.P. Anastasiou (Pissouri) LTD et al.*, the European Court of Justice was faced a question concerning the *de facto* practice of acceptance by the European Commission and the majority of Member States of movement certificates and phytosanitary certificates for agricultural goods originating in the northern, Turkish occupied part of Cyprus, a.k.a. 'The Turkish Republic of Northern Cyprus' which is only recognized by Turkey.[113] Indeed, the European Commission had actually distributed specimen of stamps etc. used by the Turkish authorities on northern Cyprus to the Member States. With regard to the movement certificates, the controlling Origin Protocol to the Association Agreement between the European Economic Community and Cyprus required that these be issued by 'custom authorities of the exporting State'.[114] The applicants in the main proceedings and the Greek government asserted that only certificates issued by the authorities of the Republic of Cyprus could attest to originating status as products of Cyprus, and hence covered by the Association Agreement. The United Kingdom and the Commission did not dispute that 'in normal circumstances' the practice of accepting certificates issued by the Turkish authorities would be incompatible with Community law. They found, however, that a special situation pertained to Cyprus.[115] The question of subsequent practice was not explicit but the arguments 'could be seen as an invocation of the subsequent practice clause of Article 31'.[116] The European Court of Justice could not accept the arguments of the United Kingdom and the Commission: Even the special situation on Cyprus did 'not warrant a departure from the clear, precise and unconditional provisions of the Protocol'.[117] The Court placed great emphasis on

---

[111] Case C-327/91, Opinion of Mr. Advocate General Tesauro, December 16, 1993, paragraph 29.

[112] Case C-327/91, paragraph 36. See also Case C-29/99, Opinion of Advocate General Jacobs, December 13, 2001, paragraph 147.

[113] Case C-432/92. For background and critique of the case, see Stefan Talmon 'The Cyprus Question before the European Court of Justice' 12 *European Journal of International Law* (2001) 727-750.

[114] Case C-432/92, paragraph 7.

[115] Case C-432/92, paragraph 19.

[116] P.J. Kuijper 'The Court and the Tribunal of the EC and the Vienna Convention on the Law of Treaties 1969' 25 *Legal Issues of European Integration* (1998) 1 at 8.

[117] Case C-432/92, paragraph 36-37.

the object and purpose of the provisions and did not give the subsequent practice great weight.[118]

In 1986, in *Deumeland v. Germany*, the European Court of Human Rights examined whether Ms Deumeland's proceedings before German social courts involved the determination of 'civil rights and obligations' in Article 6, paragraph 1 of the European Convention.[119] The majority found this to be the case. A Joint Dissenting Opinion, however, found that the state practice of the Contracting States lacked uniformity and exhibited diversity.[120] The dissenters further found that

> 'an evolutive interpretation allows variable and changing concepts already contained in the Convention to be construed in light of modern-day conditions, but it does not allow entirely new concepts or spheres of application to be introduced into the Convention: that is a legislative function that belongs to the member states of the Council of Europe'.[121]

This appears to be a clear statement that a dynamic interpretation is permissible as long as the limits of the Convention are respected ('concepts already contained in the Convention'). Conversely, the *dictum* would indicate that modification of the treaty cannot be effected by the Court even if state practice is evolving towards a modification.

In the 1988 *Johnston and Others* v. *Ireland*, the Court had to consider whether the right to marry in Article 12 could be read to include a right to divorce.[122] The Court reiterated that 'the Convention and its Protocols must be interpreted in the light of present-day conditions'. It maintained, however, that it could not 'by means of an evolutive interpretation derive from these instruments a right that was not included therein at the outset'.[123] The Court found this to be particularly evident where the omission was deliberate. In the case under consideration, the Court pointed out that the parties to the European Convention had had able opportunity to include a right to divorce in, for example, Protocol No. 7 (1984).[124]

---

[118] The practice of the Commission might not have been entirely consistent, see Stefan Talmon 'The Cyprus Question before the European Court of Justice' 12 *European Journal of International Law* (2001) 727 at 732.

[119] (1986) 8 E.H.R.R. 448.

[120] Judges Ryssdal, Bindschedler-Robert, Lagergren, Matscher, Sir Vincent Evans, Bernhardt and Gersing, (1986) 8 E.H.R.R. 448 at 479.

[121] (1986) 8 E.H.R.R. 448 at 480, paragraph 24. (footnote omitted).

[122] *Johnston v. Ireland,* (1987) 9 E.H.R.R. 203.

[123] *Johnston v. Ireland,* (1987) 9 E.H.R.R. 203 at 219, paragraph 53.

[124] Ibid. In fact, the explanatory report to said Protocol stressed that a right to divorce could not be read into obligations connected to the dissolution of marriage.

In the 1989 *Soering Case,* the Court considered the evolution in the attitude towards the death penalty within Europe.[125] It proposed the argument that 'subsequent practice in national penal policy, in the form of a generalised abolition of capital punishment, could be taken as establishing the agreement of the Contracting States to abrogate the exception provided for under Article 2(1) and hence to remove a textual limit on the scope of evolutive interpretation of Article 3'.[126] The European Court of Human Rights, however, did not find that such a process was likely. By adopting Protocol No. 6 in 1983, the parties to the European Convention indicated that they intended to achieve changes to the Convention through the 'normal method of amendment'. The Court, thus, found that 'Article 3 cannot be interpreted as generally prohibiting the death penalty'.[127]

In the 1991 *Cruz Varas v. Sweden Case*, the Court made reference to the *Johnston Case* when it found that 'subsequent practice could be taken as establishing the agreement of Contracting States regarding the interpretation of a Convention provision but not to create new rights and obligations which were not included in the Convention at the outset'.[128]

An argument similar to that raised in the *Soering* case was proposed in the recent judgment in the *Öcelan* case. Here the applicant argued that 'the Contracting States, through the practice they had been following for fifty years, had abolished the exception provided for in the second sentence of Article 2 § 1'. In this case, the Court noted that the 'concepts of inhuman and degrading treatment and punishment have evolved considerably since the Convention came into force in 1950 [*sic* the Convention was drafted in 1950 but entered into force in 1953] and indeed since the Court's *Soering v. the United Kingdom* judgment in 1989'.[129] Based on these developments, i.e. that the territories encompassed by the member States of the Council of Europe, in the Court's words, 'have become a zone free of capital punishment', (51, 195) the Court found that 'it cannot now be excluded ... that the states have agreed through their practice to modify the second sentence of Article 2 § 1 in so far as it permits capital punishment in peace time'.[130] Even if the Court emphasized that this finding was an *obiter dictum*,[131] it

---

[125] *Soering v. United Kingdom*, (1989) 11 E.H.R.R. 439.

[126] In its Öcalan decision, the Court recalled that it 'accepted in its *Soering v. the United Kingdom* judgment that an established practice within the Member States could give rise to an amendment of the Convention. In that case the Court accepted that subsequent practice in national penal policy, in the form of a generalized abolition of capital punishment, could be taken to establish the agreement of the Contracting states to abrogate the exception provided for under Article 2 § 1 and hence remove a textual limit on the scope for evolutive interpretation of Article 3', Öcalan Judgment, application no. 46221/99, delivered March 12, 2003, 50, paragraph 191.

[127] *Soering v. United Kingdom*, (1989) 11 E.H.R.R. 439 at 747, paragraphs. 102-103.

[128] *Cruz Varas v. Sweden*, March 20, 1991, (1992) 14 E.H.R.R. 1 at 42, paragraph 100.

[129] Öcalan Judgment, application no. 46221/99, delivered March 12, 2003, 51, paragraph 194.

[130] Öcalan Judgment, application no. 46221/99, delivered March 12, 2003, 52, paragraph 198.

cannot but be read as an acknowledgement of a process in international law, which allows for the informal modification of treaties.[132]

While the just mentioned *dictum* in the *Öcalan* case is quite explicit in its recognition of the possibility of modifying treaties through practice, the combined tenor of these cases from the European Court of Justice and the European Court of Human Rights appears to at least question the assertion that subsequent practice can modify conventional obligations. With regard to both courts, however, particular circumstances help to make these precedents exceptions that confirm the rule: In the case of the European Court of Justice, the unique character of the European Union must be considered, including the much more developed division of power and checks and balances, as compared to other international organizations. With regard to the Human Rights Court, the dynamism of the treaty regime itself must, as does the Court, be emphasized. As the Court pointed out on several occasions, the original 1950 treaty rights and duties can be and have been extended through protocols. This fact has at least two implications: Firstly, formal treaty modification is relatively easily attainable if the will exists and, secondly, when, as in the *Soering* case, a protocol was adopted a mere six years prior to the case, this would make it somewhat unlikely that a tacit agreement had been reached during this brief period.

3.V. The Legal Justification for the Informal Modification of Formal Treaties

Based on the extensive case material just reviewed, there can be no doubt that practice can modify a convention under certain conditions. Still, a number of questions remain. How do we legally describe what is taking place; and what are the conditions that have to be in place in order for practice to effect normative change. As Karl emphasizes, it is not, however, the outward appearance that counts. It is the legal justification.[133] Karl finds three legal justifications (Deutungen): Custom, tacit agreement and a 'legally relevant fact' (völkerrechtlicher Tatbestand) that may modify the treaty.[134] The latter includes, for example, prescription that was at issue in the 1959 case between the

---

[131] In the specific case, the Court found that 'the imposition of the death penalty on the applicant following an unfair trial amounted to inhuman treatment in violation of Article 3' (p. 55, paragraph 213) and, thus, it was 'not necessary for the Court to reach any firm conclusion' regarding the possible informal modification of the Convention 52, paragraph 198.

[132] On the *Öcelan* case, see Andrew Clapham 'Symbiosis in International Human Rights Law: The *Öcelan* Case and the Evolving Law on the Death Sentence' 1 *Journal of International Criminal Justice* (2003) 475-489 at 480-482.

[133] 'Die Besonderheit der vertragsgestaltenden Praxis liegt nicht in ihrer äußeren Erscheinungsform (in ihrem Typus), sodern in dem inneren Prinzipm das sie begleitet, d.h. ihrer *Deutbarkeit* in dogmatischer Hinsicht'. Wolfram Karl: *Vertrag und spätere Praxis im Völkerrecht: zum Einfluß der Praxis auf Inhalt und Bestand völkerrechtlicher Verträge* Springer, 1983, 246 and 386.

[134] Ibid.

Netherlands and Belgium[135] and in the boundary decision between Cameroon and Nigeria.[136] This category, the third of Karl's categories, would not appear to play a central role for the present subject area aside from recognizing the possibility of normative change through practice.[137] The remaining possible distinction is, thus, between tacit agreements and customary international law.

As is clear from the reactions to the modification of, for example, UN Charter Article 27, paragraph 3, it is not always easy to make an exact determination as to which legal justification is the correct one even if all agree that the provision in question has been changed. One may, as Karl, find that derogating treaty practice, which extends in time and is often repeated, may be best construed as a customary norm.[138] Similarly, Karl and Mützelburg consider that a customary process best explains informal modification of constitutive instruments.[139] Kontou, however, argues that if the process regarding Article 27, paragraph 3 is regarded as an amendment, as opposed to an interpretation, it should be characterized as a modification by the subsequent practice of the parties, i.e. by tacit agreement.[140] This is because the process is 'treaty-oriented', motivated by an intention to modify the treaty, and not aimed at creating a customary rule.[141]

Even if the process is treaty oriented, when we deal with universal treaties, such as the UN Charter, it would seem more correct to speak of a customary process; both because the modification will be in the character of a general legal norm and because conceiving of a tacit agreement between more than 175 states appears difficult. For these reasons and based on Karl's findings, any modification of the UN Charter to be discussed subsequently will be treated as the development of a customary rule. What

---

[135] 1959 ICJ 209.

[136] Land and Maritime Boundary Between Cameroon and Nigeria (Cameroon v. Nigeria, Equatorial Guinea Intervening), Judgment, Merits, October 10, 2002.

[137] As MacGibbon has pointed out 'prescriptive and customary rights share a common process of development which involves, on the one hand, the constant assertion of the right in question, and, on the other hand, consent in that assertion on the part of the affected States', I.C. MacGibbon 'The Scope of Acquiescence in International Law' *British Yearbook of International Law* 1954, 143-186 at 150.

[138] Wolfram Karl: *Vertrag und spätere Praxis im Völkerrecht: zum Einfluß der Praxis auf Inhalt und Bestand völkerrechtlicher Verträge* Springer, 1983, 386. See also Villiger: 'The process of modification is essentially and primarily one of *customary law*. Hence, the fulfillment of the regular conditions for the formation and existence of customary law must be ascertained', Mark E. Villiger, *Customary International Law and Treaties*, The Hague, Kluwer Law International, 1997, 205, paragraph 321.

[139] Bruno Simma (ed.) *The Charter of the United Nations: A Commentary*, Oxford University Press (1994) 1167, paragraph 11.

[140] Nancy Kontou *The Termination and Revision of Treaties in the Light of New Customary International Law* Clarendon Press, 1994, 124-125.

[141] Ibid. 27-28 and 124-125.

this exactly entails is what we now turn to: firstly with a relatively short overview of the characteristics of customary international law.[142]

3.VI. Customary International Law

The primary definition of international customary law is found in Article 38, paragraph 1(b) of the Statute of the International Court of Justice: when deciding a dispute in accordance with international law, the Court shall apply … 'international custom, as evidence of a general practice accepted as law;'. The Court has, on various occasions, elaborated on the meaning of Article 38, paragraph 1(b): 'it is of course axiomatic that the material of customary international law is to be looked for primarily in the actual practice and *opinio juris* of States …'.[143]

As for state practice, the Court, in the *North Sea Continental Shelf* cases, held that such practice might be identified even if only a short period of time has passed. It further found that the practice should have been 'both extensive and virtually uniform'.[144] In the *Nicaragua* case, the Court found that the practice did not need to be in 'absolute rigorous conformity' with the rule.[145] In cases where a state acts in a way that is prima facie inconsistent with a rule, the justification for the action is essential: the state may, as we shall see throughout this study, produce a hitherto unrecognized justification in an attempt to change the law. It may, however, defend its conduct by reference to a justification inherent in the rule itself. In the latter case, 'whether or not the State's conduct is in fact justifiable on that basis, the significance of that attitude is to confirm rather than weaken the rule'.[146]

As for the so-called subjective element, the Court found in the *North Sea Continental Shelf* cases that: 'Not only must the acts concerned amount to a settled practice, but they must also be such, or be carried out in such a way, as to be evidence of a belief that this practice is rendered obligatory by the existence of a rule of law requiring it. The need for such a belief, i.e., the existence of a subjective element, is implicit in the very notion of *opinio juris sive necessitates*. The States concerned must

---

[142] Reference may be had to numerous previous works. Among the latest contributions to the debate are Anthea Elizabeth Roberts 'Traditional and Modern Approaches to Customary International Law: A Reconciliation' 95 *American Journal of International Law* (2001) 757-791; Samuel Estreicher 'Rethinking the Binding Effect of Customary International Law' 44 *Virginia Journal of International Law* (2003) 5-17; and Jörg Kammerhofer 'Uncertainty in the Formal Sources of International Law: Customary International Law and Some of its Problems' 15 *European Journal of International Law* (2004) 523-553.

[143] 1985 ICJ 29-30, paragraph 27.

[144] 1969 ICJ 43, paragraph 74.

[145] 1986 ICJ 98, paragraph 186.

[146] 1986 ICJ 98, paragraph 186.

therefore feel that they are conforming to what amounts to a legal obligation'.[147] The Court further stressed that the frequency and habitual character of the acts is not in itself enough because acting or agreeing to act in a certain way does not of itself demonstrate anything of a juridical nature.

Even with these elaborations by the Court numerous questions remain. One might ask as to whether practice has to consist of actual acts or whether mere statements suffice. Wolfke believed that custom is based on 'material deeds and not words: custom arises from acts of conduct and not promises of such acts'.[148] Conversely, Akehurst has advocated regarding statements *in abstracto* as creative of customary international law:

> It is often supposed that the only way to change a customary rule is to break it frequently. There is no doubt that customary rules can be changed in this way, but the process is hardly one to be recommended by anyone who wishes to strengthen the rule of law in international relations. Fortunately there is a way out of the dilemma; as an alternative to changing customary law by breaking it, States can change it by repeatedly declaring that the old rule no longer exists – a much more desirable way of changing the law.[149]

A similar viewpoint may be found in the *Fisheries Jurisdiction case,* where the Court declared that it was aware 'of various proposals and preparatory documents produced in this [third Conference on the Law of the Sea] framework, which must be regarded as manifestations of the views and opinions of individual States and as vehicles of their aspirations, rather than as expressing principles of existing law'.[150] In all the examples that we will consider in Chapters 6 through 8, actual acts – attacks on alleged terrorist targets – took place.

The debate over acts versus statements ties into a more general disagreement about the correct balance between state practice and *opinio juris* that by now has preoccupied international legal scholarship for decades: In her recent article, Roberts describes the chasm between what is termed the traditional versus modern approaches to customary

---

[147] 1969 ICJ 44, paragraph 77.

[148] Karol Wolfke *Custom in Present International Law,* Martinus Nijhoff, 1993, 42.

[149] Michael Akehurst 'Custom as a Source' 47 *British Yearbook of International Law* 1977 at 8. Villiger similarly opined: 'Statements in the UN framework represent State practice constitutive of customary law. If such statements contain unequivocal proposals contradicting existing rules *in abstracto,* State in that way, at least, are not violating existing obligations with regard to other States in order to modify the law', Mark E. Villiger, *Customary International Law and Treaties*, The Hague, Kluwer Law International, 1997, 211, paragraph 332.

[150] 1974 ICJ 23, paragraph 53.

international law.[151] The two approaches have differing characteristics: The traditional seeks descriptive accuracy represented by the inductive method, whereas the modern approach relies on the deductive process, aiming for normative appeal. Hence, considering the two elements of customary international law, the traditional approach emphasizes state practice, whereas the modern version accentuates *opinio juris*. Even if various intermediary positions may be identified, the juxtaposed traditional and modern approaches pretty much reflect the crux of intellectual debate surrounding customary international law. The choice between the two is very much guided by some of the considerations on selection of method outlined in Chapter 1.

Roberts sets out to reconcile the two approaches.[152] She does this by proposing a theory of custom as a reflective interpretive concept that combines descriptive accuracy with normative considerations through a revision of an initial interpretation of practice and principles, back and forth, until everything has been done to render the interpretation coherent and justified from both ends.[153]

In order to attain descriptive accuracy, state practice is the point of departure. This initial inductive approach may end up as an apology for state action. As mentioned, however, state practice is only the point of departure and remains so only where there is one eligible interpretation due to the uniformity of practice. These cases will often mostly include facilitative customs that do not involve strong issues of principle. If, however, there are multiple eligible interpretations, *opinio juris* will play a role at the level of substance. Hence, inconsistent practice can be seen as either a breach of the rule or a seed of a new custom. The final balance, or solution, will be determined by the relative strength of the practice and the principle.

The structure developed by Roberts is interesting for the present project for at least two reasons. Firstly, by placing initial emphasis on state practice – letting state practice have the initial determinative effect, so to speak – Roberts' approach goes a long way towards allaying the complaints voiced by the critics of modern custom, i.e. that it is aloof from reality.

Secondly, the area of international law under consideration is, as has been pointed out, under stress or pressure and may be characterized as being in a state of flux, which,

---

[151] Anthea Elizabeth Roberts 'Traditional and Modern Approaches to Customary International Law: A Reconciliation' 95 *American Journal of International Law* (2001) 757-791.

[152] Anthea Elizabeth Roberts 'Traditional and Modern Approaches to Customary International Law: A Reconciliation' 95 *American Journal of International Law* (2001) 757-791 at 760.

[153] A similar attempt at reconciling the inductive and deductive approaches may be found in political science theory where John Ruggie, based on Charles Peirce, considered what is termed 'abduction': 'The successive adjusting of a conjectured ordering scheme to the available facts ... until the conjecture provides as full an account of the facts as possible', John G. Ruggie *Constructing the World Polity: Essays on International Institutionalization* Routledge 1998, 94. Recently, Finnemore applied this approach, see Martha Finnemore *The Purpose of Intervention: Changing Beliefs About the Use of Force,* Cornell University Press, 2003.

virtually by definition, makes the scenario of only one eligible interpretation unlikely. Roberts' framework is particularly useful in these circumstances because it allows for the dynamic or fluid nature of custom. Hence, one may observe developments in how states perceive the relationship between state sovereignty and (humanitarian) intervention, the designation of rogue states, weapons of mass destruction, the ban on use of force in international relations, and the increasing concerns over terrorism. The value that is attached to these issues will vary and thus influence the process of legal change. Roberts' theory incorporates this aspect, the importance of which necessitates a thorough review of the perception of terrorism in the UN setting, which is provided in chapter 4.

3.VII. The Development of Customary International Law and *ex iniuria ius oritur*

In the *Nicaragua* case, the Court described how a customary rule might develop. It considered whether a right of intervention in support of forces in opposition to the metropolitan government existed: Firstly, it considered whether a practice illustrative of a right to intervene could be identified.[154] Not only must such a settled practice be present, the acts making up this practice must be accompanied by *opinio juris,* which means that the acting state or states in a position to react must behave so that their conduct is evidence of a belief that this practice is rendered obligatory by the existence of a rule of law requiring it.[155] In the case of use of force, it would be more appropriate to describe the rule as a permissive, rather than obligatory, rule. Finally, the ICJ found that 'reliance by a State on a novel right or an unprecedented exception to the principle [of non-intervention] might, if shared in principle by other States, tend towards a modification of customary international law'.[156] Since the issue is a 'novel right' or an 'unprecedented exception', the claim or conduct is, as the Court declared, 'prima facie inconsistent with the principle of non-intervention', i.e. the law as it stood when the claim was raised.[157] Yet, as the Court went on to note, if other states accept the 'novel right', it may be vindicated. It should be noted that such an acceptance has traditionally been possible through tacit acceptance or acquiescence. See, for example, the already mentioned 1994 case between Cameroon and Nigeria where the Court noted that since Cameroon held a pre-existing title, 'the pertinent legal test is whether there was thus evidenced acquiescence by Cameroon in the passing of title from itself to Nigeria'.[158]

---

[154] 1986 ICJ 108, paragraph 206.
[155] 1986 ICJ 108-109, paragraph 207, the Court quoting from the *North Sea Continental Shelf* cases, 1969 ICJ 44, paragraph 77.
[156] 1986 ICJ 109, paragraph 207.
[157] Ibid.
[158] Land and Maritime Boundary Between Cameroon and Nigeria (Cameroon v. Nigeria, Equatorial Guinea Intervening), Judgment, Merits, October 10, 2002, paragraph 67.

MacGibbon defined the function of acquiescence as equivalent to that of consent: 'it constitutes a procedure for enabling the seal of legality to be set upon rules which were formally in process of development and upon rights which were formally in process of consolidation. The primary purpose of acquiescence is evidential; but its value lies mainly in the fact that it serves as a form of recognition of legality and condonation of illegality and provides a criterion which is both objective and practical'.[159] MacGibbon further wrote that 'the acquiescence of States affected by such a claim [i.e. a claim that is incompatible with the rule] may be interpreted as a recognition of its legality as far as they are concerned, with the result that a customary or prescriptive right to be exempted from the operation of the rule may be acquired by the participants in the exceptional claim'.[160] Again, it is particularly pertinent in the current context because acquiescence, as MacGibbon pointed out, 'provides a salutary corrective to the more exaggerated theories of State sovereignty' and 'serves to temper the apparent rigidity of certain of the cannons of positivism' in the context of development of international law.[161]

Here, when considering an 'unprecedented exception', the Court broached upon a delicate issue that has also has been vexing international legal scholarship, i.e. the apparent fact that a new rule can only be born out of a violation:[162] *ex iniuria ius oritur*?[163] Critics have ridiculed this, as well as other, aspects of customary international law: 'Practice is practice, and custom is custom; neither one is law. Customary international law changes under this definition when state practice changes, which led former Attorney General Bill Barr to opine: "Well, as I understand it, what you're saying is the only way to change international law is to break it". This telling remark shows the incoherence of treating "customary international law" as law'.[164] A great number of scholars, however, appear to accept this dynamic: 'A usual procedure to

---

[159] I.C. MacGibbon 'The Scope of Acquiescence in International Law' 31 *British Year Book of International Law* 1954, 143-186 at 145.

[160] I.C. MacGibbon 'The Scope of Acquiescence in International Law' 31 *British Year Book of International Law* 1954, 143-186 at 185.

[161] I.C. MacGibbon 'The Scope of Acquiescence in International Law' 31 *British Year Book of International Law* 1954, 143-186 at 183 and 184.

[162] Kunz referred to this as a 'challenging theoretical problem', Josef L. Kunz 'The Nature of Customary International Law' 47 *American Journal of International Law* (1953) 662-669 at 667.

[163] Byline inspired by Cassese: '*Ex iniuria ius oritur:* Are We Moving towards International Legitimation of Forcible Humanitarian Countermeasures in the World Community' 10 *European Journal of International Law* (1999) 23-30.

[164] John R. Bolton 'Is There Really "Law" in International Affairs?' 10 *Transnational Law and Contemporary Problems* (2000) 1- 48 at 6, footnotes omitted. See also Glennon: No "living constitution" worthy of the name, domestic or international, is so "alive" as to permit its most vital limits to be expunged through violation. ... No legal regime can endure if the most important proscriptions that it imposes are capable of being revised through violation by its creature', Michael J. Glennon *Limits of Law, Prerogatives of Power: Interventionism after Kosovo* Palgrave, 2201, 127.

modify customary international law is to break it and to accompany the breach by a new legal claim'.[165]

As became evident in a seminar on custom conducted by Professor D'amato, it can be difficult to determine or agree on whether certain acts by states entail breaches or, as favored by D'amato, a 'series of developmental stages'.[166] Tunkin found that 'the action of the state at this moment may contradict international law. I understand your thinking that in the future these violations may become a rule of international law. It has happened in history. In the future it may be accepted as a rule of international law, but at the moment it is a violation' ... 'it's hard to tell it's a violation until we see what the reactions are'.[167] Similarly, Higgins has noted that developments which some find to be persuasive evidence of a changing international law, others will perceive as evidence of repeated breaches.[168]

Following the 1999 NATO intervention over Kosovo, Cassese suggested that 'this particular instance of breach of international law may gradually lead to the crystallization of a general rule of international law authorizing armed countermeasures for the exclusive purpose of putting an end to large-scale atrocities amounting to crimes against humanity and constituting a threat to the peace'.[169] Recently, Kammerhofer dismissed the controversy by emphasizing the difference between the creation and the application of norms. If these are kept apart, a violation of a rule of behaviour does not disqualify the same act from constituting a building block for a modified norm.[170]

As pointed out by Henkin, the reactions by other states will primarily be guided by how deeply the acts infringe on the interests of other states.[171] Thus, the Truman Proclamation, which some thought unlawful, responded 'to a new opportunity in ways

---

[165] Michael Bothe 'Terrorism and the Legality of Pre-emptive Force' in 14 *European Journal of International Law* (2003) 227-240 at 236. See similarly Villiger: 'Modification thus originates in a derogation from – often a breach of – the conventional rule', Mark E. Villiger, *Customary International Law and Treaties*, The Hague, Kluwer Law International, 1997, 210, paragraph 329.

[166] Anthony D'amato *International law: Process and Prospect* Transnational 1995, 109.

[167] Anthony D'amato *International law: Process and Prospect* Transnational 1995, 104.

[168] Rosalyn Higgins 'The Identity of International Law' in Bin Cheng (ed.) *International Law: Teaching and Practice* Stevens and Sons 1982, 27 at 35.

[169] Antonio Cassese: '*Ex iniuria ius oritur:* Are We Moving towards International Legitimation of Forcible Humanitarian Countermeasures in the World Community' 10 *European Journal of International Law* (1999) 23-30 at 29. In a follow-up article, Casssese subsequently dismissed that the purported rulepossessed the 'requisite elements of generality and non-opposition', Antonio Cassese 'A Follow-Up: Forcible Humanitarian Countermeasures and *Opinio Necessitatis*' 10 *European Journal of International Law* (1999) 791-799 at 798. This conclusion does not, however, undermine the actual dynamic of legal change outlined in the first article.

[170] Jörg Kammerhofer 'Uncertainty in the Formal Sources of International Law: Customary International Law and Some of its Problems' 15 *European Journal of International Law* (2004) 523-553.

[171] Louis Henkin: 'Editorial Comment – Arctic Anti-Pollution: Does Canada Make – or Break – International Law?' 65 *American Journal of International Law* (1971) 131 at 133.

which did not affect the perceived rights of others; it was immediately accepted and later codified'.[172]

Depending on how one perceives this process – as positive or negative – one may see it as prevalent or rare. It is relatively rare that the process takes place in explicit terms, primarily because of the well-known fact that states always, or almost always, will produce an excuse based on a well-established justification. In some cases, however, a state has a purpose beyond the individual action, for example, an intention to develop the law through its acts. One such example, which may be sighted here, involves Canada.

Canada has on at least two occasions attracted attention due to its claims regarding the law of the sea and its simultaneous amendments of its acceptance of compulsory jurisdiction by the International Court of Justice. The first case took place in 1970.[173] The second instance occurred in 1994 when Canada amended its Costal Fisheries Protection Act[174] and, two days prior, filed an amended declaration accepting the jurisdiction of the International Court of Justice.[175] This episode is particularly interesting because the International Court of Justice had the issue before it, in the form of a complaint from Spain against Canada.[176] Although the Court only considered the question of its jurisdiction to deal with the case and did not delve on the merits, both the Court and several of the individual judges touched upon the background of the case and the motives of Canada, although the Court emphasized that 'the lawfulness of the acts which the reservation to the Canadian declaration seeks to exclude … has no relevance for the interpretation of … that reservation'.[177]

---

[172] Ibid.

[173] R. St. J. Macdonald 'The New Canadian Declaration of Acceptance of the Compulsotry Jurisdiction of the International Court of Justice' VIII *Canadian Yearbook of International Law* (1970) 3.

[174] See Costal Fisheries Protection Act as Amended in 1994, Received Royal Assent, May 12, 1994, reproduced in 33 *International Legal Materials* (1994) 1383.

[175] Among the caveats to the Court's jurisdiction was 'disputes arising out of or concerning conservation and management measures taken by Canada with respect to vessels fishing in the NAFO Regulatory Area, as defined in the Convention on Future Multilateral Co-operation in the Northwest Atlantic Fisheries, 1978, and the enforcement of such measures' see 1998 ICJ 439, paragraph 14. For general background, see 1998 ICJ 438-442. See also Barbara Kwiatkowska 'ICJ Jurisdiction under the Optional Clause – Relevance of Legality of Acts to Validity of Reservation to Jurisdiction made in Contemplation of such Acts – High Seas – Conservation and Management Measures' 93 *American Journal of International Law* (1999) 502.

[176] The Fisheries Jurisdiction Case, Spain v. Canada, 1998 ICJ 432. See also Derrick M. Kedziora 'Gunboat Diplomacy in the Northwest Atlantic: The 1995 Canada-EU Fishing Dispute and the United Nations Agreement on Straddling and High Migratory Fish Stocks' 17 *Northwestern Journal of International Law and Business* (1996-1997) 1132. Of other possible examples, see cases mentioned by Judge Kooijmans where states have modified their declaration of acceptance of the jurisdiction of the Court in anticipation of a certain dispute reaching the Court.1998 ICJ 491, paragraph 8. See also the German example mentioned by Michael Byres.

[177] 1998 ICJ 467, paragraph 85.

The case before the Court arose out of the arrest by Canadian authorities of the Spanish fishing vessel the *Estai* on March 9, 1995. The vessel was at the time some 245 miles from the Canadian coast, i.e. outside the Canadian Exclusive Economic Zone and, hence, on the high seas.[178] The European Community issued a strong condemnation of the 'lawless act against the sovereignty of a Member State' of the Community.[179] On March 25, 1995 Spain submitted an application to the Court, instituting proceedings against Canada in regard to the amendment of the law and the arrest of the *Estai*. Based on its acceptance of the Courts jurisdiction, Canada submitted that the Court 'manifestly lacked jurisdiction'. Spain submitted that, when interpreting the Canadian acceptance of the Court's jurisdiction, this must be done 'consistently with legality and that any interpretation which is inconsistent with the Statute of the Court, the Charter of the United Nations or with general international law is inadmissible'.[180] The Court, however, did not find this to be the case.

Interestingly, the Court found that 'reservations from the Court's jurisdiction may be made by States for a variety of reasons; sometimes precisely because they feel vulnerable about the legality of their position or policy'.[181] And further 'the fact that a State may lack confidence as to the compatibility of certain of its actions with international law does not operate as an exception to the ... freedom to enter reservations'.[182] These observations were echoed by President Schwebel who found that 'if States ... could withhold jurisdiction only where their measures and actions are incontestably legal, and not ... where their measures and actions are illegal or arguably illegal, much of the reason for making reservations would disappear'.[183] The Court added as a conclusion that 'whether or not States accept the jurisdiction of the Court, they remain in all cases responsible for acts attributable to them that violate the rights of other States'.[184] By a vote of twelve to five, the Court found that it lacked jurisdiction.[185]

Several of the individual judges also, more or less explicitly, commented on the propriety of the Canadian approach. Judge Bedjaoui found that the Canadian approach was not a welcome situation 'for the international community'[186] and he feared 'that the Court has endorsed Canada's action':[187] 'it is no secret that Canada ... is dissatisfied with the law of the sea as it stands and wishes to press on with reforming it. ... It has

---

[178] 1998 ICJ 443, paragraph 19.
[179] 1998 ICJ 444, paragraph 20.
[180] 1998 ICJ 455, paragraph 53.
[181] 1998 ICJ 455, paragraph 54.
[182] 1998 ICJ 456, paragraph 54.
[183] 1998 ICJ 471, paragraph 4.
[184] 1998 ICJ 456, paragraph 56.
[185] 1998 ICJ 468, paragraph 89.
[186] 1998 ICJ 535, paragraph 49.
[187] 1998 ICJ 538, paragraph 57.

then proceeded, while invoking in certain for a the idea of a "state of need", or simply of "emergency", to the point of breaking the existing law in order to secure "progress" in this regard on the part of other States. The Court has of course no bounden duty either to encourage or to discourage this strategy. The formative process of a new international legal norm need not involve wrongful conduct designed by its author to induce other States to negotiate a new law. The decision by the majority that the Court lacks jurisdiction must not be taken to mean that the Court, the guardian of international legality, offers any encouragement whatever to this strategy'.[188] Judge Oda had 'no doubt that Canada believed that it had a legitimate right to adopt and enforce certain fisheries legislation, but that it also believed, in light of the development of the law of the sea, that that right may belong to the area of *lex ferenda*'.[189] Somewhat in matter of fact, Judge Kooijmans found that 'a State taking unilateral action on a matter where international law is in a state of flux is well aware of the probability that such actions may lead to disputes with other States'.[190]

Based on the present review, it would appear to be accepted that new rules of customary international law might originate through the negation of the currently existing rule. When statements are used to achieve this, the risks to international stability are minor.

3.VIII. Customary International Law and Formal Treaties

As set out above, practice modifying a treaty is best conceived as the development of a customary rule. It remains here to describe how this new rule interacts with the earlier treaty. The issue arose in the 1986 ICJ decision on *Nicaragua*. The US argued that the Charter provisions subsumed and supervened related principles of customary and general international law.[191] On the issue of the use of force, the Court did not consider that the content of the conventional and customary rules was 'exactly identical'; the two sources did not 'exactly overlap'.[192] This was in part due to the fact that the conventional regulation of the use of force by no means covers the whole area of the regulation of the use of force in international relations. The well-recognized principles of proportionality and necessity, for example, are absent from Article 51 of the Charter and have to be found in customary rules. Therefore, it cannot be held that Article 51 subsumed or supervened customary international law.[193] Also, the mode of application of the two sources may differ.

---

[188] 1998 ICJ 539, paragraph 58.
[189] 1998 ICJ 484, paragraph 21.
[190] 1998 ICJ 492, paragraph 10.
[191] 1986 ICJ 93, paragraph 173.
[192] 1986 ICJ 93-94, paragraph 175.
[193] 1986 ICJ 94, paragraph 176.

Be that as it may, the Court concluded that even if the content and operation of the two sources were identical, both sources would still remain applicable. The Court found it to be clear that 'customary international law continues to exist and to apply, separate from international treaty law, even where the two categories of law have identical content'.[194] Although the two sets of rules did not overlap completely, the Court found that they flowed from a common fundamental principle and, implicitly, that the differences were not considerable.[195] Thus, the Court clearly found that the two sources, treaty law and customary law, exist in parallel even if they regulate the same question. As pointed out by the Court, a series of practical reasons indicate why this must be so. The Court – due to the peculiar circumstance of the case – did not address one interesting question: assuming that the two bodies of law are not identical, which source should be consulted when stating the law in a certain area? Hence, it has to be determined which of the two norms prevails.

Here one has to determine the hierarchical relationship between conventional and customary rules. Even if not all agree,[196] 'it is accepted that there is no generally established hierarchy between treaty and custom, because they both emanate from States and are equivalent expressions of their consent to be bound internationally'.[197] Similarly, Villiger observed: 'the obligation to derogate from a conventional rule in favour of applying a [more recent] customary rule is made possible because there is no hierarchy of sources in international law; and because customary law and treaties are equal sources'.[198] Some however, for example Wolfke, have warned that the far-reaching autonomy of customary and conventional law does not permit any easy presumption of their mutual derogation in the case of coexistence.[199] While the Institute of International Law in 1995 confirmed that there is no *a priori* hierarchy between treaties and custom as sources of international law, the Institute went on to hold that relevant norms deriving from a treaty will prevail between the parties over norms

---

[194] 1986 ICJ 96, paragraph 179.

[195] 1986 ICJ 96-97, paragraph 181.

[196] McGinnis argues that 'global multilateral agreements' should be given 'absolute priority' over conflicting customary international law, John O. McGinnis 'The Appropriate Hierarchy of Global Multilateralism and Customary International Law: The Example of the WTO' 44 *Virginia Journal of International Law* (2003) 229-284 at 232. See also Michael J. Glennon *Limits of Law, Prerogatives of Power: Interventionism after Kosovo* Palgrave, 2001, 125.

[197] Nancy Kontou *The Termination and Revision of Treaties in the Light of New Customary International Law* Clarendon Press, 1994, 20. See also Joost Pauwelyn who similarly concludes that there is no formal hierarchy of sources in international law, *Conflict of Norms in Public International Law: How WTO Law Relates to other Rules of International Law* Cambridge University Press, 2003, 94 et seq.

[198] Mark E. Villiger, *Customary International Law and Treaties*, The Hague, Kluwer Law International, 1997, 206, paragraph 323. He further asserted that this solution is supported by the principles *lex posterior* and *lex specialis*. Ibid. 207, 325.

[199] Karol Wolfke *Custom in Present International Law,* Martinus Nijhoff, 1993, 99.

deriving from customary law.[200] As pointed out by Pauwelyn, however, this rule is subject to some exceptions, the main being if the conflict involves a customary *jus cogens* norm.[201] This is recognized by the Institute in Conclusion 4, but the issue of supervening custom modifying or revising an earlier treaty is not addressed by the Institute. As pointed out above,[202] the members were not able to agree on the legal relationship between a treaty and later custom dealing with the same subject area. As already outlined in this chapter, however, the subsequent custom may prevail. The reason is the lack of hierarchy between the sources combined with the principle of *lex posterior*, which refers back to the basic contractual freedom of states and identifies the most current 'expression of state consent':[203] 'Hence, in respect of conflict between a treaty norm and supervening custom, one first applies the *lex posterior* rule, which is the subject, however, to the principle of *lex specialis'*.[204] Thus, *lex posterior* remains the rule of first resort. However, as pointed out by Pauwelyn, the principle of *lex posterior* does not work as well when considering supervening custom as when considering a later conventional rule because it is 'virtually impossible' to point to a date on which the custom emerged or matured.[205] Yet, for our purposes, this challenge is not serious because the Charter is as old as it is and there will not be any problem in determining that a certain custom is more recent than the Charter. As for *lex specialis*, only if it is clear that the treaty rule was agreed upon in order to head off custom in the area or if the treaty rule is indeed more specific than the supervening custom, does the treaty prevail. If we focus specifically on the UN Charter and the rules governing force, it may reasonably be proposed that the conventional rules in this case are as general as can be and that it is difficult to conceive of a situation in which the *lex specialis* principle would apply when confronting subsequent custom.

---

[200] See Institut de Droit International: 'Problems Arising from a Succession of Codification Conventions on a Particular Subject', Session of Lisbonne – 1995: *Conclusion 11: Hierarchy of Sources,*available at: http://www.idi-iil.org/idiE/resolutionsE/1995_lis_01_en.pdf.

[201] Joost Pauwelyn *Conflict of Norms in Public International Law: How WTO Law Relates to other Rules of International Law* Cambridge University Press, 2003, 134.

[202] Joost Pauwelyn *Conflict of Norms in Public International Law: How WTO Law Relates to other Rules of International Law* Cambridge University Press, 2003, 138-139.

[203] Joost Pauwelyn *Conflict of Norms in Public International Law: How WTO Law Relates to other Rules of International Law* Cambridge University Press, 2003, 388.

[204] Joost Pauwelyn *Conflict of Norms in Public International Law: How WTO Law Relates to other Rules of International Law* Cambridge University Press, 2003, 392.

[205] Joost Pauwelyn *Conflict of Norms in Public International Law: How WTO Law Relates to other Rules of International Law* Cambridge University Press, 2003, 97.

3.IX. Possible Informal Amendment of the Charter

One remaining question is whether the fact that a treaty, such as the UN Charter, contains a formal amendment procedure will preclude informal amendments?

Some have certainly suggested as much: While Judge Spender, in the *Certain Expenses Case*, accepted that subsequent practice may 'provide evidence from which to infer a new agreement with new rights and obligations between the parties, in effect superimposed or based upon the text of the treaty and amending the same', he rejected that this process may take place when the treaty contains a provision detailing how it may be amended, as for example Article 108 of the UN Charter.[206] Glennon avered that 'the Charter, after all, spells out in plain words how it is to be amended; it says nothing about amendment by practice'.[207]

Engel maintains that Articles 108 and 109 only apply to formal amendments, 'to alteration of its text, but do not apply to changes which, while affecting the substance and content of the Charter, leave its form and text intact'.[208]

Karl conducts quite an extensive analysis of the question. Initially he finds that individual amendment clauses tended to make amendments easier to achieve compared to the traditional alternative of consent of all the parties[209] (see e.g. the – limited –

---

[206] 1962 ICJ 191. South Africa, in the oral statement by Mr. Grosskopf in the 1971 *Namibia Case* relied on this *dictum* when it submitted that 'as regards modification of the Charter by conduct, that possibility seems to be excluded, in our submission, by the existence of Article 108 and 109, which expressly provide for amendment'. ICJ Pleadings, Legal Consequences for States of the Continued Presence of South Africa in Namibia (South West Africa) Notwithstanding Security Council Resolution 276 (1970), Vol. II, 208. See also Edward Gordon 'The World Court and the Interpretation of Constitutive Treaties' 59 *American Journal of International Law* (1965) 794 at 831. At the Vienna Conference, France objected to the proposed Article 38 in part because it would deprive amendment provision of all meaning 208, paragraph 63. See, finally, Fassbender who concludes that the Charter can only be amended in the procedures provided for in Articles 108 and 109, Bardo Fassbender 'The United Nations Charter as Constitution of the International Community' 36 *Columbia Journal of Transnational Law* (1998) 529 at 600.

[207] Michael J. Glennon *Limits of Law, Prerogatives of Power: Interventionism after Kosovo* Palgrave, 2201, 124.

[208] Salo Engel 'The Changing Charter of the United Nations' 7 *The Year Book of World Affairs* (1953) 71 at 73.

[209] 'The classical method of treaty amendment depends on the concurrence of all the parties to the treaty … the classical way out of this dilemma is to insert an amendment clause in the constitutive instrument providing for amendment by a majority of the member states', Karl/Mützelburg 'Commentary to Article 108' 1164-65, paragraph 1. See also Reuter: 'the unanimity rule for revision became too cumbersome to ensure the rapid adaptation of a treaty to changing needs. That is why in practice specific provisions have been introduced … in most international conventions relating to their revision'. Paul Reuter, *Introduction to the Law of Treaties*, 2nd Ed., Kegan Paul International, 1995, 134, paragraph 205. See, however, Schermers and Blokker who, while recognizing unanimity as being the rule of traditional international law, finds that 'this rule is no longer accepted', 807, paragraph 1311.

requirement of two thirds majority required in Article 108) and he finds that, in general, informal amendments are not excluded by the existence of specific amendment procedures.[210] He does, however, proceed to examine some special cases. He finds that some treaty amendments may be dependent upon the approval of a third party in which case the (often limited number of) parties to the treaty are excluded from circumventing this requirement through an informal amendment.[211] A similar concern may arise in the context of constituent instruments of international organizations. In this case, the issue may be viewed as a more philosophical problem as to whether and to what extent the Organization has taken on a life of its own and separate from the united will of its members. The other side of the coin is the argument that the member states continue to hold the ultimate power over the Organization. Fundamentally, the problem may be addressed either deductively or inductively: In the former case, theories, which emphasize the constitutional nature of the Charter, will maintain the importance of the Organization as an individual being. If, however, actual practice, whether by states or by organs of the organization, is taken as the point of departure, one will find that informal amendments do occur, the most prominent example being Article 27, paragraph 3. As is well known, the ICJ in the 1971 Namibia case confirmed this informal amendment. Based on this, Karl and Mützelburg conclude that 'it is established that the Charter may not only be subject to formal amendments under Arts. 108 and 109, but may also be changed by informal or *de facto* modifications'.[212]

In this and the previous chapter, we have examined the effect subsequent practice may have on a conventional rule. When examining claims and acts that appear to challenge *lex ferenda* we have to try to determine whether the challenge is within the interpretative radius of the rule or whether we are seeing a new norm being put forward. The evaluation of the claim, whether it succeeds or fails, depends on the answer to this question, in as much as different criteria are applicable in each case.

---

[210] Wolfram Karl: *Vertrag und spätere Praxis im Völkerrecht: zum Einfluß der Praxis auf Inhalt und Bestand völkerrechtlicher Verträge* Springer, 1983, 340-345.

[211] Karl makes reference to minority treaties under the League of Nations during the inter-war years, Wolfram Karl: *Vertrag und spätere Praxis im Völkerrecht : zum Einfluß der Praxis auf Inhalt und Bestand völkerrechtlicher Verträge* Springer, 1983, 345-346. See similar considerations in Schermers and Blokker *International Institutional Law* 722, paragraph 1163: As an example, the authors mention that amendments made to the Treaty of the European Union without respecting the required consultation procedures would be unlawful, even if the members acted unanimously. Reuter, too, finds that the parties to a treaty may unanimously agree on another amendment procedure that the one contained in the original treaty. He too, however, notes the potential problem where third parties are involved. Paul Reuter *Introduction to the Law of Treaties* Kegan Paul International (1995) 137, paragraph 210.

[212] Article 108, in Bruno Simma (ed.) *The Charter of the United Nations: A Commentary*, Oxford University Press (1994) 1167, paragraph 11. They continue, that 'to some extent ... informal modification may be considered as a viable alternative to a formal Charter amendment', ibid. 1168, 12.

Yet, we still need to address one more issue before we can proceed to the analysis of state practice. In reflections reminiscent of those just outlined by Roberts, Simma and Paulus concluded that legal problems are addressed by 'a patchwork of legal considerations' and the 'impartial mediation of attitudes, ideologies or conflicts'.[213] In the process, standards from legal sources deemed to be representative of the attitude of the community in providing a yardstick. It is to this 'attitude of the community' we now turn. In this case, to the deliberations on measures to eliminate terrorism at the United Nations.

---

[213] Bruno Simma and Andreas Paulus 'The Responsibility of Individuals for Human Rights Abuses in Internal Conflicts: A Positivist View' 93 *American Journal of International Law* 1999, 302-316 at 316.

Chapter 4

Terrorism in the Work of the United Nations

4.I. Introduction

The international community has been struggling to co-operate in order to eliminate international terrorism for decades. Early attempts failed miserably.[1] When the United Nations (UN) took up the issue in 1972, the USA proposed a comprehensive treaty.[2] It soon became clear, however, that the work at the UN was to be marred by fundamental disagreement between the member states.[3] The work on treaties proceeded on a basis dealing with different aspects of terrorism individually. By the mid-1980s some found that a review of the efforts revealed that the law on terrorism was not only flawed, it was perverse.[4]

Observations like these may help explain why the work at the UN used to attract relatively little attention. As will be documented in the present paper, however, things have changed significantly during the 1990s. These developments will be described and explanations for the observed changes will be proposed.

4.II. A General Chronological Overview of the United Nations Work on Terrorism

The UN included terrorism on its agenda in 1972.[5] The Secretary-General (SG) requested the items inclusion against a background of increasing incidence of acts of violence against national leaders, diplomatic envoys, international passengers and other innocent civilians which had created throughout the world a climate of fear from which

---

[1] The 1937 Convention for the Prevention and Punishment of Terrorism received one ratification, Hudson: *International Legislation: A Collection of the Texts of Multipartite International Instruments of General Interest*, Volume VII, 1935-1937, No. 499, 1941, 862-878.

[2] Draft Convention for the Prevention and Punishment of Certain Acts of Terrorism, Report of the Ad Hoc Committee on International Terrorism, General Assembly, Official Records, 28th Session, Supplement no. 28 (A/9028), 1973, Annex.

[3] In 1973, Dinstein concluded that 'the present atmosphere in the United Nations is not conducive to a strong stand against terrorism'. Yoram Dinstein 'Terrorism and Wars of Liberation Applied to the Arab-Israeli Conflict: An Israeli Perspective' 3 *Israel Yearbook of Human Rights* (1973) at 86.

[4] Sofaer: 'Terrorism and the Law' in 64 *Foreign Affairs*, 901-922, 902.

[5] One might argue, as does Bassiouni, that the UN undertook to examine terrorism starting in 1963, M. Cherif Bassiouni (ed.) *International Terrorism: A Compilation of United Nations Documents 1972-2001* (2002) Transnational Publishers, *xxviii*. However, as is evident from his title, the real deliberations began in 1972.

no one was immune. The item was proposed included under the title: 'Measures to prevent terrorism and other forms of violence which endanger or take innocent human lives or jeopardize fundamental freedoms'..[6] The General Assembly (GA) eventually adopted the item under the following title:

> Measures to prevent international terrorism which endanger or take innocent human lives or jeopardize fundamental freedoms, and study of the underlying causes of those forms of terrorism and acts of violence which lie in misery, frustration, grievance and despair and which cause some people to sacrifice human lives, including their own, in an attempt to effect radical change.[7]

The GA subsequently adopted its first resolution on the issue of terrorism.[8] The resolution included an invitation to states to consider the subject-matter and to submit their observations to the SG and, further, a decision to establish an Ad Hoc Committee on International Terrorism (AHC) to consider the observations of States and to submit a report with recommendations for possible co-operation for a speedy elimination of terrorism.[9]

The AHC submitted its report to the 1973 GA session. The report of the AHC showed substantial differences among the States as to how the problem of terrorism was to be approached and the report did not take any decisions or make any recommendations on the question.[10] Due to lack of time the GA decided to refer considerations of the report to the 1974 session. Similar decisions were made at the 1974 and 1975 sessions. At the 1976 session, the GA invited the AHC to continue its work in accordance with the original mandate.[11] The AHC duly presented a report to the GA 1977 session on the basis of which the GA again invited the AHC to continue its work but with a slightly different mandate by firstly studying the underlying causes of terrorism and then recommending practical measures to combat terrorism. The GA further decided to include the item in the agenda of its 1979 session.[12] For the first time, the AHC, in it report to the GA in 1979, agreed on a set of recommendations. These included urging all states to eliminate the causes of terrorism, found to be *inter alia*

---

[6] 1972 U.N.Y.B. 639.

[7] Ibid. 640. The title was amended in 1991, when the GA adopted resolution 46/51: "Measures to eliminate international terrorism'. This remains the current title.

[8] Resolution 3034 (XXVII), Ibid. 649.

[9] Ibid., paragraphs 7, 9 and 10.

[10] Report of the Ad Hoc Committee on International Terrorism, General Assembly, Official Records, 28th Session, Supplement no. 28 (A/9028). See in addition 1973 U.N.Y.B. 777-780.

[11] Resolution 31/102, paragraph 7, 1976 U.N.Y.B. 832-834.

[12] Resolution 32/147, paragraphs 7 and 12, 1977 U.N.Y.B. 968-971.

colonialism, racial discrimination, aggression, occupation and domination and an appeal for states to join existing conventions and consider the need for concluding new treaties on the subject.[13] The GA welcomed the report but did not ask the AHC to continue its work.[14]

During the following decade the GA revisited the issue biannually but did not take any action save the passing of resolutions.[15] At a general level, it is possible to discern some positive signs of convergence between the member states. Resolutions in 1981, 1983, 1985 and 1989 were adopted without a vote.[16] Particularly the negotiations concerning the 1985 resolution appear positive.[17] Throughout the 1980s there were calls for a reactivation of the AHC.[18] This, however, did not happen.

The 1990s, and especially the second half of the decade, saw a substantial increase in attempts at dealing with terrorism at the UN. In 1993, the GA began to consider the question of terrorism annually. Of particular significance, the GA approved the 'Declaration on Measures to Eliminate International Terrorism' in 1994 and the 'Declaration to Supplement the 1994 Declaration on Measures to Eliminate International Terrorism' in 1996.[19] In its 1995 resolution, the GA requested the SG to, among other things, conduct an analytical review of existing international legal instruments relating to international terrorism in order to determine whether there were aspects of international terrorism not covered by the existing corpus and which could be addressed by developing further instruments.[20] In his report, the SG found that consideration could be given to: Terrorist bombings, terrorist fund-raising, traffic in arms, money laundering, exchange of information concerning persons or organizations suspected of terrorist-linked activities etc. The report also directed attention to the risk of terrorist use of weapons of mass destruction and modern information technology for terrorist purposed.[21] Prompted by the report, the GA decided to establish an ad hoc committee to elaborate an international convention for the suppression of terrorist bombings and, subsequently, an international convention for the suppression of acts of

---

[13] 1979 U.N.Y.B. 1146.

[14] Resolution 34/145.

[15] Resolutions 36/109, 38/130, 40/61, 42/159, 44/29.

[16] The 1987 resolution was adopted by a recorded vote of 153-2-1. The United States and Israel abstained while Honduras voted against, 1987 U.N.Y.B. 1065.

[16] See for example a call in 1987 from several East European countries, 1987 U.N.Y.B 1062.

[17] 'Many felt that the text, despite certain shortcomings, represented the common will of a vast majority of Member States or was a generally acceptable compromise solution', 1985 U.N.Y.B. 1169.

[18] See for example a call in 1987 from several East European countries, 1987 U.N.Y.B 1062.

[19] Annexed to Resolutions 49/60 and 51/210 respectively.

[20] Resolution 50/53, paragraph 10.

[21] Measures to Eliminate International Terrorism, Report of the Secretary-General, A/51/336, paragraph 36.

nuclear terrorism.[22] The ad hoc committee (AHC1996) has met annually since 1997 and its work has, additionally, continued during the sessions of the GA in the framework of a working group (WG).[23] Through the efforts of the AHC1996 and the WG, the GA has adopted three recent international conventions on Terrorist Bombings, Terrorist Financing and Nuclear Terrorism.

The UN system has, through the GA and through subsidiary bodies such as International Civil Aviation Organisation (ICAO) and the International Maritime Organisation (IMO), promulgated altogether 12 international treaties[24] dealing with terrorism.[25] The United Nations, on April 15, 2005, passed resolution 59/290, adopting

---

[22] Resolution 51/210, paragraph 9. In 1998, the AHC1996 was authorised to elaborate on a French draft of an international convention for the suppression of terrorist financing, see resolution 53/108, paragraph 11.

[23] The ad hoc committee's official title is: The Ad Hoc Committee established by General Assembly Resolution 51/210 of 17 December 1996. See reports of the committee: 1997: A/52/37, 1998: A/53/37, 1999: A/54/37, 2000: A/55/37, 2001: A/56/37, 2002: A/57/37, 2003: A/58/37, 2004: A/59/37 and 2005: A/60/37. The Working Group has issued eight reports: 1997: A/C.6/52:L.3, 1998: A/C.6/53/L.4, 1999: A/C.6/54/L.2, 2000: A/C.6/55/L.2, 2001: A/C.6/56/L.9, 2002: A/C.6/57/L.9, 2003: A/C.6/58/L.10, and 2004: A/C.6/59/L.10.

[24] The number of treaties will, of course, depend upon which one finds as addressing terrorism in one way or another. Bassiouni, for example count 17, M. Cherif Bassiouni (ed.) *International Terrorism: A Compilation of United Nations Documents 1972-2001* (2002) Transnational Publishers, *xxxi*. The United Nations Treaty Collection, however, lists 12, see http://untreaty.un.org/English/Terrorism.asp, visited December 12, 2002.

[25] In chronological order, these are (I have included ratifications status as of May 2001 and May 2004 to show the increase in ratifications following September 11, 2001. The number of ratifications for the treaties in force has been found in Measures to eliminate international Terrorism, Report of the Secretary-General, A/56/160 and A/59/210.): The Tokyo Convention (Convention on Offences and Certain Other Acts Committed on Board Aircraft, signed at Tokyo September 14, 1963, entered into force December 4, 1969, ratifications as of May 1, 2001: 171; ratifications as of May 28, 2004: 178. (2 *ILM* 1042)); The Hague Convention (Convention for the Suppression of Unlawful Seizure of Aircraft, signed at The Hague December 16, 1970, entered into force October 14, 1971, ratifications as of May 1, 2001: 173; ratifications as of May 28, 2004: 177. (10 *ILM* 133)); The Montreal Convention (Convention for the Suppression of Unlawful Acts against the Safety of Civil Aviation, signed at Montreal September 23, 1971, entered into force January 26, 1973, ratifications as of May 1, 2001: 174; ratifications as of May 28, 2004: 180. (10 *ILM* 1151)); The Diplomat Convention (Convention on the Prevention and Punishment of Crimes against Internationally Protected Persons, including Diplomatic Agents, adopted in New York December 14, 1973, entered into force February 20, 1977, ratifications as of June 13, 2001: 107; ratifications as of May 28, 2004: 149. (13 *ILM* 41)); The Hostage Convention (International Convention against the Taking of Hostages, adopted in New York, December 17, 1979, entered into force June 3, 1983, ratifications as of June 13, 2001: 95; ratifications as of May 28, 2004: 140. (18 *ILM* 1456)); The Nuclear Material Convention (Convention on the Physical Protection of Nuclear Material, signed at Vienna March 3, 1980, entered into force February 8, 1987, ratifications as of April 25, 2001: 69; ratifications as of May 28, 2004: 104. (18 *ILM* 1419)); The Montreal Protocol (Protocol for the Suppression of Unlawful Acts of Violence at Airports Serving International Civil Aviation, supplementary to the Convention for the Suppression of Unlawful Acts against the Safety of Civil Aviation, signed at Montreal February 24, 1988, entered into force August 6, 1988, ratifications as of May 1, 2001: 107; ratifications as of May 28, 2004: 146. (27 *ILM* 628)); The

the International Convention for the Suppression of Acts of Nuclear Terrorism as proposed by Ad Hoc Committee established by General Assembly resolution 51/210 of 17 December 1996. The treaty will open for signature on September 16, 2005.

Rome Convention (Convention for the Suppression of Unlawful Acts against the Safety of Maritime Navigation, done at Rome March 10, 1988, entered into force March 1, 1992, ratifications as of April 30, 2001: 52; ratifications as of May 28, 2004: 104. (27 *ILM* 668)); The Rome Protocol (Protocol for the Suppression of Unlawful Acts against the Safety of Fixed Platforms Located on the Continental Shelf, done at Rome March 10, 1988, entered into force March 1. 1992, ratifications as of April 30, 2001: 48; ratifications as of May 28, 2004: 95. (27 *ILM* 685)); The Plastics Explosives Convention (Convention on the Marking of Plastic Explosives for the Purpose of Detection, signed at Montreal March 1, 1991, entered into force June 21, 1998, ratifications as of May 1, 2001: 66; ratifications as of May 28, 2004: 106 (30 *ILM* 721)). The Terrorist Bombing Convention (International Convention for the Suppression of Terrorist Bombing, adopted at New York January 9, 1998, entered into force May 23, 2001, ratifications as of May 28, 2004: 124. (37 *ILM* 249)); and The Terrorist Financing Convention (International Convention for the Suppression of the Financing of Terrorism, adopted at New York December 9, 1999, entered into force April 10, 2002, ratifications as of May 28, 2004: 118 (39 *ILM* 270)). On April 1, 2005, the Ad Hoc Committee finalized the draft for the International Convention for the Suppression of Nuclear Terrorism, see A/50/377, April 4, 2005. The draft was adopted by the General Assembly on April 13, 2005, (Resolution 59/290) and will be opened for signature on September 14, 2005. Main regional instruments:
Organization of American States (OAS): Convention to Prevent and Punish the Act of Terrorism Taking the Form of Crimes against Persons and Related Extortion that are of International Significance concluded at Washington DC, February 2, 1971, entered into force October 16, 1973. Ratified by 13 of 18 states, see Organization of American States web-site: www.oas.org, visited May 12, 2000; Inter-American Convention against Terrorism, June 3, 2002, entered into force July 10, 2003, ratifications as of June 3, 2004: 8. Council of Europe: European Convention on the Suppression of Terrorism concluded at Strasbourg January 27, 1977, entered into force August 4, 1978. Ratified by 32 of 41 states, see Council of Europe web-site: http://conventions.coe.int/treaty/EN/cadreprincipal.htm, visited May 12, 2000; Protocol amending the European Convention on the Suppression of Terrorism, adopted May 15, 2003, ratifications as of June 11, 2004: 5. Council of Europe Convention on the Prevention of Terrorism adopted May 16, 2005, signatures as of September 25, 2005: 20, ratifications as of September 25, 2005: 0. Council of Europe Convention on Laundering, Search, Seizure and Confiscation of the Proceeds from Crime and on the Financing of Terrorism, adopted May 16, 2005, signatures as of September 25, 2005: 13, ratifications as of September 25, 2005: 0. Available at http://conventions.coe.int/Treaty/Commun/ListeTraites.asp?CM=8&CL=ENG, visited September 26, 2005. The South Asian Association for Regional Co-operation (SAARC): Regional Convention on Suppression of Terrorism signed at Kathmandu November 4, 1987 and entered into force August 22, 1988. All seven members of SAARC have ratified the convention, see A/54/301. League of Arab States: Arab Convention on the Suppression of Terrorism, adopted in Cairo April 22, 1998, entered into force May 7, 1999, ratified by 17 of 22 states (including the Palestinian Authority) as of April 9, 2004, see A/59/210. Treaty on Cooperation among States Members of the Commonwealth of Independent States in Combating Terrorism, June 4, 1999, status as of June 19, 2003: 5 ratifications, see A/59/210. OAU Convention on the Prevention and Combating of Terrorism, July 14, 1999, entered into force December 6, 2002, status as of May 21, 2004: 32 ratifications, see A/59/210.

4.III. The Development Within Specific Issue-Areas

The condensed review just presented of the work on terrorism at the UN does not reveal the substantial developments; it is to these substantial developments we now turn.

The three decades, in which the GA has considered terrorism, can be summarised as: 1970s: fundamental disagreement with regard to both the overall issue and ways to address it; 1980s: continued disagreement concerning the issue but an agreement to disagree, including an implicit understanding that no progress would be made; 1990s: substantial shift to widespread agreement on the fundamentals and progress with the work on practical measures.[26] Post September 11 development have, needless to say, propelled the work at the UN to eliminate terrorism further; yet these developments are not without new tensions and ambiguities. The present suggested schematic breakdown over decades does, however, obliterate a gradual evolution that has escalated during the 1990s and particularly during the second half of that decade.

Firstly, it is only reasonable to point out that all states condemned terrorism throughout. This condemnation was based on the fact that terrorism takes innocent lives and that it jeopardises international relations and co-operation. Some, in addition, condemned terrorism based on ideological concerns.[27] Beyond this very fundamental starting point, however, agreement subsided. The lack of progress, some may even say deadlock, that has characterized the work of the UN with regard to the problem of terrorism in the 1970s and to some extend in the 1980s may, at a very general level, be explained by a basic disagreement between member states: Is terrorism to be determined based on the act or on the motive/motivation of the actor? The positions of states and the developments in these positions will be examined with now regard to a number of issues: The question about what to address first: the causes of international terrorism or the creation of remedies, the question of state versus individual terrorism, the question of self-determination, national liberation organizations and terrorism, and, finally, the issue of the political offence exception and asylum.

---

[26] The assertion that no progress was made during the 1980s primarily refers to work at the GA level and particularly to the discontinuation of the AHC. In all fairness, it should be pointed out that several conventions and protocols were agreed to within UN subsidiary organs: The Montreal Protocol, The Rome Convention and Protocol etc., see footnote 23.

[27] The Soviet Union, for example, stated that Marxism-Leninism rejected international terrorism as a 'method of revolutionary action because it weakened the revolutionary movement and deflected the workers from the mass revolutionary struggle. The entire experience of revolutionary and national liberation movements showed that the recognition of terrorism as the principal method of combat led to a division of forces and diverted active militants from their real task', see 1972 U.N.Y.B. 642. China adopted a similar stance, Ibid. 643.

4.III.A. The Causes of Terrorism Versus Measures to Eliminate Terrorism

During the early work of the UN on terrorism, a lot of time was taken up by discussion about whether to study and deal with the causes of terrorism first or whether to implement measures to eliminate it. From the very beginning in 1972, it is possible to discern a division on this question. Many states found that the study of the underlying causes was a pre-condition for the study of measures. 'How could measures be elaborated to combat a phenomenon without first trying to disclose its causes?'[28] In addition, measures to combat terrorism should above all address the underlying causes.

Other states pointed out that although the study of the causes of terrorism was important it should not postpone or prevent the elaboration of practical measures. This was justified by the fact that 'it was quite unrealistic to expect that, upon completion of that study, the underlying causes could be so eradicated as to lead to the prompt elimination of international terrorism'.[29] Part of the division on the issue had roots in the fundamental questions of: Who is a terrorist or which acts constitute terrorism? As Algeria made clear during the 1972 session: By studying the origins of the various forms of terrorism, the Committee (the AHC) would be able to determine their legality or illegality'.[30] Such an approach was, however, rejected by other states: The examination of the question of causes of international violence could not imply seeing in those causes justification of any sort for the violence experienced.[31]

During the 1970s the question remained controversial and the study of the causes in the AHC's work was given priority in 1977.[32] In 1979, Syria pointed out that it was not by mere chance that the GA, 'after a lengthy discussion, added to the original title of the topic of terrorism a reference to the necessity of a 'study of the underlying causes of those forms of terrorism and acts of violence which lie in misery, frustration, grievances and despair".[33] An operative paragraph urging states to contribute to the progressive elimination of the causes underlying international terrorism and to pay special attention to all situations, including colonialism, racism and situations involving mass and flagrant violations of human rights and those involving occupation that may give rise to international terrorism remained a permanent part of GA resolutions throughout the 1980s.[34] The title of the 1991 resolution, however, gave an indication of

---

[28] Report of the Ad Hoc Committee on International Terrorism, General Assembly, Official Records, 28th Session, Supplement no. 28 (A/9028), paragraph 42.

[29] Ibid., paragraph 43.

[30] 1972 U.N.Y.B. 642.

[31] Report of the Ad Hoc Committee on International Terrorism, General Assembly, Official Records, 28th Session, Supplement no. 28 (A/9028), paragraph 45.

[32] Resolution 32/147, paragraph 7.

[33] Analytical Study Prepared by the Secretariat in Accordance with General Assembly Resolution 32/147, A/AC.160/4, 1979, paragraph 12.

[34] See for example resolution 40/61, paragraph 9.

where the trend was heading. As noted by Syria in 1979, the title does not appear by mere chance. In 1991, the title was changed from the original to: 'Measures to Eliminate International Terrorism'. 1991 was the last resolution including the familiar phase on the causes of terrorism.[35] Throughout the 1990s, despite very elaborate declarations in 1994 and 1996, no mention was made of the need to study or eliminate the causes of international terrorism.

4.III.B. State Terrorism Versus non-State Terrorism

The discussion about whether to include state terrorism in the work of the AHC created problems similar to those caused by the issue of causes versus remedies. Some states saw state terrorism as 'the most dangerous brand of violence, the most often practiced on the most comprehensive scale'.[36] In a contribution to the AHC on the question of underlying causes, Algeria included among the reasons for state terrorism: The wish to maintain colonial domination, foreign occupation, apartheid or to intervene in or exploit another country.[37] Some states further stated that 'as long as Governments were free to inflict terror, the only retaliation available to their victims would be counter-terror'.[38] The line of argument inevitably led to the question of the legitimacy of the struggle of peoples subjected to state terrorism in the form of colonialism, occupation and apartheid, to which we shall turn shortly.

States opposed to including the question of state terrorism in the work of the AHC found that acts committed by states were already governed by the general rules of state responsibility and rules in elaborate conventions, most notably in international humanitarian law and human rights law.

The first GA resolution condemned the repressive and terrorist acts by colonial, racist and alien regimes in denying peoples their legitimate right to self-determination and operational paragraphs with this content remained in resolutions throughout the 1970s. The 1979 resolution was, however, the last to include it.

A vindication of the view that acts of states should not be dealt with in the context of the UN work on terrorism, but left to international law in general and to international humanitarian law in particular, is the recent 1997 Convention on Terrorist Bombings. Article 19 exempts, from the application of the convention, the activities of armed

---

[35] Resolution 46/51, paragraph 6.

[36] Statement by Syria: Observations of States Submitted in Accordance with General Assembly Resolution 3034 (XXVII), Analytical Study Prepared by the Secretary-General, A/AC.160/2, 1973, paragraph 16.

[37] Report of the Ad Hoc Committee on International Terrorism, General Assembly, Official Records, 28th Session, Supplement no. 28 (A/9028), Annex, B.

[38] Report of the Ad Hoc Committee on International Terrorism, General Assembly, Official Records, 28th Session, Supplement no. 28 (A/9028), paragraph 24.

forces during armed conflict and the activities undertaken by military forces of a State in the exercise of their official duties. The former are generally exempted whereas the latter are exempted inasmuch as they are governed by other rules of international law. The article caused some controversy during the negotiations and similar provisions in the Russian Draft Convention for the Suppression of Acts of Nuclear Terrorism hampered progress of that Draft Convention, but were eventually settled in a manner similar to that of the Terrorism Bombings Convention just mentioned.[39] Discussions on this topic also took place in the negotiations on the Draft Comprehensive Convention.[40] A comparison with – what was perceived by some – attempts to exempt national liberation movements from the application of the 1979 Hostage Convention (to be discussed shortly) highlights the radical shift in the approach at the UN, where it is now armed forces that are explicitly exempted.

4.III.C. Self-determination, National Liberation Organisations (NLO) and Terrorism

As was the case with the above-discussed issues of causes versus measures and state versus individual terrorism, the polarisation between states on the issues of self-determination, NLO and terrorism was present from the start of the work on international terrorism at the UN. Indeed, this is hardly surprising since the two former controversies, as alluded to above, are intimately tied to questions of self-determination and the struggle to achieve it: If state terrorism includes colonialism, racism and occupation, then state terrorism was seen by many states at the UN to be a cause of individual terrorism. Since all peoples have the right to self-determination, including the right not to be subjected to subjugation, domination and exploitation, the crucial question naturally arises as to what measures peoples denied their right to self-determination can take to remedy the situation.[41]

---

[39] See original Russian proposal: A/AC.252/L.3. The reason why the Draft Nuclear Convention has faced more resistance on the question of exempting armed forces should be found in the fact that the subject matter of the convention is nuclear weapons as opposed to conventional in the Terrorist Bombings Convention. Any general controversy over the exemption of state actors is, in the case of the nuclear convention, exacerbated by questions of the legality of nuclear weapons, the non-proliferation regime etc. As pointed out by the chairman of the AHC1996 and WG at the meeting of the Sixth Committee: The issue [of the scope of the treaty] is essentially a political rather than a legal one, A/C.6/54/SR.31. The last meeting of the AHC1996 in February 2000 failed to reach agreement on the Russian proposal.

[40] See 'Report of the Ad Hoc Committee established by General Assembly resolution 51/210 of 17 December 1996, 2001, Document A/56/37, 13.

[41] On peoples right to self-determination see for example the UN Charter, article 1, paragraph 2, GA Declaration on the Granting of Independence to Colonial Countries and Peoples, paragraphs 1 and 2, Resolution 1514 (XV), 1960, common article 1, paragraph 1 of the International Covenant on Economic, Social and Cultural Rights and the International Covenant on Civil and Political Rights, both 1966 and GA Declaration on Principles of International Law Concerning Friendly Relations and

Against an international law background in which the right to self-determination for peoples is well established, the discussion at the UN did not concern the right itself but the measures to implement it. The United States, during the first session in 1972, declared that, as a country which had emerged from a struggle for independence, it would not be party to any action that would adversely affect that right.[42] The same state, however, maintained that recourse to certain methods was unacceptable in any circumstances, whatever the aim pursued.[43] The sentiment was elaborated by New Zealand in the statement: 'No cause, however just, and no end, however worthy, can justify the terrorist in taking or risking the lives of innocent and unsuspecting people'.[44]

Among some states there was concern that attempts were made to equate the struggle for self-determination with terrorism. They felt that the original GA resolution vindicated their point of view. As Syria remarked: '... resolution 3034 (XXVII) defeated the imperialist attempt made during the twenty-seventh session to brand as terrorism acts of resistance waged by freedom-fighters in order to achieve objectives stemming from the spirit and the letter of the United Nations Charter itself, first among which is self-determination'.[45] In 1979 several governments stressed the necessity of excluding from any definition of international terrorism the acts performed by recognised national liberation movements in their struggle to obtain their goals of self-determination and independence.[46]

The ambiguities concerning self-determination, NLO and terrorism were exemplified by the negotiations surrounding the Hostage Convention. As documented by Lambert, some states argued that the convention should be inapplicable to acts of hostage taking by national liberation groups.[47] Some states proposed the following provision:

> For the purposes of this Convention, the term 'taking of hostages'
> shall not include any act or acts carried out in the process of
> national liberation against colonial rule, racist and foreign regimes,

---

Co-operation Among States in Accordance with the Charter of the United Nations, Resolution 2625 (XXV), 1970.

[42] 1972 U.B.Y.B. 642.

[43] Observations of States Submitted in Accordance with General Assembly Resolution 3034 (XXVII), Analytical Study Prepared by the Secretary-General, A/AC.160/2, 1973, paragraph 15.

[44] Ibid.

[45] Ibid., paragraph 35.

[46] Analytical Study Prepared by the Secretariat in Accordance with General Assembly Resolution 32/147, A/AC.160/4, 1979, paragraph 27.

[47] Lambert: *Terrorism and Hostages in International Law – A Commentary on the Hostage Convention 1979*, Grotius, 1990, 267.

by liberation movements recognized by the United Nations or regional organizations.[48]

Similar efforts to legitimise the struggle of NLO and remove the stigma of terrorism can be seen in the 1977 Protocol Additional to the Geneva Conventions of 12 August 1949 and Relating to Protection of Victims of International Armed Conflicts (1977 Protocol I).[49] The convention, as remarked by Lambert, was part of a trend to 'internationalise' armed conflicts of national liberation.[50] Article 1, paragraph 4 extends the scope of international armed conflict to include 'armed conflicts in which peoples are fighting against colonial domination and alien occupation and against racist regimes in the exercise of their right of self-determination'. The debates concerning the scope of the Hostage Convention *vis-a-vis* NLO were eventually settled by a quite elaborate article 12 which refers directly to article 1, paragraph 4 of the 1977 Protocol I. Although article 12 in no way exculpates acts of hostage taking by NLO, it does in some cases submit the legal regulation of such acts to international humanitarian law. Formally, acts of hostage taking during armed conflict whether committed by NLO or organised armed forces of a state are subject to the same regulation, be it the Hostage Convention or international humanitarian law. The equation of state forces and NLO, which precluded suggestions that the Hostage Convention was directed against NLO, may have been the main reason why supporters of exempting NLO altogether agreed to article 12.[51]

The first GA resolution in 1972 included the following operative paragraph: The General Assembly,

> *Reaffirms* the inalienable right to self-determination and independence of all peoples under colonial and racist regimes and other forms of alien domination and upholds the legitimacy of their struggle, in particular the struggle of national liberation movements, in accordance with the purposes and principles of the Charter and the relevant resolutions of the organs of the United Nations;[52]

The paragraph remained in subsequent resolutions, although from 1979 through 1985 it was placed in the preamble. The latter fact did not, however, change the view of its

---

[48] Ibid.
[49] 16 ILM 1391.
[50] Lambert: *Terrorism and Hostages in International Law – A Commentary on the Hostage Convention 1979*, Grotius, 1990, 293.
[51] Ibid. 272.
[52] Resolution 3034 (XXVII), paragraph 3.

supporters that the struggle of NLO could not be identified with terrorist acts.[53] Western states repeatedly argued against the paragraph because they saw it as being selective, as overemphasizing certain regimes while ignoring others whose repressive acts caused at least as much suffering, or as simply being superfluous.[54] In 1987 the paragraph returned, in a slightly different and expanded form, to operational status which created further controversy. The members of the European Community stated that the right to fight for self-determination did not include the right to resort to terrorism, while the United States felt the text was gratuitous and susceptible to misinterpretation.[55] The ambiguity was such that at the end of the 1980s, although the language of the resolutions could hardly be read as excluding NLO, several states continued to maintain a distinction between acts of NLO and acts of terrorism.[56] During the 1990s, however, the GA dispelled any lingering uncertainty concerning the issue of NLO. This was achieved partly through the elimination of the disputed paragraph, partly through the strengthening of the condemnation of terrorism.[57] Since 1985, the GA unequivocally condemns, as criminal, all acts and practices of terrorism wherever and by whomever committed, including those which jeopardize friendly relations among states and their security.[58] If there is disagreement as to what constitutes terrorism, however, this paragraph may still be ambiguous. The paragraph was elaborated during the 1990s and in the most recent resolution paragraphs 1 and 2 read: The General Assembly:

> Strongly condemns all acts, methods and practices of terrorism as criminal and unjustifiable wherever and by whomsoever committed;

---

[53] Cuba and Mali stated that they had voted in favour on the understanding that the term 'international terrorism' did not include the actions of NLO, 1979 U.N.Y.B. 1149. See also Yugoslavia in 1981, 1981 U.N.Y.B. 1220.

[54] 1981 U.N.Y.B. 1219.

[55] 1987 U.N.Y.B. 1065.

[56] Lambert: *Terrorism and Hostages in International Law – A Commentary on the Hostage Convention 1979*, Grotius, 1990, 44. Halberstam remarked that "every resolution of the General Assembly condemning terrorism has included a paragraph reaffirming the right to self-determination, as if the latter justified the former', "Terrorism on the High Seas: The Achille Lauro, Piracy and the IMO Convention on Maritime Safety in 82 *American Journal of International Law*, 269-310, 310, 1988. Higgins finds that by 1989 "the implication is clear: the right to self-determination, which constitutes an important part of United Nations policy, cannot justify acts of terror', Higgins: 'The General International Law of Terrorism' in Higgins and Flory (ed.): *Terrorism and International Law*, Routledge, 1997, 18.

[57] The paragraph concerning self-determination and NLO appears for the last time in the 1991 resolution.

[58] Resolution 40/61, paragraph 1.

> Reiterates that criminal acts intended or calculated to provoke a state of terror in the general public, a group of persons or particular persons for political purposes are in any circumstances unjustifiable, whatever the considerations of a political, philosophical, ideological, racial, ethnic, religious or other nature that may be invoked to justify them;[59]

Based on the developments in the resolutions from the GA, particularly during the 1990s, it is possible today, as opposed to ten years ago, to state without any reservations that no justification, struggle for self-determination or other, exists for employing terrorism. That having been said, some ambiguity continues to subsist, as we shall see below.

4.III.D. The Political Offence Exception (POE) and Asylum[60]

The POE is related to extradition of alleged offenders between states and has a long history.[61] The exception in its modern form originated in Europe around the middle of the 19th century.[62] The POE arose in a Europe that was gradually substituting absolutist rulers for more popularly based governments. It was in this environment that more 'enlightened' states found it objectionable to return persons sought by less 'enlightened' states on the basis of their political efforts at reforming the latter. The POE has since then attained broad acceptance and is for example included in the 1990 United Nations Model Treaty on Extradition.[63]

The practical implementation of the POE has caused problems, and several authors identify various approaches.[64] Any general problems are, however, further exacerbated when the POE encounters the issue of terrorism. This is due to the fact that acts of

---

[59] Resolution 58/81, January 8, 2004, paragraphs 1 and 2.

[60] The words 'exception' and exemption' appear to be used interchangeably.

[61] See most generally: Van den Wijngaert: *The political offence exception to extradition: The delicate problem of balancing the rights of the individual and the international public order*, Kluwer, 1980.

[62] As the first state, Belgium codified the POE in 1833, Ibid., 12.

[63] The Model Treaty on Extradition includes the POE in article 3 (a) as a mandatory ground for refusal to extradite, see: Resolution 45/120 with annex including the model treaty, 1990 U.N.Y.B. 705.

[64] Gilbert for example examines the United Kingdom, the United States, the French and the Swiss approaches, Gilbert: 'Terrorism and the Political Offence Exemption Reappraised' in 34 *International and Comparative Law Quarterly*, 695-723, 1985, whereas Phillips divides his examination into the Anglo-American 'Political Incidence' approach, the Swiss 'predominant motive approach and the 'mixed' continental approach, Phillips: 'The Political Offence Exception and Terrorism: Its Place in the Current Extradition Scheme and Proposals for Its Future' in 15 *Dickinson Journal of International Law*, 337-359, 1997.

terrorism are almost always seen as political.[65] In the United States, the close link between the POE and terrorism led to a number of instances in which members of the Irish Republican Army (IRA) sought by the British authorities for acts such as bombings of British army barracks were found to be protected by the POE. In a different case, dealing with a bombing in the Israeli town of Tiberias by a member of the Palestine Liberation Organization (PLO), extradition was granted to Israel.[66] Even accepting that the circumstances and facts of the various cases were different, the question of consistency remains.[67] Concerning the specific issue of extradition of alleged IRA terrorists from the United States and Britain, the two countries concluded a supplementary treaty in 1986 to address the problem. The supplementary treaty makes an exception to certain offences, such as murder, kidnapping, bombing etc. from the POE.[68] The United States has subsequently sought to restrict the POE in other extradition treaties.[69]

At the international level, the European Convention on the Suppression of Terrorism originally addressed the problem in a somewhat ambiguous fashion. Article 1 establishes that a number of offences related to terrorism shall not be regarded as 'a political offence or as an offence connected with a political offence inspired by political motives'. Article 13, however, allows states to 'reserve the right to refuse extradition in respect of any offence mentioned in Article 1 which it considers to be a political offence...'. As noted by Green, this makes it 'relatively easy for any state to evade the

---

[65] 'A conclusion which may be gathered from the observations sent by Governments is that a definition of international terrorism should cover acts committed for a political motive', Analytical Study Prepared by the Secretariat in Accordance with General Assembly Resolution 32/147, A/AC.160/4, 1979, paragraph 40. Of 109 definitions of terrorism collected by Alex Schmid in 1984, 65% contained "political' as a definitional element, see Hoffman: *Inside Terrorism*, Columbia University Press, 1998, 40.

[66] See the problem described in for example: Hanney: 'International Terrorism and the Political Offense Exception the Extraditon' in 18 *Columbia Journal of Transnational Law,* 381-412, 1979; Green: 'Terrorism, the Extradition of Terrorists and the 'Political Offence' Defence' in 22 *German Yearbook of International Law*, 337-371, 1988; and Sapiro: Extradition in an Era of Terrorism: The Need to Abolish the Political Offense Exception' in 61 *New York University Law Review*, 654-702.

[67] 'Without implying that those who decide on the applicability of the political offense exception consciously favor one kind of political struggle over another, the provision nevertheless remains a very loosely circumscribed set of terms open to radically conflicting interpretations', Petersen: 'Extradition and the Political Offense Exception in the Suppression of Terrorism' in 67 *Indiana Law Review*, 767-796, 787, 1992

[68] For the controvercy surrounding the supplementary treaty see for example: Sofaer: 'Terrorism and the Law' in 64 *Foreign Affairs*, 901-922, 910, 1986 and Franck: *The Power of Legitimacy Among Nations*, 69f, Oxford University Press, 1990.

[69] See Witten: 'The International Convention for the Suppression of Terrorist Bombings' in 92 *American Journal of International Law*, 774-781, 779 note 28 an accompanying text, 1998.

extradition obligation'.[70] Recent developments have, somewhat, rectified this inconsistency. In 1996, the Council (of Ministers) of the European Union approved the Convention Relating to Extradition between the Member States of the European Union. Article 5 deals with political offences. It declares that no offence shall be regarded by the requested state as a political offence. Member states may, however, make a reservation to the effect that only terrorist offences, as referred to in the European Convention on the Suppression of Terrorism, articles 1 and 2, will not be regarded as political offences. The member states can, thus, reserve to keep the POE, but not for terrorist offences.[71] It should be noted that the 1996 convention is between the members of the European Union whereas the 1977 convention is between the members of the Council of Europe. In the 2005 Council of Europe Convention on the Prevention of Terrorism, Article 20 stipulates that none of the offences covered by the convention shall be regarded as political offences.

The concern over the problem caused by the POE in the battle against terrorism has been articulated on a number of occasions during work at the UN. Among observations submitted by states in 1973, several contributions addressed the issue: Australia found that acts of terrorism should not be considered as political crimes, and Jamaica thought that extradition and asylum should be considered with a view to restricting the concept of political offences in respect of international terrorism. Canada and the Netherlands felt that states that retained the right to refuse extradition on grounds of the POE should be obligated to submit the case to its own authorities for prosecution.[72] In 1979, the United Arab Emirates pointed out, during a discussion on the definition of terrorism, that 'the connexion [*sic*] of the idea of terrorism with criminal acts on the one hand and with political offences and the right of political asylum, on the other, was one of the greatest difficulties standing in the way of the formulation of a precise and accurate definition of terrorism'.[73]

Two GA resolutions from the mid-1980s contain operational paragraphs that hint at a wish for abstention from the use of provisions such as the POE. In these the GA 'urges all states not to allow any circumstance to obstruct the application of appropriate law enforcement measures provided for in relevant conventions to which they are party

---

[70] Green: 'Terrorism, the Extradition of Terrorists and the 'Political Offence' Defence' in 22 *German Yearbook of International Law*, 337-371, 356, 1988
[71] See EUR-Lex: Community Legislation in Force: Convention relating to extradition between the Members States of the European Union – Explanatory Report: www.europa.eu.int/eur-lex/en/lif/dat/1997/en_497Y0623_01.html, visited March 11, 2000. See also: Warbrick and McGoldrick: 'Current Developments: Public International Law: I. Extradition and the European Union' in 46 *International and Comparative Law Quarterly*, 948-957, 955, 1997.
[72] Observations of States Submitted in Accordance with General Assembly Resolution 3034 (XXVII), Analytical Study Prepared by the Secretary-General, A/AC.160/2, 1973, paragraph 54.
[73] Analytical Study Prepared by the Secretariat in Accordance with General Assembly Resolution 32/147, A/AC.160/4, 1979, paragraph 19.

to persons who commit acts of international terrorism covered by those conventions'.[74] The misgivings concerning the POE were made explicit in the 1996 Declaration to Supplement the 1994 Declaration on Measures to Eliminate International Terrorism.[75] Paragraph 6 encourages states to exclude acts of terrorism from the POE when concluding or applying extradition agreements.

Until the two most recent conventions, the multilateral treaties dealing with terrorist offences do not address the issue of POE.[76] In these cases, therefore, the extradition treaties between individual states govern the application. The multilateral treaties do establish that if no bilateral extradition treaty exists between a requesting and requested state they may consider the multilateral treaty as a legal basis for extradition.[77] In such a case, the question would arise as to whether the POE would be in effect. The fact that the multilateral treaties do not deal with the question would indicate that one has to turn to customary international law and it would be fair to suggest that recent efforts to remove terrorist offences from the POE have not yet changed customary international law. Such a view would seem to be supported by the fact that the relatively recent UN Model Treaty on Extradition maintains the general POE.[78] Finally, following Byers, it can be noted that, in the absence of any active will from a substantial number of states to exempt terrorist offence from the POE, it will be a difficult change to achieve in customary international law.[79]

As a new development, the two most recent conventions on terrorist bombings and terrorist financing stipulate that none of the offences in the respective treaties shall be regarded as 'a political offence or as an offence connected with a political offence or as an offence inspired by political motives'.[80] In spite of the novelty of this approach, there does not appear to have been much resistance in neither the AHC1996/WG nor in the Sixth Committee. In his presentation to the Sixth Committee, the chairman of the AHC1996/WG pointed out that the removal of the POE had been balanced with other safeguards.[81] The primary safeguard is that there is no obligation to extradite if the requested state has substantial grounds for believing that the request is 'made for the purpose of prosecuting or punishing a person on account of that person's race, religion,

---

[74] GA resolutions 40/61, paragraph 7 and 42/159, paragraph 7.

[75] Annexed to GA resolution 51/210.

[76] See conventions in note 23.

[77] See for example the Hostage Convention, article 10, paragraph 2 and the Rome Convention, article 11, paragraph 3.

[78] See footnote 63.

[79] See Byers discussion on jurisdiction and 'internal rules', Byers: *Custom, Power and the Power of Rules: International Relations and Customary International Law*, 57, Cambridge University Press, 1999.

[80] The Terrorist Bombing Convention, article 11 and the Terrorist Financing Convention, article 14.

[81] Sixth Committe, Summary Records, A/C.6/52/SR.27, paragraph 3.

nationality, ethnic origin or political opinion …'.[82] The European Convention on the Suppression of Terrorism includes a similar provision and critics have pointed out that it is difficult to imagine the alleged offender not being prosecuted for his political opinion considering the political nature of most terrorist acts.[83] However, when read in conjunction with the provision exempting terrorist acts from the POE, the safeguard provision may be seen as a requirement for a 'fair trial'. It is, of course, possible that requested states will use the safeguard provision as an excuse not to extradite, as a substitute for the POE. In this case, it is important to note that the evaluation the requested state must make concerns two different aspects. The POE concerns the offence whereas the safeguard provision concerns the status and workings of the justice system of the requesting state. As has been pointed out, it will be somewhat more difficult for a requested state to officially determine and communicate its misgiving and displeasure with a requesting state's court system than to determine that an offence is political according to its own law.[84]

In ways similar to the POE, the institutions of refugee status and asylum have been perceived to protect persons suspected or convicted of terrorist acts and, thus, not deserving such protection. The general condition for qualifying for refugee status is found in the 1951 Convention Relating to the Status of Refugees.[85] The protection of the Convention does not apply, however, to persons who have committed certain serious crimes.[86] The crimes listed are severe and, therefore, narrowly defined. Article 1F(b) mentions serious non-political crimes and includes several 'normal' crimes but the political element, often present in terrorist acts, complicates the application.[87] Some national authorities, such as the Danish, have, however, in some cases in which the applicant admitted to terrorist acts, ruled that the use of terrorism was disproportionate to the political goal, indicating that the offence was not political.[88] It would appear difficult to fit an 'ordinary' terrorist act into the narrow crimes in article 1F (a) and (c) respectively. Yet, Canadian authorities have in some cases involving terrorism, such as complicity in suicide bombings for example, excluded applicants because it was

---

[82] Ibid., articles 12 and 15 respectively.

[83] Green: 'Terrorism, the Extradition of Terrorists and the 'Political Offence' Defence' in 22 *German Yearbook of International Law*, 337-371, 355, 1988

[84] Point made by legal advisor at the United States Department of State in interview April 17, 2000.

[85] The refugee has to have a well-founded fear of being persecuted for reasons of race, religion, nationality, membership of a particular social group or political opinion …, article 1A.

[86] Article 1F: (a): Crimes against peace, war crimes, or crimes against humanity; (b): serious non-political crimes; (c): acts contrary to the purposes and principles of the United Nations.

[87] See discussion in Goodwin-Gill: *The Refugee in International Law*, second edition, 104, 1996 and Amarasinha and Isenbecker: 'Terrorism and the Right to Asylum under the 1951 Convention and the 1967 Protocol Relating to the Status of Refugees – A Contradiction in Terms or Do Opposites Attract?' in 65 *Nordic Journal of International Law*, 223-240, 1996.

[88] Based on personal knowledge of Danish cases.

determined that the systematic murder of Israeli civilians and Palestinian collaborators amounted to crimes against humanity under article 1F(a).[89] As for article 1F(c), an Australian court in 1982 excluded an Iranian applicant based on his involvement in the take over and occupation of the United States embassy in Teheran in 1979-1980. In this case, the International Court of Justice had found that the holding of the American diplomats as hostages was manifestly incompatible with the purposes and principles of the United Nations.[90] Although the example shows that some acts will fall within the severe and narrow crimes of article 1F, the uniqueness of the embassy occupation would, at the same time, indicate that 'lesser' terrorist acts would probably not.

The GA has recently addressed the question of asylum as a haven for terrorists. In both the 1994 and 1996 Declarations, the GA urges states to ensure that an asylum seeker has not engaged in terrorist activity before granting asylum.[91] The GA, in 1994, also took steps to establish a closer link between terrorist acts and the exclusion grounds in the Refugee Convention. The 1994 Declaration stresses that 'Acts, methods and practices of terrorism constitute a grave violation of the purposes and principles of the United Nations ...'.[92] It would appear that the GA, by making this connection, has opened up for a more extensive use of article 1F(c) of the 1951 Refugee Convention. Most recently, the Draft Comprehensive Convention, proposed by India, includes a provision that requires parties to ensure that refugee status 'is not granted to any person in respect of whom there are serious reasons for considering that he or she has committed an offence referred to in Article 2', i.e. a terrorist offense.[93]

4.IV. Explanations

What explanations may be put forward to account for the developments just described? As should be clear from section 3, the developments have been gradual, although they picked up significant speed in the 1990s. Already around 1990 some progress was

---

[89] See the case of Qasem Ibrahim Qasem Hussein in 'Canada's Crimes Against Humanity and War Crimes Program, 2001-2002, Fifth Annual Report', Department of Citizenship and Immigration, Department of Justice, Solicitor General Canada, 45.

[90] See the case mentioned in Goodwin-Gill: *The Refugee in International Law*, second edition, 113, 1996

[91] Declaration on Measures to Eliminate International Terrorism, paragraph 5(f) and Supplement, preambular paragraph 6 and paragraph 3. The US Antiterrorism and Effective Death Penalty Act of 1996 denies possibilities ofr asylum to members of groups designated by the State Department as a 'foreign terrorist organisation'. It is sufficient that the asylum seeker knows that the organisation he belongs to has terrorism among its activities for him to be excluded, see Heymann: *Terrorism and America: A Commonsense Strategy for a Democratic Society*, MIT Press, 1998, 81.

[92] 1994 Declaration on Measures to Eliminate International Terrorism, paragraph 2.

[93] Quoted from the edition of the Draft Convention, Article 7 contained in Annex II in 'Measures to Eliminate International Terrorism: Report of the Working Group, 2001, Document A/C.6/55/L.2.

discernible and various authors have provided suggestions as to the reasons. Lambert found that the fact that the states could agree on the recommendations of the AHC in 1979 'represented a breakthrough of sorts'.[94] In the early 1990s Higgins was able to detect progress during the 1980s and she put this down to the fact that diplomats of the Soviet Union had become victims of terrorism, that there existed generally better relations between East and West and the fact that the Soviet Union terminated its support for radical Middle Eastern groups which led to a consensus at the UN on the condemnation of terrorism.[95] What factors may account for the developments during the 1990s.

4.IV.A. The End of Colonial and Racist Regimes and Alien Domination

If one accepts the argument that the crux of the matter and disagreement concerning terrorism at the UN was based fundamentally on the issue of self-determination and NLO, then, if colonialism etc. disappeared, disagreement would presumably also vanish. Although it may be hard to convince some, if not most people that the world of today is a world without alien domination, injustices due to predatory globalization and (neo) imperialism, the proposed argument still has some merit. Even if the majority of former colonies had achieved independence by 1972 when the UN took up the issue of terrorism, the hardest cases remained. Most of these have, however, been settled or are in the process of being settled. Angola and Mozambique became independent in 1975, Southern Rhodesia in 1980 as well as Zimbabwe, Namibia in 1990 and South Africa changed to majority rule in the early 1990s.[96] One may add East Timor in 1999. Even other protracted conflicts that have not yet been settled, such as the Palestinian and Northern Ireland conflicts have reached a stage where the parties to the conflicts have formally agreed to settle the dispute peacefully.[97]

It is clear from the negotiations at the UN that these were all conflict that were on the minds of states advocating a special role for NLO. They were also conflicts that had an international audience, paradoxically often through the use of violence and terrorism.

---

[94] Lambert: *Terrorism and Hostages in International Law – A Commentary on the Hostage Convention 1979*, Grotius, 1990, 41.

[95] Higgins: 'The General International Law of Terrorism' in Higgins and Flory (ed.): *Terrorism and International Law*, Routledge, 1997, 18. See also Checkel who documents that by 1986, Soviet support for NLO 'was downgraded in both leadership statements and actual policy', *Ideas and International Political Change: Soviet/Russian Behavior and the End of the Cold War*, Yale University Press, 1997, 85.

[96] See list of Trust and Non-Self-Governing Territories, 1945-1999 at UN web-site: www.un.org/Depts/dpi/decolonization/, visited May 15, 2000.

[97] For the conflict between Israel and the Palestinians the Oslo agreement from September 1993 and subsequent agreements and for Northern Ireland the Good Friday Agreement from 1998.

Only few 'classical' cases of conflicts belonging to the category 'colonialist and racist regimes and alien domination' remain, foremost probably being Western Sahara.

4.IV.B. The End of the Cold War

At a very general level, some fundamental shifts occurred at the end of the Cold War. For example, the end of the Cold War produced a general realignment in international politics. Studies have found radical shifts in the voting at the UN GA on issues such as self-determination.[98] The end of the Cold War also saw the world left with one superpower, or, in different parlance, a hegemon. This may lead to the conclusion that the increase in co-operation at the UN when dealing with terrorism is due to 'hegemonic stability'. The theory of 'hegemonic stability' holds that 'hegemonic structures of power, dominated by a single country, are most conducive to the development of strong international regimes, whose rules are relatively precise and well obeyed'.[99] Although few disregard the importance of power as one, albeit important, component, the of theory hegemonic stability has attracted much criticism.[100] Indeed, one may argue that hegemonic power is much less important in an era characterized by 'new sovereignty'.[101]

More specifically, however, the end of the Cold War did not only spell the demise of the bipolar system, it also caused the fragmentation of a number of states that had been held together by more or less repressive governments. The break-ups of the Soviet Union and Yugoslavia serve as prime examples. These developments seem to have triggered awareness of ethnic identity among groups throughout the world.[102] Their demands, from various degrees of autonomy to secession and independence, have often been cloaked in the rhetoric of self-determination. These developments have placed the multifaceted concept of self-determination at the top of the agenda in numerous countries. These countries, desperate to preserve the territorial integrity of the state, have been busy rejecting secessionist claims. The relevance of these developments to

---

[98] Kim and Russett: 'The New Politics of Voting Alignment in the United Nations General Assembly' in 50 *International Organization*, 1996, 629-652. The article studied voting during the 1991, 1992 and 1993 sessions.

[99] Keohane: 'The Theory of Hegemonic Stability and Changes in International Economic Regimes, 1967-1977' in Keohane: *International Institutions and State Power: Essays in International Relations Theory*, Westview, 1989, 75.

[100] See for example Grunberg: 'Exploring the 'myth' of hegemonic stability' in 44 *International Organization*, 1990, 733-477.

[101] See: Chayes and Chayes: *The New Sovereignty: Compliance with International Regulatory Agreements*, Harvard University Press, 1995. The content of the 'new sovereignty' will be discussed further under section 5.3.

[102] Also termed 'new tribalism' or ' micronationalism', see Cassese: *Self-Determination of Peoples: A Legal Reappraisal*, Grotius, 1995, 339.

the discussion of terrorism at the UN is as follows: Ambiguity concerning a possible justification of terrorism has, as noted in section 3, been tied first and foremost to the struggle for self-determination.

The right to self-determination is an 'elusive concept'.[103] Different actors can resort to the concept and advocate the interpretation that best suites their cause, be it for example territorial integrity or independence.[104] The problem is exacerbated by the fact that self-determination exists both as a legal and as a, broader, political principle.[105] Most authors seem to agree that in the context of 'classical' colonialism, an absolute right to self-determination, including the right to independence, existed.[106] The question, however, remains concerning the content of the right to self-determination in a post-colonial world. Many an ethnic group will argue that its members constitute a 'people', ergo they have a right to self-determination, and that this must equal a right to independence. The majority of authors, however, agree that the right to self-determination in its external form does not give any 'peoples' within a state the right to establish their own independent state. Notable exceptions would be any remaining colonial people and those under foreign occupation.

Quane argues that the right of peoples to self-determination, at present, is based on a territorial concept of people. 'People' refers to 'the entire inhabitants of a State or colony'.[107] Finding a similar basis, i.e. the 'self' as coinciding with the territorial state, Cox, asserts that self-determination since de-colonialisation has shifted from independence to modes of participation.[108] He sees three aspects of this shift: 1) The duty to create inclusive political processes, including the fostering of non-sectarian political institutions, 2) the duty to protect minority rights, and 3) the possibility of creating autonomy regimes.[109]

Even with these caveats to the right to self-determination, the question remains: What is the legal effect, if any, of a governing elite refusing to create modes of participation and inclusion for groups living within the state with a different ethnic, racial or cultural background? Some advocate that in such a case 'a claim of a right to

---

[103] Quane: 'The United Nations and the Evolving Right to Self-Determination' in 47 *International and Comparative Law Quarterly*, 1998, 537-572, 537.
[104] Ibid.
[105] Ibid., 538.
[106] See for example Hannum: 'Rethinking Self-determination' in 34 *Virginia Journal of International Law*, 1993, 1-70, 32.
[107] Quane: 'The United Nations and the Evolving Right to Self-Determination' in 47 *International and Comparative Law Quarterly*, 1998, 537-572, 571.
[108] Cox: 'Beigbeder, International Monitoring of Plebiscites, Referenda and National Elections: Self-Determination and Transition to Democracy' in 16 *Michigan Journal of International Law,* 1995, 733-782, 735.
[109] Ibid., 752-753.

secede from a repressive dictatorship *may* be regarded as legitimate'.[110] Kirgis has suggested that the answer to such a question would depend upon the degree to which a government is representative and the degree to which a claim of a right to self-determination is destabilizing. Such an evaluation would, of course, open a myriad of questions concerning who is to judge, on what basis etc. Most people may agree that if the repression reaches proportions resembling genocide, the persecuted ethnic minority should be allowed to secede. Fortunately, such cases are rare, which then, unfortunately, offers little help in delineating a standard for when repression equals a right to secede. Individually, all ethnic groups may see their case as special and the repression they are subjected to as intolerable. What impact would it have on the evaluation if radical elements among an ethnic minority pursued a policy, maybe including terrorist acts, calculated to provoke escalation and more repression? Even assuming that these questions can be settled, it still leaves a similar number of questions concerning how to determine the degree of destabilization.

For the present purposes, the importance of the preceding discussion is that it takes place at all. Even if a right to independence under external self-determination can be ruled out in a post-colonial era, many less than representative governments may face claims of a right to secede under internal self-determination.[111] For these governments, any ambiguities that may legitimise the use of terrorism in the pursuit of self-determination are undesirable to say the least.

Of major countries facing separatist claims, their merit untold, are India and Russia. Although India and Pakistan have been in disagreement over Kashmir since their independence in 1947, the most recent fighting was initiated in 1990 and again, in particular, in 2002 following the attack on the Indian parliament in December of 2001. As for Russia, their biggest problem with separatism can be dated to 1991. In August of that year Chechnya declared its independence following the failed coup in Moscow. In the wake of September 11 states have attempted to re-cast their particular struggles in light of events in the USA.[112] A similar development is detectable in China, which claims to be facing separatist terrorism from elements among the Muslim Uighur

---

[110] Kirgis: 'Degrees of Self-Determination in the United Nations Era' in 88 *American Journal of International Law*, 1994, 304-310, 308 (original emphasis)

[111] Note that Tappe appears to base a legal claim to independence for Chechnya on a combination of external self-determination (historical occupation) and internal self-determination (oppression) and limited destabilising effect, see: 'Chechnya and the State of Self-Determination in a Breakaway Region of the Former Soviet Union: Evaluating the Legitimacy of Secessionist Claims' in 34 *Columbia Journal of Transnational Law*, 1995, 220-295.

[112] David E. Sanger 'For Moscow, Beijing and Washington, a Common Goal' *The New York Times* October 28, 2001.

minority in the Xinjiang province in western China.[113] For states like India and Russia, and other states with heterogeneous populations, most recent examples Indonesia and the Philippines, have a clear interest in the removal of any talk of self-determination from the discourse on and regulation of terrorism.

4.V. Post-September 11 Developments

The UN work on terrorism has moved from substantial disagreement, which resulted in ambiguities regarding the scope of the work, to agreement on the fundamentals and a significant increase in the co-operation to eliminate terrorism. The focal point of the disagreement concerned the role of NLO and what means these organizations should be allowed to employ in their struggle for self-determination for the peoples they represented. As has been hinted at in the preceding paragraphs, disagreements on state versus individual terrorism and whether to address the causes of terrorism or the measures to eliminate it were essentially intimately connected to the principal questions about self-determination and NLO. Even the debates over the POE and asylum are connected to the issue of self-determination and NLO.[114]

4.V.A. A Definition of Terrorism

Two additional questions, not addressed in detail, have occupied the UN. They concern a definition of terrorism and a comprehensive treaty. Early on, it became clear that progress on these two issues was also hampered by the basic lack of agreement concerning NLOs. Thus, the question seems to remain: Is it really 'the task of trying to define what may be indefinable' and it is enough to say that 'I know it when I see it'?[115] But is this description still fitting? Arguably not. The UN has by now reached a point at which a clear operative understanding exists as to what terrorism is; an understanding

---

[113] For a background see, for example Matthew Moneyhon 'Controlling Xinjiang: Authonomy on China's "New Frontier"' 3 *Asian-Pacific Law and Policy Journal* (2002) 4-152. See also Craig S. Smith 'Fearing Unrest, China Presses Muslim Groups' *The New York Times* October 5, 2001.

[114] As noted by Van den Wijngaert in 1980: Consequently, the discussions relating to the political character of acts of 'terrorism', and its implications with respect to extradition are only the semantic veneer of an issue which goes much deeper, *i.e.* the fact that there are, on the one hand, states who want to decriminalize the phenomenon by reducing it to its underlying causes, whereas other states take the 'repressive' stand by prosecuting and punishing terrorist, regardless of their political motivations Van den Wijngaert: *The political offence exception to extradition: The delicate problem of balancing the rights of the individual and the international public order*, Kluwer, 1980, 148.

[115] Justice Potter Stewart commenting on hard-core pornography in Jacobellis v. Ohio, 878 U.S. 184 (1964) at 197. For similar reflections concerning the term 'intervention', see Fawcett who argued that 'we broadly recognize intervention when we see it' 'Intervention in International Law: A Study of some Recent Cases' 103 RC (1961-II) 343-423 at 347.

that has all but the designation 'definition'. The best example may be found in the 1999 Convention for the Suppression of Terrorist Bombings. Article 2 defines terrorist offences as those contained in a list of 9 treaties from the collection of UN treaties already discussed, in addition to

> any other act intended to cause death or serious bodily injury to a civilian, or to any other person not taking an active part in the hostilities in a situation of armed conflict, when the purpose of such act, by its nature or context, is to intimidate a population, or to compel a government or an international organization to do or to abstain from doing any act.

Of course some issues are still left unsolved by this definition, such as the question of 'state terrorism' which is dealt with elsewhere in the Convention. For all intents and purposes, however, here is a UN definition of terrorism.[116]

For another example, one may turn to the Draft Comprehensive treaty, which was originally presented by India, and which stipulates that a person commits an offence within the meaning of the Convention, i.e. a terrorist offence, if he or she, by any means, unlawfully and intentionally, does an act intended to cause:

(a) Death or serious injury to any person; or

(b) Serious damage to a State or government facility, a public transportation system, communications system or infrastructure facility with the intent to cause extensive destruction of such a place, facility or system, or where such destruction results or is likely to result in major economic loss;

> When the purpose of such act, by its nature or context, is to intimidate a population or to compel a Government or an international organization to do or abstain from doing any act.[117]

---

[116] One may also pint to GA resolution 56/88, adopted on December 12, 2001, which '*reiterates* that criminal acts intended or calculated to provoke a state of terror in the general public, a group of persons or particular persons for political purposes are in any circumstances unjustifiable, whatever the considerations of a political, philosophical, ideological, racial, ethnic, religious or other nature that may be invoked to justify them'. Another example of a true operational definition, one might turn to the Committee dealing with the pre-September 11 sanctions against Afghanistan: For the purpose of 'the Committee's [established by Security Council resolution 1333] task, "terrorists' … are the clandestine agents or sub-national groups … that are preparing or training to perpetrate premeditated, politically motivated violence against non-combatant targets … to achieve sectarian goals', see S/2001/511, 9.

[117] Quoted from the edition of the Draft Convention contained in Annex II in 'Measures to Eliminate International Terrorism: Report of the Working Group, 2001, Document A/C.6/55/L.2. Mention may

Finally, one may add the December 2004 Report of the High-level Panel, appointed a year before by the Secretary-General, on Threats, Challenges and Change. The Panel analysed a range of threats and challenges to international peace and stability and, amongst other issues, dealt with the two well-known stumbling blocks to international agreement on a definition of terrorism:

> The search for an agreed definition usually stumbles on two issues. The first is the argument that any definition should include States' use of armed forces against civilians. We believe that the legal and normative framework against State violations is far stronger than in the case of non-State actors and we do not find this objection to be compelling. The second objection is that peoples under foreign occupation have a right to resistance and a definition of terrorism should not override this right. Some contest the right to resistance. But it is not the central point: the central point is that there is nothing in the fact of occupation that justifies the targeting and killing of civilians.[118]

Following this, the Panel proposed that a definition of terrorism should include the following elements: ...[119]

---

also be had of Security Council Resolution 1566 from October 8, 2004, paragraph 3 of which recalls that 'criminal acts, including against civilians, committed with the intent to cause death or serious bodily injury, or taking of hostages, with the purpose to provoke a state of terror in the general public or in a group of persons or particular persons, intimidate a population or compel a government or an international organization to do or to abstain from doing any act, which constitute offences within the scope of and as defined in the international conventions and protocols relating to terrorism, are under no circumstances justifiable by considerations of a political, philosophical, ideological, racial, ethnic, religious or other similar nature, and *calls upon* all States to prevent such acts and, if not prevented, to ensure that such acts are punished by penalties consistent with their grave nature'.

[118] A More Secure World: Our Shared Responsibility Report of the High-level Panel on Threats, Challenges and Change, A/59/565, December 2, 2004, available at www.un.org/secureworld, visited December 4, 2004, page 48, paragraph 160.

[119] (a) Recognition, in the preamble, that State use of force against civilians is regulated by the Geneva Conventions and other instruments, and, if of sufficient scale, constitutes a war crime by the persons concerned or a crime against humanity; (b) Restatement that acts under the 12 preceding anti-terrorism conventions are terrorism, and a declaration that they are a crime under international law; and restatement that te rrorism in time of armed conflict is prohibited by the Geneva Conventions and Protocols; (c) Reference to the definitions contained in the 1999 International Convention for the Suppression of the Financing of Terrorism and Security Council resolution 1566 (2004), see A More Secure World: Our Shared Responsibility Report of the High-level Panel on Threats, Challenges and Change, A/59/565, December 2, 2004, available at www.un.org/secureworld, visited December 4, 2004, page 49, paragraph 169.

(d) Description of terrorism as 'any action, in addition to actions already specified by the existing conventions on aspects of terrorism, the Geneva Conventions and Security Council resolution 1566 (2004), that is intended to cause death or serious bodily harm to civilians or non-combatants, when the purpose of such an act, by its nature or context, is to intimidate a population, or to compel a Government or an international organization to do or to abstain from doing any act'.[120]

In comparing the three definitions, one may note the differences or the similarities just as one may prefer one to the other. Such observations, however, should not detract from the fact that broad consensus today exists concerning what qualifies as a terrorist act and that the once formidable problem of NLOs has passed away. Maybe the best example to illustrate this point is the position taken by the non-aligned movement (NAM), once the most ardent supporter of struggles for national libations. At the ministerial meeting in April of 2002, NAM-ministers issued a final document containing the following conclusions, including that NAM 'reiterates its condemnation of all acts, methods and practices of terrorism as unjustifiable whatever the considerations or factors that may be invoked to justify them'.[121] As will be recalled, such a statement reveals little.[122] The ministers, however, went on to reaffirm 'the legitimacy of the struggle of peoples under colonial or alien domination and foreign occupation for national liberation and self-determination, which does not constitute terrorism' and once again called for the definition of terrorism to differentiate it from the legitimate struggle of peoples under colonial or alien domination and foreign occupation, for self-determination and national liberation'.[123] The pertinent remark here is 'which does not constitute terrorism', which must be read as a de-legitimization of

---

[120] A More Secure World: Our Shared Responsibility Report of the High-level Panel on Threats, Challenges and Change, A/59/565, December 2, 2004, available at www.un.org/secureworld, visited December 4, 2004, page 49, paragraph 169.

[121] Ministrial Meeting of the Co-Ordinating Bureau of the Non-Aligned movement, Final Document, Durban, April 29, 2002, 22-23, paragraph 93.

[122] The Foreign Ministers of the Islamic Conference, for example, in April of 2002, adopted a Declaration which unequivocally condemned acts of international terrorism 'in all its forms and manifestations ... irrespective of motives, perpetrators or victims'.(Kuala Lumpur Declaration on International terrorism, adopted at the Extraordinary session of the Islamic Conference of Foreign Ministers on Terrorism, paragraph 7, April 1-3, 2002, available at www.oic-oci.org, visited August 3, 2002). The Foreign Ministers, however, went on to 'reject any attempt to link terrorism to the struggle of the Palestinian people' (ibid.). Yet, the Declaration also acknowledged the inarguable statement by the Malaysian Prime Minister Mahatir bin Mohamad, see immediately following.

[123] Ministrial Meeting of the Co-Ordinating Bureau of the Non-Aligned movement, Final Document, Durban, April 29, 2002, 23-24, paragraph 99.

the use of terrorism in struggles for national liberation.[124] As another example, one may point to recent statements by the then Malaysian Prime Minister who does not usually mince his words.[125]

4.V.B. Unexpected Consequences

With the massive focus on September 11, it is important to stress that most of the developments concerning the international community's discourse on terrorism had changed and developed before the tragic events of 2001. And even with the work on terrorism generated by the worldwide outrage over the attacks on the USA, one may observe some unexpected dynamics.

One is the possible shift in forum at the UN. Since 1996 the Ad Hoc Committee (and Working Group) established by the GA has worked persistently and achieved a fair measure of success. With the passing of Security Council resolution 1373, however, the center of the work would appear to have moved to the Counter-Terrorism Committee, which was established by said resolution. Many of the measures that are perceived as paramount, particularly with regard to the efforts aimed at impeding the funding of terrorist activities, have been fast tracked through the Security Council and resolution 1373.[126] The new focus may also prove to be to the detriment of the work under the GA. Many of the old grievances about, for example, state terrorism still linger and perhaps due in part to the reduced exposure of the work of the Ad Hoc Committee, some of the intransigent parties may feel they have more room to air their concerns.[127]

---

[124] In addition, one may read the remark as a protest against the designation of liberation struggles as terrorism by the incumbent government.

[125] 'Terrorism we all know has always been with us. It is not a new phenomenon. What is new is that newer and more diabolical ways have been used in order to kill and injure more people and achieve more spectacular damage. But we have always been ambiguous, regarding terrorism in other countries as not really terrorism but as the legitimate struggles of people against their oppressive Governments or alien rule. As long as it happens to other people we do not believe we should do anything. Certainly we do not feel a need for a universal effort to fight against terrorism. But we know now that no country is safe, no one is safe', Speech by Prime Minister The Hon Dato Seri Dr. Mahathir bin Mohamed at the Extraordinary Conference of Foreign Ministersof the Organization of the Islamic Conference on Terrorism in Kuala Lumpur, April 1, 2002, available at www.kln.gov.my/english/Fr-speeches.html, visited May 5, 2002. The speech was adopted as an official document of the conference, see Kuala Lumpur Declaration on International Terrorism, available at www.oic-oci.org, visited May 5, 2002.

[126] Gilbert Guillaume 'Terrorism and International Law' 53 International and Comparative Law Quarterly (2004) 537-548, finding that the Security Council played a truly legislative role. See also Paul C. Szasz 'The Security Council Starts Legislating' 96 *American Journal of International Law* (2002) 901-905.

[127] See, foe example, the dispute over the wording of draft Article 18 of the comprehensive convention draft. The Organization of the Islamic Conference has proposed new version of Article 18 that, in the words of Malvina Halberstam, would eviscerate the convention, Malvina Halberstam 'The Evolution of the United Nations Position on Terrorism: From Exempting National Liberation Movement to

The fact that bodies under the GA through more than half a decade have been unable to finalize drafts for a comprehensive convention and – until recently – a convention for the suppression of nuclear terrorism further exposes the inertia that seems to characterize the Ad Hoc Committee and Working Group since they successfully drafted the conventions on terrorist bombings and terrorist financing in the late 1990s. This reality along with a growing frustration is explicit in the 2004 report of the Ad Hoc Committee: 'It was observed that in the fight against terrorism, the United Nations should play a central role ... Given the global representative character of the General Assembly, several delagations highlighted its primary role in the fight against against terrorism and, in particular, in elaborating counter-terrorism instruments through the Ad Hoc Committee'.[128] This should be juxtaposed with, for example, Rosand's conclusion that the Counter-Terrorism Committee is currently at the center of the international community's counter terrorism efforts.[129]

Another surprise has materialized at a different level. Even if it is accepted that a definition of terrorism exists this does not mean that 'a terrorist is a terrorist is a terrorist'. It is interesting and puzzling that, while all – or almost all – have come to an agreement as to the unconditional illegality of terrorism under international law, the concerns about the legitimate aspirations of certain groups have somehow been retained.

At this point it might be interesting to briefly consider the relationship between liberation struggles and terrorism, illustrated through the example of an NLO that had very strong and broad legitimacy, i.e. the African National Congress (ANC). The reason why the ANC makes a relevant case study is the fact that the struggle has been brought to an end; the struggle was evaluated in a reasonably objective manner through the reconciliation process, which took place during the second half of the 1990s; and finally because the ANC leadership was conscions about the risks of the national struggle being tainted by employing what can only be described as terrorism.

The ANC adopted armed struggle in late 1961. The armed struggle was carried out by the armed wing of the ANC, the *Umkhonto we Sizwe* (Spear of the Nation) or MK. The ANC, in part, justified the initiation of organized armed struggle as an antidote to random acts of senseless violence. These random acts would merely 'play into the

---

Criminalizing Terrorism Wherever and by Whomever Committed' 41 *Columbia Journal of Transnational Law* 573-584 at 582.

[128] The Ad Hoc Committee established by General Assembly Resolution 51/210 of 17 December 1996, Eighth Session, 2004: A/59/37, page 5. See a similar sentiment expressed in the 2004 Report of the Working Group, A/C.6/59/L.10, page 4.

[129] Eric Rosand 'Security Council Resolution 1373, the Counter-Terrorism Committee, and the Fight Against Terrorism' 97 *American Journal of International Law* (2003) 333-341 at 341.

hands of the enemy'.[130] While terrorism as such was denounced, the ANC did acknowledge the constant 'tension between two tendencies: a strict adherence to these policies [to ensure that the moral high ground occupied by the liberation movement due to the justness of the cause must be maintained], and taking the easiest route of terrorist attacks against white civilians. ... The temptation to resort to indiscriminate attacks was always there: but at all times, the principled approach of the movement would prevail'.[131] The distinction between combatants and civilians, however, became increasingly difficult during the mid-1980s when the ANC initiated an all-out intensification of the armed struggle and the organization acknowledged that 'some incidents not entirely consistent with ANC policy did take place'.[132]

The Truth and Reconciliation Commission did not designate acts as 'terrorism' but rather as 'gross violations of human rights'. These were in turn defined as

'the violation of human rights through
(a) the killing, abduction, torture or severe ill-treatment of any person; or
(b) any attempt, conspiracy, incitement, instigation, command or procurement to commit an act referred to in paragraph (a)'

during the period between 1960 and 1994 within or out side the South African Republic and which was 'advised, planned, directed, commanded or ordered, by any person with a political motive'.[133] Based on this definition, it is fair to equate 'gross violations of human rights' with terrorism. The Truth and Reconciliation Commission found that:

The ANC has accepted responsibility for all actions committed by members of MK under its command in the period 1961 to August 1990. In this period there were a number of such actions – in particular the placing of limpet and landmines – which resulted in civilian casualties. Whatever the justification given by the ANC for such acts – misinterpretation of policy, poor surveillance, anger or

---

[130] See ANC's [First] Submission to the Truth and Reconciliation Commission, Part 5 'The ANC: Stages of Struggle and Policy Foundations, 1960-1994, Section 5.1. Available at www.anc.org.za/ancdocs/misc/trc05.html, visited August 30, 2002.
[131] See ANC's [First] Submission to the Truth and Reconciliation Commission, Part 5 'The ANC: Stages of Struggle and Policy Foundations, 1960-1994, Section 5.1. Available at www.anc.org.za/ancdocs/misc/trc05.html, visited August 30, 2002.
[132] See ANC's [First] Submission to the Truth and Reconciliation Commission, Part 5 'The ANC: Stages of Struggle and Policy Foundations, 1960-1994, Section 5.3. Available at www.anc.org.za/ancdocs/misc/trc05.html, visited August 30, 2002.
[133] Promotion of National Unity and Reconciliation Act, No. 34 of 1995, Section 1(1)(xi), available at www.doj.gov.za/trc/legal/index.htm#atcs, visited August 24, 2002.

differing interpretations of what constituted a 'legitimate military target' – the people who were killed or injured by such explosions are all victims of gross violations of human rights perpetrated by the ANC. While it is accepted that targeting civilians was not ANC policy, MK operations nonetheless ended up killing fewer security force members than civilians. With regard to actions committed during the armed struggle, the Commission makes the following findings: while it was ANC policy that the loss of civilian life should be 'avoided', there were instances where members of MK perpetrated gross violations of human rights in that the distinction between military and civilian targets was blurred in certain armed actions, such as the 1983 Church Street bombing of the SAAF headquarters, resulting in gross violations of human rights through civilian injury and loss of life.[134]

Based on the findings of the Truth and Reconciliation Commission, it can be concluded that the ANC was responsible for certain terrorist acts. During the actual events in the 1980s there may actually have been some international support for the application of terrorist tactics. That would not be the case in the year 2005 even if the aim of the struggle was legitimate because, as pointed out, today the issue is not whether a NLO may employ terrorism in their struggle; they may not. As stated recently by the British Prime Minister Tony Blair: 'terrorism is not the way to a negotiated settlement,

---

[134] Final Report, Presented to President Nelson Mandela on 19 October 1998, Vol. 5, Chapter 6: Findings and Conclusions, Findings on the African National Congress, Violations committed in the course of the armed struggle, paragraph 136. Available at www.polity.org.za/govdocs/commissions/1998/trc/5chap6.htm, visited August 24, 2002. The Commission further found that 'in the course of the armed struggle there were instances where members of MK conducted unplanned military operations using their own discretion, and, without adequate control and supervision at an operational level, determined targets for attack outside of official policy guidelines. While recognising that such operations were frequently undertaken in retaliation for raids by the former South African government into neighbouring countries, Such unplanned operations nonetheless often resulted in civilian injury and loss of life, amounting to gross violations of human rights. The 1985 Amanzimtoti shopping centre bombing is regarded by the Commission in this light. In the course of the armed struggle the ANC, through MK, planned and undertook military operations which, though intended for military or security force targets, sometimes went awry for a variety of reasons, including poor intelligence and reconnaissance. The consequences in these cases, such as the Magoo's Bar and Durban Esplanade bombings, were gross violations of human rights in respect of the injuries to and loss of lives of civilians. ... The Commission finds that, in the 1980s in particular, a number of gross violations of human rights were perpetrated not by direct members of the ANC or those operating under its formal command, but by civilians who saw themselves as ANC supporters. In this regard, the Commission finds that the ANC is morally and politically accountable for creating a climate in which such supporters believed their actions to be legitimate and carried out within the broad parameters of a 'people's war' as enunciated by the ANC.

terrorism is the obstacle to a negotiated settlement'.[135] Along similar lines, Michael Walzer found that 'terrorists cannot claim a right to self-determination'.[136]

Yet, the employment of terrorist tactics does not completely undermine a legitimate struggle. Thus, the fact that the United States and Israel ostracized Yasser Arafat because of his alleged links to terrorism may have stalled the peace process but it did not end the need for one. As the Econimist wrote at the death of Mr. Arafat: After Mr. Arafat's death, the Palestinians can again do business with Israel and the US: 'For Mr. Bush and Mr. Ariel Sharon, the animus against Mr. Arafat was personal. Though they would not deal with him, neither ruled out talking to the Palestinian Authority'.[137]

The issue has now become one, at least at the political level, aimed at describing the legitimate counter-measures. Hence, a differentiation still exists between various forms of terrorism. A much-taunted example considers the terrorism emanating from al-Qaeda and Palestinian groups respectively. Whereas Israel, and her supporters, have lang sought to equate the two, the US administration has been reluctant to do so.[138] On September 23, 2001, the State Department spokesman, in effect, described how the threat from al-Qaeda was one aimed at destroying societies, whereas the situation in the Middle East involved violence and political issues that needed to be resolved.[139] Following the start of Israel's Operation Defensive Shield, President Bush was asked: 'What's keeping you from labeling Chairman Arafat a terrorist? The President answered that: 'Chairman Arafat has agreed to a peace process'.[140] Following up the issue with the President's Press Secretary, the latter was asked whether an exception had been carved to the Bush-doctrine for Yasser Arafat, Ari Fleischer, the Press Secretary stated that 'The situation is the Middle East is, indeed, different [to the Taliban harboring al Qaeda]. What makes it different is the fact that you have parties, who themselves have agreed' to various accords. 'That was not the case with al Qaeda. And I understand you want to compare them, but that's not a comparison that the President accepts. ... The president does believe that the path to peace goes through

---

[135] Tony Blair's Press Conference with Israeli Prime Minister Ariel Sharon, December 22, 2004, available at www.number-10.gov.uk/output/Page6836.asp, visited December 24, 2004.

[136] Michael Walzer *Arguing about War* Yale University Press, 2004, 107. This finding may in part be based on the way Watzer conceives of terrorism: not as a negotiation strategy; 'it aims instead at total victory, unconditional surrender', Ibid. page 114.

[137] Editorial: 'Exit Arafat', *The Economist'* November 13th 2004, page 11.

[138] Any discussion of this issue may have to be differentiated further between those within the Palestinian camp who deny the right of Israel to exist and those who 'merely' seek an Israeli withdrawal from the West Bank, East Jerusalem and Gaza Strip. The point in this regard would be that the former are more akin to al-Qaeda in as much as their stated aim is beyond the pale.

[139] Serge Schmemann 'Is There One War Against Terrorism, or Two?' *The New York Times* October 28, 2001.

[140] Remarks by the President in Photo opportunity with New York Governor George Pataki and New York Mayor Michael Bloomberg, The Oval Office, April 1, 2002, available at www.whitehouse.gov/news/releases/2002/04/20020401-4.html, visited October 2, 2002.

Chairman Arafat'.[141] In the case of India, the US administration has also stressed the need to reach a peaceful solution.[142] The differences between 'terrorism and terrorism', for example al-Qaeda terrorism and Palestinian terrorism, or more precisely the differences in perceived legitimate responses was again accentuated in November 2002, when an unmanned US drone destroyed a car in Yemen killing six alleged al-Qaeda members.[143] The spokesman at the US Department of State was confronted with the question as to how the US could disapprove of Israeli targeted killings of alleged Palestinian terrorists when the US applied an indistinguishable technique against suspected al-Qaeda terrorists. Richard Boucher would not be drawn into a comparison, partly because he refused to acknowledge that the CIA was behind the Yemen incident, but he particularly separated the 'Israeli-Palestinian context' by stating that 'we all understand that the situation with regard to Israeli-Palestinian issues and the prospects of peace and the prospects of negotiation and the prospect of the need to create an atmosphere for progress – a lot of different things come into play there'.[144]

While these observations may seem surprising at first glance, this should not be so. After all, as pointed out by Stanley Fish, lumping various issues together under the term 'international terrorism' is unhelpful since terrorism is a style of warfare in the service of a cause. 'It is the cause, and the passions informing it, that confront us'.[145] Therefore, if the overall objective is world order, states will ignore causes at their own peril.[146] In as much as the goal of the terrorists possesses some measure of justification and

---

[141] Press Secretary Ari Fleischer, April 1, 2002, available at www.whitehouse.gov/news/releases/2002/04/20020401-6.html, visited October 2, 2002.

[142] Question: 'India … said that the terrorists who had been involved in the attack on the parliament had training camps just over the border in Pakistan, and they used a variant of the Bush doctrine that suggests that they should go after those camps. … Is it a fair invocation of the Bush doctrine in this case? Answer: India has a legitimate right to self-defense. And at the same time, the President counsels that this is a very difficult situation in the region and one that could spiral out of control' Whitehouse Press Secretary www.whitehouse.gov/news/releases/2001/12/20011217-1.html, visited October 2, 2002.

[143] See Walter Pincus 'U.S. Strike Kills Six in Al Qaeda' *The Washington Post* November 5, 2002 and David Johnston and David E. Sanger 'Yemen Killing Based on Rules Set Out by Bush' *The New York Times*, November 6, 2002.

[144] Richard Boucher, Daily Press Briefing, US Department of State, November 5, 2002, available at www.state.gov/r/pa/prs/dpb/2002/14920pf.htm, visited November 6, 2002. For an earlier discussion of targeted killings in the Israeli-Palestinian context, see press briefing August 27, 2001, available at www.state.gov/r/pa/prs/dpb/2001/4656.htm, visited November 6, 2002.

[145] Stanley Fish 'Condemnation Without Absolutes' *The New York Times* October 15, 2001. See also Franck and Senecal's discussion concerning whether to include the why and to whom when dealing with terrorism, Thomas M. Franck and Scott C. Senecal 'Porfiry's Proposition: Legitimacy and Terrorism' 20 *Vanderbilt Journal of Transnational Law* (1987) 195-234.

[146] Which they often tend to do: 'government are unwilling to consider the causes of terrorism, because they are unwilling or unable to address such causes', M. Cherif Bassiouni (ed.) *International Terrorism: A Compilation of United Nations Documents 1972-2001* Transnational Publishers (2002) xxx.

legitimacy (which does not, however, justify the use of terrorism) the risk of terrorism does not end with the death of the individual terrorist if a substantial population base identifies with the stated objective. Hence, while al-Qaeda terrorism may end if one could imagine the elimination of all al-Qaeda 'members' this is not the case as far as the Palestinian – or Kashmiri – issues are concerned because whereas most ordinary people do not envision themselves fighting against an American presence in Saudi Arabia most Palestinians do see themselves as possible fighters against an Israeli presence in the West Bank.[147]

That different forms of terrorism are not always equal appears accepted by both politicians and academics. Thus, Attorney General Ashcroft appeared to distinguish the September 11 terrorists from more traditional terrorists, describing the September 11 ones as 'motivated not by nationalism or ideology, but by hate'.[148] Among academics, Reisman notes that while 'all terrorism is unlawful' the attacks on September 11 were 'different' from terrorism aimed at changing a particular policy, such as the terrorism in Spain or Northern Ireland. The September 11 terrorism was aimed at 'destroying the social and economic structures and values of a system of world public order, along with the international law that sustains it'.[149] Somewhat similarly, Wedgwood opines that 'there are terrorist organizations whose concerted design is to violently disrupt and destroy existing governments and commerce. Against these, one may have to entertain the paradigm of ongoing conflict. An idealist's desire to address root causes will not suffice against an organization that opposes all secular regimes in the region and objects to United States protection of essential economic and political interests'.[150]

---

[147] In the specific case of the Palestinians, a note of caution is, however, necessary: The continued use of terrorist attacks against Israeli civilians, in addition to the possible active donning of the mantle of Palestinian resistance by the al-Qaeda network as has been suspected in the November 2002 attacks against Israelis in Mombassa, Kenya, cannot but undermine the legitimacy of the Palestinian struggle and make Israeli arguments about the similarities between Palestinian terrorism and al-Qaeda terrorism all the more convincing to the serious detriment of the Palestinian cause, see James Bennet 'Al Qaeda and Palestinains: Fight Against Terror: Two Conflicts or One?' *The New York Times* November 29, 2002. See also Nathan Guttman 'State Dept. report questions PA's recognition of Israel', *Haaretz* December 12, 2002.

[148] Remarks by Attorney General John Ashcroft at the Organization of American states, January 28, 2002, available at www.usdoj.gov/ag/speeches/2002/012802agpreparedremarks.htm, visited February 4, 2002.

[149] W. Michael Reisman 'In Defense of World Public Order' 95 *American Journal of International Law* (2001) 833-835 at 833.

[150] Ruth Wedgwood 'Responding to Terrorism: The Strikes Against bin Laden' 24 *The Yale Journal of International Law* (1999) 559-576 at 575-576.

PART II

The Use of Force Against Terrorists

Chapter 5

Self-defence and Terrorism

5.I. Introduction

The aim of the present chapter is to examine the historical challenges regarding the use of force in self-defence against terrorism during the 1980s and most of the 1990s. These challenges include firstly, the traditional requirement that the state against which force is used in self-defence is responsible for the preceding terrorist act; secondly, that self-defence presupposes an armed attack; thirdly, that the issue of when a terrorist act is complete and the issues of necessity, immediacy and proportionality and of distinguishing between self-defence and reprisals which is particularly pertinent when it comes to low intensity uses of force, such as terrorist acts.

5.II. Self-defence and Terrorism

It is a fact that most states resorting to force will claim self-defence: 'It is a commonplace that all states, determined to go to war, plead self-defense'.[1] As a consequence, as noted by Gray, disputes over the resort to force most often turn on the issue of facts rather than disagreement over the legal content of Article 51 of the UN Charter. In a number of areas, however, the legal technicalities are in dispute. Among these is the use of force against terrorism.

The controversy surrounding the use of force in self-defence against terrorism is due to the fact that Article 51 has difficulties recognizing terrorist attacks as 'armed attacks' legitimizing self-defence; 'The point is that terrorism, integrating domestic and international dimentions, is fraught with problems when it comes to the Article 51 self-defense mechanism'.[2] Alexandrov has set out these difficulties:

'One is whether a terrorist act can be traced and attributed to a specific state. ... A second question is whether terrorist acts, if

---

[1] Josef L. Kunz 'Individual and Collective Self-Defense in Article 51 of the Charter of the United Nations' 41 *American Journal of International Law* (1947) 872-879 at 877. See also Higgins: 'The plea of self-defence is perhaps the most frequently heard justifications for a particular use of force', Rosalyn Higgins *The Development of International Law through the Political Organs of the United Nations* Oxford University Press (1963) 197.

[2] Tawia Ansah 'War: Rhetoric and Norm-Creation in Response to Terror' 43 *Virginia Journal of International Law* 2003 797-860 at 807.

organized or sponsored by a State, can be considered an armed attack under Article 51. ... [A further] question is whether the use of force is a defensive action in response to a specific terrorist act, or rather a punishment for it or a pre-emptive action against similar acts in the future. In most cases of terrorist acts in the territory of a third State or terrorist acts committed by armed bands from neighboring States, there is no necessity for immediate action, since any action taken would be after the fact and after the harm has been done'.[3]

The various arguments concerning self-defence and terrorism are well rehearsed in the literature and it is not considered useful to conduct an in-depth examination here. It is, however, necessary to briefly outline the main positions. In general, the interpretations of Article 51 are often divided into two rough groups: the wide interpretation and the narrow interpretation.[4] The wide approach relies on the reference in Article 51 to the 'inherent' right to retain customary international law on the use of force as it stood in 1945, whereas the narrow approach emphasizes the requirement of an 'armed attack' to substantially limit the states' right to use force in self-defence.[5]

---

[3] Stanimir A. Alexandrov *Self-Defense Against the Use of Force in International Law* Kluwer Law International 1996, 182-184. See also Baker: 'Invoking the right of self-defense in response to terrorism does not fit neatly with the requirements of article 51.' Mark B. Baker 'Terrorism and the Inherent Right of Self-Defense (A Call to Amend Article 51 of the United Nations Charter) 10 *Houston Journal of International Law* (1987) 25-49 at 47. See further Terry D. Gill 'The Eleventh of September and the Right of Self-Defense' in W. P. Heere (ed.) *Terrorism and the Military: International Legal Implications* Asser Press, 2003, 23-37 at 24 and Rein Müllerson '*Jus ad bellum* and International Terrorism' 32 *Israel Yearbook of International Law* 2003, 1-52 at 36.

[4] See for example Christine Gray *International Law and the Use of Force* Oxford University Press 2000 86. See also Roberto Ago 'State Responsibility: Addendum to the eighth report on State responsibility', Document A/CN.4/318/ADD.5-7, 64-65, paragraph 110-112. For a review of the 'expansive view' and the 'restrictive view' see Norman Menachem Feder 'Reading the U.N. Charter Connotatively: Toward a New Definition of Armed Attack' 19 *New York University Journal of International Law and Politics* (1987) 395-432 at 401-412. Other designations are also used, for example 'community interest proponents' and 'statists' (James Larry Taulbee and John Anderson 'Reprisal *Redux*' 16 *Case Western Reserve Journal of International Law* (1984) 309-336 at 310). The reduction of the various interpretations into two groups is somewhat arbitrary. Arend and Beck, for example, apply three groups when analyzing the use of force, the 'legalist', the 'core interpretist' and the 'rejectionist', see Anthony Clark Arend and Robert J. Beck *International Law and the Use of Force* Routhledge (1993) 180-185. In theory, however, innumerable distinctions exist between the various interpretations and, hence, numerous groups could be outlined.

[5] Christine Gray *International Law and the Use of Force* Oxford University Press 2000 86-87.

5.II.A. The Requirement of State Involvement

Many of the authors writing and discussing self-defence against specific terrorist acts neglect to address the issue of state involvement. Such involvement has, however, traditionally been perceived as a necessary ingredient in order to establish an armed attack:[6] 'the State Responsibility of that State [the one attacked in self-defence] must have been engaged in respect of the attack'.[7]

At the most authoritative level, the ICJ in 1986 found that self-defence can only be legitimate in response to an armed attack and set out which acts could be treated as constituting an armed attack.[8] These include 'not merely action by regular armed forces across an international border, but also "the sending by or on behalf of a State of armed bands, groups, irregulars or mercenaries, which carry out acts of armed force against another State of such a gravity as to amount to" (*inter alia*) an actual armed attack conducted by regular forces, "or its substantial involvement therein"'.[9] In other words, an armed attack may take place even if the attack is not conducted by a State's regular armed forces. In this case, however, the State must be sending the irregular force or have a 'substantial involvement' in its deployment. The Court did not discuss what 'substantial involvement' might include, but it is possible to determine that, according to the Court, 'assistance to rebels in the form of the provision of weapons or logistical or other support' does not amount to 'substantial involvement' and, hence, an armed

---

[6] See for example Gray who notes that the initial controversy centers on 'the degree of state involvement that is necessary to make the actions attributable to the state' thereby justifying action in self-defense. Christine Gray *International Law and the Use of Force* Oxford University Press 2000 97. See also Rowles: 'Military responses to terrorist acts are permissible only when the acts in question are on a scale equivalent to what would be an armed attack if conducted by government forces and then only if direction and control, or very substantial complicity, on the part of the territorial state can be shown or if it refuses to act to bring such activities to a halt', James P. Rowles 'Military Responses to Terrorism: Substantive and Procedural Constraints in International Law' 81 *American Society of International Law Proceedings* (1987) 287-320 at 314.

[7] Antonio Cassese 'The International Community's "Legal" Response to Terrorism' 38 *International and Comparative Law Quarterly* (1989) 589-608 at 597.

[8] 'In case of individual self-defence, the exercise of this right is subject to the State concerned having been the victim of an armed attack. Reliance on collective self-defence of course does not remove the need for this', 1986 ICJ 103, paragraph 195. See also, for example, Ago who found that 'it is not possible to read into the text of Article 51, either explicitly or implicitly, any kind of extension of this right [of self-defense] to other cases in which the State is affected by an infringement of a right which, however important, is not held to be one of those infringed by an armed attack', Roberto Ago 'State Responsibility: Addendum to the eighth report on State responsibility', Document A/CN.4/318/ADD.5-7, 67, paragraph 114.

[9] 1986 ICJ 103, paragraph 195. The Court was quoting Article 3(g) of the Definition of Aggression, adopted by the General Assembly in 1974, Resolution 3314 (XXIX). The Court, however, did not believe assistance to rebels in the form of the provision of weapons or logistical or other support could amount to an armed attack, 1986 ICJ 104, paragraph 195.

attack.[10] The reflections of the Court appear to leave only very substantial involvement, such as the sending or organizing of irregular troops and planning by the state of irregular operations as sufficient to reach the level of an armed attack.

Among other scholars, Ronzitti and Schachter have maintained the requirement of state involvement.[11] Similarly, regarding the September 11 attacks, Myjer and White pointed out that the attacks were 'committed by individuals, not acting, directly at least, on behalf of a state. Self-defence, traditionally speaking, applies to an armed response to an attack by a state'.[12]

Some, however, argue that it is not a condition that the state subjected to the use of force in self-defence was responsible for the armed attack justifying the self-defence. Dinstein developed quite an expansive notion of self-defence, originally consisting of four categories. The third dealt with the cases where 'the employment of force within the territory of another state directed against individuals in retribution for acts committed by them – on their own responsibility – without the complicity of the government concerned:[13] 'The terrorist raids continue to be armed attacks – even if conducted from, and not by, another State [and] self-defence is permitted inside the territory of another State …against the guilty terrorists rather than the ineffective local

---

[10] 1986 ICJ 104, paragraph 195. All in all, the Court presented quite a restrictive reading of the conditions necessary in order to claim self-defense. The stringency of the Court's approach has been widely criticized. Dissenting Judge Jennings, for example, found it 'neither realistic nor just in a world where power struggles are in every continent carried on by destabilization, interference in civil strife, comfort, aid and encouragement to rebels, and the like'. He further found that 'it seems dangerous to define unnecessarily strictly the conditions for lawful self-defence', 1986 ICJ 543-544.

[11] 'In order to be able to react in self-defense, the attack must originate from a subject of international law or be ascribed to it by virtue of the norms regulating State international responsibility'. Natalino Ronzitti *Rescuing Nationals Abroad Through military Coercion and Intervention on Grounds of Humanity* Martinus Nijhoff 1985, 12. Later he emphasizes that the exercise of self-defense 'presupposes both the existence of an armed attack launched by a State, as well as its occurrence'. Ibid. 69. The requirement of state involvement is so important to Schachter that he in turn considers the necessity excuse for use of force against terrorists in large part because of incidents where no state has been involved, Oscar Schachter *International Law in Theory and Practice* Kluwer Law International 1991 162-175.

[12] Eric P.J. Myjer and Nigel D. White 'The Twin Towers Attack: An Unlimited Right to Self-Defence?' 7 *Journal of Conflict and Security Law* (2002) 5 at 7. See similarly Ulfstein: 'International law requires that a state must have been involved in one way or another in an attack. It is not easily accepted that the Security Council would do away with such a requirement' Geir Ulfstein 'SC Resolution 1368 and self-defence' available at www.ejil.org/forum_WTC/messages/5.html, visited October 13, 2002. See also Michael Byers 'Terrorism, the Use of Force and International Law after 11 September' 51 *International and Comparative Law Quarterly* (2002) 401-414 at 408.

[13] Yoram Dinstein 'A Survey of Self-Defense in International Law' in M. Cherif Bassiouni (ed.) *A Treaties on International Criminal Law, Volume I, Crimes and Punishment* Charles S. Thomas (1973) 273-286 at 279.

government'.[14] Although he acknowledges that this scenario occasionally is called 'necessity', he preferred the designation 'execution'.[15] Dinstein found and still finds that 'the distinction between self-defence and necessity ... is artificial. ... the use of cross-border counter-force against armed bands is historically tied to the subject of self-defence, and there is no reason to cut that umbilical cord'.[16] He has, however, changed the title of the sub-category of self-defence, which encompasses this situation to 'extra-territorial law enforcement'.[17] As we shall see in the final chapter, Dinstein's approach has recently found favour with individual judges at the International Court of Justice. Along similar lines, Murphy argues that 'there is nothing in Article 51 ... that requires the exercise of self-defense to turn on whether an armed attack was committed directly by another state'.[18]

At least by the end of the 18th century, the duty of a state to prevent the use of its territory for attack on its neighbours was well recognized.[19] It must be pointed out that a state may well be in breach of one or more of its international obligations even when it is not responsible for the armed attack as such. In 1928, Lauterpacht wrote that: 'international law imposes upon the state the duty of restraining persons resident within

---

[14] Yoram Dinstein 'Terrorism and Wars of Liberation Applied to the Arab-Israeli Conflict: An Israeli Perspective' 3 *Israel Yearbook of Human Rights* (1973) 78 at 90. Dinstein further argues that 'A government that is unable to repel terrorists must not try to display unwonted powess when the victim implements the law', Ibid. 91.

[15] Ibid.

[16] Yoram Dinstein *War, Aggression and Self-defence* Cambridge University Press 3rd ed. (2001) 217. Schachter answers – responding to an earlier edition of Dinstein's book containing the same argument that the umbilical cord 'has already been cut by two international legal bodies – the International Court and the International Law Commission', Oscar Schachter *International Law in Theory and Practice* Kluwer Law International (1995) 172.

[17] Yoram Dinstein *War, Aggression and Self-defence* Cambridge University Press 3rd ed. (2001) 213-221. See also Yoram Dinstein 'Ius ad bellum Aspects of the 'War on Terrorism'' in W.P. Heere (ed.) *Terrorism and the Military: International Legal Implications* Asser Press, 2003, 13-22.

[18] Sean Murphy 'Terrorism and the Concept of "Armed Attack" in Article 51 of the U.N. Charter' 43 *Harvard International Law Review* (2002) 41-51 at 50. Gaja, however, asserts that such a 'condition may be taken as implicit', Giorgio Gaja 'In What Sense was there an "Armed Attack"?' available at www.ejil.org/forum_WTC/ny-gaja.html, visited January 12, 2002. See also the 'Position Paper of Australian Section of the International Commission of Jurists on the Appropriate Response of the UN to the Attacks on the USA' available at www.ejil.org/forum_WTC/messages/17.html, visited October 13, 2002: 'It is clear that where another state ... provides bases or refuge for the attackers, the state under attack, or threat of attack, may use armed force against that other State in exercise of the right of self defence'. See further Michael N. Schmitt 'Counter-Terrorism and the Use of Force in International Law' in 32 *Israel Yearbook on Human Rights* 2003, 53-116 at 77, Rein Müllerson '*Jus ad bellum* and International Terrorism' 32 *Israel Yearbook of International Law* 2003, 1-52 at 37 and Rüdiger Wolfrum 'The Attack of September 11, 2001, the Wars Against the Taliban and Iraq: Is There a Need to Reconsider International Law on the Recourse to Force and the Rules in Armed Conflict?' in 7 *Max Planck Yearbook of United Nations Law* 2003, 1-78 at 35.

[19] Roy Emerson Curtis 'The Law of Hostile Military Expeditions as Applied by the United States' 8 *American Journal of International Law* (1914) 1-37 at 1 and 6.

its territory from engaging in such revolutionary activities against friendly states that amount to organized acts of force in the form of hostile expeditions against the territory of those states'.[20] In the context of the assassination of King Alexander of Yugoslavia on October 9 1934, the Council of the League of Nations unanimously adopted a resolution, recalling 'that it is the duty of every State neither to encourage nor tolerate on its territory any terrorist activities with a political purpose; and that every State must do all in its power to prevent and repress acts of this nature and must for this purpose lend its assistance to governments which request it'.[21] In the Corfu Channel case, the Court set out a number of obligations incumbent on Albania, including 'every State's obligation not to allow knowingly its territory to be used for acts contrary to the rights of other States'.[22] Subsequently, various bodies of the United Nations have reiterated this obligation.[23] Most prominent is perhaps the Declaration on Friendly Relations from 1970 which stipulates that 'every State has the duty to refrain from organizing or encouraging the organization of irregular forces or armed bands, including mercenaries, for incursions into the territory of another State'.[24] More recently, following the bombing of the two American embassies in Kenya and Tanzania in August 1998, the Security Council stressed 'that very Member State has the duty to refrain from organizing, instigating, assisting or participating in terrorists in another State or acquiescing in organized activities within its territory directed towards the commission of such acts'.[25]

It is, thus, not correct when Sofaer laments that under the *Nicaragua* judgment from the ICJ, a state 'can do virtually anything short of ordering a terrorist act or

---

[20] H. Lauterpacht 'Revolutionary Activities by Private Persons Against Foreign States' 22 *American Journal of International Law* (1928) 105-130 at 128.

[21] Quoted in Arthur K. Kuhn 'The Complaint of Yugoslavia against Hungary with Reference to the Assassination of King Alexander' 29 *American Journal of International Law* (1935) 87-92, at 91. In addition, a committee of experts was set up to study the question with a view to drawing up a convention to repress terrorism.

[22] 1949 ICJ 4 at 22.

[23] In the 1954 Draft Code of Offences against the Peace and Security of Mankind, 'the organization, or the encouragement of the organization, by the authorities of a State, of armed bands within its territory or any other territory for incursions into the territory of another State, or the toleration of the organization of such bands in its own territory, or the toleration of the use by such armed bands of its territory as a base of operations or as a point of departure for incursions into the territory of another State, as well as direct participation in or support of such incursions' constituted an offence against the peace and security of mankind, see Draft Code, Article 2, paragraph 4, available at www.un.org/law/ilc/texts/offebces.htm, visited October 31, 2002.

[24] Declaration on Principles of International Law concerning Friendly Relations and Co-operation among States in accordance with the Charter of the United Nations, General Assembly Resolution 2625 (XXV), October 24, 1970. A similar provision is contained in the Declaration on the Enhancement of the Effectiveness of the Principles of Refraining from the Threat or Use of Force in International relations, General Assembly Resolution 42/22, November 18, 1987, Part I, paragraph 6.

[25] Security Council Resolution 1189, S/RES/1189 (1998), August 13, 1998.

participating in its execution and still avoid being treated as responsible'.[26] As Cassese succinctly points out, if the state failed its obligation in this regard, 'the attack will not become the State's act, so there can be no question of a forcible response to it. But, as there has nevertheless been an internationally wrongful act, there are still grounds for the application of peaceful sanctions'.[27]

5.II.B. The Caroline *and the Requirement of State Involvement*

The *Caroline* case has, as noted by Gray, taken on a mythical authority,[28] and is referred to at varying length in the vast majority of articles dealing with aspects of self-defence.[29] It is appropriate at this point to attach some comments to this case because some of the arguments fielded to justify the use of force against terrorism in self-defence are drawn from this case, including the fact that it stands for 'the proposition that self-defense is permissible as a reaction to attacks by non-governmental entities'.[30]

Firstly, even authors who invoke the *Caroline* case in support of their argument allow themselves to tinker with the proscriptions of the case. O'Brien, for example, determines that 'given the duration and magnitude of Israel's was with the PLO ... the "necessity" is very different from that of a single unique incident along the U.S.-Canadian border in 1837'.[31]

---

[26] Abraham D. Sofaer 'Terrorism, the Law and the National Defense' 126 *Military Law Review* (1989) 89-123 at 100.

[27] Antonio Cassese 'The International Community's "Legal" Response to Terrorism' 38 *International and Comparative Law Quarterly* (1989) 589-608 at 597. See similarly Randelzhofer 'Article 51' in Bruno Simma (ed.) *The Charter of the United Nations: A Commentary* Oxford University Press, 2nd ed. (2002) 790, para. 4.

[28] Christine Gray *International Law and the Use of Force* Oxford University Press 2000 105.

[29] About the case, see in general R. Y. Jennings 'The Caroline and McLeod Cases' 32 *American Journal of International Law* (1938) 82- 99 and Martin A. Rogoff and Edward Collins, Jr. 'The Caroline Incident and the Development of International Law' 16 *Brooklyn Journal of International Law* (1990) 493-527. See also Occelli arguing that 'the Caroline doctrine was no more than an exchange of polite diplomatic letters in order for both Britain and the United States to keep honor, while at the same time smoothing tensions between the two states. ... The Caroline doctrine should not be quoted as the standard for the limitations on self-defense but instead be remembered as a part of history', Maria Benvenuta Occelli '"Sinking" the Caroline' 4 *San Diego International Law Journal* (2003) 467-490 at 490.

[30] Sean D. Murphy 'Terrorism and the Concept of "Armed Attack" in Article 51 of the U.N. Charter' 43 *Harvard International Law Journal* (2002) 41 at 50.

[31] William V. O'Brien *Law and Morality in Israel's War with the PLO* Routledge 1991, 120. One might actually take issue with O'Brien's description of the *Caroline* case involving only 'a single unique incident'. The circumstances took place over at least two weeks and were arguably part of a more extended conflict between anti-unionists and the British authorities. Somewhat similarly, Beard has an explanation as to why the *Caroline dictum* does not fit the situation after September 11, Jack M. Beard 'America's New War on Terror: The Case for Self-Defense under International Law' 25 *Harvard Journal of Law and Public Policy* (2002) 550-590 at 585-486.

Secondly, one should be careful not to use the Caroline precedent in an anachronistic manner. As noted by Brownlie, 'the statesman of the period used self-preservation, self-defence, necessity, and necessity of self-defence as more or less interchangeable terms and the diplomatic correspondence was not intended to restrict the right of self-preservation which was in fact reaffirmed'.[32] To answer this, it is at times pointed out that the International Military Tribunal in Nuremberg quoted from the case: 'The defense that has been made here is that Germany was compelled to attack Norway to forestall an Allied invasion and her action was therefore preventive. It must be remembered that preventive action in foreign territory is justified in case of "an instant and overwhelming necessity for self-defense, leaving no choice of means, and no moment of deliberation" (The Caroline Case, Moore's *Digest of International Law*, II, 412)'.[33]

What is generally known as the *Caroline* case actually involved two separate, albeit connected, cases and should rightly, as the title of Jennings vintage article suggests, be referred to as the *Caroline* and *McLeod* cases.[34] The significance of this observation for the present purposes is the somewhat paradoxical way in which the correspondence concerning the British attack on the *Caroline* is regarded as of immutable relevance for self-defence today, whereas all would presumably agree that the – agreed – deliberation about McLeod's situation is no longer good law. As is well known, Mr. McLeod had apparently bragged about having been party to the destruction of the *Caroline* and had been arrested for the offence in New York State. The British government complained that he could not be held responsible for a transaction of public character, planned and executed by persons duly empowered by a government. As Mr. Fox explained: 'It would be contrary to the universal practice of civilized nations to fix individual responsibility upon persons who with the sanction or by the orders of the constituted authorities of a State engage in military or naval enterprizes in their

---

[32] Ian Brownlie *International Law and the Use of Force by States* Oxford University Press (1963) 43. Brownlie further asserts that references to self-preservation usually appears as 'the window dressing of *raison d'état*'. Ibid. 42. See also Yoram Dinstein *War, Aggression and Self-defence* Cambridge University Press 3rd ed. (2001) 160. Also Ian Brownlie 'The United Nations Charter and the Use of Force, 1945-1985' in Antonio Cassese (ed.) *The Current Legal Regulation of the Use of Force* Martinus Nijhoff (1986) 491 at 493.

[33] See, The Invasion of Denmark and Norway, 'Judicial Decisions, the International Military tribunal (Nuremberg), Judgment and Sentences, October 1, 1946' 41 *American Journal of International Law* (1947) 172, 203-207 at 205. The Tribunal went on to find that the German plans were made not for the purpose of forestalling an imminent Allied invasion but, at the most, might 'prevent an Allied occupation at some future date' and that Norway was occupied in order to gain bases and not in self-defense: 'In light of all available evidence it is impossible to accept the contention that the invasions of Denmark and Norway were defensive, and in the opinion of the Tribunal they were acts of aggressive war', Ibid. 207.

[34] R.Y. Jennings 'the *Caroline* and McLeod cases' 32 *American Journal of International Law* (1938) 82-99.

country's cause'.[35] The United States' representative was in full agreement: 'The Government of the United States entertains no doubt that … as a public transaction, authorized and undertaken by the British authorities, individuals concerned in it ought not, by the principles of public law, and the general usage of civilized State, to be holden personally responsible in the ordinary tribunals of law, for their participation in it'.[36]

It is now, however, axiomatic that 'a new category of international responsibility has developed according to which individuals can be held criminally responsible under international law'.[37] Indeed, the Nuremberg trials, which are referred to as recognizing the *Caroline dictum* as relevant, were based on the very idea of individual responsibility under international law: 'Crimes against international law are committed by men, not by abstract entities, and only by punishing individuals who commit such crimes can the provisions of international law be enforced'.[38]

The preceding remarks are merely made in order to point out that, although often re-iterated, the *Caroline* case is not necessarily still good law. As a matter of fact, such an assertion would have a presumption against it. Still, this does not automatically mean that a phrase from the U.S.-British correspondence cannot capture something essential, as recognized in Nuremberg, such as the famous words of Webster about the need for the British to 'show a necessity of self-defence, instant, overwhelming, leaving no choice of means, and no moment for deliberation'.[39] What it does mean is that one ought to be careful if and when attempting to apply the facts and law from more that a century and a half ago to occurrences today. Sofaer appears to hold that the requirement that an attack is imminent in the 21st century is feasible only where the state from which the terrorists originate is able and willing to (attempt) prevents these. If this is not the case, Sofaer argues for a broader right of pre-emption.[40]

As noted by Ago, it is often adherents of a wide interpretation of Article 51 who refers back to the *Caroline* case.[41] As an aside to these considerations concerning the

---

[35] *The Caroline Case*, reproduced in Eric Heinze and Malgosia Fitzmaurice (eds.) *Landmark Cases in Public International Law* (2000) Kluwer Law International 1245-1265 at 1246.

[36] *The Caroline Case*, reproduced in Eric Heinze and Malgosia Fitzmaurice (eds.) *Landmark Cases in Public International Law* (2000) Kluwer Law International 1245-1265 at 1249.

[37] Hazel Fox 'The International Court of Justice's Treatment of Acts of the State and in Particular the Attribution of Acts of Individuals to the State' in N. Ando *et al.* (eds.) *Liber Amicorum Shigeru Oda* Kluwer Law International (2002) 147-163 at 156.

[38] 'Judicial Decisions, the International Military tribunal (Nuremberg), Judgment and Sentences, October 1, 1946' 41 *American Journal of International Law* (1947) 172 at 221.

[39] *The Caroline Case*, reproduced in Eric Heinze and Malgosia Fitzmaurice (eds.) *Landmark Cases in Public International Law* (2000) Kluwer Law International 1245-1265 at 1254.

[40] Abraham D. Sofaer 'On the Necessity of Pre-emption' 14 *European Journal of International Law* 2003 209-226.

[41] Ago remarks how those who 'remain wedded' to the wide understanding of self-defense draw on a 'relatively antiquated portion of State practice', including the *Caroline* case, Roberto Ago 'State

applicability of the *Caroline* case today, one might note the potential inconsistency presented by those who argue that Article 51 refer back to the entire gamut of customary international law vintage 1945, including the *Caroline* case. One issue is whether customary international law in 1945 was as permissive about the use of force as presumed by some or, rather, much more akin to the subsequent UN Charter as argued by, for example, Brownlie.[42] A second issue is that the proponents of this line of reasoning often belong to the group of scholars who criticize, on both legal and policy grounds the 'restrictive' interpretationists as being too static when it comes to legal interpretation, while at the same time maintaining their own interpretation of Article 51 which clings to an immutable customary international law, frozen in time in the autumn of 1945.

5.II.C. Is a Terrorist Attack an Armed Attack?

As pointed out by Alexandrov one might question whether a terrorist act amounts to an armed attack even if a state is involved. Indeed, the ICJ referred to support of terrorism in a neighboring state, albeit in a somewhat different context, as intervention involving the use of force or as a threat or use of force, not as an armed attack.[43] The issue at hand concerns the fact that run of the mill terrorist attacks, however reprehensible, often involve a limited number of casualties and rarely constitute the threat to a state that some envision necessary to legitimize self-defence.[44] In other words, they may not amount to 'the most grave forms of the use of force (those constituting an armed attack)'.[45] With regard to the quantitative requirements for an incident to become an armed attack, the ICJ has in broad terms outlined that an armed attack could be differentiated from a frontier incident by its 'scale and effects'.[46]

Critics of the Courts *dictum* have taken different avenues in their critique: some, while accepting that an armed attack is a special, severe category, argue, as does Schwebel, that 'I do not agree with a construction of the United Nations Charter which

---

Responsibility: Addendum to the eighth report on State responsibility', Document A/CN.4/318/ADD.5-7, 65, paragraph 113.

[42] Ian Brownlie *International Law and the Use of Force by States* Oxford University Press (1963) 195-196. See also Roberto Ago 'State Responsibility: Addendum to the eighth report on State responsibility', Document A/CN.4/318/ADD.5-7, 63, paragraph 108 and 67, paragraph 114.

[43] 1986 ICJ 108, paragraph 205.

[44] See, for example, Erickson who declares that 'the general rule of international is that sporadic or isolated incidents by armed groups (even with state support) do not constitute armed attacks'. Richard J. Erickson *Legitimate Use of Military Force Against State-Sponsored International Terrorism* Air University Press (1989) 143.

[45] 1986 ICJ, p. 101. para. 191.

[46] 1986 ICJ 103, paragraph 194.

would read Article 51 as if it were worded: ... if, and only if, an armed attack occurs'. [47] A different group of critics strongly disagree with the Court or interprets it's *dictum* in a manner which would all but eliminate any distinction or graduation. Dinstein, for example, maintains that, save incidents falling below a *de minimis* threshold,[48] 'small-scale armed attacks are still armed attacks'.[49] Hence, Dinstein concludes that only very few uses of force banned by Article 2, paragraph 4 would fall below a minimal threshold (outlined as use of force not 'causing human casualties and/or serious destruction of property') and not entitle the use of force in self-defence.[50]

In the context of minor cross-border attacks, others have argued that by accumulating the series of minor attacks the net effect is an attack of sufficient scale to be designated an armed attack. This argument was first advanced decades ago[51] and is of particular interest when examining responses to terrorist incidents:[52] Terrorists generally do not engage in pitched battles with government forces. As pointed out by Blum, 'more often than not, it is the avowed and declared objective of terrorist organizations engaging in needle prick tactics to achieve in this manner the results which they are incapable of achieving in one concentrated and direct blow against their

---

[47] Judge Schwebel, in his dissenting opinion in the Nicaragua case (1986 ICJ 347, paragraph 173.), endorsed Waldock's view that 'it would be a misreading of the whole intention of Article 51 to interpret it by mere implication as forbidding forcible self-defence in resistance to an illegal use of force not constituting an "armed attack"', C. H. M. Waldock 'The Regulation of the Use of Force by Individual States in International Law' 81 RC (1952) 542-517 at 497.

[48] Yoram Dinstein *War, Aggression and Self-defence* Cambridge University Press 3rd ed. (2001) 175-176.

[49] Yoram Dinstein 'Terrorism and Wars of Liberation Applied to the Arab-Israeli Conflict: An Israeli Perspective' 3 *Israel Yearbook of Human Rights* (1973) 90 and Yoram Dinstein *War, Aggression and Self-defence* Cambridge University Press 3rd ed. (2001) 176.

[50] He finds the gap between Article 2, paragraph 4 and Article 51 to be 'quite narrow', Yoram Dinstein *War, Aggression and Self-defence* Cambridge University Press 3rd ed. (2001) 174.

[51] Brownlie found that 'it is conceivable that a co-ordinated and general campaign by powerful bands of irregulars, with obvious or easily proven complicity of the government of the State from which they operate, would constitute an "armed attack"', Ian Brownlie 'International Law and the Activities of Armed Bands' 7 *International and Comparative Law Quarterly* (1958) 717-735 at 731 and Ian Brownlie *International Law and the Use of Force by States* Oxford University Press (1963) 279. Similarly, Higgins believed that if a state is subjected, over a period of time, to border raids by nationals of another state, which are openly supported by the government of that state, the former state may use force in self-defense in anticipation of the continuation of such action, Rosalyn Higgins *The Development of International Law through the Political Organs of the United Nations* Oxford University Press (1963) 201.

[52] As observed by Dinstein, 'it is ... conceivable that while each of the acts of terrorism, when viewed separately, probably does not qualify as an "armed attack", the totality of such acts does reveal such a pattern', Yoram Dinstein 'The Right of Self-defence Against Armed Attacks' in Magnus D. Sandbu and Peter Nordbeck (eds.) *International Terrorism: Report from a Seminar Arranged by the European Law Students' Association in Lund, Sweden, 1-3 October 1987* Juristförlaget I Lund (1987) 57-71 at 62.

intended victim'.[53] In the Nicaragua case, the ICJ appears to have recognized that, under unspecified conditions, 'incursions', i.e. minor uses of force, may, 'singly or collectively', amount to an armed attack.[54]

5.III. Necessity and Proportionality in the Context of Terrorist Attacks

It is well recognized that any legal use of force must be necessary and proportional. In the above-mentioned *Caroline case* the well-known *dictum* spoke of 'a necessity of self-defence, instant, overwhelming, leaving no choice of means and no moment for deliberation … [without doing anything] unreasonable or excessive'. In 1986, the ICJ reiterated that self-defense warrants 'only measures which are proportional to the armed attack and necessary to respond to it, a rule well established in customary international law'.[55] However, as pointed out by Alexandrov, the requirements of necessity and proportionality are problematic when it comes to the application of counter-terrorism force.

5.III.A. Necessity and Immediacy

As is generally recognized, the use of force in self-defence must be necessary. This primarily requires the exhaustion of peaceful means. In addition, it would rule out any use of force coming after the terrorist attack had terminated.[56] This latter part speaks to the issue of immediacy or 'instancy', which according to Gardam is the only part of the *Carolina* 'necessity' formulation that needs to be satisfied within the meaning of Article 51:[57] 'What is contemplated by the [UN] Charter is that States have the right to respond to an armed attack only for the period that it takes for the Security Council to be notified and for the necessary action to be taken to restore international peace and

---

[53] Yehuda Z. Blum 'State Response to Acts of Terrorism' 19 *German Yearbook of International Law* (1976) 223-237 at 233.

[54] 1986 ICJ 120, paragraph 231. See also Christine Gray *International Law and the Use of Force* Oxford University Press 2000 108 and 123.

[55] 1986 ICJ 94, para. 176.

[56] Ago expresses this requirement as one of self-defense having to take place immediately, Roberto Ago 'State Responsibility: Addendum to the eighth report on State responsibility', Document A/CN.4/318/ADD.5-7, 70, paragraph 122. See also Greenwood: 'The use of force in response to an attack which has already terminated cannot be intended as protection against that attack'. Christopher Greenwood 'International Law and the United States' Air Operation Against Libya' 89 *West Virginia Law Review* (1987) 933-960 at 942. In the Nicaragua case, the ICJ found that United States' measures could not be seen as necessary because 'these measures were only taken … several months after the major offensive … had been completely repulsed' 1986 ICJ 122, paragraph 237.

[57] Judith Gardam *Necessity, Proportionality, and the Use of Force by States* Cambridge University Press (2004) 149.

security'.[58] This would indicate that the right of self-defense ceases when the attack has come to an end. Hence, in normal circumstances of a guerilla or terrorist attack, as observed by Bowett, 'this military action [in self-defence] cannot strictly be regarded as self-defense in the context of previous guerilla activities: they are past, whatever damage has occurred as a result cannot now be prevented and no new military action ... can really be regarded as a defense against attacks in the past'.[59] Yet, as noted by Blum, 'under the needle-prick approach [i.e. 'accumulation of events theory'], such military action may be considered a legitimate response in anticipation of the next terrorist attack'.[60] Ago writes that in the case of 'successive acts, the requirement of the immediacy of the self-defensive action would have to be looked at in the light of those acts as a whole'.[61]

Yet, this way of identifying the issue brings forth an auxiliary controversial aspect: anticipatory self-defence. International law scholars are divided on the issue: Brownlie,[62] Gray[63] and Gardam[64] oppose a right of anticipatory self-defence under Article 51, whereas, for example, Higgins[65] and Schwebel[66] believe such a right to exist.[67] The International Court of Justice explicitly declined to address the question in

---

[58] Judith Gardam *Necessity, Proportionality, and the Use of Force by States* Cambridge University Press (2004) 149.

[59] Derek Bowett 'Reprisals Involving Recourse to Armed Force' 66 *American Journal of International Law* (1972) 3-4.

[60] Yehuda Z. Blum 'The Legality of State Response to Acts of Terrorism' in B. Netanyahu (ed.) *Terrorism: How the West Can Win* Farrar, Straus, Giroux (1986) 133-138 at 136. Similarly, Feder argue that 'a response to a "needle prick," which presumably presages further minor attacks, can be said to exhibit the very traits that identify self-defense – prevention and protection', Norman Menachem Feder 'Reading the U.N. Charter Connotatively: Toward a New Definition of Armed Attack' 19 *New York University Journal of International Law and Politics* (1987) 395-432 at 416.

[61] Ago expresses this requirement as one of self-defense having to take place immediately, Roberto Ago 'State Responsibility: Addendum to the eighth report on State responsibility', Document A/CN.4/318/ADD.5-7, 70, paragraph 122.

[62] Ian Brownlie *International Law and the Use of Force by States* Oxford University Press (1963) 275.

[63] 'This reluctance [in state practice] expressly to invoke anticipatory self-defence is in itself a clear indication of the doubtful status of this justification for the use of force' Christine Gray *International Law and the Use of Force* 2nd ed. Oxford University Press 2004, 130.

[64] Judith Gardam *Necessity, Proportionality, and the Use of Force by States* Cambridge University Press (2004) 146-147.

[65] Higgins argues that even in the case of conventional warfare, a right to anticipatory self-defense seems to be the 'only realistic interpretation', Rosalyn Higgins *Problems and Process: International Law and How We Use it* Oxford University Press (1994) 242.

[66] S.M. Schwebel 'Aggression, Intervention and Self-Defence in Modern International Law'136 *Recueil des Cours* (1972) II, 479-483.

[67] Individual writers may fall between the two well-defined positions. Dinstein, for example, rejects an alleged right to anticipatory self-defense but does allow for the use of force in self-defense before the first shot has been fired: The decisive criteria is that the attacker has embarked upon an irreversible course of action leading to the attack, Yoram Dinstein *War, Aggression and Self-defence* Cambridge University Press 3rd ed. (2001) 171-172. Dinstein terms this form of self-defense 'interceptive' self-

the Nicaragua case: 'the issue of the lawfulness of a response to the imminent threat of armed attack has not been raised. Accordingly the Court expresses no view on that issue'.[68] As noted by Gardam, state practice has not generally supported a strict or narrow view of immediacy and recent developments have accentuated this, as we shall see below.[69]

5.III.B Proportionality, Self-defence and Reprisals

Even if there has been 'consistent agreement' on the need for any forceful action to be proportionate, serious differences persist as to the exact parameters of proportionality: the assessment of proportionality is far from easy and will always depend on the specific facts.[70] Gardam has, however, outlined the following factors that are relevant to assessing proportionality:

- Geographical and destructive scope of the response,
- The duration of the response,
- The means and methods and targets selected, and
- The effect on third States.[71]

The crucial task remains the identification of the range of objectives that may legally be pursued in self-defence: 'Proportionality in coercion constitutes a requirement that responding coercion is limited in intensity and magnitude to what is reasonably necessary to promptly secure the permissible objectives of self-defense'.[72] Even if the objectives are limited to what is characterized as purely defensive, disagreement exists.[73]

---

defense and associates himself with Waldock's deliberations that would require that the attack 'being actually mounted', C. H. M. Waldock 'The Regulation of the Use of Force by Individual States in International Law' 81 RC (1952) 542-517 at 498.

[68] 1986 ICJ 103, paragraph 194

[69] Judith Gardam *Necessity, Proportionality, and the Use of Force by States* Cambridge University Press (2004) 150.

[70] Judith Gardam *Necessity, Proportionality, and the Use of Force by States* Cambridge University Press (2004) 11 and 21-22.

[71] Judith Gardam *Necessity, Proportionality, and the Use of Force by States* Cambridge University Press (2004) 162.

[72] Myers S. McDougal and Florentino P. Feliciano *Law and Minimum World Public Order: The Legal Regulation of International Coercion* Yale University Press (1961) 242, quoted in Judith Gardam *Necessity, Proportionality, and the Use of Force by States* Cambridge University Press (2004) 156.

[73] Gardam has documented how three scholars have suggested different measurements: Proportional to the danger (Bowett), to the injury being inflicted (Higgins), and to what is required for achieving the object (Waldock), see Judith Gardam *Necessity, Proportionality, and the Use of Force by States* Cambridge University Press (2004) 12.

Must the force used in self-defence be proportionate to the force use by the attacker? The ICJ appeared to imply as much when it held that United States activities against Nicaragua, in part the mining of Nicaraguan harbors, 'could not have been proportionate to that aid', i.e. the aid which Nicaragua supplied to the Salvadorian armed opposition.[74] This finding implies that force used to counter an armed attack must be proportionate to the force of the attack. This conclusion, however, appears counter-intuitive. Say that A has invaded B and occupied the province X. If B were only allowed to use an amount of force similar to that employed by A, stalemate would ensue. Rather, it would seem that legitimate force in this case would include the force required to repel the invader. By necessity this would require a degree of force, which is greater than that initially applied by A. Hence, Ago emphasizes that the defensive act may be disproportionate to the attack suffered.[75] Gardam supports this observation by emphasizing that the action needed to halt or repulse an attack may well assume dimensions that are disproportionate to the original attack's scale.[76]

The problems, however, mount when the focus becomes low-intensity warfare, a category, which is usually considered to include terrorism. Here, we again return to the 'accumulation of events' theory. The application of proportionality as a legal standard in these cases – which technically often are use of force in anticipation – is difficult because it has to be measured against a threat as opposed to a specific attack, even if the past experience may provide leads.[77] In such situations, Ago finds that the victim state may undertake one single armed action on a much larger scale in order to put an end to the escalating succession of attacks.[78] This would seem to be at odds with the practice of the Security Council, as noted by Higgins: 'once one retreats into history, self-defence begins to partake of the flavour of retaliation; so that in assessing proportionality, only the immediate illegality against which forceful self-defence is taken is relevant'.[79]

As is implicit in the outline provided by Alexandrov, an armed response to terrorism often takes on an air of punishment or reprisal either because it, as just discussed, takes place some significant time after the terrorist incident – and, hence, is

---

[74] 1986 ICJ 122, paragraph 237.

[75] State Responsibility for Internationally Wrongful Acts (Part 1), Document A/CN.4/318/ADD.8, reproduced in 2 Yearbook of the International Law Commission 1980, 13-70 at 69-70, paragraph 121.

[76] Judith Gardam *Necessity, Proportionality, and the Use of Force by States* Cambridge University Press (2004) 160-161. See similarly Christine Gray *International Law and the Use of Force* 2nd ed. Oxford University Press, 2004, 121.

[77] Judith Gardam *Necessity, Proportionality, and the Use of Force by States* Cambridge University Press (2004) 183. See also page 179.

[78] Ibid.

[79] Rosalyn Higgins *The Development of International Law through the Political Organs of the United Nations* Oxford University Press (1963) 205.

no longer necessary and as a consequence punitive – or because the response is excessive compared to the terrorist attack, i.e. disproportionate.

Reprisals[80] are generally agreed to be illegal.[81] The central 1970 General Assembly Declaration on the principles concerning friendly relations stipulated that 'States have a duty to refrain from acts of reprisals involving the use of force'.[82] In the 1970s, the US administration twice re-iterated that the US believe reprisals to be illegal. In 1974 the Department of State concluded that 'it may sometimes be difficult to distinguish the exercise of proportionate self-defense from an act of reprisal. Yet, essentially for reasons of the abuse to which the doctrine of reprisals particularly lends itself, we think it desirable to endeavor to maintain the distinction between acts of lawful self-defense and unlawful reprisals'.[83] Similarly, an examination of United States practice with regard to act of reprisal or retaliation following armed provocation, covering the period 1953 to 1975, concluded that the US 'has taken the categorical position that reprisals involving the use of force are illegal under international law'.[84] It was further found that the US was reluctant to condemn reprisals if the provocative terrorists act was not similarly condemned and that the US maintained the distinction between self-defence

---

[80] On reprisals, see in general: Falk, Richard A. 'The Beirut Raid and the International Law of Retaliation' 63 *American Journal of International Law* (1969) 415-443; Blum, Yehuda Z. 'The Beirut Raid and the International Double Standard' 64 *American Journal of International Law* (1970) 73-105; Derek Bowett 'Reprisals Involving Recourse to Armed Force' 66 *American Journal of International Law* (1972) 3-4; Robert W. Tucker 'Reprisals and Self-Defense: The Customary Law' 66 *American Journal of International Law* (1972) 586-596; Taulbee, J.L. 'Retaliation and Irregular Warfare in Contemporary International Law' 7 International Lawyer (1973) 195-204; Taulbee, James Larry; Anderson, John 'Reprisal Redux' 16 *Case Western Reserve Journal of International Law* (1984) 309-336 and William V. O'Brien 'Reprisals, Deterrence and Self-Defense in Counterterror Operations' 30 *Virginia Journal of International Law* (1990) 421-478.

[81] Reprisals should be distinguished from the concept of retorsions which are 'unfriendly, but not unlawful acts, undertaken for remedial motives. ... In contrast, a reprisal is an unlawful act that is justified in response to a prior unlawful act of another state', W. Michael Reisman and James E. Baker *Regulating Covert Action: Practices, Contexts, and Policies of Covert Coercion Abroad in International and American Law* Yale University Press (1992) 90. In the following the words reprisals and retaliation are considered interchangeable although some writers either argue that they are two different concepts (see for example Seymore who defines a reprisal as an otherwise illegal act performed in order to obtain redress, whereas retaliation has as its sole purpose to inflict punishment, Philip A. Seymore 'The Legitimacy of Peacetime Reprisals as a Tool Against State-Sponsored Terrorism' 39 *Naval Law Review* (1990) 221-240 at 225) or merely point out that they used to be separate categories (see Taulbee and Anderson who found that the joining of the two concepts have militated against clarification, James Larry Taulbee and John Anderson 'Reprisal *Redux*' 16 *Case Western Reserve Journal of International Law* (1984) 309-336 at 313-315.

[82] See General Assembly resolution 2625 (XXV) and Annex.

[83] From Acting Secretary of State Kenneth Rush's May 29, 1974 letter to Yale Professor Eugene Rostow, reproduced in Arthur W. Rovine 'Contemporary Practice of the United States Relating to International Law' 68 *American Journal of International Law* (1974) 720-736 at 736.

[84] Marian Lloyd Nash (ed.) 'Digest of United States Practice in International Law 1979' Office of the Legal Advisor, Department of States, 1749-1752 at 1752.

and reprisals even though it was recognized that this distinction was difficult.[85] Even authors who find the current legal regulation wanting acknowledge that reprisals are disallowed by Security Council practice.[86]

The legal parameters of acts of reprisal in international law are most often traced back to the 1914 *Naulilaa* incident between Germany (German South West Africa/Namibia) and Portugal (Angola). In large part due to misunderstandings caused by faulty translation, three Germans were killed at the Portuguese fort *Naulilaa*. In response, Germany launched a series of raids against Portuguese positions which it, subsequently, argued were justified as 'legitimate retaliatory measures' in response to the killing of the German officials.[87] The 1928 *Naulilaa* arbitration set out the following three conditions for a legal reprisal: a prior act, contrary to the law of nations, prior attempt at gaining redress and, while the arbitrators were unsure whether the law of nations required that the reprisal be calibrated approximately to the offense, they recognized the need for reasonable proportionality.[88]

Yet, although it may be stated with certainty that reprisals are illegal, it is, as emphasized by the just quoted statements by the US Department of State, quite difficult to distinguish between action in self-defence and reprisal action. The most quoted distinction between self-defence and reprisals would appear to be the one set out by Bowett: the difference lies in their purpose.[89] Self-defence is permissible for the purpose of protecting the security of the state, whereas reprisals are punitive in

---

[85] Ibid.

[86] William V. O'Brien 'Reprisals, Deterrence and Self-Defense in Counterterror Operations' 30 *Virginia Journal of International Law* (1990) 421-478. For practice until 1963, see Higgins who notes that reprisals involving the use of force are generally considered to be illegal and that the practice of the United Nations practice until 1963 upholds this assertion, Rosalyn Higgins *The Development of International Law through the Political Organs of the United Nations* Oxford University Press (1963) 217.

[87] Following the German raids, natives revolted against the retreating Portuguese. The revolt became quite extensive and ultimately resulted in 'a ravaged country, a decimated native population and a deadly and expensive [Portuguese military] campaign' The *Naulilaa* Case, reproduced in Eric Heinze and Malgosia Fitzmaurice (eds.) *Landmark Cases in Public International Law* (2000) Kluwer Law International 1266-1285 at 1282.

[88] The *Naulilaa* Case, reproduced in Eric Heinze and Malgosia Fitzmaurice (eds.) *Landmark Cases in Public International Law* (2000) Kluwer Law International 1266-1285 at 1280-1281. In fact, the arbitrators found that the German reprisals had failed on all three counts since no prior illegal act had taken place, no notice had been served and the German actions were obviously lack proportion to the *Naulilaa* incident.

[89] See similarly Scharf: 'Self-defense differs from reprisals, which are punitive in character, in that the purpose of self-defense is to mitigate or prevent harm', Michael P. Scharf 'Clear and Present Danger: Enforcing the International Ban on Biological and Chemical Weapons through Sanctions, Use of Force, and Criminalization' 20 *Michigan Journal of International Law* (1999) 477 at 489.

character.[90] Bowett, however, acknowledges the difficulty of his seemingly simple division and some argue that 'all actions in self-defense combine' protection and punishment.[91]

It may be suggested that an examination of the amount of force applied could, at least in theory, help differentiate between self-defence action and reprisals: different amounts of force may be necessary for defensive purposes and punitive purposes respectively. Thus, one could argue that force measuring 1 is sufficient for defence, whereas $1 + X$ is required if the objective includes a punitive aspect. Thus, the application of force, which went beyond what was necessary in order to achieve a legitimate goal must be characterized as excessive or disproportionate and, hence, as an illegal reprisal. Such an approach, while appealing in theory, might, however, not be workable. Hence, as pointed out by Ago, since the aim of a reprisal is to punish, the amount of force used in reprisal should be equivalent to the original attack, while – as we have just seen – force used in self-defense could often be disproportionate to the attack suffered.[92]

In conclusion, the central factor concerning proportionality and self-defense must remain the identification of the objectives, which may be legitimately pursued when using force in self-defense. This will be the focus when examining the cases in the subsequent chapters.

---

[90] Derek Bowett 'Reprisals Involving Recourse to Armed Force' 66 *American Journal of International Law* (1972) 1-49 at 3. See also Zoller: 'Self-defense and reprisals are not on the same level. Reprisals are related to a way or a means of acting but convey a hidden meaning of punishment. On the other hand, self-defense relates to a cause or a justification for acting but without pejorative connotations', *Peacetime Unilateral Remedies: An Analysis of Countermeasures* Transnational Publishers, 1984, 5. Others, however, such as Stuesser, differentiate between reprisals and self-defense based on the object: the focus of reprisals is the wrongdoer, whereas the focus of self-defense is the victim state. He visualizes the relationship as two circles in a 'venn diagram', where a quarter portion of each circles overlap, see Lee Stuesser 'Active Defense: State Military Response to International Terrorism' 17 *California Western International Law Journal* (1987) 1-42 at 7. Somewhat similarly, Seymore speaks of a continuum between 'pure retaliation' at one end and 'pure self-defense' at the other end, see Philip A. Seymore 'The Legitimacy of Peacetime Reprisals as a Tool Against State-Sponsored Terrorism' 39 *Naval Law Review* (1990) 221-240 at 224. The fluidity reproduced in these visual aids attests to the intricacy of drawing a clear distinction between self-defense and reprisals.

[91] Alan D. Surchin 'Terror and the Law: The Unilateral Use of Force and the June 1993 Bombing of Baghdad' 5 *Duke Journal of Comparative and International Law* (1995) 457-496 at 470.

[92] Ago quoted in Judith Gardam *Necessity, Proportionality, and the Use of Force by States* Cambridge University Press (2004) 157.

5.IV. Forcible Counter-Measures?

In its judgment in the Nicaragua case, the ICJ brought forth some considerations on the use of counter-measures which were rather ambiguous and have caused a fair amount of controversy.

The Court wondered whether 'a State has a right to respond to intervention with intervention going so far as to justify a use of force in reaction to measures which do not constitute an armed attack but may nevertheless involve a use of force'.[93] The Court's deliberations are particularly relevant to the question of using force against terrorism because, as pointed out, terrorist acts are often perceived to fall short of an 'armed attack'.

Yet, due to the subject matter of the *Nicaragua* case, the Court addressed the issued of *collective* counter-intervention. The Court initially suggested that the USA might have had a right to intervene in Nicaragua in response to the latter's intervention in El Salvador. In the following paragraph, however, the Court took pains to point out that collective counter-intervention involving the use of force can *only* take place in response to an armed attack, i.e. in self-defence. These somewhat cryptic deliberations left the issue of individual counter-intervention, including the use of force, open. On this point, the Court merely stated that it was not for it to determine what direct reaction might be lawful.

One of the confusing aspects of the 1986 Court's *dictum* is the fact that, when addressing the issue of self-defence, the Court opined that individual and collective self-defence are subjected to the same primary condition, i.e. the occurrence of an armed attack.[94] Subsequently, when addressing counter-measures against intervention of a gravity less than an armed attack, the Court suddenly distinguishes between individual and collective responses, implying a wider right of individual response.

The Court, at a later point, re-iterated these observations: 'While an armed attack would give rise to an entitlement to collective self-defence, a use of force of a lesser degree of gravity cannot ... produce any entitlement to take collective counter-measures involving the use of force'. 'The acts of which Nicaragua is accused ... could only have justified proportionate counter-measures on the part of the State which had been the victim of these acts... They could not justify counter-measures taken by a third States ... and particularly could not justify intervention involving the use of force'.[95]

---

[93] 1986 ICJ 110, paragraph 210.
[94] 'In case of individual self-defence, the exercise of this right is subject to the State concerned having been the victim of an armed attack. Reliance on collective self-defence of course does not remove the need for this', 1986 ICJ 103, paragraph 195.
[95] 1986 ICJ 127, paragraph 249.

This rendition may be seen to make slightly more sense because it implies that all collective counter-measures, including force or not, are illegal. Such an attitude would be solidly based in the history of counter-measures. As Elagab documents, 'Vattel ... observed that resort to reprisals by one State against another could not be justified by a denial of justice against which a third State was protesting'.[96] He finds that this is still the law: 'the salient features and conditions of resort to non-forcible reprisals are as follows: ... 1. It is recognized by international law that only an aggrieved State has the right to take non-forcible reprisals'.[97]

There is, however, a modification to this rule; indeed a modification which is pertinent to the case at hand, i.e. the issue of use of force. As Elagab states '... the *erga omnes* principle may be applied to widen the category of 'an aggrieved party' so as to include all States where the violated obligation has an *erga omnes* character. Accordingly, all States, including those which have not been injured directly, will be deemed to have the right to impose counter-measures against the perpetrator of the breach. That said, it needs, however, to be recognized that measures taken in such circumstances might exceed the limits of proportionality. It follows, that difficulties would arise when the legality of such measures is being considered'.[98] Since the obligations of non-interference and the prohibition on the use of force in international relations can reasonably be described as obligations having an *erga omnes* character,[99] third states would be allowed to take counter-measures against the state which was in violation of its *erga omnes* obligation.

Be this as it may, the original question remains: can the victim state take proportionate counter-measures involving the use of force? Based on the Court's ambiguous *dictum,* Reisman and Baker question the legality of 'countermeasures using force of a "lesser degree of gravity than an armed attack", but which might still be

---

[96] Omer Yousif Elagab *The Legality of Non-Forcible Counter-Measures in International Law* Oxford University Press 1988, 10.

[97] Omer Yousif Elagab *The Legality of Non-Forcible Counter-Measures in International Law* Oxford University Press 1988, 35. Similarly, he writes: Conditions: In the first, they [reprisals] could only be exercised by a State which had suffered injury to herself or to her nationals', Ibid. 15.

[98] Omer Yousif Elagab *The Legality of Non-Forcible Counter-Measures in International Law* Oxford University Press 1988, 59. In conclusion, Elagab states 'counter-measures may be taken only be an injured party. ... in cases of breach of *erga omnes* obligations, all States assume the right to take counter-measures', Ibid. 63

[99] In the present case, the US argued that 'the self-defense issues presented in this case raise matters of the highest importance to all members of the international community', quoted in the Judgment, page 22, paragraph 38. This was seconded by Judge Parra-Aranguren who found that 'there can be no doubt that matters relating to the use of force and to self-defence are of the highest importance to all members of the international community, Separate Opinion of Judge Parra-Aranguren, page 3, paragraph 10.

categorized as intervention?'[100] Their tentative answer is that 'other than the general demand that uses of coercion meet tests of proportionality, it would appear that there are, as yet, no other limitations'.[101] Separately, Reisman concluded that although most states continue to disavow the legality of reprisals, 'the notion of reprisal is generally reviving, under the guise of 'counter-measure'.[102] Similarly, Gardam found that what in previous times may have been regarded as reprisal action by the United States and its allies 'has received significant State support as constituting legitimate self-defence in response to a prior armed attack'.[103]

Sohn's interpretation of the Court's finding is similar but more direct although it has a sense of *lex ferenda*: 'If an intervention does not amount to an armed attack, a counter-intervention in the form of an armed attack is clearly prohibited. This does not mean, however, that an intervention which does not constitute an armed attack may not be countered by equally less grave measures. As long as there is compliance with the rules relating to necessity and proportionality, counter-measures *should* be allowed. This means that below the level of an armed attack, the counter-intervener *should* be entitled to take the same kind of measures as the intervener. ... If the intervener resorts to the use of force, short of an armed attack, a similar amount of force would be applied to it'.[104]

Yet, do the 1986 Court's deliberations really warrant such an interpretation? Arguably, they do not.[105] Even if the Court's discussion is somewhat equivocal, it had previously emphasized that it was not making any considerations about the measures available to the State which is the victim of an intervention. Thus, it is not reasonable to interpret the *dictum* of the Court with regard to what it does not address: The fact that the Court only explicitly ruled out counter-measures by a third State cannot logically be read to mean that such measures are open to the victim state. At most, what can be

---

[100] W. Michael Reisman and James E. Baker *Regulating Covert Action: Practices, Contexts, and Policies of Covert Coercion Abroad in International and American Law* Yale University Press (1992) 114.

[101] Ibid. 115.

[102] W. Michael Reisman 'The Raid on Baghdad: Some Reflections on its Lawfulness and Implications' 5 *European Journal of International Law* (1994) 120-133 at 127.

[103] Judith Gardam *Necessity, Proportionality, and the Use of Force by States* Cambridge University Press (2004) 182.

[104] Louis B. Sohn 'The International Court of Justice and the Scope of the Right of Self-Defense and the Duty of Non-Intervention' in Yoram Dinstein (ed.) *International Law at a Time of Perplexity: Essays in Honour of Shabtai Rosenne* Martinus Nijhoff (1989) 869 at 877-878 (emphasis added).

[105] See, for example, Dinstein: 'the counter-measures coming within the framework of [the] rubric [counter-measures analogous to but short of self-defence] cannot entail the use of force, because – however 'analogous' to self-defence – in the absence of an armed attack, they cannot constitute self-defence', Yoram Dinstein *War, Aggression and Self-defence* Cambridge University Press 3rd ed. (2001) 174. Dinstein further find that any approval of counter-measures including the use of force would be hard to reconcile with the UN Charter, Ibid. 175.

concluded is that the Court evaded the issue and, hence, has not ruled anything out. Against this background, Sohn's reflections are more in the form of a prescription than a statement of the law.

Other factors may support this finding. Firstly, it is important to note that the Court chose the word 'counter-measures'. Elagab's examination of the history of counter-measures in international law finds that 'non-forcible reprisals still retain their validity as a category of justification for wrongful conduct. It would follow, therefore, that counter-measures may be regarded as synonymous with non-forcible reprisals'.[106] An acceptance of this conclusion must, naturally, be combined with the widely recognized fact that forcible reprisals are considered illegal.

Secondly, the best indication is probably state practice subsequent to the Nicaragua decision. If the Court had indeed been perceived to have acknowledged the existence of a right of forcible counter-measures, as argued by some, one would have expected states to apply this justification. Considered, for example, the US missiles attack on Baghdad in 1993. While many observers found it unacceptable to characterize the thwarted attempt at the life of retired President Bush as an 'armed attack', it would most certainly be a breach of Iraq's international obligations, assuming the Iraqi Government was indeed involved. Based on the latter assertion, the United States would, subsequent to the making of an unfulfilled demand for redress, be allowed to take proportionate counter-measures. If said counter-measures could include forcible measures, such a justification would be more convincing than a claim of self-defence in response to an armed attack. Yet, as is well-known, the United States did not argue a right of forcible counter-measures. Neither has any other government using force. In its letter to the Security Council, the United States reported that it had exercised its right to self-defence under Article 51 of the UN Charter by responding to an Iraqi attempt at the life of former US President George Bush.[107]

We now turn to an examination of a number of cases involving the use of force against terrorists. This inquiry will be conducted in four parts: Subsequently, in Chapter 6, five

---

[106] Omer Yousif Elagab *The Legality of Non-Forcible Counter-Measures in International Law* Oxford University Press 1988, 4.

[107] S/26003, June 26, 1993. At a subsequent meeting of the Security Council, the US declared that 'the attempt against President George Bush's life ... was an attack on the United States of America', S/PV/3245, 3. 'From all the evidence available to our intelligence community, we are therefore highly confident that the Iraqi Government, at its highest levels, directed its intelligence services to carry out an assassination attempt against President Bush. We responded directly, as we are entitled to do under Article 51 of the United Nations Charter, which provides for the exercise of self-defence in such cases. Our response has been proportionate and aimed at a target directly linked to the operation against President Bush. It was designed to damage the terrorist infrastructure of the Iraqi regime, reduce its ability to promote terrorism and deter further acts of aggression against the United States', S/PV/3245, 6.

cases from the two final decades of the 20th century will be investigated. In Chapters 7 and 8 four post-September 11 cases will be subjected to analysis. In Chapter 8 the 2001 US campaign against Afghanistan will be scrutinized. In the Chapter 9, three subsequent examples of use of force against terrorists will be included. They are the 2002 Israeli incursion into West Bank towns, the 2002 Russian bombing of Georgian territory and the 2003 Israeli bombing of Syrian territory. Finally, in Chapter 9, it will be considered whether the necessity justification may be pertinent when it comes to using force against terrorists.

Chapter 6

Self-Defence and Terrorism: Cases from the 1980s and 1990s

6.I. Introduction

Following the general outline of the difficulties related to claiming self-defence against terrorism, the present chapter sets out to examine a number of incidents involving attacks in response to terrorism. The cases cover the last two decades of the 20th century.

6.II. Israel's Invasion of Lebanon in 1982

In the summer of 1981, a cease-fire of sorts was arranged ending military action between 'Lebanese and Israeli territory'.[1] Following the assassination attempt against the Israeli ambassador to London, Slomo Argov, Israel initiated a sustained bombardment of targets in Lebanon. Against this background, the Security Council called on 'all the parties to the conflict to cease immediately and simultaneously all military activity'.[2] On June 6, however, the UN Secretary-General reported that 'hostilities have escalated dangerously' and that Israeli troops were entering Lebanon in large numbers.[3]

The Israeli representative to the Council outlined the series of attacks, which Israel had been subjected to from 1979 onwards, including since the 1981 cease-fire.[4] Israel claimed to be acting in self-defence and stated that the PLO was facing a well deserved and long overdue 'retribution'.[5] The representative maintained that Lebanon, having forfeited its sovereignty and independence long before,[6] could not expect Israel to sit back idly, while being subjected to 'unending harassment'[7] and 'repeated aggression'.[8] Somewhat in contradiction to the statement concerning Lebanon's lack of control, Israel

---

[1] William V. O'Brien *Law and Morality in Israel's War with the PLO* Routledge 1991, 134.
[2] Security Council Resolution 508, June 5, 1982, operative paragraph 1.
[3] S/PV.2375, June 6, 1982, 3.
[4] Since the ceasefire, Israel claimed 141 terrorist attacks emanating from Lebanon, S/PV.2375, June 6, 1982, 12-15.
[5] S/PV.2375, June 6, 1982, 16 and S/15178, June 7, 1982. Repeated S/PV.2376, June 8, 1982, 11.
[6] S/PV.2375, June 6, 1982, 22 and 33.
[7] S/PV.2375, June 6, 1982, 31.
[8] S/PV.2375, June 6, 1982, 33.

165

maintained that it would 'hold Lebanon responsible for all acts conceived and planned in Lebanon'.[9]

The Security Council, however, saw things somewhat differently. The United Kingdom, for example, found that 'the assassination attempt, however despicable, does not in any way justify the massive attacks on Lebanese towns and villages',[10] and, later, declared that Israel had invaded Lebanon 'in flagrant violation of international law' and rejected the claim to self-defence.[11] On June 6, the Council passed a resolution demanding that 'Israel withdraw all its military forces forthwith and unconditionally'.[12]

Among authors commenting on the action of Israel, many support its legality. Feder found that the invasion was in conformity with an emerging international law of self-defence.[13] Feinstein concluded that Israel was subjected to an armed attack through PLO terrorism and that Lebanon was complicit in these actions and, hence, that Israel's invasion was one of 'legitimate self-defence'.[14] The Israeli line of argument fits very well with a conception of self-defence set out by Dinstein. Dinstein has long maintained that 'terrorist raids continue to be armed attacks – even if conducted from, and not by, another State' and that 'self-defence is permitted inside the territory of another State ... against the guilty terrorists rather than the ineffective local government'.[15] He finally asserts that 'a government that is unable to repel terrorists must not try to display unwonted powess when the victim implements the law'.[16] With regard to the Lebanon

---

[9] S/PV.2375, June 6, 1982, 28-30.

[10] S/PV.2374, June 5, 1982, 11. See also the French statement: 'how criminal and reprehensible the attack on the Israeli ambassador may have been, France can only energetically condemn 'the bombing of Lebanese territory by Israeli aircraft'. S/PV.2374, June 5, 1982, 34-35.

[11] S/PV.2379, June 18, 1982, 18. The Netherlands, likewise, found that the display of force could not 'be justified under international law', Ibid. 33.

[12] Security Council resolution 509, June 6, 1982, operative paragraph 1. As noted by O'Brien, Israel's claim to self-defence was rejected by the Security Council, William V. O'Brien *Law and Morality in Israel's War with the PLO* Routledge 1991, 137.

[13] Norman Menachem Feder 'Reading the U.N. Charter Connotatively: Toward a New Definition of Armed Attack' 19 *New York University Journal of International Law and Politics* (1987) 395-432 at 397, 402 and 431. At one point, Feder, however makes reference to the 'ambiguity of some areas of the relevant law', 402. It is somewhat difficult to understand how he, in the same sentence, unequivocally can assert that 'Israel's invasion arguably is fully within the bounds of Article 51, 402.

[14] Barry A. Feinstein 'The Legality of the Use of Armed Force by Israel in Lebanon – June 1982' 20 *Israel Law Review* (1985) 362-396 at 396. Gross found that the sporadic PLO attacks probably were insufficient to amount to an armed attack and, hence, allow for the invocation of Article 51. He does, however, find that Israel had a reasonable argument under anticipatory self-defence, Laurence M. Gross 'The Legal Implications of Israel's 1982 Invasion into Lebanon' 13 *California Western International Law Journal* (1983) 458-492. See also O'Brien who found that the condemnations of the war were unsupported by sanctions and, therefore, 'reluctantly tolerated', William V. O'Brien *Law and Morality in Israel's War with the PLO* Routledge 1991, 145.

[15] Yoram Dinstein 'Terrorism and Wars of Liberation Applied to the Arab-Israeli Conflict: An Israeli Perspective' 3 *Israel Yearbook of Human Rights* (1973) 90.

[16] Ibid., 91.

invasion, he avers that it was 'the best contemporary illustration of extra-territorial law enforcement', a category which he subsumes as included under the right of self-defence.[17]

6.III. The 1985 Israeli Raid on Tunisia

On October 1, 1985, Israeli aircraft bombed the PLO's headquarters at Borj Cedria, south of Tunis, Tunisia killing 73, including 12 Tunisians.[18] Israel stated that the raid was revenge for the killing of three Israeli tourists in Cyprus on September 25, 1985.[19] The raid was fiercely denounced by Arab states and was condemned by European Community members and Japan.[20] On October 1, a White House spokesman characterized the raid as 'retaliation against a terrorist attack' and 'a legitimate response and expression of self-defense'; subsequently, on October 2, the raid was considered 'understandable as an expression of self-defense' which, however, 'cannot be condoned'.[21]

In the Security Council, the Israeli representative argued that the action had been taken in self-defence: 'if anything can be defined as aggression, it is the action taken against us. If anything can be defined as self-defence, it is the action taken by us. It is a legitimate response to acts of terrorism'.[22] He further stated that 'as for the assertion that it was an unprovoked attack on a country not actively at war with Israel, every state has a responsibility to prevent armed attacks from its territory, especially terrorist attacks against civilians. ... Uganda, after the Entebbe rescue, offered a feeble and false excuse that it did not know of the terrorists' designs. Lebanon claimed that it was too weak to do anything about them. But Tunisia knew, and it was strong enough to stop them. It knowingly harboured the PLO and allowed it complete freedom of action in planning, training, organizing and launching murderous attacks from its soil'.[23] These statements would indicate that Israel argued that Tunisia was responsible for PLO action because it harbored the alleged terrorists.[24] Subsequently, however, the Israeli speaker appears to claim that the attack was not directed at Tunisia: 'as surely as night follows day, it is clear that our action was pinpointed against the terrorists themselves

---

[17] Yoram Dinstein *War, Aggression and Self-Defence* 3rd ed. Cambridge University Press (2001), 218.

[18] Fact on File, 1985, 723.

[19] Ibid.

[20] Ibid.

[21] Keesing's Vol. XXXI, 34076-34077. See also San Francisco Chronicle 'U.S. Softens Its Support of Israel's Raid in Tunisia', October 3, 1985 (WL 3504110).

[22] S/PV.2613, October 3, 1985, 59.

[23] S/PV.2613, October 3, 1985, 65.

[24] See also Marcelo Kohen 'The use of force by the United States after the end of the Cold War and its impact on international law' in Michael Byers og Georg Nolte (ed.) *United States Hegemony and the Foundations of International Law,* Cambridge University Press, 2003, 197-223 at 207.

and the extra-territorial base from which they operate, not against the host country, whatever its responsibility. The false assertion that we somehow violated the sovereignty of a state would appear even more ludicrous here than it appeared in the case of Entebbe'.[25]

The Security Council was, however, generally unreceptive to the Israeli interpretation of the right of self-defence. France found the attack an 'inadmissible violation of the rules of international law'.[26] Denmark, on behalf of the European Community 'vigorously condemned the bombing' and stressed that 'acts of terrorism against Israeli citizens do not justify such actions'.[27] Australia, too, found the attack to be 'clearly a breach of international law and the Charter of the United Nations' and went on to determine that 'even if we were to accept Israel's version of the events, two wrongs do not make a right.' Australia further touched on the issue of proportionality: 'There is also, of course, the question of the strength of the response to the alleged actions that were used to justify Israel's reaction'.[28] Finally, the United Kingdom found that 'arbitrary and disproportionate violence of this sort, even in retaliation, is a clear breach of this obligation [to settle conflicts peacefully]. ... even if there had been demonstrable responsibility by the PLO, this would not have justified the retaliation taken against Tunisia on 1 October'.[29] Still, Israel received some support and understanding from one of the permanent members: the representative of the United States made the following general statement, while abstaining from the vote on the resolution condemning the attack: 'we recognize and strongly support the principle that a State subjected to continuing terrorist attacks may respond with appropriate use of force to defend itself against future attacks. This is an aspect of the inherent right of self-defence'.[30]

6.IV. The 1986 Raid on Libya

On April 14, 1986, United States' aircraft attacked Libya. The United States claimed that Libya, over a considerable period of time had 'openly targeted American citizens and U.S. installations'.[31] The most recent such attack was the bombing of the West Berlin disco *La Belle* on April 5. As a result of this bombing two U.S. servicemen and a

---

[25] S/PV.2613, October 3, 1985, 166.

[26] S/PV.2611, October 2, 1985, 9.

[27] S/PV.2611, October 2, 1985, 17-18.

[28] S/PV.2611, October 2, 1985, 51-52.

[29] S/PV.2611, October 2, 1985, 111.

[30] S/PV.2615, October 4, 1985, 22, paragraph 252.

[31] S/17990, April 14, 1986. See, in addition, the April 14, 1986 statement from the White House and the Presidents address to the Nation 86 *Department of State Bulletin* (1986), June, 1-2 and Deputy Secretary of State John C. Whitehead' statement on U.S. counterterrorism policy, Ibid. 79-80.

Turkish woman were killed and numerous other persons were injured. In its presentation to the Security Council, the U.S. representative elaborated on the Libyan connection to terrorism in general[32] and to the *La Belle* bombing in particular. The U.S. maintained that 'there is direct, precise and irrefutable evidence that Libya bears responsibility for the bombing in West Berlin on April 5',[33] which was 'only the latest in an ongoing pattern of attacks by Libya'.[34] The United States further claimed to have 'clear evidence that Libya was planning a multitude of future attacks ... [which] compelled the United States to exercise its right of self-defense'.[35]

Based on these allegations the Unites States representative stated: 'On April 14, in exercise of the inherent right of self-defence recognized in Article 51 of the Charter of the United Nations, United States military forces executed a series of carefully planned air strikes against terrorist-related targets in Libya'.[36] ... Those [the targets] are the sites used to carry out Libya's harsh policy of international terrorism, including ongoing attacks against United States citizens and installations'.[37] He further stated that the 'necessary and proportionate action was designed to disrupt Libya's ability to carry out terrorist acts and to deter future terrorist acts by Libya'.[38]

The United States' claim did not, however, meet with approval. The Soviet Union spoke of a 'neo-globalism' where 'gunboat diplomacy [was replaced] with aircraft-carrier diplomacy'[39] and condemned the attack 'vigorously'.[40] Most speakers condemned the attack in general terms as a violation of the Charter, international law and Libyan sovereignty.[41] A number of states designated the attack as 'state

---

[32] See 'Contemporary Practice of the United States' 80 *American Journal of International Law* (1986) 634-635. See also Christopher Dickey 'Qaddafi Says Libya Will Prepare Arabs For Terror Missions' Washington Post, January 16, 1986 (WL 2066445).

[33] S/PV.2674, 16.

[34] S/PV.2674, 17. 15 years later, this assertion appears to have been vindicated when a German court, in November 2001, convicted four people, three of whom worked at the Libyan embassy to East Germany, of the 1986 bombing of the *La Belle* disco, upholding claims that secret Libyan agents had planned the attack. The Court, however, stopped short of blaming the Libyan leader, BBC News 'Four Jailed for Berlin Disco Bombing', November 13, 2001, available at http://news.bbc.co.uk/1/hi/world/europe/1653575.stm, visited November 12, 2002.

[35] S/PV.2674, 17. The United States representative stressed that there was evidence that Libya is planning widespread attacks Americans over the next several weeks, S/PV.2674, 18.

[36] S/PV.2674, 13.

[37] S/PV.2674, 14-15.

[38] S/PV.2674, 14-15.

[39] S/PV.2675, 7.

[40] S/PV.2675, 8.

[41] Syria described the attack as a 'brutal, premeditated act of aggression' and a 'flagrant violation of the provisions of the Charter and the rules of international law' (S/PV.2675, 11-12) while China 'condemned such an act of attacking the territory of another state and encroaching upon its sovereignty, in violation of the norms governing international relations' (S/PV.2675, 53).

terrorism'.[42] Even the states traditionally aligned with the United States and those who would later vote against the draft resolution,[43] declined to lend support to the attack. Speaking after the vote, Denmark emphasized that it 'dissociated itself clearly from and deplored the military action'.[44] Similarly, France would not 'associate itself with the United States intervention against Libya'.[45] The sole supporting voice came from the United Kingdom which declared the central issue to be terrorism.[46] It furthermore described the right of self-defence as 'plainly include[ing] the right to destroy or weaken the capacity of one's assailant, to reduce his resources, and to weaken his will so as to discourage and prevent future attacks'.[47]

Only a few states elaborated on the United States' arguments concerning self-defence and Article 51. Hungary and Afghanistan found that the United States line or argument entailed a misinterpretation of Article 51.[48] Algeria stated that 'Article 51 sets exact limits … [on the] right of self-defense, which cannot be invoked in the absence of an act of aggression, and in this case there was no such act by Libya'.[49] Ghana argued that 'the incidents described [i.e. primarily the bombing of the La Belle disco in Berlin] are not in the nature of armed invasions perpetrated against the territorial integrity or sovereign independence of the United States. Indeed, they did not occur on United States' territory. … Furthermore, the fact that a national or nationals of such a State become victims of the incidents could not in our view be sufficient to trigger the use of force in the name of self-defence'.[50] Ghana, finally, pointed out that force used in self-defence 'can only be directed against the party that has perpetrated the armed attack' and did not find that the attacks could be imputed to Libya beyond reasonable doubt.[51]

The Qatari representative sought to 'shed light on the true status of international law' with regard to self-defence.[52] Firstly, Article 51, as an exception to the general prohibition on the use of force in international relations, has to be interpreted

---

[42] See for example Democratic Yemen (S/PV.2675, 42), Poland (S/PV.2677, 27) and Iran (S/PV.2678, 21).

[43] The draft resolution condemned the 'armed attack by the United States of America in violation of the Charter of the United Nations and the norms of international conduct'. See S/18016/Rev.1, April 21, 1986, proposed by Congo, Ghana, Madagascar, Trinidad and Tobago and the United Arab Emirates. The draft resolution received nine vote in favor, five against and one abstention.

[44] S/PV.2682, 32. Denmark voted against the draft resolution because it did 'not reflect the inter-relationship between action and reaction'.

[45] S/PV.2682, 42.

[46] S/PV.2679, 29-31.

[47] S/PV.2679, 27.

[48] S/PV.2677, 32 and S/PV.2678, 6 respectively.

[49] S/PV.1676, 4.

[50] S/PV.2680, 32.

[51] S/PV.2680, 32-33.

[52] S/PV.2677, 4.

narrowly.[53] Secondly, 'under the Charter ... prior armed attacks, which justify the legitimate use of self-defence, must entail aggression by one State against another'.[54] Thirdly, acts of self-defence must be carried out 'directly following armed aggression' and if the 'aggression ceases, there is no longer any pretext for making use of force on grounds of self-defence; otherwise such use of force would be mere retaliation'.[55] Qatar also, with apparent approval, referred to international legal experts in that 'combatting so-called terrorist acts never justifies the use of force in violation of Article 2(4) of the Charter and does [not?] come under the provisions of Article 51'.[56]

On April 21, the United States, the United Kingdom and France vetoed a draft Security Council Resolution which would have condemned the US strikes as an armed attack on Libya.[57] Denmark and Australia also voted against the resolution. On November 20, 1986 the General Assembly passed a resolution condemning the 'military attack' on April 15.[58]

Among the numerous academic reflections on the Libya strike,[59] Greenwood's article provides an excellent analysis of the fundamental legal issues.[60] He concluded

---

[53] S/PV.2677, 5.

[54] S/PV.2677, 5.

[55] S/PV.2677, 6.

[56] S/PV.2677, 8.

[57] See 'Contemporary Practice of the United States' 80 *American Journal of International Law* (1986) 632.

[58] General Assembly Resolution 41/38, 79-28-33, November 20, 1986. Gray explained the less than overwhelming vote by the general international hostility to Libya, Christine Gray 'After the Ceasefire: Iraq, the Security Council and the Use of Force' 65 *British Yearbook of International Law* (1994) 135-174 at 170.

[59] See, for example, Hays Parks who provides quite a detailed and technical specific account of the attack, concluding that the credibility of the U.S. counterterrorism program was significantly enhanced by the strike, W. Hays Parks 'Crossing the Line' *Proceedings of the U.S. Naval Institute* November 1986, 40-52. More recently, Hays Parks has described the strike as neither a peacetime reprisal nor an act of retaliation but a limited act of self-defence against a continuing threat for the purpose of deterring Libya's reliance on terrorism, see W. Hays Parks 'Lessons from the 1986 Libya Airstrike' 36 *New England Law Review* (2002) 755-766 at 760. See also Gregory Francis Intoccia 'American Bombing of Libya: An International Legal Analysis' 19 *Case Western Reserve Journal of International Law* (1987) 177-213 concluding that the US legitimately acted in self-defence when it responded to ongoing Libyan-supported terrorism. McCredie is less convinced about the legal justification for the attack but finds that states like the U.S. have few options, Jeffrey Allen McCredie 'The April 14, 1986 Bombing of Libya: Act of Self-Defense or Reprisal?' 19 *Case Western Reserve Journal of International Law* (1987) 215-242 Similarly, Turndorf is not persuaded that international law permitted an attack such as the one visited upon Libya but stresses the lack of other effective remedies to eliminate state-sponsored terrorism, Davis Turndorf 'The U.S. Raid on Libya: A Forceful Response to Terrorism' 14 *Brooklyn Journal of International Law* (1988), 187. See, finally, Wallace F. Warriner 'The Unilateral Use of Coercion under International Law: A Legal Analysis of the United States Raid on Libya on April 14, 1986' 37 *Naval Law Review* (1988) 49-95, concluding that the strike was wholly justified and specifically designed to further the purposes of the United Nations.

that the attack on Libya 'falls near the uncertain border between lawful self-defence and reprisals which are unlawful but may be condoned in practice' and went on to set out the criteria according to which the attack may be seen as a lawful exercise of self-defence.[61]

6.V. The 1993 Missile Attack on Iraq

On June 26 1993, the United States of America launched a number of missiles against the headquarters of the Iraqi Intelligence Service.[62] In a letter, Iraq informed the Security Council that the United States had 'committed a cowardly act of military aggression' by firing 23 Tomahawk missiles at the head quarter of the Iraqi information service.[63]

In its letter to the Security Council, the United States reported that it had exercised its right to self-defence under Article 51 of the UN Charter by responding to an Iraqi attempt at the life of former US President George Bush.[64] At a subsequent meeting of the Security Council, the US declared that 'the attempt against President George Bush's life ... was an attack on the United States of America'.[65] 'From all the evidence available to our intelligence community, we are therefore highly confident that the Iraqi Government, at its highest levels, directed its intelligence services to carry out an assassination attempt against President Bush. We responded directly, as we are entitled to do under Article 51 of the United Nations Charter, which provides for the exercise of self-defence in such cases. Our response has been proportionate and aimed at a target directly linked to the operation against President Bush. It was designed to damage the terrorist infrastructure of the Iraqi regime, reduce its ability to promote terrorism and deter further acts of aggression against the United States'.[66]

In the Security Council, many members showed great understanding for the US position. Whereas some states took the rather neutral position of referring to the generic international law position[67] some stated slight support[68] and some voiced outright

---

[60] Christopher Greenwood 'International Law and the United States' Air Operation Against Libya' 89 *West Virginia Law Review* (1987) 933-960.

[61] Christopher Greenwood 'International Law and the United States' Air Operation Against Libya' 89 *West Virginia Law Review* (1987) 933-960 at 947 and 955.

[62] John Law 'Clinton dons the Bush mantle on Iraq' 454 *Middle East International* (1993) 3.

[63] S/26004, dated June 27, 1993. 'Today Iraq appeals to the Council to safeguard its rights as a member states and calls upon it to condemn this act of aggression and take the action necessary to prevent a repetition in the future' (S/PV.3245, 13).

[64] S/26003, June 26, 1993.

[65] S/PV/3245, 3.

[66] S/PV/3245, 6.

[67] China, for example, stated that it opposed any 'action that can contravene the Charter ... and norms of international relations. ... We cannot endorse any action that might intensify the tension in the

support: The French government fully understood 'the reaction of the United States and the reasons for the unilateral action [taken in the name of the right to self-defence] by United States forces, in the circumstance under which it was carried out. Having always condemned all forms of terrorism, my Government approves policies that combat it'[69] Hungary found 'the action taken was 'justified' according to the information available to us. Its declared purpose was to deter other similar actions in the future and to ensure that the principles of civilized behaviour shall prevail in the world'.[70] The United Kingdom believed the action to be 'proper and proportionate' and 'entirely justified'.[71] Finally, Russia declared: 'In the view of the Russian leadership, the action by the United States are justified since they arise from the right of States to individual and collective self-defence, in accordance with article 51 of the Charter of the United Nations'.[72] At the close of the debate, no proposal requiring action was suggested.

Reaction outside the Security Council was also generally supportive although clear regional differences were detectable. Western Europe was by far the most supportive group.[73] In Eastern Europe, the Czech Republic understood the US reaction and Slovakia and Russia found the strike justified.[74] In the Middle East, however, only Kuwait approved of the attack.[75] Sudan condemned the attack, as did the Jordanian parliament.[76] Libya denounced it and Iran deplored it, calling it a breach of the

---

region, including the use of force.' (S/PV.3245, 21). A similar position was taken by the Non-Aligned Caucus in the Council (Cape Verde, Djibouti, Morocco, Pakistan and Venezuela)(S/PV.3245, 16-17).

[68] See for example comments by Japan: 'Given such circumstances [as presented by the US], my Government considers that there existed an unavoidable situation in which the United States Government could not help but take action' (S/PV.3245, 16); Brazil which toke note of the information and the opinion of the United States that the action was necessary, as a last resort, with a view to preventing the further occurrences of such acts(S/PV.3245, 17); New Zealand which similarly understood why a country faced with the situation of the United States 'could feel obliged to consider responding with force' (S/PV.3245, 23); and Spain: 'we understand the action the United States Government felt forced to take in the exceptional circumstances of this case' (S/PV.3245, 24).

[69] S/PV.3245, 13.

[70] S/PV.3245, 18-19.

[71] S/PV.3245, 21.

[72] S/PV.3245, 22.

[73] Austria 'approved' (FBIS-WEU-93-122, June 28, 1993, 6), the British Prime Minister called it a 'justified act of self-defense' (Ibid. 9), Chancellor Kohl of Germany believed the strike a 'justified reaction to a detestable attempted act of terrorism' (Ibid. 11), France, Italy and Greece 'understood' the US reaction (Ibid. 24 and 34 and 49), Denmark and Finland found the strike 'justified' (ibid. 44). The Spanish Foreing Minister, Solana, found that 'with international law in one's hand and in accordance with the previous UN Security Council resolutions in relations to Iraq, one can say that there is a legal basis [for the attack], that it has legal support'. He, however, went on to say that 'one can also argue the opposite', FBIS-WEU-93-123, June 29, 1993, 53.

[74] FBIS-EEU-93-123, June 29, 1993, 20 and 24 and FBIS-SOV-93-122, June 28, 1993, 6.

[75] Fact on File, July 1, 1993, Vol. 53, no. 2744, 481.

[76] FBIS-NES-93-123, June 29, 1993, 17 and 41.

principles of the United Nations.[77] Egypt and Pakistan expressed hope that similar action would be forthcoming in Bosnia.[78] In Asia, Malaysia condemned the attack, whereas Australia and the Philippines were more supportive.[79]

In addition to works dealing with the 1993 Iraq attack in a larger context, a number of publicists have contributed specific analyses of the strike.[80] Baker compares the 1986 strike against Libya and the 1993 strike against Iraq and finds them 'remarkably similar'.[81] He then examines the reaction in the world community and finds that whereas the Libya strike was roundly condemned, the 1993 attack received a supportive, if somewhat muted response.[82] He believes the latter difference is due to a shift in the interpretation of Article 51, from a restrictive interpretation to an expansive view of the term 'armed attack'.[83] Based on the facts, Kritsiotis finds that the missile strike 'was in the classic form of an armed reprisal, given its essentially retributive (as opposed to defensive or protective) nature'[84] but since the United States relied on self-defence, he evaluates this justification, finding that the strike did not 'conform to any conventional understanding of the concept of self-defence'[85] and did not 'accord with

---

[77] FBIS-NES-93-122, June 28, 1993, 20 and 60. See also Safa Haeri 'Iranian Condemnation' 454 *Middle East International* (1993) 5.

[78] FBIS-NES-93-122, June 28, 1993, 13 and 69.

[79] FBIS-EAS-93-122, June 28, 1993, 45 and 71 and FBIS-EAS-93-124, June 30, 1993, 47.

[80] See Stuart G. Baker 'Comparing the 1993 U.S. Airstrike on Iraq to the 1986 Bombing of Libya: A New Interpretation of Article 51' 24 *Georgia Journal of International and Comparative Law* (1994) 99-116; John Quigley 'Missiles with a Message: The Legality of the United States Raid on Iraq's Intelligence Headquarters' 17 *Hastings International and Comparative Law Review* (1994) 241-274; W. Michael Reisman 'The Raid on Baghdad: Some Reflections on its Lawfulness and Implications' 5 *European Journal of International Law* (1994) 120-133; Alan D. Surchin 'Terror and the Law: The Unilateral Use of Force and the June 1993 Bombing of Baghdad' 5 *Duke Journal of Comparative and International Law* (1995) 457-496; Robert F. Teplitz 'Taking Assassination attempts Seriously: Did the United States Violate International Law in Forcefully Responding to the Iraqi Plot to Kill George Bush?' *Cornell International Law Journal* (1995) 570-617 concluding that the missile attack was legal under international law, finding that it was 'necessary, in response to an imminent threat' 617; Dina Kritsiotis 'The Legality of the 1993 US Missile Strike on Iraq and the Right of Self-Defence in International Law' 45 *International and Comparative Law Quarterly* (1996) 162-177.

[81] See Stuart G. Baker 'Comparing the 1993 U.S. Airstrike on Iraq to the 1986 Bombing of Libya: A New Interpretation of Article 51' 24 *Georgia Journal of International and Comparative Law* (1994) 99-116 at 104.

[82] Ibid. at 111.

[83] Ibid. at 112. Surchin finds that 'modern notions of self-defense ... provided a sufficient legal basis; for the attack and that Brownlie and the ICJ would have determined that the attempted assassination was an 'armed attack', Alan D. Surchin 'Terror and the Law: The Unilateral Use of Force and the June 1993 Bombing of Baghdad' 5 *Duke Journal of Comparative and International Law* (1995) 457-496 at 458 and 479

[84] Dina Kritsiotis 'The Legality of the 1993 US Missile Strike on Iraq and the Right of Self-Defence in International Law' 45 *International and Comparative Law Quarterly* (1996) 162-177, at 166.

[85] Ibid. 174-175.

the present dictates of international law'.[86] Reisman, too, finds that the raid 'fits as comfortably [as under self-defence], if not more so under the classic rubric of reprisal'.[87] Although most states continue to disavow the legality of reprisals, Reisman finds that that 'the notion of reprisal is generally reviving, under the guise of 'counter-measure'.[88] Quigley concludes that the attack was 'a reprisal' and that the Security Council 'abdicated its role as protector of international peace' when accepted the United States' assertions and declined to investigate the issue further.[89]

Although the attack received wide understanding in the international community, it is, as will be discussed below, difficult to justify legally. In this context, it is deemed useful to briefly compare the US response with the response of Egypt and the world community following the, in several ways similar, attempted assassination of the Egyptian president. On June 26, 1995, President Mubarak of Egypt escaped an assassination attempt shortly after arriving in Ethiopia.[90] The Egyptian government soon accused Sudan of being behind the attempted assassination and it, initially, appeared somewhat undecided as to how to react to the attempt on Mubarak's life. Early on, the attempt was called 'an attack against Egypt through its president'[91] and both Mubarak and several newspapers suggested reprisals.[92] Egyptian officials, however, maintained that 'we will not confront it [Sudan] by military action' and emphasized that there would be no military conflict.[93] On the contrary, it was pointed out that Egypt had 'many legal, political means without resorting to military operations'.[94] Similarly, Foreign Minister Musa, stressed that 'military action was not on the table'.[95]

Within days, however, clashes took place in the disputed border area near Halaib on the Red Sea coast in which two Sudanese were killed and ten injured[96] and in the following weeks, Egyptian forces expelled most of the Sudanese police and government

---

[86] Ibid. 176.

[87] W. Michael Reisman 'The Raid on Baghdad: Some Reflections on its Lawfulness and Implications' 5 *European Journal of International Law* (1994) 120-133 at 125. See also Randelzhofer 'Article 51' in Bruno Simma (ed.) *The Charter of the United Nations: A Commentary* Oxford University Press, 2nd ed. (2002) 794, para. 15.

[88] W. Michael Reisman 'The Raid on Baghdad: Some Reflections on its Lawfulness and Implications' 5 *European Journal of International Law* (1994) 120-133 at 127.

[89] John Quigley 'Missiles with a Message: The Legality of the United States Raid on Iraq's Intelligence Headquarters' 17 *Hastings International and Comparative Law Review* (1994) 241-274 at 274.

[90] Cherif Cordahi 'Mubarak's Escape' 504 *Middle East International* (1995) 8.

[91] FBIS-NES-95-127, July 3, 1995, 11.

[92] Keesing's June 1995, 40622-23.

[93] FBIS-NES-95-127, July 3, 1995, 12.

[94] Ibid.

[95] FBIS-NES-95-127, July 3, 1995, 14.

[96] Cherif Cordahi 'Mubarak's Escape' 504 *Middle East International* (1995) 8. Both sides claimed that they had been fired on first.

officials from Halaib.[97] In a number of letters, Sudan complained about the Egyptian acts to the Security Council.[98] These complaints appear to treat the alleged Egyptian 'aggression' as entirely related to the decades old territorial dispute within the Halaib Triangle.[99] Although Sudan does mention wrongful accusations directed against it in connection with the assassination attempt, this appears to be perceived by Sudan merely as part of a smear campaign. Such an understanding is also expressed by the Egyptian side, where Foreign Minister Musa declared that the question of Halaib was 'completely unrelated'.[100]

On September 11, 1995 the Committee on Conflict Resolution of the Organization of African Unity (OAU) determined that the assassination attempt was 'aimed not only at the Egyptian President and not only at the sovereignty, integrity and stability of Ethiopia, but also Africa as a whole'.[101] The Committee demanded that Sudan hand over the persons suspected of being behind the assassination attempt.[102] Since no progress was achieved neither bilaterally not regionally through the OAU, Ethiopia decided to bring the matter before the Security Council.[103] The Council, in turn, unanimously adopted Resolution 1044 which called on Sudan to hand over the suspects and, more generally, to desist from 'engaging in activities of assisting, supporting and facilitating terrorist activities and from giving shelter and sanctuaries to terrorist elements'.[104] During the negotiations, Ethiopia characterized 'an act of State-sponsored international terrorism undertaken in the territory of another State' as constituting 'a clear threat to international peace and security'.[105] Egypt explicitly noted that the resolution condemned the assassination attempt as 'an attempt to disturb the peace and security of the region as a whole'.[106]

The Security Council gathered again in April in order to review a report by the Secretary-General on the implementation of Resolution 1044. The report generally concluded that Sudan had not fulfilled its obligations. Sudan characterized the report as 'bizarre' and maintained that it was ready to extradite the suspects once it found

---

[97] Steve Negus 'The Seizure of Halaib' 505 *Middle East International* (1995) 11.

[98] See, for example S/1995/616, July 25, 1995.

[99] Michael Collins Dunn 'Dossier: Halaib: History of an Egypt-Sudan Flashpoint' 7 *The Estimate* July 21-August 3, 1995, 5-8. See also Associate Press report 'Sudanese President Revives Territorial Dispute with Egypt' available at www.sudan.net/news/posted/5667.html, visited November 3, 2002.

[100] FBIS-NES-95-127, July 3, 1995, 14.

[101] S/1996/10, January 9, 1996, Annex I.

[102] S/1996/10, January 9, 1996, Annex I. See also Gill Lusk 'Khartoum Beset by Multiple Crises' 509 *Middle East International* (1995) 12. The demands were re-iterated in December 1995, S/1996/10, January 9, 1996, Annex II.

[103] S/1996/10, January 9, 1996.

[104] Resolution 1044, operative paragraph 4.

[105] S/PV.3627, January 31, 1996, 3.

[106] S/PV.3627, January 31, 1996, 15. Resolution 1044, operative paragraph 2.

them.[107] By Resolution 1054, the Security Council instituted quite mild sanctions against Sudan; too mild according to Ethiopia.[108] Following an additional review period, during which it was again determined that Sudan had not complied with the request of the OAU and the UN, the Security Council strengthened the sanctions against the country.[109]

In 2001, the Council lifted the sanctions after it had determined that Sudan had taken serious steps to comply with the previous resolutions.[110] The three suspects had, however, not been extradited, a fact which caused the United States to abstain.[111]

6.VI. The 1998 Missile Attack on Afghanistan and Sudan

On August 20, 1998, the United States launched a series of attacks against targets in Sudan and Afghanistan. In a letter to the Security Council, the US reported that it had exercised its right of self-defence, responding to 'a series of armed attacks against United States embassies and United States nationals'.[112] The immediate event triggering the US response was the August 7 simultaneous bombings of the US embassies in Kenya and Tanzania.[113] These bombings, which killed nearly 300 persons, took place on the eighth anniversary of the arrival of US troops in Saudi Arabia.[114] The investigation which was conducted indicated that al-Qaeda was responsible for the bombing, which took place a few months after bin Laden had issued a *fatwa* naming the United States as a target.[115]

---

[107] S/PV.1660, April 16, 1996, 2-10. Among other things, Sudan took issue with the report's claim that all Sudan's neighbors asserted that Sudan was attempting to destabilize their territories. As the Sudanese representative noted at least one of the States 'did not say that the Sudan was attempting to destabilize its territories', Ibid. 7.

[108] S/PV.1660, April 16, 1996 10-11.

[109] Security Council Resolution 1070, August 16, 1996.

[110] Security Council Resolution 1372, September 28, 2001. Both Egypt and Ethiopia had advocated the lifting of the sanctions.

[111] S/PV.4384, September 28, 2001, 2-3. At the time of the lifting of the sanction, the three suspects were not believed to be in Sudan. Sudan has been – and remains – on the US list of state-sponsors of terrorism since August 1993, see Abdel Salam Sidamed 'Sudan on the US "terrorist" list' 460 *Middle East International* (1993) 18.

[112] S/1998/780. August 20, 1998.

[113] In response, the Security Council adopted Sc Res 1189, August 13, 1998

[114] Rohan Gunaratna *Inside Al Qaeda: Global Network of Terror* Columbia University Press (2002) 46.

[115] The *fatwa* included the ruling that 'to kill the Americans and their allies – civilians and military – is an individual duty for every Muslim', see Ahmed Rashid *Taliban: Militant Islam, oil and Fundamentalism in Central Asia* Yale University Press (2000) 134. See also Press Briefing by Secretary of State Madeleine K. Albright and National Security Advisor Sandy Berger, August 20, 1998, available at http://secretary.state.gov/www/statements/1998/980820.html, visited October 27, 2002.

Much of the debate surrounding the attacks has concerned the reliability of the allegations presented by the USA, particularly with regard to the strike against the Sudanese pharmaceutical plant. Lobel's main objective, for example, is to examine the need for 'fact-finding and evaluating standards and mechanisms' in the cases of use of force in light of his determination that the most troubling aspect of the 1998 attacks was not the legal rules the Clinton Administration asserted, but 'the manner in which it treated the factual premises underlying the legal justification'.[116]

Sudan condemned the attack as 'an iniquitous act of aggression' and found it ironic that the Unites States had relied on Article 51 since the Sudan had 'not committed any action that could be regarded as an attack or a threat against the United States of America'.[117] The Sudan went on to request the urgent convention of a meeting of the Security Council.[118] Yet, no substantial meeting of the Council was ever convened. In November 2001, during the debates in the General Assembly, the Sudan yet again raised its grievances regarding the attack in 1998.[119]

International reaction was 'mixed' but hardly 'muted'.[120] The Arab League,[121] the Organization of the Islamic Conference[122] and the Non-Aligned Movement[123]

---

[116] Jules Lobel: 'The Use of Force to Respond to Terrorist Attacks: The Bombing of Sudan and Afghanistan' 24 *Yale Journal of International Law* (1999) 537-557 at 539. See also Tim Weiner and Steven Lee Myers 'Flaws in U.S. Account Raise Questions on Strike in Sudan' *The New York Times* August 29, 1998 (WL 5424497).

[117] S/1998/786, August 21, 1998. The Sudan emphasized that the attacked Shafa factory was producing medicines for human and veterinary use and had, furthermore, been approved by the Security Council Committee on Sanctions Against Iraq to export medicine under the oil-for-food program.

[118] Ibid. Subsequently, Namibia, on behalf of the Group of African States, requested the Security Council to convene a meeting of the Council, S/1998/802. Similarly, Qatar, on behalf of the Organization of the Islamic Conference, asked the President to convene a meeting of the Council, S/1998/942.

[119] 'The Sudan also calls upon the Security Council to respond positively to its demand by dispatching a fact-finding mission in connection with the incident of the bombardment of Alshifa Pharmaceutical factory in Sudan, which was destroyed by the American Missiles in August 1998. We are of the view that the bombardment of the factory was a mistake committed by the former American Administration and should be recognized as such and corrected in order for the Member States regain confidence in the International Organization and remove grievances and injustice so that all people can live in a world of justice, equality, security and serenity'. See www.un.org/webcast/ga/56/statements/011115sudanE.htm, visited August 12, 2002. In 2002, while describing the improved relations between the US and Sudan, the latter again made reference to the 'unfortunate case of the al-Shifa pharmaceutical Plant, which was falsely alleged to produce chemical weapons'. www.un.org/webcast/ga/57statements/020918sudanE.htm, visited October 23, 2002.

[120] Jules Lobel: 'The Use of Force to Respond to Terrorist Attacks: The Bombing of Sudan and Afghanistan' 24 *Yale Journal of International Law* (1999) 537-557 at 538, finding the reaction 'mixed and muted'.

[121] S/1998/894, September 28, 1998. See also FBIS-NES-98-233, Article ID: drnes08211998001025.

[122] S/1998/942, October 12, 1998.

[123] See S/1998/879, September 22, 1998. 'The Heads of State or Government, recalling the Ten Bandung Principles, which constitute the foundations of the Movement, expressed their deep concern

178

condemned the United States' attack as an act of aggression. The Pakistani Foreign Minister found that the attack against Afghanistan encroached on the sovereignty and territorial integrity of a Muslim country and was deeply concerned and angry about the attack.[124] Pakistan further complained that the United States' attack entailed a violation of its airspace and that one of the missiles actually impacted in Pakistan.[125] The Iranian Foreign Ministry condemned the attack against Sudan.[126] The Malaysian Prime Minister was indignant about both strikes and Libya's leader denounced the attack on the Sudan.[127] The UN Secretary-General expressed concern:[128] 'Terrorism is a global menace, which clearly calls for global action' but ' individual actions by member states, whether aimed at state or non-state actors, cannot in themselves provide a solution'.[129]

In Europe, however, most states expressed support. These included the United Kingdom, Germany and Spain.[130] France expressed understanding for the US action.[131] So too did Poland and the Czech Republic.[132] One major exception was Russia, which was very critical, finding that the attack 'violated international law in the most blatant fashion'.[133] In Asia, Taiwan and Australia expressed support.[134] China stated that it stood 'for handling the explosions in Kenya and Tanzania according to the United

---

over the air attack carried out by the United States Government against the El-Shifa Pharmaceutical Plant in the Sudan on 20 August 1998, and considered this as a serious violation of the principles of international law and the United Nations Charter and contrary to the principles of peaceful settlement of disputes as well as a serious threat to the sovereignty and territorial integrity of the Sudan and the regional stability and international peace and security. They further considered this attack as a unilateral and unwarranted act. The Heads of State or Government condemned this act of aggression and the continuing threats made by the United States Government against the Sudan and urged the US Government to refrain from such unilateral acts. They further expressed support to the Sudan in its legitimate demands for full compensation for economic and material losses resulting from the attack'. 12th Summit of the Non-Aligned Movement, Durban, South Africa, 2-3 September 1998, paragraph 179. Available at http://www.nam.gov.za/xiisummit/index.html, visited August 13, 2002. In the spring of 2000, the Non-Aligned Movement reaffirmed its position 'We reaffirm the position taken by the XII Summit in Durban on the air attack carried out by the United States government against the Al-Shifa Pharmaceutical Plant in the Sudan on 20 August 1998'. 13th Ministerial Conference, Cartagena, Columbia, 8-9 April, 2000, paragraph 104. Available at http://www.nam.gov.za/xiiiminconf/index.html, visited August 13, 2002.

[124] FBIS-CHI-98-234, Article ID: drchi08221998000051.

[125] S/1998/794, August 24, 1998.

[126] FBIS-CHI-98-234, Article ID: drchi08221998000051.

[127] FBIS-CHI-98-234, Article ID: drchi08221998000051.

[128] FBIS-CHI-98-234, Article ID: drchi08221998000051.

[129] Quoted in Leah M. Campbell 'Defending Against Terrorism: A Legal Analysis of the Decision to Strike Sudan and Afghanistan' 74 *Tulane Law Review* (2000) 1067-1096 at 1085-1086.

[130] FBIS-CHI-98-234, Article ID: drchi08221998000051.

[131] FBIS-CHI-98-234, Article ID: drchi08221998000051.

[132] FBIS-EEU-98-233, Article ID: dreeu08211998000883.

[133] FBIS-SOV-98-233, Article ID: drsov08211998001221.

[134] FBIS-CHI-98-233, Article ID : drchi08211998000782 (Taiwan) and FBIS-CHI-98-234, Article ID: drchi08221998000051 (Australia).

Nations Charter and the guiding principles of international law'.[135] China further advocated strengthening international cooperation against terrorism. A number of states, including Kenya, Tanzania and Turkey explicitly expressed no opinion.[136] Below governmental level, however, support was scarcer: As noted by the State Department's own monitoring of foreign media reaction, only a few opinion makers, mainly from Europe, defended the attacks.[137]

A number of law review articles have analyzed the August 1998 attacks.[138] Lobel briefly concludes that both attacks were probably justifiable if the facts alleged, but not proven, by the Clinton Administration were indeed correct. With regard to the strike against Afghanistan, he found that one could conclude that bin Laden was engaged in an ongoing armed attack against the United States and regarding the Sudanese factory, Lobel found that if the US allegations were proven, 'the United States could conceivably justify the attack as one targeting an instrumentality of bin Laden's terror network that, in turn, was engaged in an armed attack against the United States'.[139]

---

[135] FBIS-CHI-98-233, Article ID : drchi08211998000276.

[136] FBIS-AFR-98-233, Article ID: drafr08211998001190 (Kenya and Tanzania) FBIS-WEU-98-233, Article ID: drweu08211198000746 (Turkey).

[137] United States Information Agency, Foreign Media Reaction: 'U.S. Air Strikes Against Afghanistan, Sudan: Mixed Views on Washington's Action, August 21, 1998, available at www.fas.org/man/dod-101/ops/docs/wwwh8821.html, visited November 4, 2002.

[138] See, for example, Brennan who concluded that the strikes 'probably failed to meet the requirements of the Caroline doctrine and were more in the nature of reprisal, rather than legitimate self-defense', Maureen F. Brennan 'Avoiding Anarchy: Bin Laden Terrorism, the U.S. Response, and the Role of Customary International Law' 59 *Louisiana Law Review* (1999) 1195-1223 at 1209; Bisone who found that even though the US attacks were in response to terrorists attacks not directly attributable to any state 'it is likely that the American claim of self-defense will withstand diplomatic scrutiny in the U.N. and other forums' Federica Bisone 'Killing a Fly with a Cannon: The American Response to the Embassy Attacks' 20 *New York Law School Journal of International and Comparative Law* (1999) 93-115 at 114; Campbell concluding that the bombing of Afghanistan and Sudan was 'a *prima facie* violation of international law' and that it is 'not certain that the world community has agreed to expand permissible use of force to include retaliatory strikes against terrorists', Leah M. Campbell 'Defending Against Terrorism: A Legal Analysis of the Decision to Strike Sudan and Afghanistan' 74 *Tulane Law Review* (2000) 1067-1096 at 1096; Düker who concludes that the attacks were a violation of international law because the use of force was against operations which had come to an end and punishment can be no justification. With regard to the further justification of preventing further imminent attacks, Düker finds that the strikes were not aimed at preventing a specific type of threat and, hence, were a violation of international law. Arnd Düker 'United States Bombing of Terrorist Sites in Afghanistan and the Sudan: A Sign of the Necessity of International Co-operation' 5 *International Peacekeeping* (1999) 41-42.

[139] The claim by the US was that the factory was linked to or controlled by bin Laden's network, that it was producing nerve gas precursors, and that bin Laden was engaged in a systematic terror campaign against the US, Jules Lobel: 'The Use of Force to Respond to Terrorist Attacks: The Bombing of Sudan and Afghanistan' 24 *Yale Journal of International Law* (1999) 537-557 at 543-544.

Wedgwood is the only one who addresses the lack of state involvement in some detail.[140] She finds that the bombings of the two embassies were clearly "armed attacks" and that 'there is nothing in the U.N. Charter or state practice that restricts the identity of aggressors against whom states may respond – for private actors as well as governments may be the sources of aggressive conduct'.[141] She further asserts that 'if a host country permits the use of its territory as a staging area for terrorist attacks when it could shut those operations down, and refuses requests to take action, the host government cannot expect to insulate its territory against measures of self-defense'.[142]

Next we turn to the 2001 US attack on Afghanistan.

---

[140] Lobel acknowledges the disputed legal issue and explicitly sidesteps it, assuming that 'state has a right to use proportionate force against terrorists operating within a state that cannot and will not act against those terrorists', Jules Lobel: 'The Use of Force to Respond to Terrorist Attacks: The Bombing of Sudan and Afghanistan' 24 *Yale Journal of International Law* (1999) 537-557 at 543, note 31. Campbell merely concludes that the embassy bombings were armed attacks although she does not consider the lack of state involvement. Leah M. Campbell 'Defending Against Terrorism: A Legal Analysis of the Decision to Strike Sudan and Afghanistan' 74 *Tulane Law Review* (2000) 1067-1096 at 1085-1086 at 1093.

[141] Ruth Wedgwood 'Responding to Terrorism: The Strikes Against bin Laden' 24 *The Yale Journal of International Law* (1999) 559-576 at 564.

[142] Ibid. at 565.

Chapter 7

Self-defence and Terrorism: Afghanistan 2001

7.I. Introduction

In this and the following chapter, an in-depth analysis will be conducted involving four post-September 11 counter-terrorist operations. These include the US attack on Afghanistan in October 2001, the Israeli incursion into Palestinian controlled areas in the West Bank in the early spring of 2002, the Russian bombing(s) of Georgian territory in the summer of 2002 and the 2003 Israeli air strike against Syria. In addition, some brief remarks will be made regarding the 2003 Iraq war. Other episodes might reasonably have been included in the investigation. First and foremost, the tense standoff, which stretched over several months between India and Pakistan following the terrorist attack on the Indian parliament in December of 2001, comes to mind.[1] However, even if some states explicitly recognized Indian's right to respond in self-defence, it remains notoriously difficult to draw conclusions from events that did not materialize.

The question of state involvement will now be the primary focus. This focus is determined by the paradox that in spite of the fact that the September 11 situation failed to fit traditional conceptions of state involvement, the US response received general support. The Israeli/Palestinian, the Georgian/Russian and the Israeli/Syrian incidents will be included in order to make a more precise determination of the current requirement of state involvement. In addition, the question of the definition of an armed attack will be considered, particularly the issue of whether the 'accumulation of events' theory can be considered as having been accepted and what implications it might have.

---

[1] See, for example the following question and answer from the Whitehouse press secretary: 'India ... said that the terrorists who had been involved in the attack on the parliament had training camps just over the border in Pakistan, and they used a variant of the Bush doctrine that suggests that they should go after those camps. ... Is it a fair invocation of the Bush doctrine in this case? India has a legitimate right to self-defense. And at the same time, the President counsels that this is a very difficult situation in the region and one that could spiral out of control', Whitehouse Press Secretary www.whitehouse.gov/news/releases/2001/12/20011217-1.html, visited October 2, 2002. One could further have investigated the situation between Columbia and Venezuela where the Colombian army claimed that rebels from the Revolutionary Armed Forces of Columbia [FARC] operated from bases inside Venezuela, see Andrew Selsky 'At least 38 are killed in Columbia fighting' *The Chicago Tribune* March 22, 2002 (WL 2636530).

7.II. The US Attack and World Reaction

On October 7, 2001, the Unites States reported to the President of the Security Council that it, together with other states, had 'initiated actions in the exercise of its inherent right of individual and collective self-defence following the armed attacks that were carried out against the United States on 11 September 2001'.[2] The United States further claimed to have 'clear and compelling information that the Al-Qaeda organization, which is supported by the Taliban regime in Afghanistan, had a central role in the attacks'.[3] The United States emphasized that the attacks had been made possible by 'the decision of the Taliban regime to allow the parts of Afghanistan that it controls to be used by this organization [Al-Qaeda] as a base of operation'.[4] The letter described an 'ongoing threat' to the United States and stated that the actions taken were 'designed to prevent and deter further attacks on the United States'.[5] The United Kingdom also informed the Council that it had taken action in accordance with Article 51 'to avert the continuing threat of attacks from the same source', i.e. those behind September 11.[6]

The reaction from around the world was overwhelmingly supportive of the United States: The Secretary General of the United Nations stated: 'Immediately after the 11 September attacks on the United States, the Security Council expressed its determination to combat, by all means, threats to international peace and security caused by terrorist acts. The Council also reaffirmed the inherent right of individual or collective self-defence in accordance with the Charter of the United Nations. The States concerned have set their current military action in Afghanistan in that context'.[7]

The Security Council passed resolutions 1368 and 1373, condemning the attacks on the USA. Some have pointed to the fact that the Security Council, in both Resolution 1368 and in Resolution 1373, re-recognized the inherent right of individual or collective self-defence in accordance with the Charter and argued that this constituted an endorsement of possible U.S. action against Afghanistan.[8] However, it seems useful in

---

[2] S/2001/946, October 7, 2001. See also Michael R. Gordon 'Routine Start in Novel War' *The New York Times* October 8, 2001.

[3] Ibid.

[4] Ibid.

[5] Ibid.

[6] S/2001/947, October 7, 2001. See also Alan Cowell 'Blair Depicts the Attack as Act of Self-Defense' *The New York Times* October 8, 2001.

[7] Statement made on October 7, 2001 by Secretary-General Kofi Annan, Press Release, SG/SM/7985, AFG/149, available at http://www.un.org/News/Press/docs/2001/sgsm7985.doc.htm, visited August 25, 2002.

[8] See, for example Bassiouni who avers that Resolution 1373 'was intended to provide a legal basis for [*inter alia*] ... action by Member States under Article 51 of the Charter', M. Cherif Bassiouni (ed.) *International Terrorism: A Compilation of United Nations Documents 1972-2001* Transnational Publishers (2002) 3. See also Said Mahmoudi 'Comment on Fox Addendum' available at www.asil.org/insights/insigh77.htm, visited October 2, 2002.

this context to compare the two resolutions to the 1990 Resolution 661, as do Myjer and White. In the latter case, the Security Council explicitly connected the right of self-defence to the situation at hand, i.e. the 'armed attack by Iraq against Kuwait'.[9] It would thus appear that the general reference to self-defence in the two resolutions is insufficient evidence for Council support for the U.S. self-defence claim.[10]

In addition to the deliberations in the Security Council, it may be helpful to examine the statements delivered by government leaders during the General Debate of the 56th session of the General Assembly in order to gauge international reaction.[11] The General Debate was postponed in 2001 and took place between November 10 and 16, after the initiation of the U.S. attack on Afghanistan but before the conclusion of the campaign, i.e. while fighting was still taking place. The relevance of this forum is further emphasized by the fact that it appears that only one state failed to comment on the situation relating to Afghanistan and terrorism.[12]

Summarizing the exchanges in the General Assembly, one can conclude that there was a large group of states which explicitly endorsed the U.S. action in Afghanistan. These states included Argentina,[13] Australia,[14] Brazil,[15] Chile,[16] India,[17] Norway,[18] and

---

[9] Eric P.J. Myjer and Nigel D. White 'The Twin Towers Attack: An Unlimited Right to Self-Defence?' 7 *Journal of Conflict and Security Law* (2002) 5 at 10.

[10] Mary Ellen O'Connell 'Evidence of Terror' 7 *Journal of Conflict and Security Law* (2002) 19-36 at 29. See similarly Geir Ulfstein 'SC Resolution 1368 and self-defence' available at www.ejil.org/forum_WTC/messages/5.html, visited October 13, 2002. Franck opined that resolution 1368 recognized a right to respond in self-defense, see Thomas M. Franck 'Terrorism and the Right of Self-Defense' 95 *American Journal of International Law* (2001) 839-843 at 840. Kohen, however, found that the resolutions 'neither adds nor subtracts anything' Marcelo Kohen 'The use of force by the United States after the end of the Cold War and its impact on international law' i Michael Byers og Georg Nolte (ed.) *United States Hegemony and the Foundations of International Law,* Cambridge University Press, 2003, 197-223 at 209.

[11] Serge Schmemann 'Near Unity At the U.N. On Opposing Terrorism' *The New York Times* November 17, 2001.

[12] See Kazakstan statement, http://www.un.org/webcast/ga/56/statements/011115kazakstanE.htm

[13] 'At the hemispheric level, we have put into practice the regional system of self-defense and collective security established in the Inter-American Treaty of Regional Assistance. At the same time, we have fostered the full operation of the Inter-American Counterterrorism Committee and the drafting of an Inter-American Convention, which will supplement those at the universal level, as well as the convening of a special conference on hemispheric security'. http://www.un.org/webcast/ga/56/statements/011110argentinaE.htm

[14] 'Australia has joined the international coalition against terrorism. We have invoked our mutual security pact with the United States. We are contributing military forces to the campaign against those responsible for the 11 September attacks'. http://www.un.org/webcast/ga/56/statements/011116australiaE.htm

[15] 'In our understanding, the American hemisphere as a whole was attacked. That is why we suggested convening the consultative organ of the Inter-American Treaty of Reciprocal Assistance. Terrorism negates all that the United Nations stands for. It undermines the very principles of civilized behavior. It fosters fear and threatens the security of all countries. ... The Charter of the United Nations

Sweden.[19] The United States received particularly unequivocal support from countries like France and the United Kingdom.[20] Another substantial group of states expressed more cautious support while also emphasizing other concerns connected to the effort of eliminating international terrorism. Among these states were Cambodia,[21] China,[22]

---

acknowledges the right of Member States to act in self-defense'.http://www.un.org/webcast/ga/56/statements/011110brazilE.htm.

[16] 'Chile supports the coalition of countries which, in exercise of the right of self-defense, have embarked on a campaign aimed at eradicating terrorism'. http://www.un.org/webcast/ga/56/statements/011110chileE.htm. See also Erik Eckholm 'China Offers Its Wary Support for Attacks' *The New York Times*, October 8, 2001.

[17]'India supports the current campaign against the terrorist networks in Afghanistan'. http://www.un.org/webcast/ga/56/statements/011110indiaE.htm

[18] 'Norway pledges its full support to the broad global coalition against terrorism. We are part of the Atlantic Alliance. We fully support the United States in defending itself against international terrorism. We are implementing the provisions of Security Council Resolution 1373 by taking concrete steps to dry out the financial resources of terrorist networks. The Taliban regime has refused to adhere to mandatory Security Council decisions. It is harbouring and supporting terrorists in blunt contradiction of Council resolutions. Taliban is refusing to cooperate with the international community in our common efforts to eradicate international terrorism. The use of military force is therefore the only option left. The military operations in Afghanistan are aimed at the terrorists and those who harbour them. They are not aimed at innocent civilians. Not at Afghanistan as a country. They are aimed at a group of extremists exploiting a world religion for their own evil purposes'. http://www.un.org/webcast/ga/56/statements/011111norwayE.htmxx

[19] 'We support the right to self-defence of the US Government, in accordance with international law'. http://www.un.org/webcast/ga/56/statements/011113swedenE.htm

[20] France: 'The unprecedented scale and gravity of the terrorist attacks on New York and Washington on September 11 warranted an exceptional response. In its Resolution 1368, which was unanimously adopted, the Security Council rightly called this an act of aggression, and situated it within the logic of self-defence, and hence legitimate riposte, in accordance with Article 51 of the Charter. In its military response, therefore, the United States is thus entirely within its legal and political rights in targeting the terrorist organisations responsible for these acts'. http://www.un.org/webcast/ga/56/statements/011110franceE.htm. The United Kingdom: 'When the nations of the world agreed the UN Charter, they recognized the right of self-defense in Article 51. It is in exercise of this right that the military coalition is now engaged in action against Al-Qa'ida and the Taliban regime which harbors them'. http://www.un.org/webcast/ga/56/statements/011111ukE.htm

[21] 'Cambodia fully supports the UN resolutions in condemning acts of terrorism against the United States. Cambodia, also, fully endorses the international efforts in combating terrorism in all its forms and manifestations. However, Cambodia is disturbed over the loss of innocent civilian lives as a result of the bombings in Afghanistan. We must do everything possible to avoid civilian casualties and loss of lives. ... In order to find solutions to the current problems facing our world, especially terrorism, I believe that we need to look into not only the root causes of terrorism but also the other contributing factors to terrorism that are confronting the world today'. http://www.un.org/webcast/ga/56/statements/011111cambodiaE.htm

[22] China strongly believes that military actions against terrorism should have clearly defined targets and avoid any harm done to the innocent. All such actions should be consistent with the purposes and principles of the UN Charter and other universally recognized norms of international law and should

186

Malaysia,[23] Oman,[24] and South Africa.[25] Although one can observe the outlined division in two large groups, one roughly consisting of countries from the Western hemisphere[26] (but also, for example, India) and the other consisting more or less of Asian and African states, it merits emphasis that no country from either group opposed the U.S. action. Only two governments condemned the U.S. action in Afghanistan

serve the long-term interests of peace in the region and the world at large'. http://www.un.org/webcast/ga/56/statements/011111chinaE.htm

[23] 'Malaysia is ready to contribute to the global effort to combat the scourge of terrorism. In dealing with the issue there is a need for the international community, through the United Nations, to work out a sound strategy incorporating all aspects of the problem. While we understand the natural urge for retribution against the people who were believed to be behind the heinous attacks and their supporters, we do not think military actions are the best and most effective solution, nor politically a wise one. We are concerned that military actions may raise more problems than they solve. A sound strategy should include, aside from the military option, political/diplomatic efforts, legal, economic and other measures. It should be a long and sustained campaign in an effort to get at and destroy, once and for all, each and every root of the terrorist organization or organizations behind the these attacks'. http://www.un.org/webcast/ga/56/statements/011113malaysiaE.htm

[24] 'The world was shocked by the dangerous goals of the terrorist operation in their attempt to destroy vital locations in New York and in Washington resulting in thousands of victims and vast destruction of properties. While we would like, at this time, to express our solidarity with the friendly U.S.A. to combat terrorism and to defend its territories and people, as well as our understanding for the reasons of launching military operations in Afghanistan, we hope that no effort will be spared to protect the innocent civilians from the scourge of war and destruction, and to prevent more tragedy befalling them. The international society should play its role to protect these civilians. Furthermore, we should not ignore the role of other possible peaceful means in dealing with issues of terrorism, and make every effort and sincere endeavor in order to eradicate this epidemic which threaten to destroy human and civilized achievements if no countermeasures are taken to study its causes and tackle them in a way to eliminate it from its roots. We need to ensure that the utilization of military force is not the only ideal solution to eradicate terrorist groups, and we call upon the prevailing logic of farsightedness to all elements that encourage such behavior'. http://www.un.org/webcast/ga/56/statements/011111omanE.htm

[25] 'Immediately, it is correct that we must achieve global security cooperation so that the perpetrators of the September 11 acts of terrorism are apprehended and punished. Correctly, the Government of the United States has emphasized that all action that is carried out must be clearly targeted against the terrorists. It has stated that such actions, including military actions, should not degenerate into collective punishment against any people on any grounds whatsoever, including those of religion, race or ethnicity. Accordingly, it is necessary that humanitarian assistance should be extended to the people of Afghanistan. We fully agree with the approach. The US Government has also said that these actions should be of the shortest duration possible, consistent with the objective that must be achieved. Again, we agree with this without reservation'. http://www.un.org/webcast/ga/56/statements/011110safricaE.htm

[26] This geographical distribution is further emphasized by the endorsement of the United States' self-defense claim from NATO (Statement by the North Atlantic Council, September 12, 2001, Press Release 124, available at www.nato.int/docu/pr/2001/p01-124e.htm, visited April 23, 2002), by the European Union (Conclusion and Plan of Action of the Extraordinary European Council, September 21, 2001) and from the Organization of American States (Meeting of Consultation of Ministers of Foreign Affairs: Terrorist Threat to the Americas, OEA/Ser.F/II.24, RC.24/RES.1/01, September 21, 2001, available at www.oas.org/OASpage/crisis/RC.24e.htm, visited October 22, 2002).

outright: Cuba stated that 'the war in Afghanistan must be stopped. The Government of the United States must acknowledge that it has made a mistake – and must halt its ineffective, unjustifiable bombing campaign against that people. ... As to its doubtful purposes, this war will never be justified from the point of view of ethics and International Law. ... Cuba has opposed this war from the very beginning as an absurd, inefficient method to eradicate terrorism – and reiterates that it can only bring more hatred and ever-increasing dangers of new terrorist actions. No one has the right to continue murdering children, aggravating the humanitarian crisis, visiting impoverishment and death on millions of refugees'.[27] Even stronger denunciation was heard from Iraq: 'The United States, however, has once again resorted to the logic of brute force; hence, its aggression against Afghanistan'.[28]

Thus, whereas arguing that the international reaction exhibited 'compelling evidence of the international community's assessment [i.e. acceptance] of the applicability of Article 51 of the U.N. Charter to America's new war on terror'[29] might be pressing the case too far, the reaction may reasonably be taken as a sanctioning the somewhat narrower case of US action against Afghanistan. Even skeptics, like Myjer and White who expressed some disquiet about the categorization of the September 11 attacks as an 'armed attack' within the meaning of Article 51, concede that the U.S. position 'quickly found broad support'.[30]

As asserted by, for example, Kirgis, 'the absence of challenge to the US asserted right of self-defense could be taken to indicate acquiescence in an expansion of the right to include defense against governments that harbor or support organized terrorist groups that commit armed attacks in other countries'.[31] As is implicit in Kirgis assessment and as has by now been remarked upon by numerous authors, the broad acceptance and endorsement of US actions against Afghanistan creates a number of problems or challenges for international law.[32] Yet, in spite of the fact that 'it is not easily accepted that the Security Council would do away with' the requirement that a state must be involved,[33] it would be unacceptable to ignore the endorsement, in both the Security

---

[27] http://www.un.org/webcast/ga/56/statements/011113cubaE.htm.

[28] http://www.un.org/webcast/ga/56/statements/011114iraqE.htm

[29] Jack M. Beard 'America's New War on Terror: The Case for Self-Defense under International Law' 25 *Harvard Journal of Law and Public Policy* (2002) 550-590 at 573 and 590.

[30] Eric P.J. Myjer and Nigel D. White 'The Twin Towers Attack: An Unlimited Right to Self-Defence?' 7 *Journal of Conflict and Security Law* (2002) 5 at 8.

[31] Frederic L. Kirgis 'Israel's Intensified Military Campaign Against Terrorism' *ASIL Insights*, available at www.sil.org/insights/insigh78.html, visited October 14, 2002.

[32] Antonio Cassese 'Terrorism is Also Disrupting Some Crucial Legal Categories of International Law' 12 *European Journal of International Law* (2001) 993-1001.

[33] Geir Ulfstein 'SC Resolution 1368 and self-defence' available at www.ejil.org/forum_WTC/messages/5.html, visited October 13, 2002.

Council and the General Assembly, of the US claim of having been subjected to an armed attack

Having established that the international community ratified the US claim of self-defence and hence its interpretation of Article 51, it becomes paramount to delimit this new interpretation to the extent that it varies from previous interpretations. As noted by Travalio, 'there is no obvious limiting principle once it is determined that … an armed attack can occur when a state merely harbors those who have committed violent criminal acts against another state'.[34] Similarly, Kohen found that 'enlarging the concept of aggression so as to include the harboring of terrorists confuses different internationally wrongful acts and opens the door to increased unilateral uses of force, and thus escalation'.[35] In other words, even for those who understood it as inevitable that al-Qaeda had to be attacked in Afghanistan, and the Taliban regime with it, it becomes necessary to develop some criteria for why this was the case. What exactly did the international community accept?

In order to trace the developments of international law regarding the use of force caused by events on and following September 11 it is necessary, firstly, to delineate exactly how and where Operation Enduring Freedom was a challenge to a traditional interpretation of international law. Thus, it is proposed initially to examine the September 11 attacks under the traditional understanding of an armed attack as set out by the ICJ in the Nicaragua case. As may be expected, it is difficult to match the traditional requirement for justified self-defence with the events of September 11. This explains the skepticism which, for example, Thomas Franck encountered at a meeting of mainly German international lawyers.[36]

---

[34] Gregory M. Travalio 'Terrorism, International Law, and the Use of Force' 18 *Wisconsin International Law Journal* (1999) 145-191 at 156. He also admonishes: 'The point is that by expanding the definition of "armed attack" to include harboring … creates a great degree of uncertainty and unpredictability in applying this critical standard', Ibid., 156-157, note 45. See also Antonio Cassese 'Terrorism is Also Disrupting Some Crucial Legal Categories of International Law' 12 *European Journal of International Law* (2001) 993-1001 at 997 and Surchin who argues that 'concomitant with an increased ability to use force under international law comes an increased need to define the limits of the permissible use of force', Alan D. Surchin 'Terror and the Law: The Unilateral Use of Force and the June 1993 Bombing of Baghdad' 5 *Duke Journal of Comparative and International Law* (1995) 457-496 at 496.

[35] Marcelo Kohen 'The use of force by the United States after the end of the Cold War and its impact on international law' i Michael Byers og Georg Nolte (ed.) *United States Hegemony and the Foundations of International Law,* Cambridge University Press, 2003, 197-23 at 207.

[36] Thomas M. Franck 'Terrorism and the Right of Self-Defense' 95 *American Journal of International Law* (2001) 839-843 at 839.

7.III. Focus on States or Non-governmental Actors

Before turning to this question, it is appropriate to briefly address the issue of non-governmental actors in international law in the present context. It may reasonably be argued that to continue to focus solely on states in the evaluation of the legitimacy of uses of force is out of touch with reality, a reality in which non-governmental entities, including terrorists groups or networks, proliferate as never before and are more powerful than ever before.[37] Some might argue that the real question is 'can I attack the training camps of terrorist group X'. These training camps must, however, necessarily be located on the territory of some state.[38] Hence, any cross-border use of force must necessarily involve another sovereign state. Furthermore, even authors who appear to circumvent the issue of state involvement do in fact include the state. When Dinstein, for example, argues that 'it does not follow that Utopia must patently endure painful blows, only because no sovereign State is to blame', he is in fact arguing that Utopia can take action because Arcadia is unable to prevent the 'painful blows'.[39] One might as well assert that Dinstein is arguing that an armed attack is attributable to Arcadia if it is unable to prevent it. Such an argument is not, however, in line with the traditional rules of state responsibility.

Moreover, in the present context when examining the uses of force against Afghanistan (and, as examined below, the Palestinian self-rule areas), force was actually employed against the governing authorities, the Taliban (and the Palestinian Authority).[40] Such a use of force runs counter to the argument that the state was not involved. Dinstein, for his part, maintains that the counter-terrorism operation is to be 'directed exclusively against the armed bands of terrorists' and that 'even the ... armed

---

[37] As often noted by the US administration: 'the terrorists find allies in outlaw regimes, but themselves have no land or capital or standing army to defend', President Bush Salutes Veterans at White House Ceremony, November 11, 2002, available at www.whitehouse.gov/news/releases/2002/11/20021111-2.html, visited November 13, 2002.

[38] 'Non-state actors necessarily reside on the territory of a state' Michele L. Malvesti 'Bombing Bin Laden: Assessing the effectiveness of Air Strikes as a Counter-Terrorism Strategy' 26 *Fletcher Forum of World Affairs* (2002) 17-28 at 26. Megret asserts that, whether one wants it or not, self-defence will be directed against a state, Frederic Megret ';War'? Legal semantics and the Move to Violence' 13 *European Journal of International Law* (2002) 361-399 at 379. Ronzitti briefly considers the use of force against terrorists who are present outside of national jurisdictions, such as on the high seas. While it cannot be ruled out that such situations may arise, they appear rather marginal and will not be dealt with in the following. also Natalino Ronzitti *Rescuing Nationals Abroad Through military Coercion and Intervention on Grounds of Humanity* Martinus Nijhoff 1985, 135.

[39] Yoram Dinstein *War, Aggression and Self-defence* Cambridge University Press 3rd ed. (2001) 215.

[40] Indeed, in both cases it was emphasized that the local government was to blame, in part for 'harboring' the terrorists.

forces and installations [of the host state] ought not to be harmed'.[41] Similarly, following the September 11 attacks, but, presumably, before the operations in Afghanistan, Cassese accentuated that the purpose of any action in self-defence had to be limited to the detention of persons allegedly responsible for September 11 and the destruction of military objectives, such as training camps used by the terrorists: 'Force *may not* be used to wipe out the Afghan leadership or destroy Afghan military installations or other military objectives that have nothing to do with the terrorist organizations, unless the Afghan central authorities show by words or deeds that they approve and endorse the action of the terrorists organizations'.[42] Finally, if the current analysis determines that the threshold for attributing acts by terrorists to states has been lower by recent events, this would, in and of itself, be a recognition of the growing power and importance of non-governmental actors.

7.IV. The Traditional Test

As pointed out above, the 1986 ICJ judgment in the Nicaragua case appears to leave only very substantial involvement, such as the sending or organizing of irregular troops and planning by the state of irregular operations as sufficient to reach the level of an armed attack.[43] Such substantial involvement in an armed attack appears quite similar to the involvement, which the Court considered necessary in the context of state responsibility, in order to attribute acts of the *Contra* forces to the United States. As noted by Byres, 'the [International] Court [of Justice] held that an 'armed attack' exists only when the link between the State and the non-State actor is very close ... This position is consistent with the law of State responsibility insofar as it concerns the attribution of the acts of non-State actors to a State'.[44] In the Nicaragua case, Nicaragua

---

[41] Yoram Dinstein *War, Aggression and Self-defence* Cambridge University Press 3rd ed. (2001) 220. Elsewhere, Dinstein describes the targets of an 'extra-territorial law enforcement' operation as the 'bases of the hostile armed bands or terrorists' and stresses that the use of force is only permitted as long as 'the destruction of the bases is the 'sole object' of the expedition', Ibid. 216. See also Coll: 'the military measures should be directed at the actual "terrorist" sanctuaries', Alberto R. Coll 'The Legal and Moral Adequacy of Military Responses to Terrorism' 81 *American Society of International Law Proceedings* (1987) 287-320 at 305.

[42] Antonio Cassese 'Terrorism is Also Disrupting Some Crucial Legal Categories of International Law' 12 *European Journal of International Law* (2001) 993-1001 at 999 (emphasis in original).

[43] See also, for example, Condorelli who notes that imputability may be excluded 'even if it is proved that a certain State has given substantial help and support to the terrorists, but without precisely directing their criminal activity', Luigi Cordorelli 'The Imputability to States of Acts of International Terrorism' 19 *Israel Yearbook of Human Rights* (1989) 233-246 at 244.

[44] Michael Byers 'Terrorism, the Use of Force and International Law after 11 September' 51 *International and Comparative Law Quarterly* (2002) 401-414 at 408. Slaughter and Burke-White, for example, also examines the issue of state responsibility. They seem to break new ground by asserting that 'the traditional "effective control" test for attributing an act to a state seems insufficient to the

alleged that the United States 'conceived, created and organized a mercenary army, the *contra* force'.[45] Based on this, Nicaragua submitted that the USA should be held responsible for the acts of the *contras*. The Court held that for the conduct of the *contras* 'to give rise to legal responsibility of the United States, it would in principle have to be proved that that State had effective control of the military or paramilitary operations'.[46] After reviewing the facts, however, the Court found that 'there is no clear evidence of the United States having actually exercised such a degree of control in all fields as to justify treating the *contras* as acting on its behalf'.[47] The pertinent test is generally referred to as one of 'effective control'.

In the Tadic case before the ICTY, the Appeals Chamber, however, found that the test of 'effective control', which the International Court of Justice promulgated in the Nicaragua Case, had to be differentiated according to circumstances: 'The extent of the requisite State control varies' according to whether the acts are perpetrated by individuals or an organized group.[48] The Appeals Chamber found the 'effective control' test, including the requirement of specific instructions, to be too stringent when it comes to acts of organized military or paramilitary groups. The Chamber found that 'the State wields overall control over the group, not only by equipping and financing the group, but also by coordinating or helping in the general planning of its military activities'.[49] In the specific case, the Chamber applied its test to the armed forces of *Republika Srpska* and determined that these 'were to be regarded as acting under the overall control of and on behalf of the FRY [Federal Republic of Yugoslavia]'.[50]

Hence, under the traditional test, the Taliban regime of Afghanistan could only become responsible, and the September 11 attack only become an armed attack within the meaning of Article 51, if the Taliban exercised 'overall control' over al-Qaeda, i.e. if the Taliban had actually sent the terrorists, or had organized them and/or had planned

---

threats posed by global criminals and the states that harbor them'. Subsequently, however, they appear to repeat the traditional rules: 'Where a government and the terrorists ... are distinguishable, the traditional test of effective control could still apply'. Where they are indistinguishable, however, 'attacks on the state apparatus could be legitimized either as a direct attack on the terrorists or as a direct response to a state act', Anne-Marie Slaughter and William Burke-White 'An International Constitutional Moment' 43 *Harvard International Law Journal* (2002) 1-21 at 20.

[45] 1986 ICJ 53, paragraph 93.

[46] 1986 ICJ 65, paragraph 115.

[47] 1986 ICJ 62, paragraph 109. For a comment, see, for example, Francis A. Boyle, 'Determining U.S. Responsibility for Contra Operations under International Law' 81 *American Journal of International Law* (1987) 86-93.

[48] Prosecutor v. Tadic, Case IT-94-1-A, Appeals Chamber, Judgment July 15, 1999, paragraph 137, available at www.un.org/icty, visited August 21, 2002.

[49] Prosecutor v. Tadic, Case IT-94-1-A, Appeals Chamber, Judgment July 15, 1999, paragraph 131, available at www.un.org/icty, visited August 21, 2002.

[50] Prosecutor v. Tadic, Case IT-94-1-A, Appeals Chamber, Judgment July 15, 1999, paragraph 162, available at www.un.org/icty, visited August 21, 2002.

the operation. In the present case, however, it has been asserted that 'the new enemy [is] different. Osama bin Laden's organization, al Qaeda, flew no flag – it was the ultimate NGO'.[51] Similarly, Myjer and White found that the attacks were 'committed by individuals, not acting, directly at least, on behalf of a state. Self-defence, traditionally speaking, applies to an armed response to an attack by a state'.[52] The next issue will therefore be to determine, as exactly as possible, the relationship between the Taliban and al-Qaeda.

7.IV.A. The Relationship Between the Taliban and al-Qaeda

An examination of the relationship between the Taliban and al-Qaeda will inevitably be somewhat tentative since the exact relationship between al-Qaeda and the ruling Taliban regime is not entirely known. Some have actually argued that al-Qaeda in reality controlled the Taliban and Afghanistan was more correctly described as a terrorist-sponsored state than a state sponsor of terrorism.[53] Against this background, it could be suggested that al-Qaeda was actually an organ of the Afghan state but such a suggestion has not been made and will not be pursued here.

In October 2001, with an update in November, the British government issued a dossier containing its case against bin Laden.[54] The government found that 'Usama bin Laden's Al Qa'ida and the Taliban régime have a close and mutually dependent alliance. … The Taliban régime allows bin Laden to operate his terrorist training camps and

---

[51] Strobe Talbott and Nayan Chanda 'Introduction' in Strobe Talbott and Nayan Chanda (eds.) *The Age of Terror: America and the World after September 11* Basic Books (2001) xi.

[52] Eric P.J. Myjer and Nigel D. White 'The Twin Towers Attack: An Unlimited Right to Self-Defence?' 7 *Journal of Conflict and Security Law* (2002) 5 at 7.

[53] Gunaratna describes how al-Qaeda, before October 2001, became the first terrorist group to control a state, Rohan Gunaratna *Inside Al Qaeda: Global Network of Terror* Columbia University Press (2002) 61-62. Both U.S. Intelligence reports and the former Taliban deputy interior minister have described how bin Laden bankrolled the Taliban to the tune of 100 million dollars, see Peter baker 'Defector Says Bin Laden Had Cash, Taliban In His Pocket', *The Washington Post*, November 30, 2001. See also Responsibility for the terrorist atrocities in the United States 11 September 2001, paragraph 12: 'Usama bin Laden has provided the Taliban régime with troops, arms, and money to fight the Northern Alliance. He is closely involved with Taliban military training, planning and operations. He has representatives in the Taliban military command structure. He has also given infrastruture assistance and humanitarian aid. Forces under the control of Usama bin Laden have fought alongside the Taliban in the civil war in Afghanistan'. Available at http://www.fco.gov.uk/servlet/Front?pagename=OpenMarket/Xcelerate/ShowPage&c=Page&cid=102 7020898997&a=KArticle, visited August 12, 2002. See also Gaja who considers that the situation might have been one of 'a [terrorist] group giving support and to some extent controlling a state', Giorgio Gaja 'In What Sense was there an "Armed Attack"?' available at www.ejil.org/forum_WTC/ny-gaja.html, visited January 12, 2002.

[54] Patrick E. Tyler 'British Detail bin Laden's Link to U.S. Attacks' *The New York Times* October 5, 2001.

activities from Afghanistan, protects him from attacks from outside, and protects the drugs stockpiles. Usama bin Laden could not operate his terrorist activities without the alliance and support of the Taliban régime.'[55] ... 'In return for active Al Qa'ida support, the Taliban allow Al Qa'ida to operate freely, including planning, training and preparing for terrorist activity'.[56] ... 'The [September 11] attack could not have occurred without the alliance between the Taliban and Usama bin Laden, which allowed bin Laden to operate freely in Afghanistan, promoting, planning and executing terrorist activity'.[57]

Various UN resolutions have described the relationship in the following terms: 'harbouring and training terrorists',[58] 'sheltering and training'[59] and 'providing sanctuary',[60] providing 'safe haven' and allowing bin Laden 'to operate a network of training camps'[61] and allow Afghan territory to be 'used for terrorists installations and camps' and 'for the preparation or organization of terrorist acts'.[62] It has further been found that 'a large proportion of foreign 'terrorists' fight on the side of the Taliban' in the Afghan civil war and some 'terrorists receive some or part of their training in 'regular' Taliban military facilities'.[63] It is not entirely clear from the latter observation whether the Taliban supervised the training or merely allowed the use of facilities. Academics have similarly described how the Taliban and al-Qaeda had a reciprocal relationship, which included the Taliban providing al-Qaeda with sanctuary, weapons, equipment and training facilities in addition to the use of Afghanistan's national aircraft in exchange for al-Qaeda support for Taliban military and other efforts.[64] Based on these sources, it may be concluded that the Taliban and al-Qaeda had an alliance, that the Taliban allowed al-Qaeda to stay in Afghanistan, which included the Taliban

---

[55] Responsibility for the terrorist atrocities in the United States 11 September 2001, 'Background' available at http://www.fco.gov.uk/servlet/Front?pagename=OpenMarket/Xcelerate/ShowPage&c=Page&cid=1027020898997&a=KArticle, visited August 12, 2002.

[56] Ibid., paragraph 13.

[57] Ibid., paragraph 74. Similarly, during the General Debate in the General Assembly, Germany commented on 'the unprecedented symbiosis between the terrorists of the Al Qaida group and the Taliban regime', http://www.un.org/webcast/ga/56/statements/011112germanyE.htm, visited August 24, 2002.

[58] Security Council Resolution 1193, 1998.

[59] Security Council Resolution 1214, 1998.

[60] Ibid.

[61] Security Council Resolution 1267, 1999.

[62] Ibid.

[63] *Report of the Committee of Experts appointed pursuant to Security Council resolution 1333 (2000), paragraph 15(a), regarding monitoring of the arms embargo against the Taliban and the closure of terrorist training camps in the Taliban-held areas of Afghanistan*, S/2001/511, May 22, 2001, 9, paragraph 41.

[64] Rohan Gunaratna *Inside Al Qaeda: Global Network of Terror* Columbia University Press (2002) 40-41.

allowing al-Qaeda to plan, train and prepare for terrorists operations.[65] Finally the Taliban protected al-Qaeda (presumably by allowing the network to stay in Afghanistan) and provided unspecified 'support'.

Even if one agrees with the ICTY Chamber and endorses the less rigorous test, the conditions for attributing private acts to a state are still relativly stringent: Although specific instructions or directions for the specific attack are not necessary, the state must still have '*a role in organizing, coordinating or planning the military actions* of the military group, in addition to financing, training and equipping or providing operational support to that group'.[66] This test was referred to by the Chamber as one of 'overall control'. This is the test to which the British and other assertions must be subjected. According to the British report, the Taliban regime allowed al-Qaeda to operate, plan, train and prepare for terrorist operations and afforded the network protection. Fundamentally, the situation was one of the Taliban allowing al-Qaeda use of Afghan territory for whatever purpose. It should be reasonably clear that the relationship between the Taliban regime and al-Qaeda was not one that can convincingly be characterized as one in which the Taliban government had a role in organizing, coordinating or planning the September 11 attacks and, thus, did not exert overall control over al-Qaeda: as far as we know, the Taliban did not send the terrorists nor did the Taliban initiate or plan/organize the September 11 attacks. [67] According to a staff report from the 9/11 Commission, the Taliban leader, Mullah Omar, actually opposed attacking the United States. The opposition was due in part to ideological concerns, in

---

[65] Molly Moore and Peter Baker 'Inside Al Qaeda's Secret World: Bin Laden Bought Precious Autonomy' *The Washington Post* December 23, 2001.

[66] See footnote 48 (emphasis in original).

[67] See also Scharf, speaking on September 20, 2001: 'we haven't seen evidence yet that the Taliban government's involvement in the Osama bin Laden organization [al-Qaeda] rises to this level [of effective control]', Michael Scharf 'International Legal Implications: Teach-In on Terrorism' 8 *New England Journal of International and Comparative Law* (2002) 81-102 at 86. O'Connell finds otherwise, concluding that 'the case may have been made for attribution, especially under the *Tadic* case' (Mary Ellen O'Connell 'Evidence of Terror' 7 *Journal of Conflict and Security Law* (2002) 19-36 at 32). She bases this, tentative, conclusion primarily on the British Report which has also be taken as the basis for the present discussion. She quotes excerpts according to which a close mutual relationship or alliance existed on a personal level between bin Laden and Mullah Omar and on an institutional level between al-Qaeda and the Taliban Regime. However, the question of which side supported which is not insignificant. According to the British Dossier, bin Laden, and his network, appears to have supported the Taliban relatively more than vice versa. That bin Laden allegedly was 'closely involved with Taliban military training, planning and operations' (British Report as quoted in Mary Ellen O'Connell at 31) is not decisive since the crucial question is whether Afghanistan through the Taliban organized, coordinated and planned al-Qaeda operations, including the September 11 attacks. It seems unrealistic to give an affirmative answer to this latter question based on the British findings.

part to pressure from the Pakistani government to keep al Qaeda from engaging in operations outside Afghanistan.[68]

7.IV.B. Adoption by the State of Private Acts

The articles on State Responsibility set out that acts, which are perpetrated by private individuals and, hence, initially not attributable to a state, may, nonetheless, be considered an act of a state if the state *post facto* acknowledges and adopts the action as it own.[69] In the Diplomatic and Consular Staff Case, the ICJ did not find that the militant who occupied the embassy 'had any form of official status' and their conduct was, therefore, not imputable to the Iranian state.[70] Subsequent to the take over of the embassy, however, expressions of approval came from numerous Iranian authorities with 'the seal of official approval' coming in the form of a decree from Ayatollah Khomeini.[71] This endorsement of the initial occupation and the decision to perpetuate it 'translated continuing occupation of the Embassy and detention of the hostages into acts' of the Iranian state.[72]

The ILC Commentary emphasizes the distinction between adoption of an act and mere support or endorsement.[73] Thus, if the Taliban authorities had stated that the attacks on the US were appropriate or even laudable, this would probably not suffice in order to determine that the Afghan government had adopted the attacks. In actual fact, Wakil Ahmed Muttawakil, the Taliban's foreign minister, said the attacks on New York, Washington and elsewhere in the United States 'were 'from a humanitarian point of view surely a loss and a very terrifying incident'. Asked whether the Taliban condemned the attacks, he said: 'We have criticized and we are now again criticizing terrorism in all its forms''.[74] Similarly, the Los Angeles Times reported that Muttawakil

---

[68] See Staff Report No. 16: 'Outline of the 9/11 Plot', June 16, 2004, page 19, available at www.9-11commission.gov, visited July 4, 2004.

[69] Article 11.

[70] 1980 ICJ 3 at 29, paragraph 58.

[71] 1980 ICJ 3 at 34, paragraph 73.

[72] 1980 ICJ 3 at 35, paragraph 74.

[73] 122-123. Dinstein notes that 'a Government may be responsible for t the mere toleration of acts of international terrorists against another state'. Yoram Dinstein 'The Right of Self-defence Against Armed Attacks' in Magnus D. Sandbu and Peter Nordbeck (eds.) *International Terrorism: Report from a Seminar Arranged by the European Law Students' Association in Lund, Sweden, 1-3 October 1987* Juristförlaget I Lund (1987) 57-71 at 69. This is beyond dispute. He does, however, appear to imply that this is what happened in the *Diplomatic and Consular Staff Case*. In this context it must be stressed, as does the ILC, that mere support or toleration is not sufficient for the attribution of private acts to a state.

[74] Kathy Gannon 'Taliban Condemn Attacks in U.S.' The Associated Press, September 11, 2001 (WL 27335959).

sent 'condolences and condemnation'.[75] The Taliban's ambassador to Pakistan, Abdul Salam Zaeef added 'We want to tell the American children that Afghanistan feels your pain'.[76] At the same time, however, the Taliban refused to extradite bin Laden both before and after September 11.[77] Although there were some stories about the Taliban considering the idea of extraditing him for a trial in a neutral country, [78] the UN Secretary-General concluded that 'while the Taliban offered condolences for the terrorist attacks, they denied Osama bin Laden's involvement, and upheld their refusal to comply with Security Council resolutions, despite repeated attempts, including by Pakistan ... to persuade them to hand him over'.[79]

One might wonder whether earlier statements and/or threats would be enough to attribute a subsequent attack to the threatening state. A question akin to such a scenario arose in the recent *Case Concerning Oil Platforms*.[80] In the context of an missile attack on October 16, 1987 against the *Sea Isle City*, a Kuwaiti tanker, which had been reflagged to the United States, the United States, *inter alia*, made reference to an announcement by the Iranian President Ali Khameini some three months earlier indicating that Iran would attack the United States if it did not leave the region.[81] According to the U.S. this statement or threat could help substantiate the U.S. claim that Iran was behind the attack. The Court, however, found that this statement was 'evidently not sufficient to justify the conclusion[82] that any subsequent attack on the United States in the Persian Gulf was indeed the work of Iran'.

7.IV.C. The Effect of UN Resolutions

The efforts at bringing bin Laden to justice must be viewed in the context of the increasing international disenchantment with the Taliban regime as documented, *inter alia*, in the successive Security Council resolutions. In 1996, the Security Council

---

[75] Carol J. Williams 'World Leaders Condemn 'New Evil' Response: Allies rush to boost security as embassies, military posts and banks go on high alert. U.S.-bound flights are canceled, diverted' *Los Angeles Times*, September 12, 2001.

[76] Ibid.

[77] Luke Harding 'Taliban will not sacrifice Bin Laden', *The Guardian* March 31, 2001.

[78] 'Afghanistan's ruling Taliban said Sunday it might be willing to extradite Osama bin Laden to stand trial in a neutral country outside US or Taliban influence', see 'Taliban offers Bin Laden trial in neutral country', *Agence France-Presse*, October 14, 2001 (WL 25037460).

[79] 'The Situation in Afghanistan and its Implications for International Peace and Security', Report of the Secretary-General, A/56/681-S/2001/1157, December 6, 2001, 6. See also 'Taliban says Bin Laden will be "the last to leave" Afghanistan: newspaper', *Agence France-Presse*, September 20, 2001 (WL 25017258).

[80] *Case Concerning Oil Platforms* (Islamic Republic of Iran v. United States of America) ICJ Judgment (Merits) November 6, 2003.

[81] Paragraph 60.

[82] Ibid.

reiterated that the continuation of the conflict in Afghanistan provided a fertile ground for terrorism ... which destabilized the region, and beyond.[83] In 1998, the Council expressed its great concern at the continuing presence of terrorists in the territory of Afghanistan and demanded that the Afghan factions refrain from harboring and training terrorists.[84] Later in 1998, the Council was deeply disturbed by the continuing use of Afghan territory, especially the area controlled by the Taliban, for the sheltering and training of terrorists and the panning of terrorist acts and demanded that the Taliban stop providing sanctuary and training for international terrorists and their organizations, and that all Afghan factions cooperate with efforts to bring indicted terrorists to justice.[85] In October 1999, the United States submitted a summary of a November 1998 indictment of bin Laden to the United Nations, claiming that US requests for the extradition of bin Laden had been rejected more than 20 times since the August 1998 attack on the US embassies in Kenya and Tanzania.[86] Subsequently, the Council, acting under Chapter VII, adopted Resolution 1267 which determined that the Taliban had failed to respond to Resolution 1214 and imposed sanctions against the Taliban.[87] The Council further established a Committee to oversee the sanctions.[88] Since the Taliban took no steps to comply with Resolution 1267,[89] the sanctions regime was further strengthened in December 2000 by Resolution 1333.[90] Only weeks before September 11, 2001 the Council acknowledged receipt of the most recent monitoring report and restated its previous position.[91]

One of the central concerns in the pre-September 11 deliberations at the UN was the extradition of bin Laden. It remained pertinent even after October 7, i.e. in the early stages of the war: 'I will say it again – if you [the Taliban] cough him up, and his people, today, ... we'll reconsider what we're doing to your country. You still have a

---

[83] Security Council Resolution 1076, October 22, 1996.

[84] Security Council Resolution 1193, August 28, 1998.

[85] Security Council Resolution 1214, December 8, 1998, preamble and operative paragraph 13.

[86] S/1999/1021, October 4, 1999.

[87] Security Council Resolution 1267, October 15, 1999, operative paragraph 4, and S/PV.4051, October 15, 1999. The sanctions instituted a flight ban on any aircraft owned, leased or operating by or on behalf of the Taliban and froze Taliban finances.

[88] Security Council Resolution 1267, October 15, 1999, operative paragraph 6. The Committee issued its first report on December 29, 2000, S/2000/1254.

[89] S/PV.4251, December 19, 2000.

[90] Security Council Resolution 1333, December 19, 2000. Among the additional sanctions was the prevention of the supply of arms. As it turned out, paradoxically, the Taliban apparently possessed more than enough weapons and weapons were in fact 'exported' from Afghanistan to the neighboring countries, see *Report of the Committee of Experts appointed pursuant to Security Council resolution 1333 (2000), paragraph 15(a), regarding monitoring of the arms embargo against the Taliban and the closure of terrorist training camps in the Taliban-held areas of Afghanistan*, S/2001/511, May 22, 2001, 8, paragraph 29-30.

[91] Security Council Resolution 1363, July 30, 2001.

second chance. Bring him in. And bring his leaders and lieutenants and other thugs and criminals with him'.[92]

In the present context, one may ask whether the refusal to extradite bin Laden made the Taliban regime responsible for the September 11 attacks. Beard appears to be making this argument when he argues that no other government has been so universally condemned for its support for terrorism and closely linked with terrorist activities: 'With this status comes more easily assigned and more certain international legal responsibility for the horrific attacks' on September 11 'and a clearer case for self-defense under Article 51'.[93]

On this account, one may ask whether the refusal to extradite results in future acts of the candidate for extradition will be attributed to the refusing state. This would seem unlikely since a refusal to extradite, *mutatis mutandis*, constitutes a lesser form of assistance to the terrorists than, for example, material assistance, which, under the traditional test, did not lead to attribution. Refusal to extradite prior to September 11 could, therefore, probably not result in the attribution of the attacks to Afghanistan. As for the situation after September 11, one may inquire whether refusal to extradite at this point would have consequences similar to an adoption of the attack by the Taliban regime. In many ways, the refusal to extradite would constitute a more concrete act than the issuance of an official statement adopting the attack. Yet, although it is debatable, the refusal to extradite does not appear to be equivalent to an adaptation of the act itself. Still, the issue at hand is very important. The current examination indicates that the traditional 'substantial involvement' threshold is being lowered; rhetorically to one described as the 'harboring of terrorists'. However, when opening up for a more liberal regulation of the use of force, it is important to be careful and not to merely chose the lowest common denominator. In this regard, it makes more sense to ask, in addition to the determination of the fact of a state harboring terrorists, whether that particular state has to be informed or warned or requested to mend its ways before it can be considered as responsible for an armed attack perpetrated by the terrorists it harbors.[94] Hence, the fact that repeated warnings and/or extradition requests have been made may be an important element in a new regime of attributing terrorist acts to states.

---

[92] President Bush at Prime Time Press Conference, October 11, 2001, available at www.whitehouse.gov/news/releases/2001/10/20011011-7.html, visited October 12, 2002. See also Patrick E. Tyler and Elisabeth Bumiller 'President Hints He Will Halt War if bin Laden Is Handed Over' *The New York Times* October 12, 2001.

[93] Jack M. Beard 'America's New War on Terror: The Case for Self-Defense under International Law' 25 *Harvard Journal of Law and Public Policy* (2002) 550-590 at 583.

[94] See, for example, Rowles who maintains state responsibility if the state ' refuses to act to bring such activities to a halt', James P. Rowles 'Military Responses to Terrorism: Substantive and Procedural Constraints in International Law' 81 *American Society of International Law Proceedings* (1987) 287-320 at 314.

This brief survey indicates that Afghanistan did not incur direct responsibility under the traditional test for the attacks. As pointed out, however, the US action against Afghanistan received broad support as an exercise of self-defence and this, in turn, raises some serious questions about the resultant regulation of the use of force. Even for people who are convinced about the legitimacy of the US action in Afghanistan, it becomes necessary to delineate the boundaries of this new reading of Article 51.

The world has, however, witnessed other post-September 11 counter-terrorist operations that might suggest that the threshold has actually been lowered even further. In order to examine this assertion, in the next chapter, we turn to consider three other terrorist related incidents: the 2002 Israeli incursions into Palestinian controlled areas of the West Bank, the 2002 conflict between Georgia and Russia and the 2003 Israeli air strike against Syria. Finally, brief mention will be made of the 2003 Iraq war.

Chapter 8

Self-defence and Terrorism:
Three further post-9/11 Cases

8.I. Introduction

Following the investigation into the 2001 U.S. campaign against Afghanistan, we now turn to three other terrorist related incidents: the 2002 Israeli incursions into Palestinian controlled areas of the West Bank, the 2002 conflict between Georgia and Russia and the 2003 Israeli air strike against Syria. Finally, brief mention will be made of the 2003 Iraq war.

8.II. The Israeli Incursions into Palestinian Controlled Areas of the West Bank

In dealing with the conflict between Israel and the Palestinians in the present context, one preliminary problem arises: Since the Palestinian Authority is not recognized as a state, how are Israel's incursions into territory under the exclusive control of the Palestinian Authority to be evaluated?[1] The matter is further complicated by the fact that even under the Oslo-corpus, Israel may still possess certain powers in areas under Palestinian jurisdiction, including the 'overriding responsibility for security for the purposes of protecting Israelis and confronting the threat of terrorism'.[2]

Kirgis skirts the question and determines tentatively that as 'a political body [that] has the attributes of a government of a population in a reasonably well defined territory, it [the Palestinian Authority] could be considered capable of perpetrating an armed attack under international law'.[3]

---

[1] As a consequence of the various agreements between Israel and the PLO, in particular the 1995 Interim Agreement, the Palestinian Authority is in control of approximately 18 % of the territory in the West Bank, designated as 'Area A'. For an early review of the Oslo process, see 'The Peace Process' 28 *Israel Law Review* (1994) 207-576. On the status of the Palestinian Authority, see Eyal Benvenisti 'The Status of the Palestinian Authority' in Eugene Cotran and Chibli Mallat (ed.) *The Arab-Israeli Accords: Legal Perspectives* Kluwer Law International (1996) 47-66 and Yoram Dinstein 'The International Legal Status of the West Bank and the Gaza Strip – 1998' 28 *Israel Yearbook on Human Rights* (1998) 37-49
[2] 1995 Interim Agreement, Article XIII, paragraph 2(a), quoted in Raja Shehadeh *From Occupation to Interim Accords: Israel and the Palestinian Territories* Kluwer Law International (1997), 62-63.
[3] Frederic L. Kirgis 'Israel's Intensified Military Campaign Against Terrorism' *ASIL Insights*, available at www.asil.org/insights/insigh78.html, visited October 14, 2002.

In its Advisory Opinion on the Legal Consequences of the Construction of a Wall in the Occupied Palestinian Territory,[4] the ICJ, after concluding that the construction of the wall constituted an action not in conformity with various international legal obligations incumbent on Israel, considered whether Israel could use self-defence as a possible excuse for the found violation. However, as the Court had limited the possible use of Article 51 to armed attacks imputable to another state, it found that this provision had 'no relevance in this case' since Israel did 'not claim that the attacks against it are imputable to a foreign State'.[5] Judge Higgins objected to what she found to be the Court's unpersuasive contention that,

> as the uses of force emanate from occupied territory, it is not an armed attack "by one State against another". I fail to understand the Court's view that an occupying Power loses the right to defend its own civilian citizens at home if the attacks emanate from the occupied territory – a territory which it has found not to have been annexed and is certainly "other than" Israel. Further, Palestine cannot be sufficiently an international entity to be invited to these proceedings, and to benefit from humanitarian law, but not sufficiently an international entity for the prohibition of armed attack on others to be applicable. This is formalism of an unevenhanded sort. The question is surely where responsibility lies for the sending of groups and persons who act against Israeli civilians and the cumulative severity of such action.[6]

Finally, it may be noted that the Israeli Supreme Court described the character of for example operation Defensive Wall in March 2002 as 'combat operations', which are 'not regular police operations, but embody all the characteristics of armed conflict'.[7]

For the present purposes, the following choice has been made: It seems clear that Israel does not have a right to enter Palestinian territory at will. If by nothing else, this tentative conclusion is supported by the fact that Israel feels obliged to present a justification for its incursions, i.e. self-defence. It would similarly appear from the Security Council records that many other states judge the Israeli incursions as if they

---

[4] Advisory Opinion, Legal Consequences of the Wall.
[5] Advisory Opinion, Legal Consequences of the Wall, page 56, paragraph 139.
[6] Advisory Opinion, Legal Consequences of the Wall, Separate Opinion by Judge Higgins, page 7, paragraph 34.
[7] Beit Sourik Village Council v. The Government of Israel, HCJ 2056/04, Judgment, June 30, 2004, page 3, paragraph 2, available at www.court.gov.il, visited July 12, 2004.

were against, in some sense, a 'sovereign' territory.[8] For these reasons, an analysis of the Israeli incursions can arguably help illuminate the larger issue of the use of force against terrorism, even if, in a strictly formal sense, the incursions do not take place between two states.[9]

Since the outbreak of the second Palestinian uprising – *intifada* – in late September 2000, the violence between Israelis and Palestinians has escalated. Each escalation has often been seen as a new phase in the conflict.[10] On March 29, 2002, the Israeli government approved a 'wide-raging operational action plan' to counter Palestinian terrorism.[11] With explicit reference to the September 11 attacks, the Israeli Prime Minister told Israelis that 'Israel is in a war, a war against terror'.[12] The aim of the operation – Operation Defensive Shield – was to 'crush the Palestinian terrorist infrastructure' and conduct an 'all-out war against terrorism'.[13] The operations, which followed the hitherto deadliest suicide bombing in Netanya, which killed 29, was estimated by the Minister of Defense to last days, 'possibly weeks'.[14] As part of the operation, Israeli forces entered and re-occupied the majority of the major Palestinian cities in the West Bank, cities it had left as part of agreements between Israel and the

---

[8] China actually articulated the issue as one between two states: an 'aggression of Israel against Palestine', S/PV.4503, March 29, 2002, 16.

[9] See, for example, Gross who argues that 'even if it is not possible to turn to international law directly [when considering the relationship between Israel and the Palestinian areas] one may still learn from it by way of analogy about the laws applicable to the prevailing situation in the context of the fight against terrorism', Emanuel Gross 'Thwarting Terrorist Acts by Attacking the Perpetrators or Other Commanders as an Act of Self-Defense: Human Rights Versus the State's Duty to Protect its Citizens' 15 *Temple International and Comparative Law Journal* (2001) 195-246 at 199-200.

[10] For example, after a mortar attack on a school bus in November 2000 in the Gaza Strip which killed two and injured nine, Israel conducted a three hour assault from the air and the sea of Palestinian installations throughout the Gaza Strip. Graham Usher "War in Gaza' 638 *Middle East International* November 24, 2000, 4.

[11] Cabinet Communiqué, March 29, 2002, available at www.mfa.gov.il/mfa/go.asp?MFAH0ldw0, visited October 30, 2002. See also Graham Usher 'Sharon Launches the Endgame?' 672 *Middle East International* (2002) 4.

[12] PM Sharon's Address to the Nation, March 31, 2002 available at www.mfa.gov.il/mfa/go.asp?MFAH0ldfe0, visited October 30, 2002.

[13] Statements by Prime Minister Ariel Sharon and Defense Minister Binyamin Ben-Eliezer at Press conference following Cabinet Meeting, March 29, 2002, available at www.mfa.gov.il/mfa/go.asp?MFAH0ldy0, visited October 30, 2002.

[14] Ibid. The operation was officially concluded on April 21, 2002, although Arafat di not emerge from his besieged compound until May 13. See Cabinet Communiqué, April 21, 2002, available at www.mfa.gov.il/mfa/go.asp?MFAH0ll80, visited October 30, 2002 and Graham Usher 'Ashes to Ashes' 675 *Middle East International* (2002) 6. According to Human Rights Watch, March 2002 was the bloodiest month to date, i.e. October 2002, Human Rights Watch *Erased in a Moment: Suicide Bombing Attacks against Israeli Civilians*, October 2002, 13 and 29.

PLO in 1995.[15] Following the conclusion of Operation Defensive Shield, Israeli forces have made several subsequent incursions into Palestinian areas.[16] Defensive Shield, however, stands out at the time of writing as the most sustained and comprehensive operation.

The UN Security Council debated the Israeli operation on March 30. The Israeli representative stated that in the given circumstances, 'Israel is compelled to take the measures Chairman Arafat and the Palestinian leadership has steadfastly refused to take. We will exercise our basic right of self-defence and target the vast terrorist infrastructure that the Palestinian Authority continues to nurture and sustain in its territory. ... We have no intention of occupying any territory under Palestinian control. Our intention is to uproot the terrorist network that exists there'.[17] While all the speakers condemned terrorism in general and suicide bombings in particular, many also rebuffed Israel's arguments. Furthermore, most speakers expressed concern over Israel's use of excessive force. France found the Israeli action 'unacceptable' and 'leading to a disastrous cycle of violence'.[18] While condemning 'suicidal acts against Israeli civilians', China found 'the massive military offensives by Israel' 'still more alarming' and condemned 'the barbaric aggression of Israel against Palestine'.[19] Norway strongly objected to the military operations.[20] Spain, speaking for the European Union recognized Israel's legitimate fight against terrorism but found that this fight had to leave in place an effective Palestinian Authority and called for an 'immediate withdrawal' of Israeli forces from Ramallah.[21] The United States expressed most understanding for the fact 'that Israel has a right to self-defence', but called on 'Prime Minister Sharon and his Government to carefully consider the consequences of their actions'.[22] In its closing comment, Israel rejected calls for Israeli withdrawal 'without an equivalent appeal to the Palestinian side to put an end to the suicide attacks and destroy the terrorist infrastructure'.[23] Such a one-sided appeal misrepresented 'the

---

[15] Ramallah was occupied on March 29; Tulkarem and Qalqilya on April 1; Bethlehem on April 2 and Jenin and Nablus on April 3.

[16] On June 20, 2002, for example, Israel initiated what was termed Operation Determined Path, which again witnessed extensive incursions into Palestinian territory. See also, for example, Security Council Resolution 1435, which was a reaction to the Israeli Operation Matter of Time, mounted on September 19. The resolution, among other things, called for 'the expeditious withdrawal of the Israeli occupying forces from Palestinian cities', S/RES/1435 (2002), September 24, 2002, see S/PV.4614, September 23, 2002.

[17] S/PV.4503, March 29, 2002, 6.

[18] S/PV.4503, March 29, 2002, 9.

[19] S/PV.4503, March 29, 2002, 16.

[20] S/PV.4503, March 29, 2002, 19.

[21] S/PV.4503, March 29, 2002, 24.

[22] S/PV.4503, March 29, 2002, 12.

[23] S/PV.4503, March 29, 2002, 35.

Israeli operation, which is one of legitimate self-defence'.[24] At the end of the deliberations, the Council adopted Resolution 1402 which called for a ceasefire, withdrawal of Israeli troops from Palestinian cities, a return to the Tenet work plan and a cessation of violence, including all acts of terror.[25]

Subsequently, the Council met separately in closed sessions with the representative of Israel and the permanent observer of Palestine.[26] The Council met again on April 4. At the meeting, members again condemned terrorism. Israel reiterated its claim to self-defence.[27] South Africa, on behalf of the Non-Aligned Movement expressed its distress over the fact that 'the Israeli Government [had] chosen to respond to the symptoms of its own military occupation by using disproportionate lethal force'.[28] Cuba, moreover, found that 'oppression and the illegal occupation of territories are justified under the right of self-defence'.[29] While Canada recognized Israel's right of self-defence against terrorist acts, it found that the Israeli inclusions fed the spiral of violence.[30] The United Kingdom and France called for a quick withdrawal of Israeli forces.[31] Similarly, Norway called for an immediate halt to the Israeli campaign.[32] At the close of the meeting, the Secretary General of the UN took the floor. He lamented Israeli actions since the adoption of Resolution 1402: 'Israel has justified its acts as self-defence and counter-terrorism measures. However, we need to be very clear that self-defence is not a blank cheque. It is important to understand that responding to terrorism does not in any way free Israel from its obligations under international law'.[33] Resolution 1403 demanded the implementation of Resolution 1402 without delay.[34] Subsequently, on

---

[24] Ibid.

[25] Security Council Resolution 1402, March 30, 2002, S/RES/1402 (2002).

[26] S/PV.4504 and S/PV.4505, April 2, 2002.

[27] S/PV.4506, April 4, 2002, 4.

[28] S/PV.4506, April 4, 2002, 16.

[29] S/PV.4506, April 4, 2002, resumption, 2.

[30] S/PV.4506, April 4, 2002, resumption, 24.

[31] S/PV.4506, April 4, 2002, resumption, 29 and 33.

[32] S/PV.4506, April 4, 2002, resumption, 32.

[33] S/PV.4506, April 4, 2002, resumption 2, 4-5.

[34] Security Council Resolution 1403, April 4, 2002, S/RES/1403 (2002). On April 6, the US President and the British Prime Minister stated: 'We agree that the Palestinian leadership must order an immediate and effective cease-fire and crackdown on terrorist networks. And we agree that Israel should halt incursions in the Palestinian controlled areas and begin to withdraw without delay from those cities it has recently occupied', Remarks by President Bush and Prime Minister Tony Blair in Joint Press Availability, Crawford High School, Crawford, Texas, Available at http://www.whitehouse.gov/news/releases/2002/04/20020406-2.html, visited October 30, 2002. The persistent but unheeded American calls for a withdrawal 'without delay' caused some rather comic exchanges:
Q Ari, much as I'm reluctant to belabor this issue, the President did say to a key American ally, withdraw without delay. And the Israelis, although they have withdrawn from some areas, have

205

April 10, the Quartet, i.e. the United Nations Secretary General, Russia, the United States and the European Union, called for an immediate halt to Israeli military operations, an immediate, meaningful ceasefire and an immediate Israeli withdrawal from Palestinian cities.[35]

Israel claimed to be acting in self-defence in response to a continuing attack by suicide bombers: 'This is a right that any State would exercise under the conditions that we have been facing, and in fact, several States have already done so'.[36] In addition, Israel continues to claim that the Palestinian Authority is failing its responsibility by not acting against the suicide bombers and the people sending them. Hence, in legal terms, Israel is claiming to be subjected to an armed attack in the form of a continuous stream of suicide bombers.[37] Again, starting from the traditional point of departure, the state attacked in self-defence must be responsible for the initial armed attack. Since the Israeli Government has consistently maintained that it holds the Palestinian Authority responsible and has in practice directed its attacks against Authority institutions, most notable by besieging the late Yasser Arafat, it again becomes necessary to inquire how this responsibility originated: what is the relationship between those who perpetrate terrorist acts and the PA?

---

redeployed in others. My question to you is, is withdrawal, the word you have used, is that an accurate description of the sum total of what Israel's doing if they're still in major cities and towns?

MR. FLEISCHER: Israel is continuing its withdrawal, as the President asked. The Palestinian Authority has responsibilities they have not yet taken. Arab nations in the region have responsibilities that the President has called for which he is still looking for results.

So again, I remind you, it is not only one nation; it is all of them and that's the President's focus.

Q But you said that the Israelis are heeding what the President called for. He said, withdraw without delay -- and you're satisfied that's what they're doing?

MR. FLEISCHER: I simply said that the withdrawal the President called for is continuing. I did not put a value on it one way or another beyond that. I think it's an accurate statement.

Q How can you call it a withdrawal? How can you call it a withdrawal? They've pulled out of a few small towns and they haven't pulled all the way out of any town. How the hell is it a withdrawal?

MR. FLEISCHER: With all due respect for your editorial, how can you not? It is a withdrawal from those towns. Press Briefing by Ari Fleischer, April 11, 2002, available at http://www.whitehouse.gov/news/releases/2002/04/20020411-1.html, visited October 30, 2002.

Subsequently, the American President accepted the Israeli re-occupation, see Press Conference by the President July 7, 2002, available at www.whitehouse.gov/news/releases/2002/07/20020708-5.html, visited October 3, 2002. See also David E. Sanger 'Citing Israel's Need for Security, Bush Accepts Occupation' *The New York Times* July 9, 2002.

[35] Joint Statement, April 10, 2002, Annex to document S/2002/369, April 10, 2002.

[36] S/PV.4506, April 3, 2002, 4.

[37] Human Rights Watch has documented that 'the frequency and intensity of suicide bomb attacks on civilians soon [following the first suicide attack during the recent uprising, taking place on January 1, 2001] increased, and the tactic has been embraced by large sections of the Palestinian public, making these attacks a key feature of the current Palestinian-Israeli clashes', Human Rights Watch *Erased in a Moment: Suicide Bombing Attacks against Israeli Civilians*, October 2002, 12.

8.II.A. The Relationship Between the PA and the Terrorists

Human Rights Watch issued an extensive report in October 2002 dealing with various aspects of suicide bombings.[38] One of the main objectives of the report was to investigate if and to what extent Palestinian political leaders incured command responsibility under international criminal law for the acts of suicide bombers. In this context, the report sets out the relationship between several Palestinian armed groups and the PA leadership. In the present context it may be objected that different criteria govern possible individual criminal responsibility and 'state' responsibility (in this case of the Palestinian Authority).[39] However, it is merely the factual relationship between the PA and the various groups as documented in the report that will be applied in this analysis.

The Human Rights Watch report documents suicide attacks by four different Palestinian groups: Hamas, Islamic Jihad, the Popular Front for the Liberation of Palestine (PFLP), and the al-Aqsa Martyr's Brigades.[40] Whereas the three former groups can be described as being in opposition to the PA, the latter is associated with the Fatah movement which is the largest faction in the PLO and also the main source of power in the PA.[41] It is, therefore, most useful to examine the relationship between the PA and the al-Aqsa Martyr's Brigades first.[42]

Were the al-Aqsa Martyr's Brigades' suicide bombers sent by the PA? The HRW report found that no high degree of organizational coherence exists between the al-Aqsa Martyr's Brigades and Fatah and, while not disavowing or disowning the Brigades and their actions,[43] no superior-subordinate relationship existed.[44] The report concluded that

---

[38] Human Rights Watch *Erased in a Moment: Suicide Bombing Attacks against Israeli Civilians*, October 2002. See also the earlier report by Amnesty International 'Israel and the Occupied Territories and the Palestinian Authority: Without Distinction: Attacks on Civilians by Palestinian Armed Groups', July 2002, MDE 02/003/2002.

[39] Prosecutor v. Tadic, Judgment of the Appeals Chamber, July 15, 1999, 41, paragraph 103.

[40] Human Rights Watch *Erased in a Moment: Suicide Bombing Attacks against Israeli Civilians*, October 2002, 62.

[41] Human Rights Watch describes the al-Aqsa Martyr's Brigades as being 'linked to the ruling faction in the Palestinian Authority', Human Rights Watch *Erased in a Moment: Suicide Bombing Attacks against Israeli Civilians*, October 2002, 77.

[42] For the present purposes, Fatah and the Palestinian Authority are treated as identical structures, although this is not formally the case.

[43] See, however, the disassociation following attack on Likud election station in the town of Beit Shean, during Likud primary elections in November 2002, Arnon Regular 'PA says it has no connection with Al Aqsa Martyrs Brigades' *Haaretz* November 28, 2002.

[44] Human Rights Watch *Erased in a Moment: Suicide Bombing Attacks against Israeli Civilians*, October 2002, 62 and 78. The report finds that the al-Aqsa Martyr's Brigades have 'a loose personality driven local command structure with autonomy and improvisation' (p. 63), finds no evidence of chain of military command (p. 82) and no control by the political leadership (p. 84). By contrast, the Israeli security service, Shin Bet, that it was only with the arrest of Mustafa Barghouti during Operations

---

there is no evidence that Arafat or other senior PA officials 'ordered, planned, or carried out such [suicide] attacks'.[45] Similarly, based on the HRW report, it does not seem reasonable to characterize the al-Aqsa Martyr's Brigades as *de facto* agents of the PA. One may, however, inquire as to whether agents of the PA participated in terrorist acts: a state may be responsible for the conduct of persons empowered to exercise governmental authority, even if that person contravenes instructions.[46] According to HRW findings, the PA had a policy against the participation of security forces in armed confrontations with Israeli forces. This policy led to a number of resignations from the PA.[47] Nonetheless, HRW documents that at least a small number of low-level employees of the PA organized or carried out suicide attacks.[48] The evidence in this regard, however, seems too sketchy to be able to attribute suicide attacks to the PA.

It remains to be investigated whether the PA may have, *post facto*, adopted the suicide attacks as their own.[49] HRW establishes that Yassir Arafat routinely condemned suicide bombings against civilians.[50] However, the report notes that seeming public justification of the bombings came from persons close to Arafat.[51] More serious, however, has been the consistent failure of the PA either to stop the suicide attacks or to prosecute the people responsible. This, HRW concludes, has contributed to 'an atmosphere of impunity'.[52] As noted by the UN Secretary-General, 'the Palestinian

---

Defensive Shield, that contacts between the central authority and local groups weakened, see Amos Harel 'Shin Bet: Fatah 'Splinter' cell responsible for attack' *Haaretz*, November 12, 2002.

[45] Human Rights Watch *Erased in a Moment: Suicide Bombing Attacks against Israeli Civilians*, October 2002, 140. It may not be surprising that Israel draws a different conclusion. The Israeli Defense Forces concludes that 'Arafat is personally directing and funding terror' and that 'there is identity between the Fatah infrastructure and the Tanzim and Al-Aqsa Brigades infrastructure. They are all controlled and financed by Arafat and his associates', 'Documents Captured by the IDF Indicating Arafat's Support and Funding of the Fatah/Tanzim Infrastructure Perpetrating Terrorist Attacks from the Tulkarm Area in Accordance with PA Policy', available at www.idf.il/arafat/english/index1.stm, visited July 5, 2002.

[46] The International Law Commission's Articles on State Responsibility, Article 7.

[47] Human Rights Watch *Erased in a Moment: Suicide Bombing Attacks against Israeli Civilians*, October 2002, 135.

[48] Human Rights Watch *Erased in a Moment: Suicide Bombing Attacks against Israeli Civilians*, October 2002, 135. Similarly, the US Department of State found 'strong evidence that some members of the PA security forces were allowed to continue serving even though their participation in terrorist incidents was well known', see Nathan Guttman 'State Dept. report questions PA's recognition of Israel', *Haaretz* December 12, 2002.

[49] The International Law Commission's Articles on State Responsibility, Article 11.

[50] Human Rights Watch *Erased in a Moment: Suicide Bombing Attacks against Israeli Civilians*, October 2002, 32.

[51] Id, 32 and 35-37. Without pursuing an argument in this regard, one may question the difference between explaining why suicide attacks take place in the Palestinian-Israeli context and justifying such attacks, Ibid. 28.

[52] Human Rights Watch *Erased in a Moment: Suicide Bombing Attacks against Israeli Civilians*, October 2002, 110.

Authority seems to believe that failing to act against terrorism and inducing turmoil, chaos and instability will cause the Government and people of Israel to buckle'.[53] In an international criminal law context, HRW found that the lack of prosecution cannot entail command responsibility.[54] Yet, to the extent that the PA had the ability to prosecute terrorist suspects, which it arguably did have during the first year of the uprising (September 2000-September 2001), it does not require a leap of faith to assert that the inactivity of the PA in this regard amounted to endorsement.[55]

Still, having examined the traditional modes of attributing an armed attack to a state entity, it is difficult to unequivocally attribute suicide attacks – and, by extension, other acts of terrorism – to the PA. However, as has been pointed out, the PA tolerated the presence of alleged terrorists in territory under its control and has, moreover, provided some financial support to individuals and groups engaging in terrorism in addition to failing to halt substantial financial assistance to such groups from other Arab states and non-governmental groups. HRW concludes that Arafat and other senior Fatah officials did provide financial assistance to people involved in planning and carrying out armed attacks that included attacks on civilians (other than suicide bombings).[56]

If one takes the reaction of the UN Secretary-General as a reasonable indication of international reaction, one might conclude that there was an understanding for an Israeli need to react to the onslaught of terrorist attacks. Consequently, the Secretary-General can reasonably be read as implicitly acknowledging that Israel could invoke the right of self-defence. Although the PA might not have been as supportive towards the Palestinian terrorists as the Taliban were towards al-Qaeda, it might be argued that the two situations were analogous and that the international community, thus, accepted the use of force in self-defence against a state-entity that harbors and supports terrorists. On the other hand, the Palestinian case does not indicate a further lowering of the threshold compared with what was found in the examination of the US attack on Afghanistan. In other words, the reaction to Operation Defensive Shield merely confirms the already found lower threshold compared to the traditional formula. In addition, and similar to what was found in the Afghan case, the Palestinian authority had, on numerous

---

[53] S/PV.4506, resumption 2, April 3, 2002, 5.
[54] Human Rights Watch *Erased in a Moment: Suicide Bombing Attacks against Israeli Civilians*, October 2002, 140.
[55] To the lack of prosecution, one may add the use of honorific terms such as *shaheed* (martyr) for persons killed while carrying out suicide bombings, praise in the Palestinian media and the fact that families of suicide bombers receive governmental monetary support equivalent to that of persons killed in clashes with Israeli troops. With regard to the latter, HRW finds that 'even payments that do not privilege the families of suicide bombers should not be made to such families in any manner that confers social honor', Human Rights Watch *Erased in a Moment: Suicide Bombing Attacks against Israeli Civilians*, October 2002, 106.
[56] Human Rights Watch *Erased in a Moment: Suicide Bombing Attacks against Israeli Civilians*, October 2002, 132.

occasions been warned and made aware of its obligations to prevent terrorists acts and to investigate and prosecute terrorists.[57] To mention but one example, the EU in December of 2001 declared that what was required by the Palestinian Authority was 'the dismantling of Hamas' and Islamic Jihad's terrorist networks, including the arrest and prosecution of all suspects'.[58]

The following additional case study may help to further cement the current level of required state involvement. This example originates in the margins of the Russian-Chechen conflict.

8.III. The Russian Action Against Georgia During the Summer of 2002

It is not the intention here to deal with the Chechen conflict in detail.[59] From a formal point of view, Chechnya is part of the Russian Federation and the fighting taking place there is thus not *a fortiori* an international armed conflict although Waldock noted already in 1952 that 'resort to force internally by a State ... may become a matter of international concern when seceding elements form themselves into a new State'.[60] Indeed, the conflict in and over Chechnya has, on occasion, spilled over into the neighboring states, recently, in particular, into the Republic of Georgia. An examination of the incidents taking place in the summer of 2002 and international reaction may serve as a guide to how the law dealing with the use of force against terrorists is developing.

Although relations between Russia and Georgia became very strained in the summer of 2002, tension has, for a number of reasons, existed for some years and clashes along the border between Georgia and Russia had taken place in 2001.[61] The most recent tension was caused by Russian frustration with what Russia saw as Georgian lack of action against separatist Chechens who allegedly had sough refuge in

---

[57] In general, and particularly during the period from spring 1996 until the summer of 2000, the PA made some effort at halting terrorists attacks, although Watson, considering the situation before the outbreak of violence in late summer of 2000, concluded that 'in sum, the Palestinian Authority has a disappointing record on its obligation to prevent and punish terror and other forms of violence', Geoffrey R. Watson *The Oslo Accords: International Law and the Israeli-Palestinian Peace Agreements* Oxford University Press (2000) 236. However, following the outbreak of the second Palestinian uprising in September of 2000, any Palestinian effort has waned substantially.

[58] Declaration by the European Council on the Situation in the Middle East, December 15, 2001, 15474/01 (Presse 487), P.193/01.

[59] For a Russian view, see Yuri V. Ushakov 'Humanitarian and Legal Aspects of the Crisis in Chechnya' 23 *Fordham International Law Journal* (2000) 1155-1168.

[60] C. H. M. Waldock 'The Regulation of the Use of Force by Individual States in International Law' 81 RC (1952) 542-517 at 492.

[61] See, for example, 'Russia and Georgia: Smiles all round – till the next time' *The Economist*, October 12th, 2002, 46 and 'Is Georgia Ready for the U.N.?', *Time Magazine*, September 13, 2002, available at www.time.com/time/europe/eu/printout/0,9869,338996,00.html, visited September 13, 2002.

the Pankisi Gorge in Eastern Georgia.[62] On July 31, 2002, Russia sent a letter to the Secretary General of the UN concerning the 'attempts by international terrorists to effect an armed breakthrough' into Russia from Georgia and asking the Secretary General to circulate the letter in the General Assembly under the agenda 'Measures to eliminate international terrorism'.[63] In the letter, the Russian Federation stressed that 'the responsibility for the consequences of the armed incursion by bandits … lies fully with the Georgian side'.[64]

Georgia has regularly complained that Russian aircraft have violated Georgian airspace. On August 12, after alleged violations of Georgian airspace by Russian aircraft, the EU issued a CFSP statement calling for 'all parties to exercise restraint and to respect their international obligations, including territorial integrity of all countries in the region'.[65] On August 23, monitors from the Organization for Security and Co-operation in Europe confirmed that Russian planes had conducted at least one bombing raid inside Georgia.[66] Russia, however, denied that any attack had taken place.[67] The Georgian president, Eduard Shevardnadze denounced the raids as 'aggressive acts' that were 'absolutely inadmissible'.[68] The White House spokesman said that the United States 'deplores the violation of Georgia's sovereignty'.[69] The US has consistently

---

[62] 'As is known, in the Pankisi Gorge of Georgia there have amassed, in particular by Georgian authorities' estimates, a considerable number of armed Chechen militants and international terrorists who are making continuous sallies from Georgian territory into the territory of the Russian Federation, creating a direct threat to its security', Statement by Russia's Ministry of Foreign Affairs Concerning the New Exacerbation of the Situation on the Russian-Georgian Border, 1659-24-08-2002, August 26, 2002. Available at www.mid.ru, visited August 28, 2002. See also Patrick E. Tyler 'In Caucasus Gorge, a Haven for Muslim Militants' *The New York Times* February 28, 2002.

[63] A/57/269 and S/20002/854.

[64] A/57/269 and S/20002/854, Annex.

[65] Declaration by the Presidency on behalf of the European Union on recent violations of Georgian airspace, August 12, 2002, www.eu2002.dk/news/news_read.asp?Information ID=21513 (visited August 25, 2002). The Central and Eastern European countries associated with the European Union, the associated countries Cyprus, Malta and Turkey, and the EFTA countries Liechtenstein and Norway, members of the European Economic Area align themselves with this declaration.

[66] 'OSCE Chairmanship deeply disturbed over Georgian bombing reports', Press Release, August 23, 2002, available at www.osce.org/news/generate.pf.php3?news_id=2665, visited August 25, 2002.

[67] See for example Interfax 'Russian military insistently denies bombing Georgian territory', August 25, 2002, at www.themoscowtimes.com/doc/HotNews.html#24338. See also Press Release 1665-27-08-2002, August 28, 2002 in which a spokesman for Russia's Ministry of Foreign Affairs announced that Russia possessed 'materials of objective control which attest that there were no violations of the air border with Georgia by Russia'.

[68] Steven Lee Myers 'Georgia Moves Agiants Rebels and Accuses Russia of Airstrikes' *New York Times* August 24, 2002.

[69] 'The United States regrets this loss of life and deplores the violation of Georgia's sovereignty. The United States strongly supports Georgia's independence and territorial integrity …', http://www.whitehouse.gov/news/releases/2002/08/20020824-2.html, August 24, 2002.

stressed that it saw the issue as one for Georgia to deal with, possibly in co-operation with Russia.[70] The US Secretary of Defense stated that 'it's important that Georgia's sovereignty be respected. We do not favor bombing in that area'.[71] The Organization for Security and Co-operation in Europe (OSCE) Chairmanship declared that it was 'deeply disturbed' by reports of Russian bombings.[72] On August 29, 2002, the EU expressed its serious concern and called for the respect of the territorial integrity of all states in the region[73] and on September 5, while expressing its expectation that Georgia make further efforts to restore order in the Pankisi Valley, the EU reaffirmed its support for Georgia's sovereignty and territorial integrity.[74]

Following the bombing on August 23, Georgia sent troops into the Pankisi Gorge.[75] Russia, however, kept complaining about the Georgian efforts[76] culminating with several statements by the Russian President Putin, [77] including a letter to the

---

Reuters 'Russia Mulls Response to U.S. Rebuke over Georgia' August 25, 2002 available at www.nytimes.com/reuters/international/international-russia-usa.html, visited August 25 2002.

[70] US Department of State, Daily Press Briefing, Richard Boucher, Spokesman, August 27, 2002, available at www.state.gov/r/pa/prs/dpb/2002/13102.htm, visited August 28, 2002. See also US Department of State, Daily Press Briefing, Richard Boucher, Spokesman, September 24, 2002, available at www.state.gov/r/pa/prs/dpb/2002/13645.htm, visited September 28, 2002.

[71] Secretary Rumsfeld's Press Conference in Warsaw, September 25, 2002.

[72] OSCE, Press Release, Chairman-in-Office 'OSCE Chairmanship deeply disturbed over Georgian bombing reports' August 23, 2002, available at www.osce.org/news/generate.pf.php3?news_id=2665, visited August 25, 2002.

[73] Declaration by the Presidency on behalf of the European Union on the violations of Georgian Airspace', August 29, 2002, available at www.eu2002.dk/news/news_read.asp?ilnformationID=21779&, visited August 30, 2002.

[74] 'OSCE Permanent Council: EU Statement in Response to Ambassador Lacombe, Head of the OSCE Mission in Georgia', www.eu2002.dk/news/news_read.asp?informationID=22014&, visited September 17, 2002.

[75] Steven Lee Myres 'Georgia Moves Against Rebels and Accuses Russia of Airstrikes' *The New York Times*, August 24, 2002, available at www.nytimes.com/2002/08/24/international/europe, visited August 25, 2002.

[76] See 'On President of the Russian Federation Vladimir Putin's Message to President Eduard Shevardnadze of Georgia on Topical Issues in Russian-Georgian Relations, 2002-09-05-001, September 5, 2002, available at www.mid.ru, visited September 5, 2002.

[77] See 'Appeal of President Putin of the Russian Federation to the UN Secretary General, the Leaders of States – Permanent Members of the UN Security Council and OSCE Heads of State and Government', 12-09-2002, September 12, 2002, available at www.mid.ru, visited September 12, 2002. In the appeal, Putin stated that 'the problem [of terrorism in Chechnya] is not confined to the territory of Chechnya. The success of the anti-terrorist operation has forced remnants of the militants to make a base for themselves on Georgian territory, where, with the connivance of the Georgian authorities, they feel free and comfortable and continue to enjoy outside military, financial and other support. ... In this connection [the 'grievous' failure of Tbilisi to comply with UN Resolution 1373], Russia may have to avail itself of the right granted under UN Security Council Resolution 1368 ... the right to individual and collective self-defense under the UN Charter. And I would like to especially stress that we are not talking about actions aimed at undermining the sovereignty and territorial integrity of a country or a change of political regime. What we are talking about is that if the Georgian leadership does not take

United Nations. In the letter, coinciding with the first anniversary of the September 11 attacks, President Putin describes how terrorist enclaves continue to exist outside the control of national governments due to inability or unwillingness to counteract the terrorist threat.[78] He then turns to alleged presence in Georgian territory 'of hundreds of terrorists and illegal armed units'. Putin then states that if the Georgian leadership is unable to control these elements, Russia 'reserves the right to act in accordance with Article 51', including special operations designed to eliminate bandit units and carrying out strikes against reliably identified terrorist bases. Georgia reacted angrily, and fearfully, denouncing the 'undisguised threat of force', pointing out the 'unaptness of the reference to article 51'.[79]

The crisis of the summer of 2002 came to an end with the meeting between the two president on October 6 at which they agreed to the extradition of certain Chechens from Georgia to Russia and closer co-operation, including joint patrols.[80] That having been said, Russia has continued to employ quite strong rhetoric against neighboring states when it comes to issues related to Chechnya. In the autumn of 2002, Russia requested that Denmark arrest and extradite the Chechen leader Ahmed Sakajev on terrorism related charges. When, after the initial arrest, Denmark released Sakajev, Russia spoke of how Denmark, with the 'obvious connivance of authorities' is becoming a 'strong point for Chechen terrorists and their accomplices'.[81]

---

concrete actions to destroy the terrorists and bandit sorties continue from its territory, Russia, acting strictly under international law, will take adequate measures to oppose to terrorist threat'. See also 'The Statement of the State Duma of the Federal Assembly of Russia "Concerning the State of Russian-Georgian Relations"', September 16, 2002. See furthermore Steven Lee Myres 'Echoing Bush, Putin Asks U.N. to Back Georgia Attack' *The New York Times*, September 13, 2002, available at www.nytimes.com/2002/09/13/international/europe/13RUSS.html, visited September 13, 2002 and 'Putin Warns of 'Self-Defence' Strikes' *BBC News*, September 11, 2002, available at http://news.bbc.co.uk/1/hi/world/Europe/2252056.stm, visited September 12, 2002.

[78] also 'Statement by President Putin of the Russian Federation', September 11, 2002 S/2002/1012, September 12, 2002.

[79] See letter from the Georgian President Shevardnadze, S/2002/1033, September 14, 2002. See also statement by the Georgian Foreign Minister, S/2002/1035, September 16, 2002.

[80] 'Georgians to Extradite 5 Chechen Fighter' *The New York Times* October 5, 2002 available at www.nytimes.com/2002/10/05/international/europe/05REBE.html, visited October 6, 2002. Interestingly, some of the persons slated for extradition complained to the European Court of Human Rights, which, in turn, indicated to Georgia that it was 'desirable' not to extradite the Chechens until the Court had examined their complaint. Press Release issued by the Registrar at the European Court of Human Rights, 486, October 10, 2002, www.echr.coe.int/Eng/Press/2002/oct/ChechensvGeorgia&Russia.htm, visited October 11, 2002. See also Russia's reaction expressing bewilderment: 'Press release Conerning Recommendation of the European Court of Human Rights that Georgian Authorities Not Extradite to Russian Justice the Persons Detained in Georgia in Connection with Their Involvement in Terrorist Bands', 2027-08-10-2002, October 9, 2002, available at www.mid.ru, visited October 11, 2002.

[81] Press Release 'On Denmark's Policy of "Double Standards" in the Antiterrorist Sphere', Ministry of Foreign Affirs of the Russian Federation, 2517-06-12-2002, December 6, 2002.

Initially, one may ask why the incident just sketched out has been included. The justification is that both the acting claimant, i.e. Russia and the responders, i.e. the US, the EU and the OSCE all seem to accept the likelihood of terrorist elements being present in the Pankisi Gorge. Hence, when reacting to Russian statements and acts, they react on the basis of a possible presence of terrorists within Georgian territory. Based on the somewhat cursory review of the case, it may be suggested that the Georgian example provides the following conclusion: Although Russia denied having bombed Georgian territory, it appears established that at least one, and possibly more, bombings in fact took place. If Russia had acknowledged the bombing, it would presumably have argued self-defence under Article 51 as indicated by subsequent communications to the UN. Other states, reacting to the bombing, however, did not accept its legality and stressed the importance of respecting the territorial integrity of Georgia. In other words, the presence of the alleged terrorists on Georgian territory, an allegation not dismissed by Western states, was not seen as justifying Russian armed action against Georgia.

To apply this case in our survey, one must again inquire as to the relationship between the possible terrorists and the Georgian authorities. At one end, Russia has claimed that the terrorists are present in the Pankisi Gorge with the connivance of the Georgian authorities. Even from the Russian side, however, no accusations have been put forward about potential Georgian support for the terrorists. Thus, at most it is a situation of tolerance and unwillingness on the part of the Georgian authorities to take action against the alleged terrorists.

At the other end, it might be argued that the Georgian authorities were unable to confront the alleged terrorists in the Pankisi Gorge. This view might be supported by the fact that the autumn 2002 offensive, which the Georgians launched into Pankisi Gorge, followed US training of Georgian troops. In recognition of the threat terrorism posed to Georgia, 20 US service personnel arrived in the Georgian capital Tbilisi in April 2002 to launch the Georgia Train and Equip program. Altogether, 150 Americans have been involved.[82] The program was aimed at training more than 2000 Georgian soldiers help Georgia solve 'Georgian internal problems', according to the Georgian Defense Minister Davis Tevzadze.[83]

Hence, the Georgian example straddles categories 2 – inability – and 3 – unwillingness. In conclusion, indications are that the Georgian authorities were more unable than unwilling to confront the alleged terrorists in Pankisi Gorge. In any case, the conclusion to be drawn from the example is that an allegedly aggrieved state is not justified in using force against terrorists in a state where they are present but that it is unable to contain and detain them.

---

[82] See Linda D. Kozaryn: 'Republic of Georgia: Global Partner in Anti-Terror War' *American Forces Information Service, News Articles*, May 15, 2002, available at www.defenselink.mil/news/May2002/n05152002_200205152.html, visited August 24, 2002.
[83] Ibid.

8.IV. The 2003 Israeli Air Strike on Syria

On October 4, 2003, a female suicide bomber blew herself up in a restaurant in the Israeli city of Haifa.[84] At least 19 people were killed and more than 60 wounded. The Palestinian group 'Islamic Jihad' claimed responsibility for the attack.[85] On October 5, 2003,[86] the Israeli Air Force (IAF) carried out an air attack in Syrian territory against, according to the IDF (Israeli Defense Forces) spokesman, a 'training base used by terrorist organizations, including the Islamic Jihad'.[87] A subsequent Cabinet Communiqué stated that 'Israel attacked Syria because the latter not only sponsors Lebanese terrorist groups such as Hizbollah but provides active support, financing and assistance to centers of terrorism in Judea and Samaria [i.e. the West Bank] and Gaza'.[88] International reaction was mixed: China[89] and the Organization of the Islamic Conference[90] condemned the attack, the UN Secretary-General deplored the air strike,[91] while the EU was more cautious.[92] Russia limited itself to urging all parties to exert maximum restraint.[93]

---

[84] Davis Ratner *et al* '19 dead, 60 wounded in Haifa restaurant bombing', *Haaretz*, October 5, 2003.

[85] Ibid.

[86] See also Christine Gray *International Law and the Use of Force* 2nd ed. Oxford University Press 2004, 172-175.

[87] 'IDF Action in Syria', Communicated by the IDF Spokesman, available at www.mfa.gov.il/mfa/go.asp?MFAH0nug0, visited on October 9, 2003. The statement went on the assert that 'the Islamic jihad, like other terrorist organizations operating in the West Bank and Gaza Strip, enjoys support and backing of countries in the region, foremost among them Iran and Syria. Syria is a country, which sponsors terrorism and systematically tries to undermine any attempt at peace and stability in the region. Syria gives cover to terrorist organizations within the country, including in Damascus, while Iran provides funding and direction'. See also John Ward Anderson: 'Israeli Airstrike Hits Site in Syria' *The Washington Post*, October 6, 2003 and Greg Myre 'Israel Attacks What It Calls a Terrorist Camp in Syria' *The New York Times* October 6, 2003.

[88] Cabinet Communiqué, October 8, 2003, available at www.mfa.gov.il/mfa/gg.asp?MFAH0nv70, visited October 10, 2003.

[89] 'China is shocked at the Israeli military attack on the targets within Syria's territory and strongly condemns it', Spokesperson's Remarks on Israel's assault on a training camp of Palestinian Islamic Jihad near Damascus of Syria, October 6, 2003, available at www.fmprc.cn/eng/xwfw/2510/t26782.htm, visited October 9, 2003.

[90] Press Release: 'Organization of the Islamic Conference Condemns Israeli Aggression on Syria', October 5, 2003, available at www.oic-oci.org/press/english/, visited October 20, 2003.

[91] Statement attributable to the Spokesman for the Secretary-General on Israeli air strike on Syrian territory, available at www.un.org/apps/sg/sgstats.asp?nid=543, visited October 20, 2003.

[92] 'Javier Solana, EU High Representative for CFSP, calls for respect of international law, after Israel's operation in Syria', Brussels, 6 October 2003, SO194/03, available at www.europa.eu.int, visited October 8, 2003.

[93] 'Regarding Israel's Missile-Bomb Strike at a Target on Syrian Territory Near Damascus', Statement by Alexander Yakovenko, the official spokesman of Russia's Ministry of Foreign Affairs, 2207-05-10-2003, October 5, 2003, available at www.in.mid.ru, visited October 6, 2003.

Following the attack, Syria requested a meeting of the Security Council.[94] In the letter, Syria advised the Secretary-General 'that the Israeli air force, on the morning of Sunday, 5 October, violated the Lebanese and Syrian airspaces and committed an act of aggression by launching guided missiles inside the territory of the Syrian Arab Republic. The target was a civilian site in the village of Ein Saheb, north-west of the capital, Damascus. That act of aggression caused physical damage'.[95]

The Israeli representative started out by describing the attack on the restaurant in Haifa. He pointed out that Islamic Jihad 'has headquarters in Damascus, Syria'.[96] He then went on to outline Syria's involvement with terrorism more generally: 'The encouragement, safe harbour, training facilities, funding and logistical support offered by Syria to a variety of notorious terrorist organizations is a matter of public knowledge. … Safe harbour and training facilities are provided throughout Syria for terrorist organizations such as Islamic Jihad, Hamas and Hizbollah, both in separate facilities and in Syrian army bases. The Ein Saheb base, which was targeted in Israel's measured defensive operation today, is just one of those facilities sponsored by Syria and Iran. Recruits at camps such as Ein Saheb come from Islamic Jihad, Hamas and other terrorist groups. … Syria has itself facilitated and directed acts of terrorism by coordination and briefings via phone and Internet and by calling activists to Damascus for consultations and briefings. … Instructions are also given to halt terrorist activity when it suits Syrian or Iranian interests to avoid the spotlight, such as following the terrorist attacks of 11 September in the United States. … Syria uses its State-run media and official institutions to glorify and encourage suicide bombings against civilians in restaurants, schools, commuter buses and shopping malls. … Syrian complicity in and responsibility for suicide bombings are as blatant as they are repugnant'.[97] Finally, the Israeli representative declared that 'Israel's measured defensive response to the horrific suicide bombings against a terrorist training facility in Syria is a clear act of self-defence in accordance with Article 51 of the Charter. … it is designed to prevent further armed attacks against Israeli civilians in which Syria is complicit, with a view to encouraging Syria to resolve its dispute through bilateral negotiations in accordance with Security Council resolutions 242 (1967) and 338 (1973), as it is legally required to do'.[98]

---

[94] S/2003/939, October 5, 2003. Lebanon also called for a meeting of the Security Council due to the fact that Israeli planes violated Lebanese airspace en route to Syria, see S/2003/943 and S/PV.4836, October 5, 2003, 15-16. See in general Press Release SC/7887, October 5, 2003, available at www.un.org/News/Press/docs/2003/sc7887.doc.htm, visited October 6, 2003. See also 'Syria's decision to use diplomacy instead of retaliation is wise – UN envoy', available at www.un.org/apps/news/printnews.asp?nid=8505, visited October 10, 2003.
[95] See S/PV.4836, October 5, 2003, 3.
[96] See S/PV.4836, October 5, 2003, 5.
[97] See S/PV.4836, October 5, 2003, 5-6.
[98] See S/PV.4836, October 5, 2003, 7.

A number of speakers in the Council condemned Israel's strike: Pakistan,[99] Spain,[100] China,[101] Chile,[102] Mexico,[103] Angola,[104] and Guinea.[105] Similarly, and maybe expectedly, a number of Arab states, as well as the representative of the Arab League and the Permanent Observer of Palestine, all condemned the attack on Syria.[106] Cuba and Iran, too, condemned Israel.[107] Four European states, the United Kingdom, Germany, France and Bulgaria, described the Israeli attack as unacceptable.[108] Russia and Cameroon presented less direct remarks.[109]

The United States called 'on all sides to avoid heightening the tensions in the Middle East and to think carefully about the consequences of their actions'.[110] The U.S.

---

[99] 'The attack perpetrated by Israel against the territory of the Syrian Arab Republic on 5 October did not meet these strict requirements set out in the Charter with regard to the use of force. This was an arbitrary attack, and in legal and political terms it is clearly a violation of the Charter', S/PV.4836, October 5, 2003, 8.

[100] 'However, that [the suicide bombing] cannot cause us to overlook or minimize the extreme gravity of the attack perpetrated against Syria today. That attack is clearly a patent violation of international law', S/PV.4836, October 5, 2003, 9.

[101] 'We also condemn Israel's air attack against Syria. Israel's action is a violation of the norms of international law', S/PV.4836, October 5, 2003, 9.

[102] 'First of all, we condemn the Israeli air force bombing on Syrian territory, which is an outrage against international law and the principles and purposes of the United Nations Charter', S/PV.4836, October 5, 2003, 11.

[103] 'The reprisals taken by Israel in consequence of that attack are equally reprehensible. Israel gains nothing by such reprisals; they only contribute to the spiral of violence of which Israel and its citizens are the victims. The Israeli attack on Syrian territory was a clear violation of the United Nations Charter; it was a grave act that endangers international peace and security', S/PV.4836, October 5, 2003, 11.

[104] My delegation unequivocally condemns such acts [the suicide bombing and the Israeli strike]', S/PV.4836, October 5, 2003, 12.

[105] 'Nothing — absolutely, nothing — can justify such an act, which is contrary to all acceptable standards of international conduct, and whose sole purpose is to extend the strategy of chaos already imposed on the people of Palestine to all the neighbouring Arab Islamic states', S/PV.4836, October 5, 2003, 12.

[106] See S/PV.4836, October 5, 2003: The Arab League (14), Lebanon (15), Algeria (16), Morocco (17), Jordan (17), Egypt (18), Tunisia (19), Palestine (19), Kuwait (19), Saudi Arabia (20), Bahrain (22), Libya (23), Yemen (23), Qatar (24) and Sudan (24).

[107] S/PV.4836, October 5, 2003, 21.

[108] S/PV.4836, October 5, 2003, 9 (United Kingdom), 10 (Germany), 10 (France) and 11 (Bulgaria). The French representative stated that 'the Israeli operation today that targeted a site near Damascus is a grim business and an unacceptable violation of international law and the rules of sovereignty' (10).

[109] Russia: 'Russia urges all parties to the conflict to show maximum restraint and to act in a balanced and responsible way so as to avert any further escalation in the spiral of violence and to prevent regional destabilization, the tragic results of which would be difficult to foresee', S/PV.4836, October 5, 2003, 10; Cameroon: 'Similarly, Cameroon, which is resolutely committed to combating that scourge, is convinced that our common struggle must be undertaken with full respect for fundamental human rights and international law', S/PV.4836, October 5, 2003, 13.

[110] S/PV.4836, October 5, 2003, 13. See also Douglas Jehl 'U.S. Avoids Criticism of Raid, but Urges Caution on Israel' *The New York Times* October 6, 2003.

representative, however, went on to single out Syria for criticism: 'The United States believes that Syria is on the wrong side of the war on terrorism. We have been clear of the need for Syria to cease harbouring terrorist groups. Specific directions for terrorist acts continue to be issued from terrorist groups based in Syria. ... We believe that it is in Syria's interest and in the broader interests of Middle East peace for Syria to stop harbouring and supporting the groups that perpetrate terrorist acts such as the one that occurred in Haifa yesterday'.[111] Speaking on October 6, 2003, U.S. president George Bush declared that 'I made it very clear to the prime minister [of Israel], like I have consistently done, that Israel's got a right to defend herself, that Israel must not feel constrained in terms of defending the homeland'.[112] It is publication, *Patterns of Global Terrorism*, the US State Department wrote in 2003 that Syria 'continued to provide political and material support to Palestinian rejectionist groups'.[113]

Syria had presented a draft resolution that 'strongly condemns the military aggression carried out by Israel against the sovereignty and territory of the Syrian Arab Republic ... in violation of the Charter of the United Nations, the rules and principles of international law and relevant Security Council resolution'.[114] The Security Council, however, took no action.[115]

Subsequent to the attack, Israeli officials repeatedly warned Syria of a further attack if Syria kept 'aiding terrorists'.[116] The US, too, has continued to criticise Syria for supporting terrorist groups.[117] In September 2004, Sheikh Kahlil, an alleged leader in Hamas, was killed when his car exploded in Damascus.[118] Many saw the killing as a response to a double suicide bombing in the Israeli Beersheba on August 31, 2004 that killed 16 people. In contrast to the air strike one year earlier, Israel did not claim official

---

[111] S/PV.4836, October 5, 2003, 14.

[112] See www.whitehouse.gov/news/release/2003/10/print/20031006-3.html, visited October 7, 2003. See also Richard W. Stevenson and Carl Hulse 'Bush Tells Israel It Has the Right to Defend Itself' *The New York Times*, October 7, 2003.

[113] *Patterns of Global Terrorism*, 2003, 93, available at www.state.gov, visited December 23, 2004.

[114] S/2003/340, October 5, 2003.

[115] Press Release SC/7887, October 5, 2003: 'Security Council Meets in Emergency Session Following Israeli Air Strike Against Syria: Syria Asks Council to Condemn Attack; Israel Says Attack Response for Islamic Jihad's Bombing in Haifa'

[116] 'Report: Mofaz warns Syria of attack if it keeps aiding terror' by Haaretz Service and News Agencies, *Haaretz*, November 11, 2003, available at www.haaretzdaily.com, visited November 11, 2003. Amos Harel 'Ya'alon: We might attack Syria again' *Haaretz* November 17, 2003. According to the article, the chief of staff noted that 'Syria and Iran continue to maintain they are innocent of murder, even after the Maxim restaurant bombing in Haifa – despite the fact that the attack was coordinated from the Islamic Jihad headquarters in Damascus, as organization that enjoys strong backing from Iran'.

[117] 'U.S. Asks Syria for "Concrete Action" Towards Regional Peace", September 11, 2004, available at www.usinfo.state.gov, visited December 30, 2004.

[118] Arieh O'Sullivan 'Damascus: Casr Bombing is 'Israeli State Terrorism'' *Jerusalem Post* September 26, 2004.

responsibility. According to the Israeli newspaper Haaretz, however, Israeli security sources said that the operation was carried out by Israel.[119]

What did Syrian involvement actually amount to? This is a difficult question to answer specifically. There is no doubt that at the time of the air strike, Syria did allow various Palestinian groups to have offices in Damascus. It can also reasonably be established that political support has been forthcoming from the Syrian government if in no other way then by its opposition – shared with the so-called rejectionist groups – to the substantial parts of the peace process. Things become sketchier when one considers possible material and other support. Reasonably, the Syrian case may be seen as one of unwillingness to confront the terrorists at least until recently when the offices in question apparently were closed.[120] Also, even if the will was there, it is obviously rather difficult for Syria to have a direct influence on events taking place in the West Bank and Gaza. At this point the Syrian case is certainly different from the PA situation. All in all, these elements help explain the quite widespread criticism of the Israeli attack even among Western states such as the UK and Spain.

8.V. Iraq 2003

Brief mention finally has to be made of the 2003 invasion of Iraq by an American/British led coalition. In the present context, the main point of interest is the Iraqi regime's possible connections to terrorist groups and, in particular, to bin Laden and al-Qaeda.

Before the war, a number of statements were made regarding the Iraqi regime's connections to international terrorists, including al-Qaeda. In September 2002, Secreatry of Defense Rumsfeld stated: 'Since we began after September 11th, we do have solid evidence of the presence in Iraq of al Qaeda members, including some that have been in Baghdad. We have what we consider to be very reliable reporting of senior level contacts going back a decade, and of possible chemical and biological agent training. And when I say contacts, I mean between Iraq and al Qaeda. The reports of these contacts have been increasing since 1998. We have what we believe to be credible information that Iraq and al Qaeda have discussed safe haven opportunities in Iraq, reciprocal nonaggression discussions. We have what we consider to be credible evidence that al Qaeda leaders have sought contacts in Iraq who could help them acquire weapon of weapons of mass destruction capabilities. We do have I believe it's one report indicating that Iraq provided unspecified training relating to chemical and/or

---

[119] 'Car Bomb Kills Hamas Leader in Syria' September 26, 2004 at www.ict.org.il/spotlight/tod_prev_frame.htm, visited December 23, 2004.
[120] Khaled abu Toamed 'Syria Closes Offices of Palestinian Terror Groups' *Jerusalem Post* September 26, 2004, reporting that all offices were closed and phone lines cut off.

biological matters for al Qaeda members. There is, I'm told, also some other information of varying degrees of reliability that supports that conclusion of their cooperation'.[121]

Immediately before the war, Secretary of State, Colin Powell, told the UN Security Council that 'Iraq and terrorism go back decades'. Powell then pointed to the presence of Abu Musab al-Zarqawi and other 'al-Qaeda affiliates', based in Baghdad as the possible nexus between Iraq and al-Qaeda and went on to state that 'We are not surprised that Iraq is harbouring Zarqawi and his subordinates. This understanding builds on decades long experience with respect to ties between Iraq and al-Qaeda'.[122] However, in January 2003, the CIA described the relationship between Iraq and al-Qaeda as one that 'appears to more closely resemble that of two independent actors trying to exploit each other ... The Intelligence Community has no credible information that Baghdad had foreknowledge of the 11 September attacks or any other al-Qaeda strike...'.[123]

Following the war, some within the US administration, in particular the Vice President, maintained the argument about the connection between the Iraqi regime and terrorists, including al-Qaeda: 'In Iraq, we took another essential step in the war on terror. ... Saddam had a lengthy history of reckless and sudden aggression. He cultivated ties to terror, hosting the Abu Nidal organization, supporting terrorists, making payments to the families of suicide bombers in Israel. He also had an established relationship with Al Qaeda, providing training to Al Qaeda members in the areas of poisons, gases, making conventional bombs. ... If Saddam Hussein were in power today, there would still be active terror camps in Iraq, the regime would still be allowing terrorist leaders into the country and this ally of terrorists would still have a hidden biological weapons program capable of producing deadly agents on short notice'.[124] The President stated that 'We've had no evidence that Saddam Hussein was

---

[121] Secretary of Defense Donald H. Rumsfeld, Department of Defense News Briefing, September 26, 2002, available at http://www.defenselink.mil/transcripts/2002/t09262002_t0926sd.html

[122] Secretary of State Colin Powell, Speech at United Nations Security Council, Feruary 5, 2003, available at www.whitehouse.gov/news/release/2003/02/print/20030205-1.html, visited July 2, 2004.

[123] CIA assessment in 'Iraqi Support for Terrorism', January 2003, reproduced in 'Report on the U.S. Intelligence Community's Prewar Intelligence Assessments on Iraq' Select Committee on Intelligence, United States Senate, Ordered Reported on July 7, 2004, 322, available at www.intelligence.senate.gov, visited July 12, 2004.

[124] Remarks by the Vice President to the Heritage Foundation, October 10, 2003. www.heritage.org/Research/MiddleEast/hl800.cfm?renderforprint=1, visited January 7, 2004. See also Eric Schmitt 'Cheney Lashes Out at Critics of Policy on Iraq' *The New York Times* October 11, 2003 and Dana Milbank and Walter Pincus 'Cheney Goes on Offensive Over Iraq' *The Washington Post* October 11, 2003.

involved with the September 11th. ... there is [however] no question that Saddam Hussein had al Qaeda ties'.[125]

Various bi-partisan congressional investigations have, however, failed to uncover any substantial link between al-Qaeda and Iraq: The US Senate Select Committee on Intelligence issued a report concluding *inter alia* that 'The Central Intelligence Agency reasonably assessed that several instances of contacts between Iraq and al-Qaeda were likely throughout the 1990s, but that these contacts did not add up to an established formal relationship'.[126] The National Commission on Terrorist Attacks Upon the United States (The 9-11 Commission) found that 'There have been reports that contacts between Iraq and al Qaeda also occurred after Bin Ladin had returned to Afghanistan, but they do not appear to have resulted in a collaborative relationship. ... We have no credible evidence that Iraq and al Qaeda cooperated on the attacks against the United States'.[127]

When the US had to justify the invasion to the Security Council, neither terrorists nor weapons of mass destruction were at the center. Rather, the legality of the campaign hinged on the violation of a series of UN resolutions going back to 1990:

> The responsibility for the current situation lies in the hands of the Iraqi regime, a regime which launched two bloody wars and which has refused for 12 years to give up weapons of mass destruction and join its neighbours in peace. Iraq has repeatedly refused to respond to diplomatic overtures, economic sanctions and other peaceful means designed to bring about Iraqi compliance with its obligations to disarm. The actions that coalition forces are undertaking are an appropriate response. The military campaign in Iraq is not a war against the people of Iraq, but rather against a regime that has denied the will of the international community for more than 12 years. It was regrettable that the Government of Iraq decided not to take the final opportunity for compliance provided in Security Council resolution 1441 (2002). The coalition response is legitimate and not unilateral. Resolution 687 (1991) imposed a series of obligations on Iraq that were the conditions of the ceasefire. It has

---

[125] Remarks by the President After Meeting with Members of the Congressional Conference Committee on Energy Legislation, September 17, 2003, available at www.whitehouse.gov/news/releases/2003/09/print/20030917-7.html, visited September 22, 2003.

[126] 'Report on the U.S. Intelligence Community's Prewar Intelligence Assessments on Iraq, Conclusion 93' Select Committee on Intelligence, United States Senate, Ordered Reported on July 7, 2004, 346, available at www.intelligence.senate.gov, visited July 12, 2004.

[127] Staff Report No. 15: 'Overview of the Enemy', June 16, 2004, page 5, available at www.9-11commission.gov, visited July 4, 2004.

long been recognized and understood that a material breach of those obligations removes the basis of the ceasefire and revives the authority to use force under resolution 678 (1990). Resolution 1441 (2002) explicitly found Iraq in continuing material breach. In view of Iraq's additional material breaches, the basis for the existing ceasefire has been removed and the use of force is authorized under resolution 678 (1990).[128]

The UN Security Council debated the war a few days after its commencement, on March 26 and 27, 2003. Speaking on behalf of the Non-Aligned Movement, the Malaysian representative found that 'the war against Iraq has been carried out without the authorization of the Security Council. This war is being carried out in violation of the principles of international law and the Charter'.[129] Similarly, the representative of the Arab League, referring to ministerial decision adopted by the Council of the League of Arab States on 24 March 2003, held that 'this aggression [the invasion of Iraq] [should be deemed] a violation of the Charter of the United Nations and the principles of international law, a departure from international legitimacy, a threat to international peace and security and an act of defiance against the international community and world public opinion ...'.[130] Greece, speaking on behalf of the European Union, including acceding[131] and associated[132] countries, reiterated their 'commitment to the fundamental role of the United Nations in the international system and to the primary responsibility of the Security Council for the maintenance of international peace and stability'.[133] The statement was broad enough for both Germany – an opponent of the war – and the United Kingdom – a participant in the war – to endorse it. Russia found the invasion 'an unprovoked military action has been undertaken, in violation of international law and in circumvention of the Charter, against Iraq, a sovereign State and Member of the United Nations'.[134] Similarly, China found the invasion to be an

---

[128] S/PV.4726, Resumption 1, March 27, page 25. For more justifications, see Letter to the President of the Security Council, March 21, 2003, S/2003/351: 'The actions being taken are authorized under existing Council resolutions ...'. See also William H. Taft IV and Todd F. Buchwald: 'The Council [in resolution 1441, paragraph 4] that ... any such violations [material breach, i.e. failure to cooperate] by Iraq would mean that the use of force to address this threat was consistent with Resolution 678' in 'Preemption, Iraq and International Law 97 *American Journal of International Law* (2003) 557-563. See further comments in the Agora: Law 97 *American Journal of International Law* (2003) 553-642.

[129] S/PV.4726, March 26, page 7.

[130] S/PV.4726, March 26, page 8.

[131] Cyprus, the Czech Republic, Estonia, Hungary, Latvia, Lithuania, Malta, Poland, the Slovak Republic and Slovenia.

[132] Bulgaria, Romania and Turkey.

[133] S/PV.4726, March 26, page 19.

[134] S/PV.4726, Resumption 1, March 27, page 26.

action that constituted 'a violation of the basic principles of the Charter of the United Nations and of international law'.[135] As for the precedent setting value of the Iraq war, it must be regarded to be limited, primarily due to the US justification. Iraq can be seen as a unique case in this regard.[136]

In spite of the official US justification, the Iraq campaign has been viewed as an example of the implementation of the pre-emptive doctrine, which the US administration recently elaborated. In the Security Council a small number of states made this connection: Malaysia found that the doctrine of pre-emptive strikes has no foundation in international law and wished to underline that the pre-emptive use of force threatens the very foundation of international law, making war once again the tool of international politics and of the powerful in subjugating the weak and defenceless. It also erroneously asserts the notion that might is right.[137] Yemen held that a pre-emptive war, based on mere doubts about the intentions of others, leads to chaos that will undermine the basis of international relations.[138] Finally, Iran stated that the stated goal of regime change in Iraq runs flagrantly counter to the norms and principles of international law; and so does the concept of arbitrary pre-emptive strike, which openly negates the provisions of the Charter of the United Nations.[139] If one were to view the Iraq campaign as an example of pre-emptve use of force, the international reaction quite clearly rejected the existence of such a right in international law.

Although some argue that the seeds of the strategy of pre-emptive force may be found in the 1992 'Defense Planning Guidance',[140] President Bush first announced the idea when he told graduates at West Point Military Academy: 'And our security will require all Americans to be forward-looking and resolute, to be ready for preemptive

---

[135] S/PV.4726, Resumption 1, March 27, page 27.

[136] See Kritsiotis: 'The legal case for Operation Iraqi Freedom must therefore either stand or fall on its reliance on Security Council Resolutions 678 (1990), 687 (1991) and 1441 (2002)... as a matter of law and legal justification, the tenuous nature of proof rendered on the relationship between Iraq and al Qaeda should not serve as a counter-point to the validity of the justification advanced for Operation Iraqi Freedom' Dino Kritsiotis 'Arguments of Mass Confusion' 15 *European Journal of International Law* 2004, 233-278 at 253 and 259.

[137] S/PV.4726, March 26, page 8.

[138] S/PV.4726, March 26, page 13.

[139] S/PV.4726, March 26, page 33.

[140] According to the program 'Frontline' from Public Broadcasting Service, 'Policy analysts note that there are many elements in the 2002 NSS [National Security Strategy] document which bear a strong resemblance to recommendations presented in Paul Wolfowitz's controversial Defense Planning Guidance draft written in 1992 under the first Bush administration', including the ideas that containment was a relic of the Cold War and the need to use military force to preempt provocations from rogue states with weapons of mass destruction, see www.pbs.org/wgbh/pages/ frontline/shows/iraq/etc/cron.html, visited August 13, 2003. On the controversy caused by Wolfowitz's initial draft, see Patrick E. Tyler 'Pentagon Drops Goal of Blocking New Superpowers' in *The New York Times* May 23, 1992.

action when necessary to defend our liberty and to defend our lives'.[141] The President's thoughts have now been codified in the National Security Strategy (NSS), according to which 'we will disrupt and destroy terrorist organizations by ... identifying and destroying the threat before it reaches our borders. ... we will not hesitate to act alone, if necessary, to exercise our right of self-defense by acting preemptively against such terrorists, to prevent them from doing harm against our people and our country'.[142]

As is clear from the text just quoted, the drafters of the NSS document perceive 'acting preemptively' as being within 'our right of self-defense'. The legal side of the argument is subsequently elaborated upon: 'For centuries, international law recognized that nations need not suffer an attack before they can lawfully take action to defend themselves against forces that present an imminent danger of attack. Legal scholars and international jurists often conditioned the legitimacy of preemption on the existence of an imminent threat – most often a visible mobilization of armies, navies, and air forces preparing to attack'.[143] Here the NSS document finds that anticipatory self-defense is permissible in international law, which is generally a fair statement, even if not all international law scholars agree. There is, however, a problem of 'imminent', which

---

[141] 'For much of the last century, America's defense relied on the Cold War doctrines of deterrence and containment. In some cases, those strategies still apply. But new threats also require new thinking. Deterrence -- the promise of massive retaliation against nations -- means nothing against shadowy terrorist networks with no nation or citizens to defend. Containment is not possible when unbalanced dictators with weapons of mass destruction can deliver those weapons on missiles or secretly provide them to terrorist allies. We cannot defend America and our friends by hoping for the best. We cannot put our faith in the word of tyrants, who solemnly sign non-proliferation treaties, and then systemically break them. If we wait for threats to fully materialize, we will have waited too long. Homeland defense and missile defense are part of stronger security, and they're essential priorities for America. Yet the war on terror will not be won on the defensive. We must take the battle to the enemy, disrupt his plans, and confront the worst threats before they emerge. In the world we have entered, the only path to safety is the path of action. And this nation will act'. President Bush Delivers Graduation Speech at West Point, Remarks by the President at 2002 Graduation Exercise of the United States Military Academy West Point, New York, June 1, 2002 available at www.whitehouse.gov/news/releases/2002/06/20020601-3.html, visited June 13, 2003.

[142] *National Security Strategy*, September 2002, 6, available at www.whitehouse.gov, visited June 12, 2003. The National Security Strategy to Combat Weapons of Mass Destruction similarly states that US military forces ‚ust have the capability to defend against WMD [Weapons of Mass Destruction] armed adversaries, including 'in appropriate cases through preemptive measures', *National Security Strategy to Combat Weapons of Mass Destruction*, December 2002, 3, available at www.whitehouse.gov, visited June 12, 2003.

[143] *National Security Strategy*, September 2002, 15, available at www.whitehouse.gov, visited June 12, 2003. See also the statement by then National Security Advisor Condoleezza Rice: 'Well, I would say that the idea of preventive action is not a new concept. In fact, the idea that you have to wait to be attacked to deal with a threat seems to us simply to fly in the face of common sense. ... Now, to be sure, anticipatory self-defense, or preemption has to be used carefully', Interview with National Security Advisor Condoleezza Rice, Newshour September 25, 2002, available at www.pbs.org/newshour/bb/international/july-dec02/rice_9-25.html, visited September 26, 2002.

also may be seen as the distinguishing point between anticipatory self-defense and a preemptive strike, although the NSS document conflates the two concepts.[144] Thus, the document continues: 'We must adapt the concept of imminent threat to the capabilities and objectives of today's adversaries'.[145] The document goes on to describe the new threats, concluding: '[] in an age where the enemies of civilization openly and actively seek the world's most destructive technologies, the United States cannot remain idle while dangers gather'.[146] Presidential spokesman Ari Fleischer put it as follows: 'Preemptive doctrine, of course, as laid out by the President at West Point ... says that time is not on America's side. We don't have time to wait for them to develop these weapons and attack us without any warning. And therefore, the doctrine of preemption, as the President laid it out, is a way to continue America's efforts to promote peace around the world by denying them the ability to inflict damage on us'.[147] In the Case Concerning Armed Activities on the Territory of the Congo, the Court indirectly addrssed the NSS and its reasoning stating that self-defence under Article 51 of the Charter 'does not allow the use of force by a State to protect perceived security interests' outside the strict confines in Article 51.[148]

---

[144] Then with National Security Advisor Condoleezza Rice also appeared to conflate the two: 'Well, I would say that the idea of preventive action is not a new concept. In fact, the idea that you have to wait to be attacked to deal with a threat seems to us simply to fly in the face of common sense. ... Now, to be sure, anticipatory self-defense, or preemption has to be used carefully'.Interview with National Security Advisor Condoleezza Rice, Newshour September 25, 2002, available at www.pbs.org/newshour/bb/international/july-dec02/rice_9-25.html, visited September 26, 2002.

[145] *National Security Strategy*, September 2002, 15, available at www.whitehouse.gov, visited June 12, 2003.

[146] Ibid.

[147] Press Gaggle with Ari Fleischer, Crawford Elementary School, Crawford, Texas, August 27, 2002, available at http://www.whitehouse.gov/news/releases/2002/08/20020827.html, visited September 5, 2002. See also remarks by Vice President Cheney: 'Some claim we should not have acted because the threat from Saddam Hussein was not imminent. Yet, as the president has said, "Since when have terrorists and tyrants announced their intention, politely putting us on notice before they strike?"' I would remind the critics of the fundamental case the president has made since September 11th. Terrorist enemies of our country hope to strike us with the most lethal weapons known to man and it would be reckless in the extreme to rule out action and save our worries until the day they strike. As the president told Congress earlier this year, if threats from terrorists and terror states are permitted to fully emerge, all actions, all words and all recriminations would come too late. That is the debate. That is the choice set before the American people', Remarks by the Vice President to the Heritage Foundation, October 10, 2003.
www.heritage.org/Research/MiddleEast/hl800.cfm?renderforprint=1, visited January 7, 2004. See also Eric Schmitt 'Cheney Lashes Out at Critics of Policy on Iraq' *The New York Times* October 11, 2003 and Dana Milbank and Walter Pincus 'Cheney Goes on Offensive Over Iraq' *The Washington Post* October 11, 2003.

[148] Case Concerning Armed Activities on the Territory of the Congo (Democratic Republic of the Congo v. Uganda), Judgment, December 19, 2005, paragraph 148.

Many of the arguments presented for and against the pre-emptive strategy were already rehearsed more than 20 years earlier when the premier example of pre-emptive use of force was conducted: the Israeli air strike on the Osirak reactor near Baghdad, Iraq on June 7, 1981. The attack caused a very extensive debate in the Security Council of the UN. With the dispute over the 2002 US National Security Strategy (NSS) and the Iraq war in fresh memory, it is interesting to read how very similar arguments were rehearsed in 1981, ultimately resulting in the rejection of the Israeli argument.

At a basic legal level, Israel claimed self-defence: 'In destroying Osiraq, Israel performed an elementary act of self-preservation, both morally and legally. In doing so, Israel was exercising its inherent right of self-defence as understood in general international law and as preserved in Article 51 of the United Nations Charter'.[149] In a way to be replicated in the NSS, Israel attempted to present the attack as being within the confines of traditional anticipatory self-defence.[150] Israel, however, found that the time has moved beyond the *Caroline* case, the historical reference point when it comes to anticipatory self-defence: That incident 'occurred almost a century and a half ago. It occurred precisely 108 years before Hiroshima. To try and apply it to a nuclear situation in the post-Hiroshima era makes clear the absurdity the position of those who base themselves upon it. To assert the applicability of the Caroline principles to a State confronted with the threat of nuclear destruction would be an emasculation of that State's inherent and natural right of self-defence'.[151] According to Mr. Blum, the Israeli representative, Israel only acted when it found out that there was 'less than a month to go before Osiraq might have become critical'.[152] The phrase 'might have become critical' appeared to refer not to a certain weapons status but rather a stage after which 'any attack on it [Osiraq] would have blanketed the city of Baghdad with massive radioactive fallout'.[153] Finally, Israel pointed to the character of the Iraqi regime, which was described as 'an irresponsible, ruthless and bellicose regime ... [that] has amply demonstrated its total disregard for innocent human life both at home and in its war with Iran'.[154]

Several of the speakers dismissed Israel's interpretation of international law. The Algerian representative, Mr. Bedjaoui, addressed the 'new theory of "preventive" aggression' on principle and described it as 'the very negation of law and of morality; it is diametrically opposed to peace and reason. Permeated by a suicidal subjectivism, it

---

[149] S/PV.2280, June 12, 1981, page 37. See similarly S/PV.2280, page 52.
[150] S/PV.2280, June 12, 1981, pages 53-55.
[151] S/PV.2280, June 12, 1981, page 32. Israel further argued that the scope of a State's right to self-defence has 'broadened with the advance of man's ability to wreak havoc on his enemies', S/PV.2280, June 12, 1981, page 36.
[152] S/PV.2280, June 12, 1981, page 56.
[153] S/PV.2280, June 12, 1981, page 52.
[154] S/PV.2280, June 12, 1981, page 52.

would in future authorize any State to attack another for whatever reason it considers valid – that is, in the final analysis, for no reason at all. ... Even the least imaginative mind can easily envisage the world-wide consequences, which we run the risk of legitimising, if any justification whatsoever should by misfortune be given to the intolerable Israeli example which would then become a precedent'.[155]

The United States voted in favour of the Security Council resolution that strongly condemned 'the military attack by Israel in clear violation of the Charter of the United Nations and the norms of international conduct'.[156] The US was, however, not very specific about how it viewed the attack in legal terms: 'Our judgement that Israeli actions violated the United Nations Charter is based solely on the conviction that Israel failed to exhaust peaceful means for the resolution of this dispute'.[157] For this statement it may be deduced that the US found that, at a minimum, the requirement that an attack is necessary was violated in regard to the strike and, hence, that the treat was not imminent. Rosalyn Higgins found that 'a nuclear weapons programme falls short of being a threat to use force. ... The alleged threat to Israel was not seen as instant – far short of the test of *The Caroline*'.[158]

It may be posited that the question of what is 'imminent' is the crux of the matter: The US efforts at broadening the concept of 'imminent' is the central legal issue in the new strategy of preemptive use of force. This is what caused some legal scholars to object to the NSS strategy: '*De lege lata*, however, the expansion of the right of anticipatory self-defence proposed in the National Security Strategy is not acceptable'.[159] It is probably fair to assert that the majority of scholars agree with Bothe.[160] Among the voices of concern, one may add that of the Secretary General of the United Nations, who on September 23, 2003 declared that the logic of using force pre-emptively 'represents a fundamental challenge to the principles on which, however imperfectly, world peace and stability have rested for the last fifty-eight years'.[161]

---

[155] S/PV.2280, June 12, 1981, page 81.

[156] Security Council resolution 487 (1981), operative paragraph 1.

[157] S/PV.2288, June 19, 1981, pages 58-60.

[158] Rosalyn Higgins 'The Attitude of Western States Towards Legal Aspects of the Use of Force' in A. Cassese (ed.) *The Current Legal Regulation of the Use of Force* Martinus Nijhoff (1986), 443.

[159] Michael Bothe 'Terrorism and the Legality of Pre-emptive Force' in 14 *European Journal of International Law* (2003) 227-240 at 232.

[160] See, for example, Kirgis' brief comment that if the new US policy reserves the right to act in self defense even when the terrorist threat is not imminent, the Caroline test – and thus the test under Article 51 – would not be met, Frederic L. Kirgis 'Pre-emptive Action to Forestall Terrorism' *ASIL Insights* June 2002, available at www.asil.org/insights/insigh88.htm, visited August 19, 2003.

[161] The Secretary-general: Address to the General Assembly, New York, September 23, 2003, available at www.un.org/webcast/ga/58/statements/sg2eng030923.htm, visited September 24, 2003: 'Since this Organisation was founded, States have generally sought to deal with threats to the peace through containment and deterrence, by a system based on collective security and the United Nations Charter. Article 51 of the Charter prescribes that all States, if attacked, retain the inherent right of self-defence.

Many, who have been weary of the US strategy, have pointed to the fact that other countries might also chose to adopt the doctrine. Indeed, at a meeting in Reykjavik on October 6, 2003, the Russian Defence Minister stated that Russia could use preventive military force in cases where a threat is growing and is "visible, clear, and unavoidable".[162] The Russian President subsequently backed his minister: 'As to preventive strikes, we proceed from the priority of international law in the first place. Any use of force may take place only in the case of a decision of the UN Security Council. But you are right, the Defense Minister indeed talked about the possibility of preventive strikes. What he meant, and this is also my opinion – we are against such policies. But if such behaviour continues to be affirmed in the practice of international life as a priority, then Russia reserves the right to act in a similar manner'.[163] These statements are in harmony with professor Nikitin's earlier analysis: 'on the level of general political sense, Moscow seems not to welcome doctrinalization of preemptive use of force'. Russia was happy with earlier designations, such as anti-terror counter operations. And Russia formally maintains the need for Security Council

---

But until now it has been understood that when States go beyond that, and decide to use force to deal with broader threats to international peace and security, they need the unique legitimacy provided by the United Nations. Now, some say this understanding is no longer tenable, since an "armed attack" with weapons of mass destruction could be launched at any time, without warning, or by a clandestine group. Rather than wait for that to happen, they argue, States have the right and obligation to use force pre-emptively, even on the territory of other States, and even while weapons systems that might be used to attack them are still being developed. According to this argument, States are not obliged to wait until there is agreement in the Security Council. Instead, they reserve the right to act unilaterally, or in ad hoc coalitions. This logic represents a fundamental challenge to the principles on which, however imperfectly, world peace and stability have rested for the last fifty-eight years. My concern is that, if it were to be adopted, it could set precedents that resulted in a proliferation of the unilateral and lawless use of force, with or without justification. But it is not enough to denounce unilateralism, unless we also face up squarely to the concerns that make some States feel uniquely vulnerable, since it is those concerns that drive them to take unilateral action. We must show that those concerns can, and will, be addressed effectively through collective action'.

[162] Sophie Lambroschini 'Russia: Moscow Struggles To Clarify Stance On Preemptive Force' *Radio Free Europe/Radio Liberty* October 14, 2003, available at www.rferl.org/nca/features/2003/10/14102003171155.asp, visited October 21, 2003. See also Yuri Zarakhovich 'On the Offensive: The Kremlin backs preemptive military strikes' Time/Europe, October 13, 2003, Vol. 162, No. 14, available at www.time.com, visited October 13, 2003. See also Seth Mydans 'Russia's Antiterror Tactics: Reward and a First Strike' *The New York Times* September 9, 2004.

[163] 'Russian President Vladimir Putin's Interview with Al-Jazeera, Kuala Lumpur, October 16, 2003, available at www.ln.mid.ru, visited October 21, 2003.

involvement.[164] Georgian President Shevardnadza took Ivanov's comments as a direct threat to Georgia: 'Russia means Georgia when it talks about preemptive strikes'.[165]

Finally, it should be noted that if the Iraq war were to be seen as an exercise of pre-emptive use of force, the US President has, of late, broadened the scope of the doctrine. This is due to the fact that no weapons of mass detruction were found combined with continuing support for the war from the President. When the Duefler Report was published, which found no concrete weapons of mass destruction, the President stated:

> The Duelfer report also raises important new information about Saddam Hussein's defiance of the world and his intent and capability to develop weapons. The Duelfer report showed that Saddam was systematically gaming the system, using the U.N. oil-for-food program to try to influence countries and companies in an effort to undermine sanctions. He was doing so with the intent of restarting his weapons program, once the world looked away. Based on all the information we have today, I believe we were right to take action, and America is safer today with Saddam Hussein in prison. He retained the knowledge, the materials, the means, and the intent to produce weapons of mass destruction. And he could have passed that knowledge on to our terrorist enemies. Saddam Hussein was a unique threat, a sworn enemy of our country, a state sponsor of terror, operating in the world's most volatile region. In a world after September the 11th, he was a threat we had to confront. And America and the world are safer for our actions.[166]

If the war can still be justified on this basis, as indicated by the President, the pre-emptive strategy requires very little transgression – defiance, intent of restarting a

---

[164] Alexander I. Nikitin 'Preemptive Military Action and the Legitimate Use of Force: A Russian View' Prepared for the Center for European Policy Studies, European Security Forum, Brussels January 13, 2003, available at www.eusec.org/nikitin.htm, visited October 21, 2003.

[165] Sophie Lambroschini 'Russia: Moscow Struggles To Clarify Stance On Preemptive Force' *Radio Free Europe/Radio Liberty* October 14, 2003, available at www.rferl.org/nca/features/2003/10/14102003171155.asp, visited October 21, 2003.

[166] President Bush Discusses Iraq Report, October 7, 2004, available at http://www.whitehouse.gov/news/releases/2004/10/20041007-6.html, visited October 12, 2004.

weapons program, retained the knowledge, the materials, the means, and the intent to produce weapons of mass destruction – by a potential target of a pre-emptive strike.[167]

---

[167] See David E. Sanger 'A Doctrine Under Pressure: Pre-emption Is Redefined' *The New York Times* October 11, 2004 (Arguing that subtle changes in language appear to have expanded the conditions for a pre-emptive military strike) and Glenn Kessler 'Bush Recasts Rationale For War After Report' *The Washington Post* October 10, 2004.

Chapter 9

The Use of Force and (the State of) Necessity

A strict observance of the written law is doubtless one of the high duties of a good citizen, but not the highest. The laws of necessity, of self-preservation, of saving our country when in danger, are of higher obligation. To lose our country by a scrupulous adherence to written law, would be to lose the law itself, with life, liberty, property and all those who are enjoying them with us; thus absurdly sacrificing the end to the means.
Thomas Jefferson[1]

Not kennt kein Gebot!
von Bethmann-Hollweg[2]

To say that a power is necessary, that it logically results from a certain situation, is to admit the non-existence of any legal justification. Necessity knows no law, it is said; and indeed to invoke necessity is to step outside the law.
Judge Gros[3]

It [international law] rejects the idea that necessity knows no law.
Oscar Schachter[4]

---

[1] Quoted in Robert F. Turner 'State Sovereignty, International Law and the Use of Force in Countering Low-Intensity Aggression in the Modern World' in John Norton Moore (ed) *Deception and Deterrence in "Wars of National Liberation," State-Sponsored Terrorism and Other Forms of Secret Warfare* Carolina Academic Press 1997, 195-257 at 196.

[2] German Chancellor in speech in the German Reichstag on August 4, 1914 justifying the occupation of Belgium and Luxembourg in order to forestall an alleged attack by France against Germany through Belgium and Luxembourg. Quote in Addendum to Eight Report on State Responsibility by Mr. Roberto Ago, Document A/CN.4/318/ADD.5-7, 1980, reproduced in 2 *Yearbook of the International Law Commission* (YILC) 1980, part one, page 38, note 110. See also Burleigh Cushing Rodick: *The Doctrine of Necessity in International Law*, Columbia University Press, New York, 1928, 112. See also the editorial comment in the American Journal of International Law: 'It therefore appears that the Chancellor knew and admitted that the occupation of Belgium and Luxemburg was contrary to international law, but he justified the act by the statement that the German Empire was "in a state of necessity" and that "necessity knows no law"'. Editorial Comment 8 *American Journal of International Law* (1914) 877 at 880. See, finally, Basdevant, who described the episode as one of 'strategic convenience' and not necessity, Jules Basdevant, 'Règles Générales du Droit de la Paix' 58 RC 1936-IV, 473 at 551-552.

[3] Dissenting Opinion of Judge Gros in Legal Consequences for States of the Continued Presence of South Africa in Namibia (South West Africa) Notwithstanding Security Council Resolution 276 (1970), 1971 ICJ 16 at 339.

9.I. Introduction

As has been documented, the right to use force against terrorists has primarily been justified by reference to the inherent right of self-defense. As was pointed out, however, acts of terrorism have not traditionally provided a neat fit with the conditions and criteria contained in Article 51 of the UN Charter. Even if it accepted, as asserted in the preceding chapters, that the threshold for attributing an armed attack to a state has been lower as a consequence of action following September 11, situations may still arise where the conditions for self-defense are not present. Against this background, scholars and policy-makers searched for other justifications and some, foremost among them Roberto Ago in the context of the International Law Commission and the late Oscar Schachter of Columbia University Law School suggested that the necessity defense be (re)examined in light of international terrorist violence. Recently, Johnstone, too, has considered whether the "necessity" concept might 'fill the gap' where self-defence is unavailable.[5]

Necessity in international law may provide an excuse for a state's breach of its obligation or, in other words, the state of necessity may be a circumstance precluding wrongfulness in the parlance of state responsibility. Throughout the years, necessity has been a controversial and contested concept. It has, however, not attracted much academic examination in its own right. Writing in 1928, in what would seem to be the most recent monograph on the topic, Rodick could not find any earlier attempts to deal critically with the doctrine of necessity in international law.[6] All this may soon change, though, now that the latest and last Special Rapporteur, James Crawford, has 'rescued' the topic of state responsibility.[7] In addition to the work of the ILC, a recent judgement of the International Court of Justice has dispelled any doubt about whether the necessity excuse exists in international law. In 1997, in the Gabcíkovo-Nagymaros Project case, the Court held that 'the state of necessity is a ground recognized by customary international law for precluding the wrongfulness of an act not in conformity with an international obligation'.[8]

---

[4] Schachter, Oscar: *International Law in Theory and Practice*, Martinua Nijhoff, Dordrecht, 1991, 173.
[5] Ian Johnstone 'The Plea of "Necessity" in International Legal Discourse: Humanitarian Intervention and Counter-Terrorism' 43 *Columbia Journal of Transnational Law* 2005, 337-388 at 368.
[6] Rodick, Burleigh Cushing: *The Doctrine of Necessity in International Law*, Columbia University Press, New York, 1928, 1. Basdevant, however, mentions a 'célèbre brochure' by Kohler: *Not kennt Kein Gebot: Die Theorie des Notrechtes und die Ereignisse unserer Zeit* 1915, Jules Basdevant, 'Règles Générales du Droit de la Paix' 58 RC 1936-IV, 473 at 551.
[7] Allott, Philip: 'State Responsibility and the Unmaking of International Law' in 29 *Harvard International Law Journal*, 1988, 1 at 9.
[8] Gabcíkovo-Nagymaros Project (Hungary/Slovakia), Judgement, I.C.J. Reports 1997, 7 at 40, paragraph 51.

The legal development relating to the status of necessity in international law will now be examined, specifically the relationship between necessity and the use of force. Firstly, the work at the ILC will be outlined because the most concerted discussions on the issue have taken place over several years under the auspices of the Commission. After examining the treatment of the necessity excuse by various international tribunals, in state responses to the ILC and by scholars, the cumulative conditions of the necessity defense will be set out based primarily on the ICJ's judgment in the Gabcíkovo-Nagymaros Project case. Finally, the options for claiming necessity when using force generally and against terrorists particularly will be scrutinized.

9.II. The Work of the International Law Commission

Work on the codification of the international legal rules of state responsibility has taken place in the International Law Commission (ILC) since the very beginning.[9] In 1949, state responsibility was selected as a topic suitable for codification and in 1953 the United Nations General Assembly (GA) requested that the ILC proceed with the codification of the principles of international law governing state responsibility.[10] The initial work of the ILC and of its first Special Rapporteur Garcia Amador was partly based on earlier deliberations under the auspices of the League of Nations and was concentrated on the content of substantive rules of 'responsibility of the state for injuries caused in its territory to the person or property of aliens'. In his third report, Garcia Amador discussed necessity:

---

[9] On the general work of the ILC, see: Sinclair, Ian: *The International Law Commission*, Cambridge, Grotius Publishers, 1987 and Watts, Arthur: *The International Law Commission 1949-1998*, 3 vol., Oxford, Oxford University Press, 1999. On the topic of State Responsibility, see Spinedi, Marina and Bruno Simma (ed.): *United Nations Codification of State Responsibility*, New York, Oceana Publications, 1987 and Rosenne, Shabtai (ed.): *The International Law Commission's Draft Articles on State Responsibility, Part 1, Articles 1-35*, Dordrecht, Martinus Nijhoff, 1991, and, more recently, 'Symposium: State Responsibility' in 10 *European Journal of International Law*, 1999, 339-460; Crawford, James, Pierre Bodeau and Jacqueline Peel: 'The ILC's Draft Articles on State Responsibility: Toward Completion of a Second Reading' in 94 *American Journal of International Law*, 2000, 660 and 'Symposium: The ILC's State Responsibility Articles' in 96 *American Journal of International Law*, 2002, 773-890. On Chapter V of Part 1, see: Jean J.A. Salmon 'Faut-il codifier l'etat de necessite en droit international?' in Jerzy Makarczyk (ed.) *Essays in International Law in Honour of Judge Manfred Lachs* Martinus Nijhoff (1984) 235, Jagota, S.P.: 'State Responsibility: Circumstances Precluding Wrongfulness' in 16 *Netherlands Yearbook of International Law*, 1985, 249, and Lowe, Vaughan: 'Precluding Wrongfulness or Responsibility: A Plea for Excuses' in 10 *European Journal of International Law*, 1999, 405.

[10] See GA Resolution 799 (VII) of December 7, 1953. For an overview of the ILC work on state responsibility see ILC web-site: www.un.org/law/ilc/guide/9_6.htm.

It is undeniable that great uncertainty surrounds the subject of necessity; in other words, it is a controversial question what circumstances have to attend the imputable act or omission in order that that state of necessity can justify full exoneration from responsibility or extenuate responsibility for the purposes of reparation. Nevertheless, it is precisely and principally because of this uncertainty, and because of the contradictions encountered in diplomatic and other documents, that necessity ought be mentioned as a defence in the draft. If state of necessity is recognized in international law, as in fact it is, it needs a definition to forestall as far as possible a recurrence of past controversies concerning the circumstances in which it is admissible as a defence.[11]

In his sixth and final report as Special Rapporteur included the following paragraph 2 to Article 17: Exonerating and extenuating circumstances:

Likewise, an act shall not be imputable to the state if it is a consequence of a state of necessity involving grave danger and imminent peril threatening some vital interest of the State, provided that the State did not provoke that peril and was unable to counteract it by other means and so to prevent the injury.[12]

When Garcia-Amador, in 1961, ceased to be a member of the Commission, a Sub-Committee chaired by Roberto Ago, who would subsequently be appointed the next Special Rapporteur, recommended that priority be given to the general aspects and rules governing the international responsibility of the State, i.e. general secondary rules of the international law of obligations, without neglecting the experience and material gathered, particularly concerning responsibility for injuries to persons or property of aliens.

As Special Rapporteur, Ago submitted eight reports and an addendum to the last report, dealing *inter alia* with necessity. Ago concluded his extensive survey of necessity with the observation that 'the concept of "state of necessity" is far too deeply rooted in the consciousness of the members of the international community and of individuals within States. If driven out of the door it would return through the window,

---

[11] Document A/CN.4/111, International responsibility. Third report by F.V. Garcia Amador, Special Rapporteur: Responsibility of the state for injuries caused in its territory to the person or property of aliens, Part II: The International Claim, paragraph 13, reporduced in 2 *YILC*, 1958, 47, at 53.

[12] Document A/CN.4/134 and Add. 1, International responsibility. Sixth report by F.V. Garcia Amador, Special Rapporteur: Responsibility of the state for injuries caused in its territory to the person or property of aliens, Reparation of the injury, reproduced in 2 *YILC*, 1961, 1, at 48.

if need be in other forms'.[13] In 1980, draft Article 33 was adopted by the ILC.[14] Subsequent Special Rapporteurs, Willem Riphagen and Gaetano Arangio-Ruiz, have dealt with Parts Two (Content, forms and degrees of international responsibility) and Three (Settlement of disputes) of the Draft Articles and Part One, including necessity was only revisited by the last Special Rapporteur in 1999.[15]

Overall, Crawford found that the concerns as to the possible abuse of necessity had not been borne out by experience. The ILC, furthermore, found that 'on balance, State practice and judicial decisions support the view that necessity may constitute a circumstance precluding wrongfulness under certain very limited conditions' and recommended retaining the content of article 33 (eventually article 25) with few alterations which will be noted subsequntly when examining the conditions in more detail.[16] The Drafting Committee adopted the following new and final wording of the article concerning necessity:

Article 25: Necessity

1. Necessity may not be invoked by a State as a ground for precluding the wrongfulness of an act not in conformity with an international obligation of that State unless the act:

(a) Is the only way for the State to safeguard an essential interest against a grave and imminent peril; and

---

[13] Addendum to Eight Report on State Responsibility by Mr. Roberto Ago, Document A/CN.4/318/ADD.5-7, 1980, reproduced in 2 *Yearbook of the International Law Commission* (YILC) 1980, part one, page 51, paragraph 80.

[14] 1. A State of necessity may not be invoked by a State as a ground for precluding the wrongfulness of an act of that State not in conformity with an international obligation of the State unless:
(a) the act was the only means of safeguarding an essential interest of the State against a grave and imminent peril; and
(b) the act did not seriously impair an essential interest of the State towards which the obligation existed.
2. In any case, a State of necessity may not be invoked by a State as a ground for precluding wrongfulness:
(a) if the international obligation with which the act of the State is not in conformity arises out of a peremptory norm of general international law; or
(b) if the international obligation with which the act of the State is not in conformity is laid down by a treaty which, explicitly or implicitly, excludes the possibility of invoking the State of necessity with respect to that obligation; or
(c) if the State in question has contributed to the occurrence of the State of necessity.

[15] Second Report on State Responsiblity by Mr. James Crawford, Document A/CN.4/498/Add.2, 1999, 24-33, paragraphs 275-291.

[16] Ibid., 33 paragraph 291 and James Crawford *The International Law Commission's Articles on State Responsibility: Introduction, Text and Commentary* Cambridge University Press, 2002, 183, paragraph 14.

(b) Does not seriously impair an essential interest of the State or States towards which the obligation exists, or of the international community as a whole.

2. In any case, necessity may not be invoked by a State as a ground for precluding wrongfulness if:

(a) The international obligation in question excludes the possibility of invoking necessity; or

(b) The State has contributed to the situation of necessity.[17]

9.III. International Decisions Involving Necessity

As is clear from the extensive review of older practice in Ago's Commentary, the necessity defense has a long pedigree. Of more recent international decisions examining, in one way or the other, the necessity excuse, mention should be made of the European Court of Justice, which, on occasion, has considered whether the necessity defense existed in Community law. In a 1980 case concerning the illegal sale of concrete reinforcement bars at prices below the minimum prices laid down in a Commission Decision, the defendants, in part, claimed that they found themselves in a state of (financial) necessity:[18] They found their conduct 'justified by the principle that 'necessity makes the law''.[19] Both the Advocate General and the Court dismissed the necessity defense. This was, however, apparently not done because neither the Advocate General nor the Court believed the necessity defense to be absent from Community Law:[20] The Court found that since none of the undertakings which complied with the Commission Decision was in danger of bankruptcy or liquidation or

---

[17] Draft articles on Responsibility of States for internationally wrongful acts adopted by the International Law Commission at its fifty-third session (2001) (extract from the Report of the International Law Commission on the work of its Fifty-third session, *Official Records of the General Assembly, Fifty-sixth session, Supplement No. 10* (A/56/10), chp.IV.E.1) available at: http://www.un.org/law/ilc/texts/State_responsibility/responsibilityfra.htm, visited September 22, 2002. Also found in James Crawford *The International Law Commission's Articles on State Responsibility: Introduction, Text and Commentary* Cambridge University Press, 2002, 178-186.

[18] Re Concrete Reinforcement Bars: SpA Ferriera Valsabbia and Others v. E.C. Commission (Joined Cases 154, 205-206, 226-228, 263-264/78, 31, 39, 83 & 85/79) Forges de Thy-Marcinelle et Monceau SA v. E. C. Commission (Joined Cases 26 & 86/79), The Court of Justice of the European Communities, March 18, 1980, 1980 ECR 907 see 1981 *Common Market Law Review* 613.

[19] 1981 *Common Market Law Review* 613 at 702, paragraph 142.

[20] The Advocate General, Francesco Capotorti, outlined the criteria for the necessity defense as: 'a grave and imminent danger which it is impossible to avoid otherwise than by acting in a manner which, objectively considered, is unlawful'. 1981 *Common Market Law Review* 613 at 660, paragraph 17. He further stressed that 'it seems to me indisputable that extreme caution must be exercised in interpreting the concepts, as recognition of the existence of a state of necessity is tantamount to exempting a person from compliance with particular obligations, which may be done only in exceptional cases'. Ibid.

their existence threatened, it was unnecessary to 'examine whether the threat of which they have spoken was capable of creating a state of necessity such as to justify their conduct'.[21] With regard to one of the defendants which had made 'an erroneous evaluation of an unfavourable economic situation which was known to all' the Court noted 'that personal conduct does not entitle it to rely on a state of necessity', thereby implicitly recognizing the existence of the necessity defense in certain circumstances.[22]

It may be suggested that the principles behind the necessity excuse were accepted in the Nachfolger Navigation Case although necessity was not explicitly invoked. In this case, the French navy sank a cargo ship, the *Ammersee*, 25 nautical miles off the coast, i.e. in international waters. The ship was carrying 200 tons of dynamite. During a storm the ship caught fire and the crew abandoned ship. Although the fire subsequently appears to have been extinguished, the French authorities destroyed the ship because it posed a danger to shipping and to installations along the French coast. The case before the Conseil d'Etat concerned a demand by the owners and insurers for compensation. The Court found that the destruction did not violate any principle of international law because the *Ammersee* constituted a 'grave and immediate danger' to the safety of the French coast, French territorial waters and navigation in these waters and 'no other measure would have been sufficient to remove the danger'.[23]

In the second *Rainbow Warrior* case, the Arbitration Tribunal touched upon the question of necessity but seemed unconvinced as to its authority: 'Article 33 (now Article 25) which allegedly authorizes a State to take unlawful action invoking a state of necessity [and] refers to situations of grave and imminent danger to the State as such and to its vital interests' and that the content of Draft Article 33 was of 'controversial character'.[24]

---

[21] 1981 *Common Market Law Review* 613 at 702, paragraph 143.

[22] 1981 *Common Market Law Review* 613 at 702, paragraph 144. See also the more recent decision in Case C-235/92, Judgment of the Court (Sixth Chamber) of 8 July 1999, Montecatini SpA v. Commission of the European Communities, European Court Reports 1999, I-04539: 'it must be stated that, although a situation of necessity might allow conduct which would otherwise infringe Article 85(1) [now Article 81(1)EC] of the Treaty to be considered justified, such a situation can never result from the mere requirement to avoid financial loss', at 143.

[23] See *Nochfolger Navigation Company Ltd. and Others,* October 23, 1987, 89 *International Law Reports*, 3-5.

[24] The primary proceedings connected with the Rainbow Warrior case were a criminal case before the New Zealand High Court, April 22, 1985 (74 *International Law Reports*, 241) then a Report by the United Nations Secretary-General, July 6, 1986 (Ibid., 256) and an implementing agreement between France and New Zealand (Ibid., 274). The subsequent case involving the Arbitration Tribunal concerned France's alleged breach of the implementing agreement, April 30, 1990 (82 *International Law Reports*, 449) here at 554, paragraph 78. For a brief discussion of the case, see Micahel Pugh 'Legal Aspects of the Rainbow Warrior Affair' 36 *International and Comparative Law Quarterly* (1987) 655-669. See also Jodi Wexler 'The Rainbow Warrior Affair: State and Agent Responsibility

The LAFICO-Republic of Burundi Arbitral Tribunal did not wish to express a view on the appropriateness of seeking to codify rules on "state of necessity" and the adequacy of the concrete proposals made by the International Law Commission 'which has been a matter of debate in the doctrine'.[25]

The issue of necessity was also broached in the 1998 Fisheries Jurisdiction Case at the ICJ.[26] Yet, since the decision dealt with the question of the Court's jurisdiction in light of a 1994 Canadian declaration,[27] the merits of the case were not discussed in detail.[28] Canadian authorities had, however, stated that 'the arrest of the *Estai* was necessary in order to put a stop to the overfishing of Greenland halibut by Spanish fisherman'[29] and, as pointed out by Judge Bedjaoui in his dissenting opinion, Canada had, in various fora, invoked 'emergency' or even a 'state of necessity'.[30] Academic writers have debated the merits of the Canadian case and although they disagree as to whether Canada could reasonably have claimed necessity, they appear to agree that the necessity defense does exist.[31]

---

for Authorized Violations of International Law' 5 *Boston University International Law Journal* (1987) 389-412.

[25] Libyan Arab Foreign Investment Company (LAFICO) and The Repiblic of Burundi, March 4, 1991 in 96 *International Legal Reports*, 282, at 318-319.

[26] 1998 ICJ 432.

[27] On May 10, 1994, Canada amended its acceptance of the Court's jurisdiction by submitting a new declaration of acceptance of the compulsory jurisdiction of the Court, see 1998 ICJ 432 at 438.

[28] Some judges could, however, not help but hint at the real issue: 'Was there really no other way than to embarrass the Court, which clearly discerns illegality in Canada's conduct on the high seas, but must nonetheless play Pontius Pilate and wash its hands of the case? This is an unwelcome situation for a Court which knows that it must render justice but cannot do so.' Dissenting opinion by Judge Bedjaoui, 1998 ICJ 432 at 537-538.

[29] 1998 ICJ 432 at 443.

[30] 1998 ICJ 432 at 518 and 539. Among these fora was a background paper entitled 'Backgrounder: Greenland Halibut' in which the Canadian government argued that it had 'a legal right to take action against the Spanish [which was] established under the doctrine of necessity', quoted in Peter G. G. Davies 'The EC/Canadian Fisheries Dispute in the Northwest Atlantic' 44 *International and Comparative Law Quarterly* (1995) 917-939 at 936.

[31] See for example Okon Akiba 'International Law of the Sea: The Legality of Canadian Seizure of the Spanish Trawler (*Estai*) 37 *Natural Resources Journal* (1997), 809-828. Akiba concludes that 'all the particularly strict conditions for a genuine plea of necessity were in existence when Canada arrested the Spanish vessel *Estai*', Ibid. 826. Contrary to this conclusion, Schaefer finds that the assertion that Canada fulfilled the conditions required for claiming necessity 'would not likely wash' for a number of reasons, the immediate one being that 'Canada in fact helped cause the threat [to the essential interest]', Andrew Schaefer '1995 Canada-Spain Fishing Dispute (the Turbot War)' 8 *Georgetown International Environmental Law Review* (1996) 437-449 at 447. Similarly Davies points out that the Canadian authorities previously had tolerated over fishing by Canadian fishermen and concludes that it is 'ceratinly debatable' whether circumstances of the case justified the invocation of necessity, Peter G. G. Davies 'The EC/Canadian Fisheries Dispute in the Northwest Atlantic' 44 *International and Comparative Law Quarterly* (1995) 917-939 at 937.

In another case concerning the law of the sea, the necessity defense was recently claimed by Guinea in a case before the International Tribunal for the Law of the Sea.[32] The facts of the case are as follows: An oil tanker, the M/V *Saiga*, flying the flag of St. Vincent and the Grenadines supplied oil to some fishing vessels in the Exclusive Economic Zone (EEZ) of Guinea.[33] The *Saiga* was arrested by Guinean customs patrol boats and brought into the port of Guinea. Guinea justifies this action by maintaining that the prohibition in article 1 of Law L/94/007 "can be applied for the purpose of controlling and suppressing the sale of gas oil to fishing vessels in the customs radius according to article 34 of the Customs Code of Guinea".[34] Saint Vincent and the Grenadines, on the other hand, claimed that, 'in applying its customs laws to the *Saiga* in its customs radius, which includes parts of the exclusive economic zone, Guinea acted contrary to the Convention'.[35] The Tribunal agreed with Saint Vincent and the Grenadines and found that 'the Convention does not empower a coastal State to apply its customs laws in respect of any other parts of the exclusive economic zone not mentioned above'.[36] It remained, however, for the Tribunal to consider 'whether the otherwise wrongful application by Guinea of its customs laws to the exclusive economic zone can be justified under general international law by Guinea's appeal to "state of necessity"'.[37] After making reference to the Gabèíkovo-Nagymaros Project Case and the criteria set out therein, the Tribunal concludes that 'no evidence has been produced by Guinea to show that its essential interests were in grave and imminent peril. But, however essential Guinea's interest in maximizing its tax revenue from the sale of gas oil to fishing vessels, it cannot be suggested that the only means of safeguarding that interest was to extend its customs laws to parts of the exclusive economic zone'.[38]

Finally, necessity was briefly considered recently by the ICJ in the case concerning the legal consequences of the construction of a wall in the occupied Palestinian territory. Here, the Court made reference to the Gabcíkovo-Nagymaros Project case and to the ILC draft articles, emphasizing that the necessity defence requires that the act being challenged be the only way for the State to safeguard an essential interest against a grave and imminent peril.[39] With regard to the Israeli barrier, the Court was 'not convinced that the construction of the wall along the route chosen was the only means

---

[32] THE M/V "*Saiga*" (No. 2) Case (St. Vincent and the Grenadines v. Guinea). The case is reproduced in 120 *International Law Reports* (2002) 43-353 and in 38 *International Legal Materials* (1999) 1323.

[33] For a summary of the facts and the case, see 120 *International Law Reports* (2002) 144-156.

[34] 120 *International Law Reports* (2002) 187, paragraph 116.

[35] 120 *International Law Reports* (2002) 189, paragraph 123.

[36] 120 *International Law Reports* (2002) 190, paragraph 127.

[37] 120 *International Law Reports* (2002) 191, paragraph 132.

[38] 120 *International Law Reports* (2002) 191-192, paragraph 135.

[39] Legal Consequences of the Construction of a Wall in the Occupied Palestinian Territory, Judgment 9 July 2004, paragraphs 140-142, available at www.icj.org, visited August 2, 2004.

to safeguard the interests of Israel against the peril which it has invoked as justification for that construction'.[40] Hence, the necessity defence was not available to Israel.

9.IV. States' Reactions

In the context of the British intervention in Egypt in 1956 in connection with the Suez Crisis, the then legal advisor to the British Foreign Office and member of the ILC, later Judge at the ICJ, Sir Gerald Fitzmaurice described the doctrine of so-called necessity as a 'rather back-handed doctrine, since it is founded on the maxim that necessity knows no law, but one to which international law does, nevertheless, within pretty stringent limits, afford recognition'.[41] States have, in their responses to the ILC, exhibited some ambivalence toward the concept of a state of necessity. Mongolia held that the criterion "essential interest" used in the article 'not only fails to solve the problem, but may even create new problems'.[42] Sweden found that the limitations on the invocation of necessity were 'rather vague'.[43] Czechoslovakia expressed the view that the formulations in draft Article 33, such as "essential interest" and "grave and imminent peril" were 'unclear' and that the draft article 'even extends the concept of a state of necessity to cases where there is no immediate threat to the existence of the State as a sovereign and independent entity'. Czechoslovakia further stated that the inclusion of the necessity provision 'raises serious doubts, since, with reference to safeguarding an "essential interest", it actually enables States to violate their international obligations'.[44] More recently, the United Kingdom viewed 'with extreme circumspection the introduction of a right to depart from international obligations in circumstances where the State has judged it necessary to do so in order to protect an interest that it deems "essential". A defence of necessity would be open to very serious abuse across the

---

[40] Ibid.

[41] See Marston, Geoffrey: 'Armed Intervention in the 1956 Suez Canal Crisis: The Legal Advice Tendered to the British Government' in 37 *International and Comparative Law Quarterly*, 1988, 773, at 785. Special Rapporteur Ago adds that 'if the two governments [United Kingdom and France] responsible for the action had invoked the ground of necessity, the absence in this case of the requisite conditions would have been argued against them.' See Addendum to Eight Report on State Responsibility by Mr. Roberto Ago, Document A/CN.4/318/ADD.5-7, 1980, reproduced in 2 *Yearbook of the International Law Commission* (YILC) 1980, part one, page 42, note 132.

[42] Comments from Governments, Mongolia, Document A/CN.4/492 and Add. 1-4, reproduced in 2 *Yearbook of the International Law Commission*, part one, 1981, 76.

[43] Comments from Governments, Sweden, ibid., 77.

[44] Comments from Governments, Czechoslovakia, Document A/CN.4/362, reproduced in 2 *Yearbook of the International Law Commission*, part one, 1983, 2. Similarly, Byelorussia SSR found that the provisions 'contradicts the essential meaning of the international responsibility of States and are therefore unacceptable', in 2 *Yearbook of the International Law Commission*, part one, 1982, 18.

whole range of international relations. There is a grave risk that the provision would weaken the rule of law'.[45]

9.V. Scholars' Views

A brief examination of scholarly writing on necessity also reveals doubt. Even among pre-World War II writer unease is evident. Thus Stowell found that 'this doctrine of necessity strikes at the very root of international society, and makes the preservation of the separate states of greater importance than the preservation of the community of states'.[46] Basdevant stressed that the question as to whether necessity constituted an excuse for not fulfilling an international obligation was much debated among authors.[47] Waldock describes the doctrine of necessity as 'a rejection of law'[48] and Brownlie is very critical of the necessity defense, seeing it as a relic from previous centuries, as window dressing for *raison d'etat* and susceptible to selfish interpretation.[49] Similarly, Higgins asserts that 'it is a concept which cannot be kept within proper bounds'.[50] Partly based on Krylov's opinion in the Corfu Channel case, Jiménez de Aréchaga, in 1968 wrote that it may be concluded that 'there is no general principle allowing the defence of necessity'.[51] More recently, Allott lamented that 'among the clearest lessons of our collective experience is that the concept of state of necessity is the most persistent and formidable enemy of a truly human society' and the concept is 'enough to destroy any possibility of an international rule of law.'[52] Other scholars have,

---

[45] Comments from Governments, United Kingdom, Document A/CN.4/488, 1998, 87-88, available at: http://www.un.org/law/ilc/archives/statfra.htm. These concerns were repeated in 2001: Comments from governments, United Kingdom, Document A/CN.4/515, 2001, 32-33.

[46] Ellery C. Stowell *Intervention in International Law* John Byrne & Co. (1921) 392-393.

[47] Jules Basdevant, 'Règles Générales du Droit de la Paix' 58 RC 1936-IV, 473 at 551. He further states that 'Il ne semble donc pas qu'il existe une règle de droit international positif justifiant l'inobservation d'une règle de droit international par l'excuse de nécessité', Ibid. at 553.

[48] C.H.M. Waldock 'The Regulation of the Use of Force by Individual States in International Law' 81 RC (1952) 542-517 at 461-462. In the sixth edition of Brierly's textbook, which was edited by Waldock, it was found that 'the doctrine [of self-preservation/necessity] would destroy the imperative character of any system of law in which it applied, for it makes all obligation to obey the law merely conditional', J.L. Brierly *The Law of Nations: An Introduction to the International Law of Peace* 6th ed. Oxford University Press (1963) 404.

[49] Ian Brownlie *International Law and the Use of Force by States* Oxford University Press 1963 42-49.

[50] Rosalyn Higgins *The Development of International Law through the Political Organs of the United Nations* Oxford University Press (1963) 218.

[51] Jiménez de Aréchaga, Eduardo: 'International Responsibility' in Sørensen, Max (ed.) *Manual of Public International Law*, New York, St. Martin Press, 1968, 531 at 542. He does recognize particular rules making allowance for varying degrees of necessity, but ' these cases have a meaning and a scope entirely outside the traditional doctrine', ibid.

[52] Allott, Philip: 'State Responsibility and the Unmaking of International Law' in 29 *Harvard International Law Journal*, 1988, 1 at 17 and 21.

however, accepted necessity as part of international law. Barboza, for example, found that, 'purged of some of the erroneous notions which burdened it', necessity is 'a useful concept'.[53]

9.VI. The Gabcíkovo-Nagymaros Project Case and the Cumulative Conditions

Against this background, one can understand that it was with some trepidation that Hungary's advocates pleaded necessity in the Gabcíkovo-Nagymaros Project case.[54] As it turned out, they needn't have worried. In spite of the somewhat ambiguous attitude towards necessity exhibited in previous cases, the International Court of Justice found necessity to be part of customary international law.

Today, after the work of the ILC and the endorsement of the International Court of Justice, it is fair to echo Schachter's observation that international law rejects the idea that necessity knows no law. Decades of study has found that necessity exists in international law and that the best safeguard against abuse of the concept is its codification in the Draft Articles on State Responsibility with appropriate, strictly defined and cumulative circumscriptions. Additionally, the International Court emphasized that 'the State concerned is not the sole judge' of whether the conditions have been met.[55] It is to these conditions we now turn.

In the Gabcíkovo-Nagymaros Project case, the International Court of Justice based itself on the conditions enumerated by the ILC in the 1980 Draft Article 33. Outlining the conditions, the Court held:

---

[53] Barboza, Julio: 'Necessity (revisited) in International Law' in Makarczyk, Jerzy (ed.): *Essays in International Law in Honour of Judge Manfred Lachs*, The Hague, Martinus Nijhoff, 1984, 27 at 28. See also: Cheng, Bin: *General Principles of Law as Applied by International Courts and Tribunals*, Cambridge, Grotius Publications Limited, 1987 (originally 1953), 69, and Buza, L.: 'The State of Necessity in International Law' in 1 *Acta Juridica Academiae Scientiarum Hungarica*, 1959, 205-228. More recently, see Kohen, Marcelo G.: 'The Notion of "State Survival" in International Law' in Boisson de Chazournes, Laurence and Philip Sands (ed.): *International Law, The International Court of Justice and Nuclear Weapons*, Cambridge, Cambridge University Press, 1999, 293 at 306, and Boed, Roman: 'State of Necessity as a Justification for International Wrongful Conduct' in 3 *Yale Human Rights and Development Law Journal*, 2000, 1, and Zemanek, Karl: 'New Trends in the Enforcemnet of erga omnes Obligations' in 4 *Max Planck Yearbook of United Nations Law*, 2000, 1 at 31.

[54] For a brief discussion of the case, see Phoebe N. Okowa 'Case Concerning the Gabcíkovo-Nagymaros Project (Hungary/Slovakia) 47 *International and Comparative Law Quarterly* (1998) 688-697. See also Mari Nakamichi 'The International Court of Justice Decision Regarding the Gabcíkovo-Nagymaros Project' 9 *Fordham Environmental Law Journal* (1998) 337-372 and Daniel Dobos 'The Necessity of Precaution: The Furture of Ecological Necessity and the Precautionary Principle' 13 *Fordham Environmental Law Journal* (2002) 375-408.

[55] I.C.J. Reports, 1997, 40, paragraph 51

In the present case, the basic following conditions set forth in Draft Article 33 are relevant: it must have been occasioned by an "essential interest" of the State which is the author of the act conflicting with one of its international obligations; that interest must have been threatened by a "grave and imminent peril"; the act being challenged must have been the "only means" of safeguarding that interest; that act must not have "seriously impair[ed] an essential interest" of the State towards which the obligation existed; and the State which is the author of that act must not have "contributed to the occurrence of the state of necessity". Those conditions reflect customary international law.[56]

In taking as its point of reference Draft Article 33, the Court diverged slightly from the new draft by the ILC.[57] In the following examination, however, the point of departure will be the most recent and final Article 25:

Necessity may not be invoked by a State as a ground for precluding the wrongfulness of an act not in conformity with an international obligation of that State unless the act:
(a) Is the only way ...

According to the Draft article on necessity, the conduct not in conformity with an international obligation must be the 'only means of warding off' the peril: 'the peril must not have been escapable by any other means, even a more costly one, that could be adopted in compliance with international obligations'.[58] The ICJ found that Hungary had other means than suspending and abandoning works under the 1977 treaty with Czechoslovakia, even though – 'and this is not determinative of the state of necessity' – these other means (e.g. water purification) would 'have been a more costly technique'.[59] As mentioned above, the International Tribunal for the Law of the Sea found 'it cannot be suggested that the only means of safeguarding that interest [Guinea's interest in

---

[56] Ibid., paragraph 52.

[57] The Court, for example, reiterates that the balancing of interests is vis-a-vis 'the State towards which the obligation exited'. As will be further elaborated upon below, the most recent ILC draft expanded this weighing of interest in light of *erga omnes* obligations.

[58] See Report of the International Law Commission, reproduced in 2 *Yearbook of the International Law Commission* (YILC) 1980, part two, page 33. According to Ago, the conduct must 'truly be the only means', Addendum to Eight Report on State Responsibility by Mr. Roberto Ago, Document A/CN.4/318/ADD.5-7, 1980, reproduced in 2 *Yearbook of the International Law Commission* (YILC) 1980, part one, page 20, paragraph 14.

[59] I.C.J. Reports, 1997, 42, paragraph 55.

maximizing its tax revenue from the sale of gas oil to fishing vessels] was to extend its customs laws to parts of the exclusive economic zone'.[60]

... for the State to safeguard an essential interest ...

Since any invocation of necessity can only be conceived of in conditions of an absolutely exceptional nature, it naturally follows that the interest which is protected by breaching an international obligation must be essential. According to both Ago's and the ILC's 1980 reports the interest should, however, not be limited to the very existence of the state.[61]

What more can specifically be said to constitute 'an essential interest' for a state is somewhat harder to spell out in generalities: The ILC decided that 'it would be pointless to try to spell them [essential interests] out any more clearly and to lay down pre-established categories of interests'.[62] It would depend on the circumstances and the totality of the conditions in which the state finds itself in the particular case.[63] Similarly, the ILC, in its final Commentary, found that 'the extent to which a given interest is "essential" depends on all the circumstances, and cannot be prejudged'.[64] In 1980, some broad categories are nonetheless suggested: the existence of the state, its political or economic survival, the continued functioning of its essential services, the maintenance of internal peace, the survival of a sector of its population, the preservation of the environment of its territory or a part thereof.[65] The 2001 Commentary lists similar interests as potentially essential.[66]

---

[60] 120 *International Law Reports* (2002) 191-192, paragraph 135.

[61] Addendum to Eight Report on State Responsibility by Mr. Roberto Ago, Document A/CN.4/318/ADD.5-7, 1980, reproduced in 2 *Yearbook of the International Law Commission* (YILC) 1980, part one, page 19, paragraph 12 and Report of the International Law Commission, reproduced in 2 *Yearbook of the International Law Commission* (YILC) 1980, part two, page 49, paragraph 32.

[62] Report of the International Law Commission, reproduced in 2 *Yearbook of the International Law Commission* (YILC) 1980, part two, page 49, paragraph 32.

[63] Addendum to Eight Report on State Responsibility by Mr. Roberto Ago, Document A/CN.4/318/ADD.5-7, 1980, reproduced in 2 *Yearbook of the International Law Commission* (YILC) 1980, part one, page 19, paragraph 12.

[64] James Crawford *The International Law Commission's Articles on State Responsibility: Introduction, Text and Commentary* Cambridge University Press, 2002, 183, paragraph 15.

[65] Addendum to Eight Report on State Responsibility by Mr. Roberto Ago, Document A/CN.4/318/ADD.5-7, 1980, reproduced in 2 *Yearbook of the International Law Commission* (YILC) 1980, part one, page 14, paragraph 2 and Report of the International Law Commission, reproduced in 2 *Yearbook of the International Law Commission* (YILC) 1980, part two, page 35, paragraph 3. Curiously, Ago finds a not so different enumeration of categories 'of little use' to help determine a specific situation, see Addendum to Eight Report on State Responsibility by Mr. Roberto Ago, Document A/CN.4/318/ADD.5-7, 1980, reproduced in 2 *Yearbook of the International Law Commission* (YILC) 1980, part one, page 19, paragraph 12, note 24. It may be noted that first Ago and then the ICL provided their examples of essential interests in the beginning of the Commentary and

Although the state claiming to have acted in a state of necessity must be able to point to an essential interest under threat, it would seem that reference to one of the broad categories just outlined would suffice. Such a conclusion seems to be supported by the International Court of Justice in the Gabcíkovo-Nagymaros Project (Hungary/Slovakia) Judgement. In this case, the Court – quite quickly – acknowledged that the concerns expressed by Hungary for its natural environment 'related to an "essential interest" of that State [Hungary], within the meaning given to that expression in Article 33' of the 1980 ILC Draft.[67] Justifying this, the Court referred to the inclusion of 'the preservation of the environment' in the ILC report and to its own findings in the 1996 Nuclear Weapons Advisory Opinion concerning 'the great significance that it [the Court] attaches to respect for the environment, not only for States but also for the whole of mankind'.[68]

One may, furthermore add that it may be difficult for an international judicial authority to overrule or second-guess the claim of a state, save if it is completely disingenuous. This attitude seems to be reflected in the following dictum from the International Tribunal for the Law of the Sea, considering that maximizing a country's tax revenues may be important but hardly essential: '*however essential* Guinea's interest in maximizing its tax revenue from the sale of gas oil to fishing vessels, it cannot be suggested that the only means of safeguarding that interest was to extend its customs laws to parts of the exclusive economic zone'.[69] This would indicate that the actual judicial test with regard to the interest under threat is not its 'essential' character but rather the presence of one or more of the additional cumulative conditions, in particular the graveness and imminence of the peril and the question of own fault.

An interesting question is whether essential interest may include events that do not have a direct impact on the State claiming to act under necessity. This appears to be what Belgium is arguing when it claims before the ICJ that 'necessity is the cause which justifies the violation of a binding rule in order to safeguard, in face of grave and

---

Report respectively to illustrate the difference between necessity and other categories of Chapter V: 'Circumstances precluding wrongfulness' and not when discussing essential interests. Ago, however, indicates in a footnote that the examples provided are 'often invoked in this context as "essential" or "particularly important" interests of the State' (Addendum to Eight Report on State Responsibility by Mr. Roberto Ago, Document A/CN.4/318/ADD.5-7, 1980, reproduced in 2 *Yearbook of the International Law Commission* (YILC) 1980, part one, page 14, paragraph 2, note 4) and the ICJ picked from the selection when finding the natural environment an essential interest, I.C.J. Reports, 1997, 41, paragraph 53.

[66] James Crawford *The International Law Commission's Articles on State Responsibility: Introduction, Text and Commentary* Cambridge University Press, 2002, 183, paragraph 14.

[67] I.C.J. Reports, 1997, 41, paragraph 53.

[68] Ibid., referring to Legality of the Threat or Use of Nuclear Weapons, Advisory Opinion, I.C.J. Reports, 1996, 241-242.

[69] 120 *International Law Reports* (2002) 191-192, paragraph 135 (emphasis added).

imminent peril, *values* which are higher than those protected by the rule which is breached'.[70] Although referring explicitly to Article 33, the Belgium advocate provides the Court with a definition of necessity where essential interest is substituted by 'values'. The Commentary of Ago and the ILC Report both appear to accept such an interpretation of 'essential interest' although the wording of Article 33 does not carry this out.[71] However, both of the narratives address interventions for humanitarian purposes 'such as saving the lives of nationals or foreigners threatened' or interventions in cases of 'grave and imminent danger ... simply to people'.[72] Citing these examples, Verwey writes that it 'must be assumed therefore, that the ILC, when it was drafting Article 33 within the context of a document on State responsibility, may have lost sight of acts of a State aimed at safeguarding essential interests of a non-national nature, without intending to exclude the potential applicability of the principle of necessity to such acts'.[73] The latest re-drafting would appear to follow these considerations. Paragraph 1(a) now reads 'safeguard an essential interest against a grave and imminent peril' as opposed to the original, 1980 version: 'safeguarding an essential interest of the State against a grave and imminent peril'.

... against a <u>grave and imminent peril</u>; and...

Although the final article adopted by the ICL only stipulates that the peril which threatens the essential interest must be 'grave', both Ago's commentary and the 1980 ILC Report point out that the peril must be 'extremely grave'.[74] In addition, the threat to the essential interest must be 'imminent', 'representing a present danger', 'at the actual time'.[75] This is also reflected in the 2001 Commentary according to which the

---

[70] See uncorrected transcript of Belgium's Oral Pleadings, CR 99/15, May 10, 1999, available at www.icj-cij.org, visited September 22, 2002 (emphasis added).

[71] 'Essential State interest' in Addendum to Eight Report on State Responsibility by Mr. Roberto Ago, Document A/CN.4/318/ADD.5-7, 1980, reproduced in 2 *Yearbook of the International Law Commission* (YILC) 1980, part one, page 51 and 'essential interest of the State' in the version adopted by the ILC, Report of the International Law Commission, reproduced in 2 *Yearbook of the International Law Commission* (YILC) 1980, part two, page 49, paragraph 32.

[72] Addendum to Eight Report on State Responsibility by Mr. Roberto Ago, Document A/CN.4/318/ADD.5-7, 1980, reproduced in 2 *Yearbook of the International Law Commission* (YILC) 1980, part one, page 43, paragraph 69. and Report of the International Law Commission, reproduced in 2 *Yearbook of the International Law Commission* (YILC) 1980, part two, page 41, paragraph 23.

[73] Verwey, W.D.: 'Humanitarian Intervention under International Law' in 32 *Netherlands International Law Review*, 1985, 357 at 413.

[74] Addendum to Eight Report on State Responsibility by Mr. Roberto Ago, Document A/CN.4/318/ADD.5-7, 1980, reproduced in 2 *Yearbook of the International Law Commission* (YILC) 1980, part one, page 19, paragraph 13. and Report of the International Law Commission, reproduced in 2 *Yearbook of the International Law Commission* (YILC) 1980, part two, page 48, paragraph 33.

[75] Ibid.

'peril has to be objectively established and not merely apprehended as possible'.[76] Beyond these somewhat general observations, the Commentary and Report are rather parsimonious.

The ICJ held that peril evokes the idea of "risk" and that the peril has to be established 'at the relevant point in time' and, hence, not be a mere 'possibility'.[77] The Court, however, added that a peril appearing in the long term may well be imminent if the realization of the peril 'however far off [temporally] it might be, is not thereby any less certain and inevitable'.[78] Similarly, the 2001 Commentary holds that 'a measure of uncertainty about the future does not necessarily disqualify a state from invoking necessity, if the peril is clearly established on the basis of the evidence reasonably available at the time'.[79] As pointed out by both the International Court and by the ILC, long-term predictions and prognoses are particularly pertinent to questions concerning threats to, for example, the environment.[80] Although not spelled out by the Court, it is possible to discern what is termed the 'precautionary principle' from international environmental law in the Court's deliberations.[81] However, the fact that Hungary had some "uncertainties", meaning some concerns over the potential ecological impact of the Gabcíkovo-Nagymaros project, could not, serious as they were, establish the objective existence of a "peril" in the context of the necessity defense.[82]

(b) Does not seriously impair an essential interest of the State or States towards which the obligation exists, or of the international community as a whole.

The interest which is protected by the international obligation breached due to the state of necessity 'must obviously be inferior to' the threatened essential interest of the State

---

[76] James Crawford *The International Law Commission's Articles on State Responsibility: Introduction, Text and Commentary* Cambridge University Press, 2002, 183, paragraph 15. See also I.C.J. Reports, 1997, 42, paragraph 54.

[77] I.C.J. Reports, 1997, 42, paragraph 54.

[78] Ibid. In the concrete case, the Court found that although an 'essential interest', i.e. the environment was involved, the threat was in the case of Nagymaros neither grave nor imminent (paragraph 55) and in the case of the Gabcíkovo sector not imminent, its graveness untold (paragraph 56 and concluding in paragraph 57).

[79] James Crawford *The International Law Commission's Articles on State Responsibility: Introduction, Text and Commentary* Cambridge University Press, 2002, 184, paragraph 16.

[80] Ibid.

[81] According to the Rio-Declaration, Principle 15, the precautionary principle holds that 'In order to protect the environment, the precautionary approach shall be widely applied by States according to their capabilities. Where there are threats of serious or irreversible damage, lack of full scientific certainty shall not be used as a reason for postponing cost-effective measures to prevent environmental degradation'. The Rio-Declaration may be found at the United Nations Environment Programme website, www.unep.org, visited August 12, 2003.

[82] 1997 ICJ 7 at 42, paragraph 54.

claiming necessity and, consequently, 'cannot be one which is comparable and equally essential to the foreign State concerned'.[83] As the 2001 Commentary notes: 'the interest relied on must outweigh all other considerations, not merely from the point of view of the acting state but on a reasonable assessment of competing interests'[84]. During the recent review, the Special Rapporteur, James Crawford, proposed an amendment of Article 33 (1) (b) which would open for a balancing adjusted to contemporary international law which includes obligations *erga omnes*.[85] This proposal has been codified in the reference to 'the international community as a whole'. Boed, in arguing for exactly such an amendment, notes that the bilateral paradigm, which was evident in the original wording, 'fails to account for the advent of human rights law from the middle of the twentieth century and the resulting creation of *erga omnes* obligations'.[86]

2. In any case, necessity may not be invoked by a State as a ground for precluding wrongfulness if:
(a) The international obligation in question excludes the possibility of invoking necessity; or ...

In some cases, the international obligation in question may, explicitly or by inference, exclude a plea of necessity. This is particularly the case in regard to certain humanitarian obligations.[87] Below, it will briefly be considered whether the UN Charter

---

[83] Addendum to Eight Report on State Responsibility by Mr. Roberto Ago, Document A/CN.4/318/ADD.5-7, 1980, reproduced in 2 *Yearbook of the International Law Commission* (YILC) 1980, part one, page 20, paragraph 15. In the words of the ILC: '... The interest sacrificed on the alter of "necessity" must obviously be less important than the interest it is thereby sought to save', Report of the International Law Commission, reproduced in 2 *Yearbook of the International Law Commission* (YILC) 1980, part two, page 50, paragraph 35. The ICJ found that there was 'no need' to consider this criteria since Hungary had already failed other parts of the necessity test, I.C.J. Reports, 1997, 46, paragraph 58.
[84] James Crawford *The International Law Commission's Articles on State Responsibility: Introduction, Text and Commentary* Cambridge University Press, 2002, 184, paragraph 17.
[85] See Second Report on State Responsiblity by Mr. James Crawford, Document A/CN.4/498/Add.2, 1999, 32, paragraph 290. See also James R. Crawford 'Responsibility to the International Community as a Whole' 8 *Indiana Journal of Global Legal Studies* (2001) 303 'it seems clear that there are standards of conduct in international law that cannot be reduced to the interstate realm'. At 306.
[86] Boed, Roman: 'State of Necessity as a Justification for International Wrongful Conduct' in 3 *Yale Human Rights and Development Law Journal*, 2000, 1 at 19. Addressing the specific issue of the use of necessity to justify a state's closure of its borders in face of a large number of asylum seekers, Boed suggests that, with the new wording, 'the interest of the international community in having non-refoulment honored, then, could possibly outweigh the interest of a single state in closing its borders to protect an essential interest and, in consequence, necessity would not be available to justify border closure in the face of an influx of asylum-seekers', ibid., 41.
[87] James Crawford *The International Law Commission's Articles on State Responsibility: Introduction, Text and Commentary* Cambridge University Press, 2002, 185, paragraph 19.

by explicitly allowing for one exception to the ban on use of force implicitly excluded any other exceptions.

(b) The State has contributed to the situation of necessity.

The State claiming to be acting under a state of necessity 'must not itself have provoked' the situation or have helped 'by act or omission to bring it about'.[88] In the case before the European Court of Justice mentioned previously, the Court noted that one defendant had made 'an erroneous evaluation of an unfavourable economic situation which was known to all' and, thus, the Court noted 'that personal conduct does not entitle it to rely on a state of necessity'.[89] Similarly, in the Gabcíkovo-Nagymaros Project Case, the Court concluded that Hungary could not rely on a state of necessity that 'it had helped, by act or omission to bring it about'.[90] In the case of the Kosovo conflict and the use of force against the FRY, Belgium has, as noted, for its defense in front of the ICJ, in part, relied on the necessity excuse.[91] Brownlie and Apperley seem to find such a defense precluded because the 'crisis in Kosovo originated in the deliberate fomenting of civil strife in Kosovo and the subsequent intervention by NATO States in the civil war. In such conditions those States responsible for the civil strife and the intervention are estopped from pleading humanitarian purposes.'[92]

9.V. Peremptory Norms and Necessity and the Use of Force

The weariness and concern often expressed about the necessity excuse is primarily due to the past, and potential future, abuse of the excuse, particularly involving the use of force.[93] This concern was reflected in the dissenting opinion of Judge Krylov in the Corfu Channel case, where he wrote that since the coming into force of the UN Charter, 'the so-called right of self-help, also known as the law of necessity (*Notrecht*) which

---

[88] Report of the International Law Commission, reproduced in 2 *Yearbook of the International Law Commission* (YILC) 1980, part two, page 50, paragraph 34 and I.C.J. Reports, 1997, 45-46, paragraph 57: The Court found that this, also, precluded Hungary from relying on a state of necessity excuse.

[89] 1981 *Common Market Law Review* 613 at 702, paragraph 144.

[90] 1997 ICJ 46, paragraph 57.

[91] See uncorrected transcript of Belgium's Oral Pleadings, CR 99/15, May 10, 1999, available at www.icj-cij.org, visited September 22, 2002.

[92] Brownlie, Ian and C.J. Apperley: 'Kosovo Crisis Inquiry: Memorandum on the International Law Aspects' in 49 *International and Comparative Law Quarterly*, 2000, 878 at 903.

[93] Jean J.A. Salmon 'Faut-il codifier l'état de necessité en droit international?' in Jerzy Makarczyk (ed.) *Essays in International Law in Honour of Judge Manfred Lachs* Martinus Nijhoff (1984) 235 at 258.

used to be upheld by a number of German authors, can no longer be invoked. It must be regarded as obsolete'.[94]

In his review of the positions taken by authors of scholarly works, Ago found that writers, who opposed necessity as being part of international law, partly did so due to practical considerations based the outright abuses of the necessity excuse by some governments.[95] Ago, and the ILC, sought to allay the fears of abuse by observing 'an outright rejection of the idea that a "plea of necessity" could absolve a State of the wrongfulness attaching to an act of aggression committed by this State'.[96] In the proposed Article 33, this was done by stipulating that necessity may not be invoked as a ground precluding wrongfulness if the breached obligation arose from a peremptory norm. The fact that the reference to peremptory norms in the final version has been given its own article (26) does not seem to change the substantial issue.[97] Additionally, the necessity excuse is also not available if the obligation being breached excludes the possibility of invoking necessity. As for the latter, one may ask whether the UN Charter by explicitly allowing for one exception to the ban on use of force, i.e. self-defense under article 51, implicitly excluded any other exceptions, including necessity. Ago asserts that it does not logically follow from the inclusion of Article 51 that the intention was to absolutely exclude other circumstances precluding wrongfulness.[98]

More interesting and controversial is the general question as to whether the use of force is prohibited by a peremptory norm. Ago devotes a substantial part of his Commentary to the question of use of force and the necessity excuse. He asserts that the

---

[94] The Corfu Channel case, I.C.J. Reports, 1949 at 77. See also the observation by Mrazek concerning Draft Article 33: 'The standpoint of the International Law Commission calls into question the peremptory character of the principle of the non-use of force. The right of necessity must not be misused to undermine the stability of international legal order', Josef Mrazek 'Prohibition of the Use and Threat of Force: Self-Defense and Self-Help in International Law' in XXVII *Canadian Yearbook of International Law* (1989) 81 at 107.

[95] Addendum to Eight Report on State Responsibility by Mr. Roberto Ago, Document A/CN.4/318/ADD.5-7, 1980, reproduced in 2 *Yearbook of the International Law Commission* (YILC) 1980, part one, page 47, paragraph 71. Ago paraphrased the critical position as follows: 'we are opposed to recognizing the ground of necessity as a principle of general international law because States use and abuse that so-called principle for inadmissible and often unadmittable purposes; but we are ultimately prepared to grant it a limited function in certain specific areas of international law less sensitive than those in which the abuses we deplore usually occur', ibid. page 50, paragraph 76.

[96] Addendum to Eight Report on State Responsibility by Mr. Roberto Ago, Document A/CN.4/318/ADD.5-7, 1980, reproduced in 2 *Yearbook of the International Law Commission* (YILC) 1980, part one, page 51, paragraph 79.

[97] Article 26 states 'Compliance with peremptory norms: Nothing in the Chapter precludes the wrongfulness of any act of a State which is not in conformity with an obligation arising under a peremptory norm of general international law'.

[98] Addendum to Eight Report on State Responsibility by Mr. Roberto Ago, Document A/CN.4/318/ADD.5-7, 1980, reproduced in 2 *Yearbook of the International Law Commission* (YILC) 1980, part one, page 41, paragraph 59.

prohibition on the use of force in international relations found in the UN Charter, Article 2(4) not only covers 'aggression', i.e. the most serious use of force, but also other, less serious acts besides those which merit being classified as acts of aggression.[99] Hence, whereas Ago acknowledges that even uses of force that are 'circumscribed in magnitude and duration' and carried out for 'limited purposes' and 'without true aggressive intentions' are prohibited, he questions whether all uses of force are prohibited by a peremptory norm. He found that to claim that all uses of force are prohibited *jus cogens* 'might be to expand beyond what is at present accepted by the legal conviction of States, either the concept of "aggression" or the concept of "peremptory norm" as defined in article 53 of the Vienna Convention on the Law of Treaties'.[100]

The 1980 ILC Report echoes Ago's findings: 'It remained to consider the problem of the possible existence of conduct which, although infringing the territorial sovereignty of a State, need not necessarily be considered as an act of aggression or not, in any case, as a breach of an international obligation *jus cogens*.'[101] As Ago, the ILC maintained that it is for the organs charged with interpreting the UN Charter to determine whether the differentiation is valid.[102] As is evident from the quotes, Ago employs very careful language although it is clear from the context that he believed the differentiation of the prohibition of use of force into two categories was possible: Ago 'hesitated to ascribe the same force of *jus cogens* as must, in our view, be accorded to the prohibition of aggression'.[103]

A few scholars have built on the foundation provided by Ago and the ILC.[104] Ronzitti emphasizes the requirement for a peremptory norm in Article 53 of the Vienna

---

[99] Ibid. pages 40-41, paragraph 58

[100] Ibid. page 41, paragraph 59. Article 53 of the Vienna Convention defines a peremptory norm as 'a norm accepted and recognized by the international community of States as a whole as a norm from which no derogation is permitted ...'

[101] Report of the International Law Commission, reproduced in 2 *Yearbook of the International Law Commission* (YILC) 1980, part two, page 43, paragraph 23. See also Alexandrov: 'According to such definitions [aggression as any illegal use of force], since the use or threat of force is allowed only in self-defense or if decided upon by a competent organ of the United Nations, every other use of force should be considered aggression. Such proposals, however, ignore the views that not every unlawful use of force is necessarily aggression' Stanimir A. Alexandrov *Self-Defense Against the Use of Force in International Law* Kluwer Law International (1996) 108. He does, however, warn against adopting the doctrine of necessity due to the risk of reviving theories of self-preservation, Ibid. 182, note 298.

[102] Ibid., 24.

[103] Addendum to Eight Report on State Responsibility by Mr. Roberto Ago, Document A/CN.4/318/ADD.5-7, 1980, reproduced in 2 *Yearbook of the International Law Commission* (YILC) 1980, part one, page 44, paragraph 66.

[104] See the recent comments on this issue in Ole Spiermann 'Humanitarian Intervention as a Necessity and the Threat or Use of *Jus Cogens*' 71 *Nordic Journal of International Law* (2002) 523-543 at 535-542.

Convention, i.e. that the norm must be accepted as peremptory by the international community of States as a whole. Based on this he finds that the 'peremptory rule banning the use of force does not exactly coincide with the corresponding rule contained in Art. 2(4) of the UN Charter', or, in other words, some uses of force, although prohibited under 2(4) are not prohibited by a peremptory norm.[105]

Raby, considering the use of force to protect nationals, found that 'the considerable number of states which claim that the right of intervention is valid , as well as the numerous writers who think likewise, demonstrate that intervention to protect nationals cannot certainly be seen as a violation of a norm of *jus cogens*.[106] He goes on the point out that a State cannot consent to the violation of a peremptory norm: 'Therefore, if an intervention to protect nationals constituted a violation of a rule of *jus cogens,* the territorial state's consent to such an intervention would be an irrelevant consideration in assessment of the operation's legality. However, there is unanimity among states and writers that an intervention by consent is legal, by virtue of that consent alone'.[107]

Conversely, however, one might argue that it is misplaced to speak of consent to a violation of a *jus cogens* norm. Fundamentally, the norm is not violated if the intervention is consensual. As stated by Schachter 'when a recognized government invites foreign armed forces to assist it in maintaining internal security, the foreign troops would not, as a rule, be used "against the territorial integrity" or "political independence" of the inviting State nor would their role normally be inconsistent with any of the purposes of the United Nations. If those stated conditions are met, there is no violation of Article 2(4)'.[108] Schachter further found that 'the distinction drawn by the Commission appears to be in keeping with the views generally expressed on the peremptory character of the rule against force'.[109]

One may inquire as to whether developments subsequent to 1980, the date of Ago's Commentary, have clarified the issue. Firstly, there is no doubt that international law recognizes a graduation of the use of force with some uses being less grave than

---

[105] Ronzitti, Natalino: 'Use of Force, Jus Cogens and State Consent' in Cassese, A. (ed.): *The Current Legal Regulationof the Use of Force,* Dordrecht, Matinus Nijhoff, 1986, 147 at150. See also Natalino Ronzitti *Rescuing Nationals Abroad Through military Coercion and Intervention on Grounds of Humanity* Martinus Nijhoff 1985, 74-75.

[106] Raby, Jean: 'The State of Necessity and the Use of Force to Protect Nationals' in XXVI *Canadian Yearbook of International Law,* 1988, 253 at 267. Referring to Raby's article, the Commentary of the UN Charter dismisses that the concept of necessity can provide a valid basis for protective measures involving the use of force, Randelzhofer's commentary to Article 2(4) in Simma, Bruno (ed.): *The Charter of the United Nations, A Commentary,* Oxford, Oxford University Press, 1994, 125, paragraph 55.

[107] Raby, ibid., 268. See also Natalino Ronzitti *Rescuing Nationals Abroad Through military Coercion and Intervention on Grounds of Humanity* Martinus Nijhoff 1985, 86-88.

[108] Oscar Schachter *International Law in Theory and Practice* Kluwer Law International (1995) 114.

[109] Ibid. 171.

others: one may distinguish between 'the most grave forms of the use of force (those constituting an armed attack) and other less grave forms'.[110] The International Court of Justice, however, quoted the ILC with approval to the effect that 'the law of the Charter concerning the prohibition of the use of force in itself constitutes a conspicuous example of a rule in international law having the character of *jus cogens*.[111] In the 1987 Declaration on the Enhancement of the Effectiveness of the Principle of Refraining from the Threat or Use of Force in International Relations, it is emphasized that 'No consideration of whatever nature may be invoked to warrant resorting to threat or use of force in violation of the Charter'.[112] Similarly, during the most recent reexamination of the draft article on necessity, both the Special Rapporteur and the Commission expressed that in their views, the prohibition on the use of force is a peremptory norm.[113] Likewise, some authors have criticized the differentiation proposed by Ago and the 1980 Commission.[114]

The question of use of force and necessity attracted particular interest and concern in 1999 due to the debates over humanitarian intervention. In his review of Ago's Commentary, Crawford found that the differentiation - between the peremptory status of some aspects of the rules relating to the use of force and the non-peremptory status of other aspects - raised complex questions 'beyond the scope of the draft article' and he emphasized the distinction between "primary" and "secondary" rules.[115] With regard to this latter distinction, it was pointed out that 'it is one thing to define a rule and the content of the obligation it imposes, and another to determine whether that obligation has been violated and what should be the consequence of the violation'.[116] Based on the distinction, it was stipulated that the question of humanitarian intervention is 'not one which is regulated, primarily or at all, by article 33'.[117] Interpreting this distinction, it

---

[110] 1986 ICJ 191.

[111] Ibid. 190. This was supported by both Nicaragua and the United States in their respective submissions, Ibid.

[112] Declaration annexed to GA Resolution 42/22, Section I(3). Recall that Ago's point of departure was a recognition that even the 'less grave' use of force violated the Charter.

[113] Spe Rap: rules relating to the use of force referred to in Article 2(4) and 51 of the Charter certainly rank among peremptory norms of international law, paragraph 286. ILC: 'it was generally agreed that the rules governing the use of force in the Charter were jus cogens', para 375.

[114] See, for example, Jean J.A. Salmon 'Faut-il codifier l'état de necessité en droit international?' in Jerzy Makarczyk (ed.) *Essays in International Law in Honour of Judge Manfred Lachs* Martinus Nijhoff (1984) 235

[115] Second Report on State Responsibility by Mr. James Crawford, Document A/CN.4/498/Add.2, 1999, 24-33, paragraphs 275-291 at 287. On the distinction between primary and secondary rules, see First Report on State Responsibility by James Crawford, A/CN.4/490, April 24, 1998, 4, paragraphs 12-18.

[116] Ibid.

[117] Second Report on State Responsibility by Mr. James Crawford, Document A/CN.4/498/Add.2, 1999, 24-33, paragraphs 275-291 at 287. The distinction was present in Ago's Commentary as well

can be concluded that the final Article 25 does not and cannot act as a source of authority for e.g. humanitarian intervention or for use of force against terrorists.

In response to a suggestion by the Netherlands, the Special Rapporteur, however, presented a somewhat equivocal comment on this issue. The Netherlands, in brief, suggested that Chapter V concerning circumstances precluding wrongfulness should include an article on humanitarian intervention.[118] In his comment, the Special Rapporteur firstly pointed out the distinction between primary and secondary rules, emphasizing that Chapter V does not deal with substantial law issues. He then added: 'Cases not otherwise provided for may be dealt with in accordance with the criteria in article 26 (necessity) [now article 25]'.[119] The most reasonable interpretation of this

---

and has been reiterated in several cases: Ago pointed out that the answer 'depends primarily on the interpretation to be placed on certain provisions of the Charter, an instrument of conventional origin, or, in other words, on certain primary rules enunciated in that instrument. The task of deciding what that answer will be therefore rests with the various organs responsible for such interpretation, and not with a draft concerning the definition of "secondary" rules on international responsibility on which the Commission is working'. (Addendum to Eight Report on State Responsibility by Mr. Roberto Ago, Document A/CN.4/318/ADD.5-7, 1980, reproduced in 2 *Yearbook of the International Law Commission* (YILC) 1980, part one, page 44, paragraph 66). In the France – New Zealand Arbitration Tribunal in the Rainbow Warrior case, France and New Zealand disagreed on the question of which branch of general international law should be given primary emphasis in the determination of the primary obligations of France. New Zealand held that the customary Law of Treaties should decide, while France favored the customary Law of State Responsibility. The Tribunal found that both the customary Law of Treaties and the customary Law of State Responsibility were relevant and appropriate. The fundamental provision of *pacta sunt servanda* 'is applicable to the determination whether there have been violations of that principle ...'. On the other hand, 'the legal consequences of a breach of a treaty, including the determination of the circumstances that may exclude wrongfulness ... are subjects that belong to the customary Law of State Responsibility'. (82 *International Law Reports*, 548-550, paragraphs 72-75). Similarly, in Gabcíkovo-Nagymaros Project case the International Court of Justice established that a state of necessity does not terminate a treaty but may be 'invoked to exonerate from the responsibility of the State which failed to implement the treaty. Thus, the Court implicitly held that the (primary) rules of treaty termination are found in the law of treaties and not in the (secondary) rules of state responsibility. (Gabcíkovo-Nagymaros Project (Hungary/Slovakia), Judgement, I.C.J. Reports 1997, 7 at 63, paragraph 101).

[118] 'In connection with this chapter, which deals with circumstances precluding wrongfulness, the Netherlands would draw attention to the debate currently under way, for example, in the Security Council about the concept of humanitarian intervention. This is because humanitarian intervention, without prior authorization by the Security Council and without permission from the legitimate Government of the State on whose territory the intervention takes place, can be seen — in exceptional situations, because of large-scale violations of fundamental human rights or the immediate threat of such violations — as a potential justification for an internationally wrongful act, namely the actual or threatened use of force if this is required for humanitarian ends and satisfies a series of conditions. The Netherlands takes the view that an article containing such a ground for justification should be included'. State responsibility: Comments and observations received from Governments: Netherlands, A/CN.4/515, 19 March 2001, 30.

[119] Fourth report on State responsibility by Mr. James Crawford, Special Rapporteur, Addendum, A/CN.4/517/Add.1, 3 April 2001, 4.

comment would seem to be the following: In light of the previous discussion about humanitarian intervention and necessity, the Special Rapporteur appears, again, to say 'Look, this is not an issue we are going to decide here. Maybe specific cases can be excused under the necessity defense, maybe not. You try and see whether the criteria fit in each individual case'. Indeed, in the final commentary, it was pointed out that 'the question whether measures of forcible humanitarian intervention, not sanctioned pursuant to Chapters VII or VIII of the Charter of the United Nations, may be lawful under modern international law is not covered by article 25'.

The last re-reading by Crawford and the ILC, thus, does not address the question upon which Ago wanted to shed light: whether or not the wrongfulness, which is in principle accepted as undeniable, of any such action might, by way of exception, be precluded where the State which committed it is able to show that it acted on a real "state of necessity", with all the conditions for the recognition of the existence of that circumstance being fulfilled'.[120]Against this background, it would be fair to conclude that Crawford and the ILC found that necessity was not an appropriate framework for addressing the question of humanitarian intervention, or, more generally, exceptions to article 2(4) of the UN Charter. In other words, necessity cannot function as a source of authority. The ILC did not, however, disown Ago's Commentary as such.[121] If one accepts this rendition of the relationship between Ago's and Crawford's commentaries, it is not precluded to attempt to justify the use of force under the necessity excuse, although such a justification may not be accepted by for example the International Court of Justice. The necessity excuse can, however, only be sought and invoked as an excuse *ex post facto* and not as a source of authority.

The necessity excuse appears to have been put forward as justification in at least three cases of use of force in international relations: In 1960, Belgium dispatched a contingent of troops to the Congo less than two weeks after the Republic of Congo became independent. Subsequent to independence, mutinies broke out and European residents were perceived to be at risk. In the Security Council, the Belgium Minister of Foreign Affairs said that Belgium had been forced by necessity to take this purely humanitarian action.[122] The debate in the Security Council primarily concerned the facts

---

[120] Addendum to Eight Report on State Responsibility by Mr. Roberto Ago, Document A/CN.4/318/ADD.5-7, 1980, reproduced in 2 *Yearbook of the International Law Commission* (YILC) 1980, part one, page 42, paragraph 61.

[121] For the same conclusion, see Ian Johnstone 'The Plea of "Necessity" in International Legal Discourse: Humanitarian Intervention and Counter-Terrorism' 43 *Columbia Journal of Transnational Law* 2005, 337-388 at 339.

[122] See discussion in Ago, ibid. page 43, paragraph 64. In the Security Council, the Belgian representative argued among other things that 'the intervention of Belgium metropolitan troops is thus justified, first by the total inability of the Congolese national authorities to ensure respect for fundamental rules which must be observed in any civilized community and by the Belgian Government's sacred duty to take the measures required by morality and by public international law'

and no principled discussion took place about the legality or otherwise of Belgium's justification. Ago, however, notes as 'not unimportant' that there was 'no denial of the principle of the plea of necessity as such'.[123]

Following the conclusion of the Gulf War in 1991 and throughout the 1990's, Turkey has conducted numerous operations against Kurdish groups, primarily the Kurdish Workers Party (PKK), in northern Iraq without the authorization of the Iraqi government. Initially, the Turkish operations consisted of air strikes and small troop incursions.[124] Iraq protested these incursions in letters to the Security Council.[125] In the autumn of 1992, thousands of Turkish troops crossed into Iraq and by November 1, 20.000 troops were in northern Iraq.[126] In 1995, Turkey launched Operation Steel during which a massive Turkish military force on March 20 crossed into Iraq to eliminate several guerrilla strongholds of the PKK. An estimated 35.000 troops supported by tanks and combat airplanes took part.[127] The incursion was alleged to be in response to a March 18 PKK attack on Turkish troops in South West Turkey. After the attack, the PKK forces retreated back into Iraq. The Turkish Prime Minister Tansu Ciller described the aim of the operation to be 'to rip out the roots of the terror operations aimed at innocent people'.[128] A White House spokesman on March 20 said that the administration understood 'Turkey's need to deal decisively' with the terrorists and on March 21, the US States Department spokesman said that Turkey was not in violation of international law if it used necessary and appropriate force to protect itself.

(S/PV.873, July 13-14, 1960, 35, paragraph 192) and further that 'it is justified by the complete absence of interference by the Belgian Government in the internal affairs of the Republic of Congo' (S/PV.873, July 13-14, 1960, 35, paragraph 193) and finally that 'the Belgian Government can only interpret the statement just made by Mr. Hammarskjold as recognition of the material necessity for Belgian military intervention in the Congo, and indeed as an implicit acknowledgement of the legality of the action my country was compelled to take in order to protect its nationals and in the interest of the Congo and the international community at large. This intervention, which was, I believe I have shown, imperative and unavoidable, is strictly proportional to the objective in view' law' (S/PV.873, July 13-14, 1960, 36, paragraph 196).

[123] Ibid.

[124] See Douglas Jehl 'U.S. Puts Mild Pressure on Turks to End Attacks' The Los Angeles Times, August 9, 1991 (WL 2246031) and The Washington Post 'Turkey Tells Why Its Troops Are in Iraq', August 9, 1991 (WL 4199979): A Turkish spokesman said 'This is not a war. This is just an operation against terrorists'.

[125] See S/23141, October 14, 1991 'registering the protest of Iraq' and S/23152, October 17, 1991 complaining over 'further violations committed by Turkish aircraft against the territorial integrity and national sovereignty and security' of Iraq.

[126] Keesings (1992) 39163 and Facts on File (1992) 967. See also Caryle Murphy 'Turkish Army Presses Offensive in Iraq; Troops escalate Fight Against Kurdish Rebels; Iraqi Kurds Help Reluctantly' The Washington Post, October 25, 1992 (WL 2160046).

[127] See Nicole Pope 'The Turkish Invasion of Northern Iraq' 497 *Middle East International* (1995) 3 and Nicole Pope 'A Deal with Iraq's Kurds?' 498 *Middle East International* (1995) 7.

[128] Keesing (1995) 40473.

The French foreign minister, however, condemned the attack as a violation of Iraq's sovereignty.[129] The Iraqi foreign ministry spokesman said on March 22 that the operation was 'a violation of Iraq's sovereignty' and the EU troika (France, Germany and Spain) traveled to Turkey and urged the Turks to end the offensive.[130] Subsequently, the critique of Turkey's actions increased and especially the relationship between Europe and Turkey deteriorated.[131] Finally, on May 4, the Turkish Defense Minister, Mr. Mehmet Golan, announced that all 35.000 Turkish troops had left northern Iraq.[132] As early as the beginning of the summer of 1995, Turkey had, however, subsequently resumed its recurrent incursions and Iraq had continued to complain to the United Nations' Security Council.[133]

Beyond rather general statements, Turkish authorities have been rather parsimonious when it comes to presenting any legal justifications for the frequent forays into Iraq. As pointed out by Gray, spokespersons of the U.S. administration appear to articulate more consistent legal arguments than the Turks themselves.[134] As a matter of fact, Libya responded to the claim by the United States that the Turkish action was taken in self-defense, calling it an act of aggression.[135] Turkey replied to the Libyan accusations by stressing that Turkey was 'resorting to legitimate measures which are imperative to its own security [and which] cannot be regarded as a violation of Iraq's sovereignty'.[136] These measures were taken because 'Iraq has been unable to exercise its authority [and, hence] Turkey cannot ask the Government of Iraq to fulfil its

---

[129] Facts on File (1995) 217. See also Agence France-Presse: 'France condemns Turkish offensive against Kurds in Iraq, March 21, 1995. (WL 7781954) The French Foreign Minister Alain Juppe said that 'Turkey ... has to respect the basic principles of human rights, democracy and the right to self-defense'. The French, who chaired the rotating EU presidency, did not find that Turkey respected these principles.

[130] Keesing (1995) 40474. See also Shada Islam 'Europe's Stern Warning' 497 *Middle East International* (1995) 4.

[131] On March 27, the German foreign Minister, Mr. Kinkel announced that a 100 million USD government subsidy to Turkey had been suspended because of the possibility that the offensive would drag on. The EU foreign Ministers on April 10 issued a joint statement which called on Turkey to withdraw "without delay". The ministers, however, also acknowledged the gravity of 'terrorist problems' facing Turkey (Keesing (1995) 40552). The US Secretary of State similarly stated that U.S. and international support only would be forthcoming only if troops were promptly withdrawn and the Council of Europe passed a resolution that would suspend Turkish membership unless it showed significant progress toward ending it military operations in Iraq (Facts on File (1995) 315).

[132] Keesing (1995) 40563.

[133] See for example the 'strong condemnation' of Turkey's territorial incursions issued by the Council of the League of Arab States, September 14, 1996 (S/1996/796). See also the incursion initiated on May 13, 1997 which was condemned by the League of Arab States and the Coordinating Bureau of the Movement of Non-Aligned Countries, (S/1997/461).

[134] Christine Gray *International Law and the Use of Force* Oxford University Press (2000) 104.

[135] S/1995/566, July 12, 1995.

[136] S/1995/605, July 24, 1995.

obligations under international law, to prevent the use of its territory for the staging of terrorist acts against Turkey'.[137] Authors, too, appear inclined to treat the incursions as self-defense, although they find them unacceptable. Alexandrov, for example, concludes that 'the reaction of the international community made it clear that the self-defense justification was found unacceptable and that Turkey's action had pre-emptive and punitive purpose'.[138]

In spite of the fact that the United States volunteered the right of self-defense as a justification for the Turkish actions, the Turkish statements, few as they are, however, would appear more consistent with a claim of necessity.[139] One reason why the necessity excuse comes to mind when reading the Turkish letters to the Security Council is the emphasis placed on the fact that Iraq, since 1991, has been unable to exercise its authority over the northern part of the country.[140] Under the circumstances, Turkey found that its resort to 'measures imperative to its own security [the incursions into Iraq] originating from the principle of *self-preservation and necessities*, cannot be regarded as a violation of Iraq's sovereignty'.[141]

Overall, one may briefly examine whether the Turkish incursions fulfill the criteria for a state of necessity. It can certainly be argued that terrorist cross-border attacks may threaten an essential interest. This issue will be addressed below. Whether the specific situation in Southeast Turkey is serious enough to constitute a grave and imminent peril is, of course, debatable. Turkey claimed that 'every day, many innocent citizens of Turkey have lost their lives and suffered incalculable damage because of the violent terrorist attacks coming from Iraqi territory'.[142] Also debatable is the question of whether the only way to deal with the situation is through military means. Conversely, the fact that the incursions have continued over most of a decade would indicate that

---

[137] S/1995/605, July 24, 1995. In later letters to the Security Council, Turkey emphasized that it 'continues to stand for Iraq's rights as a sovereign State' and pointed to the inability of the Iraqi authorities 'to exercise its authority over the northern parts of its territory' which 'continues to provide room for frequent violations of Turkish borders and territory in the form of terrorist infiltrations' (S/1997/7, January 3, 1997). See also S/1996/479, July 2, 1996 and S/1997/552, July 18, 1997.

[138] Stanimir A. Alexandrov *Self-Defense Against the Use of Force in International Law* Kluwer Law International (1996) 181.

[139] See also Dinstein who categorizes the Turkish actions under 'extra-territorial law enforcement', which, as discussed previously, covers the situations where armed bands or terrorists operate from a certain territory but without the complicity of the territorial sovereign, i.e. what is here referred to as necessity, Yoram Dinstein *War, Aggression and Self-defence* Cambridge University Press 3rd ed. (2001) 218.

[140] See, for example, S/1995/605, July 24, 1995, S/1996/479, July 2, 1996 and S/1997/7, January 3, 1997.

[141] S/1996/479, July 2, 1996 (emphasis added). It should be noted that the necessity defense is only applicable if an otherwise wrongful act has been committed, i.e. the violation of Iraqi sovereignty.

[142] S/1997/7, January 3, 1997. Turkey further argued that the terrorist attacks constituted a threat to regional peace and security, Ibid. and S/1997/552, July 18, 1997.

military means in and of themselves are unsuccessful. The question as to whether the incursions seriously impair a countervailing essential interest is closely tied to the issue whether the use of force is possible under the necessity excuse. Hence, an answer to this question depends on how one views this latter problem as discussed above. Finally, one may ask whether Turkey had contributed to the situation of necessity. It is certainly possible to argue that the political and bureaucratic intolerance and suppression of the Kurdish minority, caused by the perceived threat to the unity of the Turkish Republic, have pushed some Kurds to armed resistance, including the use of terrorism. This argument would, however, run afoul of the, by now, generally accepted principle that no excuses exist for the use of terrorism. More plausibly, perhaps, one could argue that the reason the Iraqi government is unable to exercise its authority in the North is the imposition of no-fly zones, patrolled by the United States and United Kingdom. The planes are stationed in Turkey and, hence, the no-fly zones can only operate with Turkish approval and assistance. In one of its letters, however, Turkey stress that it 'bears no responsibility' for the situation in northern Iraq.[143]

In 1999, Belgium, again, in part relied on the necessity excuse for justification of use of force, this time before the International Court of Justice. Having been charged by the Federal Republic of Yugoslavia with *inter alia* 'taking part in the bombing of the territory of the Federal Republic of Yugoslavia ... in breach of its obligation not to use force against another State', Belgium primary claimed that the NATO intervention was 'entirely legal' and 'compatible with Article 2, paragraph 4 of the Charter'.[144] Belgium, however, in the alternative raised the state of necessity justification in case the Court remained unconvinced that humanitarian intervention as described by Belgium was justified by international law. Although explicitly referring to draft Article 33, Belgium offered the following, different definition of necessity: A state of necessity is the cause which justifies the violation of a binding rule in order to safeguard, in face of grave and imminent danger, values which are higher than those protected by the rule which has been breached.[145]

Belgium alludes briefly to the balancing of interests: 'What rule has been breached? We do not accept that any rule has been breached. However, for the sake of argument, let us say that it is the rule prohibiting the use of force'. Subsequently, the question is asked: 'What are the higher values which this intervention attempts to safeguard? They are rights of *jus cogens*, It is the collective security of an entire region'. Later the Belgium representative adds: 'The Court is dealing with an

---

[143] S/1997/7, January 3, 1997.
[144] See uncorrected transcript of Belgium's Oral Pleadings, CR 99/15, May 10, 1999, available at www.icj-cij.org, visited September 22, 2002.
[145] See uncorrected transcript of Belgium's Oral Pleadings, CR 99/15, May 10, 1999, available at www.icj-cij.org, visited September 22, 2002.

intervention to save an entire population in peril, a population which is the victim of severe, widespread violations of its rights, rights which have the status of a norm of *jus cogens*'.[146]

It should be pointed out that Belgium's reply was given in the context of a hearing about preliminary measures. Yugoslavia delivered applications against ten NATO member states to the Court and only Belgium, and the United Kingdom, in part, addressed the substantial law underlying the dispute during the hearings concerning preliminary measures. Belgium, however, did not really address the modalities and cumulative conditions of necessity nor did it relate to the complicated question of use of force under necessity, including Ago's differentiation. On December 15, 2004, the Court found that it lacked jurisdiction and dismissed the case.[147]

9.VI. Necessity and Terrorism

When addressing various aspects of the issue of terrorism in the 21st century, it appears both sensible and necessary to distinguish between what might be termed 'traditional' terrorism, i.e. the terrorism known to the world in the 1970's through the 1990's, and what has variously been termed 'the new terrorism' or 'megaterrorism'.[148] Whatever the designation, this new terrorism is recognizable by the infliction of mass casualties or mass destruction/disruption of property or infrastructure. This distinction is particularly prudent when reviewing the legal literature from the late 20th century, which when dealing with terrorism, in the most cases, did not consider mass casualty terrorism.

9.VI.A. 'Traditional' Terrorism and Necessity

In his 1991 book *International Law in Theory and Practice*, based on his Hague Academy Lectures, Oscar Schachter discusses the options for using force against terrorists.[149] For the most part, these are thoughts developed after the Hague Lectures in 1982.[150] He first analyzes self-defense as legitimization for using force against terrorists but finds that the legal limits of self-defense may preclude the use of force in some

---

[146] See uncorrected transcript of Belgium's Oral Pleadings, CR 99/15, May 10, 1999, available at www.icj-cij.org, visited September 22, 2002.

[147] For Belgium, see Press Release 2004/39, available at http://www.icj-cij.org/icjwww/idocket/iybe/iybeframe.htm, visited on September 3, 2005.

[148] See, for example, Andrew Tan and Kumar Ramakrishna (ed.) *The New Terrorism: Anatomy, Trends and Counter-Strategies* Eastern University Press, 2002 and Richard Falk *The Great Terror War* Olive Branch Press, 2003 respectively.

[149] Schachter, Oscar: *International Law in Theory and Practice*, Dordrecht, Martinus Nijhoff, 1991, 162-173.

[150] See, for example Oscar Schachter 'The Extraterritorial Use of Force Against Terrorist Bases' 11 *Houston Journal of International Law* (1989) 309-316.

cases, particularly where the host state is not substantially involved and, secondly, where the terrorist attack has not yet taken place but involves a grave threat.[151] Based on this, Schachter queries as to whether a state injured or threatened by terrorist attacks can use force.

At once, when considering necessity in this context, which is Schachter's purpose, one may wonder how a state already injured by an attack can consider the state of necessity. As pointed out above, necessity addresses a situation of 'grave and imminent' danger to an essential interest. Hence, necessity cannot be invoked by an injured state, i.e. after the danger has materialized. The explanation is to be found in Schachter's assumption that the terrorist attack forms part of a pattern of attacks.[152] The question is

---

[151] Schachter, Oscar: *International Law in Theory and Practice*, Dordrecht, Martinus Nijhoff, 1991, 169.

[152] Ibid., 164. Some, however, have disputed Schachter's conclusion in this regard. Dinstein develops quite an expansive notion of self-defense, originally consisting of four categories. The third dealt with the cases where 'the employment of force within the territory of another state directed against individuals in retribution for acts committed by them – on their own responsibility – without the complicity of the government concerned (Yoram Dinstein 'A Survey of Self-Defense in International Law' in M. Cherif Bassiouni (ed.) *A Treaties on International Criminal Law, Volume I, Crimes and Punishment* Charles S. Thomas (1973) 273-286 at 279): 'The terrorist raids continue to be armed attacks – even if conducted from, and not by, another State [and] self-defence is permitted inside the territory of another State …against the guilty terrorists rather than the ineffective local government' (Yoram Dinstein 'Terrorism and Wars of Liberation Applied to the Arab-Israeli Conflict: An Israeli Perspective' 3 *Israel Yearbook of Human Rights* (1973) 78 at 90. Dinstein further argues that 'A government that is unable to repel terrorists must not try to display unwonted powess when the victim implements the law', Ibid. 91) Although he acknowledges that this scenario occasionally is called 'necessity', he preferred the designation 'execution' (Ibid.). Dinstein found and finds that 'the distinction between self-defence and necessity … is artificial. … the use of cross-border counter-force against armed bands is historically tied to the subject of self-defence, and there is no reason to cut that umbilical cord' (Yoram Dinstein *War, Aggression and Self-defence* Cambridge University Press 3rd ed. (2001) 217. Schachter answers – responding to an earlier edition of Dinstein's book containing the same argument – that the umbilical cord 'has already been cut by two international legal bodies – the International Court and the International Law Commission', Oscar Schachter *International Law in Theory and Practice* Kluwer Law International (1995) 172). He has, however, changed the title of the sub-category of self-defense which encompasses this situation to 'extra-territorial law enforcement' (Yoram Dinstein *War, Aggression and Self-defence* Cambridge University Press 3rd ed. (2001) 213-221). Along similar lines, Murphy argues that 'there is nothing in Article 51 … that requires the exercise of self-defense to turn on whether an armed attack was committed directly by another state' (Sean Murphy 'Terrorism and the Concept of "Armed Attack" in Article 51 of the U.N. Charter' 43 *Harvard International Law Review* (2002) 41-51 at 50. Gaja, however, asserts that such a 'condition may be taken as implicit', Giorgio Gaja 'In What Sense was there an "Armed Attack"?' available at www.ejil.org/forum_WTC/ny-gaja.html, visited January 12, 2002. See also the 'Position Paper of Australian Section of the International Commission of Jurists on the Appropriate Response of the UN to the Attacks on the USA' available at www.ejil.org/forum_WTC/messages/17.html, visited October 13, 2002: 'It is clear that where another state … provides bases or refuge for the attackers, the state under attack, or threat of attack, may use armed force against that other State in exercise of the right of self defence').

whether the necessity excuse provides a vehicle for dealing with such terrorist attacks that forms part of a pattern.

The first question is whether a terrorist attack would threaten an essential interest. Schachter holds that terrorist acts which 'take lives, disrupt internal order or interfere with essential services' would qualify as threats to essential interests.[153] As noted above, it would appear difficult to challenge a State's assertion, within reasonable limits, that a certain act or omission threatens its essential interests.

If this is accepted, the central condition under Article 25 would be the gravity of the threat to the essential interest. Indeed, a national interest may arguably become essential if the threat is grave enough. This is in harmony with Schachter's assumption the terrorist attacks in question are 'sufficiently grave to jeopardize the essential interest of the State in protecting its citizens and political order'.[154] Furthermore, according to Schachter, the threat would have to go beyond 'acts of a sporadic character that cause occasional harm and inconvenience'.[155] Terrorist attacks such as those, which took place on September 11, or attacks involving some form weapons of mass destruction (WMD) would doubtlessly reach the required level. In addition, it may be argued that the accumulation of a series of attacks also might be one way of reaching a sufficient level of seriousness. This is in agreement with Schachter's assumption of 'a pattern of attacks'. Against this observation, one may inquire whether, based on principled considerations, an emergency response such as necessity is correct or adequate for a systematic problem?

As it turns out, there appear to be several structural problems connected to the application of the necessity excuse to a systematic problem, such as a pattern of attacks. The whole discourse about patterns of attacks is reminiscent of similar arguments in the context of self-defense, i.e. the accumulation of events theory according to which several 'small' attacks which each in their own right would not amount to an 'armed attack' under Article 51, can, nevertheless, be treated as an armed attack when taken together, accumulated. In the case of necessity, the grave and imminent danger, which may trigger the invocation of the necessity excuse, would not seem to be the function of a possible previous series of attacks. The necessity response is an emergency response to deal with the immediate grave peril at hand, not the five previous attacks during the past six month in addition to the imminent attack. That the State considering invoking the state of necessity has been the victim of previous attacks would not seem to add anything towards fulfilling the cumulative conditions in Article 25.

The fact that Schachter bases his discussion on the occurrence of several or a pattern of terrorist attacks indicates that the problem is systemic, which causes further problems with regard to the necessity excuse. As international law has developed,

---

[153] Ibid.
[154] Ibid.
[155] Ibid., 171.

particularly through the 20th century, an increasing range of issues and problems are now regulated by international law, be it customary or conventional. Rodick informs us that some questions concerning extraterritorial jurisdiction once were legitimated by necessity: 'The plea of necessity has also been employed to excuse the action of a state in assuming criminal jurisdiction over aliens in respect to acts not committed within its territory.' Rodick mentions counterfeiting of currency, plotting against its ruler' and 'Russia, Greece and Mexico have gone even further and declared that circumstances of exceptional necessity will excuse the action of a state in providing for the punishment of serious extraterritorial offences against their subjects'. These bases for jurisdiction are today known as the protective or security principle and the passive personality principle respectively.[156] Ago, too, provides an example of how a situation originally dealt with under necessity today is explicitly regulated: 'The lesson of the *Torrey Canyon* incident did not go unheeded. In view of the fact that such incidents might recur at any time, it seemed essential to ground the right of the coastal State to take protective measures on positive rules which would be more precise than the mere possibility of relying on a "state of necessity" as a circumstance precluding the international wrongfulness of certain measures taken on the high seas'.[157]

International security and the use of force are regulated under the UN Charter. It has often been argued that the in-operability or poor functioning of the collective security system grants greater authority for states to use force than is allowed under the Charter rules. Such arguments have, however, been refuted by the International Court of Justice.[158] In this context, one may also quote the following excerpt from the International Court's President Winiarski's dissenting opinion:

> The intention of those who drafted it was clearly to abandon the possibility of useful action rather than to sacrifice the balance of carefully established fields of competence, as can be seen, for example, in the case of the voting in the Security Council. It is only by such procedures, which were clearly defined, that the United Nations can seek to achieve its purposes. It may be that the United Nations is sometimes not in a position to undertake action which would be useful for the maintenance of international peace and security or for one or another of the purposes indicated in Article 1

---

[156] Burleigh Cushing Rodick: *The Doctrine of Necessity in International Law*, Columbia University Press, New York, 1928, 35. See for example Brownlie, Ian: *Principles of Public International Law*, Oxford, Oxford University Press, fourth edition, 1990, 303-304.

[157] Addendum to Eight Report on State Responsibility by Mr. Roberto Ago, Document A/CN.4/318/ADD.5-7, 1980, reproduced in 2 *Yearbook of the International Law Commission* (YILC) 1980, part one, page 29, paragraph 36.

[158] 1986 ICJ 99 paragraph 188.

of the Charter, but that is the way in which the Organization was conceived and brought into being.[159]

The perceived problems attaining in particular to the functioning of the Security Council were again raised in the context of the Kosovo crisis and, albeit in a different form, in the recent case of Iraq. As recently pointed out by Crawford and the ILC, the state of necessity excuse cannot be invoked as a source of authority; it does not provide an adequate framework for authorizing the use of force for example in the context of humanitarian intervention. A similar conclusion must apply to the potential use of force against terrorism. As pointed out above, however, the state of necessity may provide an ad hoc excuse, as opposed to a source of authority, for exceptional threats to essential interests. A systematic problem concerning a pattern of attacks would, however, appear to be at odds with this function of the necessity excuse and the exception risks becoming a rule.[160]

9.VI.B. 'New' Terrorism and Necessity

Although the so-called 'new' terrorism does not by definition involve weapons of mass destruction (WMD), a scenario involving such weapons is often what comes to mind. In lieu of a reasonable self-defense argument, the necessity excuse may provide a legal basis for a forceful response to an imminent 'single massive attack against a large number of victims'. Romano has advocated the potential use of the doctrine of necessity in case of use of force against such threats.[161] Depending on the circumstance and assuming that the use of force is not completely ruled out under Article 25, the cumulative conditions would appear fulfilled if a real and immediate threat of deployment of WMD could be established. There would certainly be a grave peril to an essential interest and balancing of interests would also come out on the side of the state threatened by a WMD attack.

A hypothetical legal advisor from the State Department may, however, encounter problems when attempting to fit a preemptive strike under the necessity excuse. As in the case of self-defense, the question of immanency remains central. Article 25 speaks of a 'grave and imminent peril'. As mentioned, the ICJ has determined that the peril has to be established 'at the relevant point in time' and, hence, not be a mere 'possibility'.[162] If, however, the realization of the peril is certain and inevitable the peril

---

[159] Dissenting Opinion of President Winiarski, Certain Expenses, 1962 ICJ 151 at 230.
[160] Eyal Benvenisti 'The US and the Use of Force: Double-edged Hegemony and the Management of Global Emergencies' 15 *European Journal of International Law* 2004 677-700 at 696.
[161] Romano, John-Alex: 'Combating Terrorism and Weapons of Mass Destruction: Reviving the Doctrine of a State of Necessity' in 87 *Georgetown Law Journal*, 1999, 1023.
[162] I.C.J. Reports, 1997, 42, paragraph 54.

may still be said to be imminent even if the realization will only come about in the long term.[163] Similarly, the 2001 Commentary holds that 'a measure of uncertainty about the future does not necessarily disqualify a state from invoking necessity, if the peril is clearly established on the basis of the evidence reasonably available at the time'.[164] As pointed out by both the International Court and by the ILC, long-term predictions and prognoses are particular pertinent to questions concerning threats to, for example, the environment.[165] As outlined above, the Court implicitly employed the precautionary principle in the Gabcíkovo-Nagymaros Project case.

However, as observed by Bothe in the context of self-defense, transferring the precautionary principle to the field of legitimization of the use of force provides for a 'weird' conclusion: 'in case of uncertainty, strike'.[166] This reading of how the precautionary principle might function in the legal regime regulating the use of force may be too mordant.

One might ask whether the legal concept of immanency might be adjusted. The National Security Strategy (NSS) document may be seen to anticipate the problems arising vis-à-vis international law and proposes that 'We must adapt the concept of imminent threat to the capabilities and objectives of today's adversaries'.[167] This proposal is based on the assertion that if and when an attack by terrorists or a rogue state employing WMD becomes imminent in the conventional sense, it is too late to react. This proposal is not *prima facie* unreasonable even if the exact legal modalities and practical implications have to be studied and debated. However, *lex lata* the bottom line is that a preemptive attack as envisioned by the NSS and other documents goes beyond the bounds of the necessity excuse. If the immanency requirement were fulfilled, however, the necessity excuse would appear to be suitable as a legal excuse for using force against terrorists attempting to deploy WMD.

---

[163] Ibid. In the concrete case, the Court found that although an 'essential interest', i.e. the environment was involved, the threat was in the case of Nagymaros neither grave nor imminent (paragraph 55) and in the case of the Gabcíkovo sector not imminent, its graveness untold (paragraph 56 and concluding in paragraph 57).

[164] James Crawford *The International Law Commission's Articles on State Responsibility: Introduction, Text and Commentary* Cambridge University Press, 2002, 184, paragraph 16.

[165] Ibid.

[166] Michael Bothe 'Terrorism and the Legality of Pre-emptive Force' in 14 *European Journal of International Law* (2003) 227-240 at 232.

[167] *National Security Strategy*, September 2002, 15, available at www.whitehouse.gov, visited June 12, 2003.

Conclusion

Chapter 10

Analyses and Conclusions

10.I Introduction

In March, 2005, the Secretary-General of the United Nations submitted his report 'In Larger Freedom: towards Development, Security and Human Rights for All' and urged Member States to adopt a package of specific, concrete proposals to tackle global problems and enable the Organization to better respond to current challenges.[1] In the report, he stated:

> [A]n essential part of the consensus we seek must be agreement on when and how force can be used to defend international peace and security. In recent years, this issue has deeply divided Member States. They have disagreed about whether States have the right to use military force pre-emptively, to defend themselves against imminent threats; whether they have the right to use it preventively to defend themselves against latent or non-imminent threats; and whether they have the right — or perhaps the obligation — to use it protectively to rescue the citizens of other States from genocide or comparable crimes. ... Agreement must be reached on these questions if the United Nations is to be — as it was intended to be — a forum for resolving differences rather than a mere stage for acting them out. And yet I believe the Charter of our Organization, as it stands, offers a good basis for the understanding that we need.[2]

Again, however, it proved difficult to reach any agreement on when and how force can be used. Thus, the community of states, at the September 2005 World Summit, was merely able to 'reaffirm that the relevant provisions of the Charter are sufficient to address the full range of threats to international peace and security'.[3]

---

[1] See Press Release GA/10334, March 21, 2005, available at http://www.un.org/News/Press/docs/2005/ga10334.doc.htm, visited August 4, 2005.

[2] 'In larger freedom: towards development, security and human rights for all', A/59/2005, March 21, 2005, paragraphs 122 and 123, available at http://www.un.org/largerfreedom/, visited August 4, 2005.

[3] 2005 World Summit Outcomes, A/60/L.1, paragraph 77, available at http://daccessdds.un.org/doc/UNDOC/GEN/N05/511/30/PDF/N0551130.pdf?OpenElement, visited Sepetember 17, 2005.

269

Yet, as pointed out in the opening chapter, the international legal regulation of the use of force has been challenged a number of times during the past decade. What is the legal consequence of the challenges to and alleged violations of the Charter? Is Michael Glennon correct when he pronounces the death of international law regulating the use of force? Or, is it possible that a different kind of dynamic is in play?

In order to formulate answers to these questions, I sought to discover how a treaty reacts to challenges and violations. Through an extensive analysis of cases dealing with these issues, it was found that subsequent practice could function as an aid in the interpretation of a conventional rule and, under certain conditions, modify the treaty provision.

The importance of subsequent practice in the application of a treaty as an element of interpretation is 'obvious' and 'well established'. The practice has to be related to the treaty and has to be conducted with a conviction that it is in accordance with the treaty proscriptions. It does not, however, have to take on a particular form, i.e. it may consist of statements or acts, and no specific time span can be set; the central issue is whether the practice evidences a certain understanding, i.e. an agreement. Finally, parties can be seen to have accepted such an agreement if they do not object, i.e. by acquiescence.

It has been argued that subsequent practice may not only act as an aid when interpreting a conventional provision but may effect a normative change in a treaty. Through a thorough study of international cases, it was concluded that subsequent practice can indeed produce legal changes. Examples of the three ways, identified by Karl, in which this may happen, were found among the cases examined: custom, tacit agreement and prescription. In the present context, it seems most correct to speak of a customary process; the well-known elements of custom being state practice and *opinio juris*. The balance between these two elements is disputed; a dispute that goes to the heart of the question the concept of international law. Roberts has proposed an approach to reconcile the various theories, which starts with the practice. If, however, the practice is not clear or uniform, *opinio juris* will play a role at the level of substance. The final balance, or solution, will be determined by the relative strength of the practice and the principle. In order to engage in a specific analysis concerning terrorism, it is therefore necessary to outline how the attitude towards terrorism has developed among the states of the world. In this regard, it may be concluded that the attitude of the international community, as expressed at and through the UN, has moved from substantial disagreement that resulted in ambiguities regarding the scope of the work to agreement on the fundamentals and a significant increase in the co-operation to eliminate terrorism. Of particular note is the fact that the member states have agreed on an unconditional condemnation of terrorism no matter the justification and have agreed on a definition in all but name. These developments have further been confirmed by the recent adoption by the Security Council of resolution 1624 that calls on all states to implement measures that will outlaw the incitement to terrorism.[4]

10.II. Challenges to the Charter and Their Consequences

Having identified the dynamics of how subsequent practice may interact with a preexisting treaty, the focus turned to the actual instances where states have used force against terrorists. Initially, in Chapter 5, a number of 'problem areas' when it comes to the use of force against terrorists, were identified. These were the question of state involvement, whether a terrorist attack constitutes an 'armed attack' in the meaning of Article 51 and the requirements that the use of force has to be necessary and proportional. Chapters 6 to 8 documented and described state practice during the past two decades. Finally Chapter 9 considered the invocation of necessity to excuse or justify the use of force.

This state practice will now be analysed further in the context of the aforementioned 'problem areas'. In each case the legal implications of any subsequent practice will be assessed on the basis of the formulas identified in Part 1. In addition, relevant practice from the ICJ will be considered. As not all the cases examined in this thesis speak to all the aspects of self-defence in equal measure, the following sub-analyses will involve aspects from the different cases where relevant.

Finally, it is necessary to adopt a point of legal departure for an assessment of recent developments. Therefore, the consideration of developments within each of the 'problem areas' will be done on the basis of the 1986 judgment of the ICJ in the *Nicaragua* case.

10.III. State Involvement

In 1986, the ICJ required that for the conduct of the *contras* 'to give rise to legal responsibility of the United States, it would in principle have to be proven that that State had effective control of the military or paramilitary operations'.[5] In its December 2005 judgment in the case between the Democratic Republic of the Congo and Uganda, the Court appeared to reiterate this level of control.[6]

Of the five early cases – between 1982 and 1998 – three were allegedly aimed at non-state actors: the two Israeli (1982 and 1985) and the 1998 strike at Afghanistan and

---

[4] See, S/RES/1624, paragraph 1, adopted September 14, 2005 available at http://daccessdds.un.org/doc/UNDOC/GEN/N05/510/52/PDF/N0551052.pdf?OpenElement, visited September 17, 2005.

[5] 1986 ICJ 65, paragraph 115.

[6] Case Concerning Armed Activities on the Territory of the Congo (Democratic Republic of the Congo v. Uganda), Judgment, December 19, 2005, paragraph 160.

Sudan. In the first two, Israel, in part, argued that its actions were directed at non-state actors within the territory of Lebanon and Tunisia respectively and not against the territorial integrity of said states. Still, Israel's justifications for its 1982 and 1985 actions are somewhat equivocal. In each case, the Israeli representative appears to justify the Israeli action on two, partly contradictory legal arguments. On the one hand, it is argued that, based on its own prior acts, the attacked state had lost some of its sovereignty and, thus, can be legally attacked. This is in reality an argument speaking to Article 2, paragraph 4 of the Charter. On the other hand, it is asserted that the territorial state, through its harboring of the alleged terrorists, becomes responsible for their acts. This argument relies on a certain interpretation of Article 51 and has until recently only been supported by a small number of states besides Israel, including the United States and pre-1990 South Africa.

International reaction also relates itself to the violation of Tunisian sovereignty in the 1985 case. Here, the United Kingdom outlined the general attitude when its representative stated that 'even if there had been demonstrable responsibility by the PLO, this would not have justified the retaliation taken against Tunisia'.[7] Israel's argument under Article 51 – that, contrary to the initial perception, squarely relates itself to the territorial state, as opposed to non-governmental actors, and holds that state responsible for 'harboring' terrorists – was not accepted. Thus, in the 1980s, the attribution of terrorist acts to a state required a more substantial involvement than mere harboring. As we shall see later, an expansive interpretation of attribution has subsequently developed.

Turning to the 1998 attacks, one may discuss whether the legal evaluation should focus on the non-state actors within a given territory or, conversely, on the fact that the territorial integrity of the state was violated. It may be suggested that focus on non-state actors is only made possible because the target states were weak, if not failed, states, with fragile central governments that struggled to exert their authority throughout their formal territory. In addition, both were under UN pressure and serious scrutiny for their dealings with terrorists. Furthermore, both official declarations and academic analyses are unable to do away with some form of state connection. In its letter reporting the attacks to the Security Council, the United States stresses that the attacks only took place 'after repeated efforts to convince the Government of the Sudan and the Taliban regime in Afghanistan to shut these terrorist activities down and to cease their cooperation with the Bin Ladin Organization'.[8] Wedgwood, too, found it necessary to complement her analysis justifying the US attack with a reference to the territorial states' complicity, partly through inaction, in the bin Laden enterprise.[9]

---

[7] S/PV.2611, October 2, 1985, 111.

[8] S/1998/780, August 20, 1998.

[9] Ruth Wedgwood 'Responding to Terrorism: The Strikes Against bin Laden' 24 *The Yale Journal of International Law* (1999) 559-576 at 565.

The continued centrality of the state was reiterated by the ICJ in its Advisory Opinion on the Legal Consequences of the Construction of a Wall in the Occupied Palestinian Territory.[10] Here, the Court removed any doubt as to its opinion on the requirement of state involvement, stating that 'Article 51 … recognizes the existence of an inherent right of self-defence in case of an armed attack by *a State against another State*'.[11] Some of the judges, however, distanced themselves from the majority on this point: Judge Higgins found that there is 'nothing in the text of Article 51 that *thus* stipulates that self-defence is available only when an armed attack is made by a State'.[12] Similarly, Judge Buergenthal, maintained that the UN Charter 'does not make its [the inherent right of self-defence] exercise dependent upon an armed attack by another State'.[13]

Recently, in its judgment in the Case Concerning Armed Activities on the Territory of the Congo, the Court maintained this approach by finding that – since the acts of the Allied Democratic Forces (ADF) were not attributable to the Democratic Republic of the Congo (DRC) – 'the legal and factual circumstance for the exercise of a right of self-defence by Uganda against the DRC were not present'.[14] It should be noted that in their separate opinions, judges Kooijmans and Simma both found in favor of a right to use force in response to an 'armed attack' by irregular, non-state affiliated forces.[15]

The 1998 attacks are the most 'pure' attacks on non-governmental targets where no governmental institutions were targeted. As we shall see below, this contrasts with both the US attack on Afghanistan on October 7, 2001 and Israeli actions in the West Bank in the early spring of 2002. Although the coming analysis of the post-September

---

[10] Legal Consequences of the Construction of a Wall in the Occupied Palestinian Territory, Advisory Opinion, July 9, 2004, (hereinafter Advisory Opinion, Legal Consequences of the Wall), not yet published, all references are to the version published on the ICJ website, www.icj-cij.org, visited July 10, 2004.

[11] Advisory Opinion, Legal Consequences of the Wall, page 56, paragraph 139 (emphasis added).

[12] Advisory Opinion, Legal Consequences of the Wall, Separate Opinion of Judge Higgins, page 7, paragraph 33 (emphasis in original). Judge Higgins, however, went on to accept that the majority opinion 'is to be regarded as a statement of the law as it now stands'.

[13] Advisory Opinion, Legal Consequences of the Wall, Declaration of Judge Buergenthal, page 2, paragraph 5. See similarly Judge Kooijmans, Advisory Opinion, Legal Consequences of the Wall Separate Opnion, paragraph 35.

[14] Case Concerning Armed Activities on the Territory of the Congo (Democratic Republic of the Congo v. Uganda), Judgment, December 19, 2005, paragraph 147.

[15] Case Concerning Armed Activities on the Territory of the Congo (Democratic Republic of the Congo v. Uganda), Judgment, December 19, 2005, Separate Opinion of Judge Kooijmans, paragraphs 26-35 and Separate Opinion of Judge Simma, paragraphs 4-15. While Judge Simma appeared to find this right in Article 51, Judge Kooijmans was more equivocal: 'Whether such a reaction by the attacked State should be called self-defence or an act under the state of necessity or be given a separate name … is a matter which is not relevant for the present purpose', Separate Opinion of Judge Kooijmans, paragraph 31.

11 developments will shift the focus back to the harboring states, the 1998 example illustrates that the threat to international peace and security posed by private actors has become pertinent enough for the international community to exhibit substantial understanding for the need to strike against these forces; an understanding either not present or not accepted during the 1980s. Based solely on the 1998 attacks, it was, however, still difficult to determine how to legally conceptualize this emerging understanding.

10.IV. How Much State Involvement is Required?

One may subdivide the various degrees of state involvement in different ways.[16] For present purposes, the following degrees are chosen: (1) Unawareness of the presence of terrorists within the municipal territory (2) inability to control terrorists within the municipal territory, (3) unwillingness to control or the toleration of terrorists within the municipal territory, (4) financial, material and other support for terrorists within the municipal territory, (5) cooperation with and some control over the terrorists within the municipal territory in planning and organizing terrorists acts, and (6) effective control as outlined in the *Nicaragua* judgment. Of these, situation no. 5 resembles 'overall control' that under the *Tadic* judgment criteria would make the territorial state responsible for the terrorists' acts. This situation is, therefore, reasonably straightforward, which is even more the case in regard to situation 6. These two scenarios will not be pursued further.

The other end of the spectrum, i.e. situation no. 1, unawareness, may also be examined in brief. One may suggest that the mere presence of a terrorist group, which had committed a terrorist act amounting to an armed attack, is sufficient for holding the municipal government and state responsible. This does not, however, seem to be correct. First, it is well established that if the authorities are unaware of a certain situation, the state cannot be responsible for it: 'It cannot be concluded from the mere fact of the control exercised by a State over its territory and waters that that State necessarily knew, or ought to have known, of any unlawful act perpetrated therein, nor yet that it necessarily knew, or should have known, the authors. This fact, by itself and apart from other circumstances, neither involves prima facie responsibility nor shifts the burden of proof'.[17] Before engaging in a discussion about whether this *dictum* is still

---

[16] See, for example, Ian Brownlie 'International Law and the Activities of Armed Bands' 7 *International and Comparative Law Quarterly* (1958) 712-735 at 712-713 and Antonio Cassese 'The International Community's "Legal" Response to Terrorism' 38 *International and Comparative Law Quarterly* (1989) 589-608 at 598.
[17] 1949 ICJ 18. See similarly the comments by Fox: 'The commission of unlawful acts or causing a state of affairs contrary to international law within a State's territory is insufficient of itself, in the absence of some element of knowledge, to result in imputation of responsibility to the territorial State'.

good law in the post-September 11 world, it might be useful to mention another finding by the Court in the *Corfu Channel Case*: It found that the territorial state's exclusive control inhibits the gathering of direct proof and, thus, opens for the admission of indirect evidence. Based on this, the Court concluded that the laying of the minefield 'could not have been accomplished without the knowledge of the Albanian Government'.[18] In the 21st century it may be suggested that it is implausible for any government to argue that it did not know of the presence within its territory of terrorists, particularly terrorists that would be strong enough to launch an armed attack. Arguably, this statement may be modified by the experience following September 11 and the apparent disappearance of bin Laden. In any case, after other governments have informed the state, it is in the know. If the use of force is considered against a state which does not know of the presence of terrorists within its border, the principles of necessity and proportionality would dictate that the state first be notified and given a chance to address the problem.

Based on these observations, the situation concerning an oblivious state does not seem likely to arise. This leaves the three core situations (2) inability, (3) unwillingness and (4) material support.

10.V. Is the Harboring of Terrorists to be Equated with Substantial Involvement?

Already on the evening of September 11, President Bush established the tenets of what would later be known as the Bush Doctrine when he assured the American public that 'we will make no distinction between the terrorists who committed these acts and those who harbor them'.[19] As is clear from these remarks, the President's doctrine *in spe* was still limited to the perpetrators of the September 11 attacks. Days later, however, in his address to a joint session of Congress, the President stated:

Hazel Fox 'The International Court of Justice's Treatment of Acts of the State and in Particular the Attribution of Acts of Individuals to the State' in N. Ando *et al.* (eds.) *Liber Amicorum Shigeru Oda* Kluwer Law International (2002) 147-163 at 155. See also Dinstein: 'As long as Arcadia does not 'knowingly' allow its territory to be used contrary to the rights of Utopia, Arcadia incurs no international responsibility towards Utopia under the *Corfu Channel* ruling', Yoram Dinstein *War, Aggression and Self-defence* Cambridge University Press 3rd ed. (2001) 215.

[18] 1949 ICJ 22.

[19] Statement by the President in His Address to the Nation, September 11, 2001, available at www.whitehouse.gov/news/releases/2001/09/print/20010911-16.html, visited October 21, 2002. This Bush doctrine has subsequently been broaden to include states that might threaten the US with weapons of mass destruction, see Michael R. Gordon 'Pointing Finger, Bush Broadens His 'Doctrin'' *The New York Times* January 30, 2002.

> Our war on terror begins with al Qaeda, but it does not end there. It will not end until every terrorist group of global reach has been found, stopped and defeated. ... we will pursue nations that provide aid or safe haven to terrorism. Every nation, in every region, now has a decision to make. Either you are with us, or you are with the terrorists. From this day forward, any nation that continues to harbor or support terrorism will be regarded by the United States as a hostile regime.[20]

Before considering the implications that the American approach has had for international law, it of interest to point out that the accusation that a state 'harbors' terrorists has been employed in order to justify the use of force in the past.[21] Several states, that have used force against alleged terrorists, have emphasized that the state subjected to the force had implicated itself by harboring the terrorists.

When Israel, in 1985, bombed the PLO headquarter in Tunisia, the Israeli representative told the Security Council that 'Tunisia knew [of the presence of the PLO], and it was strong enough to stop them. It knowingly harboured the PLO and allowed it complete freedom of action in planning, training, organizing and launching murderous attacks from its soil'.[22] In 1986, the South African representative to the United Nations explained that 'the South African Government has issued frequent

---

[20] Address to a Joint Session of Congoress and the American People, September 20, 2001, available at www.whitehouse.gov/news/releases/2001/09/print/20010920-8.html, visited October 21, 2002. The President and members of his administration have subsequently repeated the Doctrine innumerable times. A few examples are 'The United States of America will fight terror, and fight its sponsors, and will uphold doctrine. One doctrine says, either you're with us, or you're with them. And the other doctrine says, if you harbor a terrorist, if you feed a terrorist, you're just as guilty as the terrorist who committed the murders on September the 11th' Remarks by the President at Hutchinson for Senate Dinner, Little Rock Convention Center, Little Rock, Arkansas, August 29, 2002, available at http://www.whitehouse.gov/news/releases/2002/08/20020829-8.html, visited September 5, 2002; 'see, there was a doctrine that said, if you harbor a terrorist, if you feed a terrorist, if you hide a terrorist, you're just as guilty as the terrorist' President Highlights Education Reform at Back to School Event, Parkview Arts and Science Magnet High School, Little Rock, Arkansas, August 29, 2002, available at http://www.whitehouse.gov/news/releases/2002/08/20020829-7.html, visited September 5, 2002; 'In this war, we have assembled a broad coalition of civilized nations that recognize the danger and that are working with us on all fronts. The President has made very clear that there is no neutral ground in the fight against terror. Those who harbor terrorists share guilt for the acts they commit. And under the Bush Doctrine, a regime that harbors or supports terrorists will be regarded as an enemy of the United States' Vice President Honors Veterans of Korean War, Marriott River Front Hotel, San Antonio, Texas, August 29, 2002, available at http://www.whitehouse.gov/news/releases/2002/08/20020829-5.html, visited September 5, 2002.

[21] See also Scharf who pointed out that the Bush doctrine is no new doctrine; it is like the Sofaer Doctrine from 1986, Michael Scharf 'International Legal Implications: Teach-In on Terrorism' 8 *New England Journal of International and Comparative Law* (2002) 81-102 at 87-88.

[22] S/PV.2611, 65, October 2, 1985.

warnings that it will have to take action if Governments tolerate the harbouring of terrorists engaged in hostile actions against South Africa'. He explained that South African forces had attacked terrorist operational and transit centers in three neighboring countries because of the attacked government's toleration of 'the harbouring of terrorists engaged in violent actions against civilians in South Africa'.[23]

The concept of harboring also entered United States thinking on the matter in the mid-1980s. In a widely publicized speech, Secretary of State George Shultz stated: 'The Charter's restrictions on the use or threat of force in international relations include a specific exception for the right of self-defense. It is absurd to argue that international law prohibits us from capturing terrorists in international waters or airspace; from attacking them on the soil of other nations, even for the purpose of rescuing hostages; or from using force against states that support, train and harbor terrorists or guerrillas. International law requires no such result. A nation attacked by terrorists is permitted to use force to prevent or pre-empt future attacks, to seize terrorists or to rescue its citizens when no other means are available'.[24]

If the word 'harbor' is taken as the decisive element, what exactly does 'to harbor' a terrorist mean? The support provided by the Taliban to al-Qaeda, following the US action in Afghanistan, appears to fall within the category 'to harbor' and make the state responsible for the terrorist acts. It is worth remembering, though, that this form of 'harboring' included various kinds of actual material support and not merely inactive tolerance of al-Qaeda's presence. This is analogous with the statement by then Secretary of State Schultz, who made the test one of 'states that support, train and harbor terrorists'. But what can be said about the required substantial state involvement post-2001?

As argued above, only the three core categories are of immediate interest – material, financial and/or logistic support (4), unwillingness to confront (3), and inability to confront (2). Where is *lex lata* situated today?

If we start from the lowest level, the Georgian example would indicate that inability to confront within a state's territory does not suffice. This was also held by the ICJ in the Case Concerning Armed Activities on the Territory of the Congo where the Court concluded that the involved states were unable – and not necessarily unwilling – to 'put an end' to the activities of the irregular forces.[25] For this reason, there was no

---

[23] S/PV.2684, 22.

[24] George Shultz 'Low-Intensity Warfare: The Challenge of Ambiguity' Address before the Low-Intensity Warfare Conference, National Defense University, Washington DC, January 15 1986, reprinted in 25 *ILM* 204 at 206 (1986). During the Security Council debate over the 1985 raid on Tunisia, the US representative made similar comments, S/PV.2615, October 4, 1985, 22, paragraph 252.

[25] Case Concerning Armed Activities on the Territory of the Congo (Democratic Republic of the Congo v. Uganda), Judgment, December 19, 2005, paragraph 301.

responsibility. As noted by Judge Koroma in that case: 'if a State is powerless to put an end to the armed activities of rebel groups despite the fact that it opposes them, that is not tantamount to use of force by that State, but a threat to the peace which calls for action by the Security Council'.[26] Although a number of other factors, including several political ones, naturally played a role, the US, the EU and the OSCE exhibited no understanding for Russian assertion of justifying incursions into Georgian territory under Article 51; this in spite of a common understanding that Russian allegations that terrorists had a presence in Georgia probably were correct.

It has been insinuated by Russia that the Georgians were not only unable but also unwilling to deal with the alleged terrorists. It is, however, very difficult to verify such allegations. In regard to Syria, there was undoubtedly an unwillingness to confront the alleged terrorist offices in Damascus. On the other hand, more active support is difficult to document, and the international community did not approve the Israeli strike. If we turn to the Palestinian case, some form of unwillingness may be identified. The Palestinian Authority has been unwilling to confront the terrorists who have a presence within the areas under its control. And, it should be added, these terrorists were operative in quite a different way from the 'office' terrorists in Damascus. There are many reasons for this and, at a political level, one may be able to explain the situation. Still, this does not alter the basic fact that the PA has been more than reluctant to react and may even have attempted to capitalize politically on the wave of terrorism directed against Israel. Partly in contrast to these observations, Israel argued that the PA was not only unwilling to confront terrorism but also supported it and even instigated and planed it. If we take the findings of Human Rights Watch as our guide, however, the tentative conclusion is that the PA has been unwilling to confront terrorism and to a lesser extent provided some form of mainly financial support. Finally, the Afghan episode certainly provides an example of a state that is unwilling to confront the terrorists as well as an example of a state that supports the terrorists in various ways.

While the Georgian case thus rules out inability (category 2) as sufficient to engage state responsibility for an armed attack, we are left with the Syrian example of tolerance but probably no substantial support, the Palestinian case of unwillingness with some amount of support and the Afghan case with substantial support.

Firstly, if the Syrian case is accepted as mere tolerance, i.e. unwillingness to confront, it may be concluded that this does not suffice: even if Syria is culpable, its actions, or lack thereof, did not justify the Israeli attack. In the Case Concerning Armed Activities on the Territory of the Congo, Uganda pleaded that tolerance of armed bands 'creates a susceptibility to action in self-defence by neighbouring States'.[27] The fact that

---

[26] Case Concerning Armed Activities on the Territory of the Congo (Democratic Republic of the Congo v. Uganda), Judgment, December 19, 2005, Declaration by Judge Koroma, paragraph 9.

[27] Quoted in the Case Concerning Armed Activities on the Territory of the Congo (Democratic Republic of the Congo v. Uganda), Judgment, December 19, 2005, Separate Opinion by Judge Kooijmans, paragraph 21.

the Court found no need to respond to this contention was interpreted by Judge Kooijmans as an implicit rejection of the Ugandan argument.[28]

This brings us to the Afghan and Palestinian campaigns and the respective international reaction. In the former case, support has been widespread. In the latter case – although the statement by the UN Secretary-General is taken as our guide, i.e. an acceptance of an Israeli claim to self-defense – it must be noted that a large number of states were reluctant to give general support for Israel's claims. This was only in part due to the disproportionate nature of the Israeli operation, which, as will be considered below, placed it outside the scope of self-defense.

The international community may have various reasons for differentiating between the two cases, including the considerations outlined in the conclusions of Chapter 4. Be that as it may, the reactions have implications for the legal interpretation. In summary, we have two cases, one with extensive support and one with sporadic support. While self-defense in the former case gained general acceptance, it was more reluctant with regard to the latter.

These findings lead to the following conclusions: in order for a state to be held responsible for an armed attack perpetrated by non-state actors, it must have provided some form of support for these individuals.[29] Mere unwillingness to confront their presence within the territory of the state is not sufficient, although this, as has been pointed out, still may engage the general responsibility of the state. This conclusion does indeed indicate a lowering of the threshold compared to that which the ICJ stipulated in the ICJ judgement in the *Nicaragua* case and the ICTY judgment in *Tadic*.[30] Crucially, the new threshold would not require any form of state control, whether 'effective control' as stipulated by the ICJ or 'overall control' as elaborated by the ICTY.

As we have seen, there is disagreement between authors as to whether state involvement is required under Article 51, some finding that the condition of state involvement is 'taken as implicit'[31] whereas other hold that there is nothing in the text

---

[28] Quoted in the Case Concerning Armed Activities on the Territory of the Congo (Democratic Republic of the Congo v. Uganda), Judgment, December 19, 2005, Separate Opinion by Judge Kooijmans, paragraph 22.

[29] See also Jinks who came to a similar conclusion but went on to express his reservations about the effects of what he termed the 'harbor or support' rule (HSR), Derek Jinks 'State Responsibility for Sponsorship of Terrorist and Insurgent Groups: State Responsibility for the Acts of Private Armed Groups' 4 *Chicago Journal of International Law* (2003) 83-95.

[30] As pointed out by Ratner, the US claims differed significantly from the findings in either the ICJ or the ICTY, Steven R. Ratner '*Jus ad bellum* and *Jus in bello* after September 11' 96 *American Journal of International Law* 2002, 905-921 at 908-909. See also Jutta Brunnee and Stephen J. Toope 'The Use of Force: International Law after Iraq' 53 *International and Comparative Law Quarterly* 2004 785-806 at 794-795

[31] Giorgio Gaja 'In What Sense was there an "Armed Attack"?' available at www.ejil.org/forum_WTC/ny-gaja.html, visited January 12, 2002.

of Article 51 that 'requires the exercise of self-defense to turn on whether an armed attack was committed directly by another state'.[32] Similarly, Judge Simma spoke about 'a restictive reading' and ' prevailing interpretation' although he then went on to consider state practice and *opinio juris*.[33] Cassese, for one, appears to believe that a potential shift in the reading of Article 51 in this regard amounts to a normative change; he briefly wonders whether a 'customary rule widening the scope of self-defence' can have originated, possibly, through 'instant custom'.[34] This would indicate that the bar that has to be passed is the higher bar of normative change or, in other words, it has to be substantiated that the requirements related to the development of customary rule have been fulfilled. In the opinion of the present writer, however, the developments outlined are within the radius of Article 51 and, hence, merely a new interpretation. Still, if the change in the law is considered a normative change – that is to say, it would need to fulfill the conditions relevant for customary international law as outlined in Chapter 3 – the overwhelming support for the US action in the General Assembly regarding its Afghan campaign as documented in Chapter 7, would indicate a vindication of these.

10.VI. An Additional Issue: Threshold Only for Terrorism?

A pertinent question, following this finding, concerns the more general application of the present conclusions. For example, considering the attribution of armed attacks perpetrated by what initially are perceived as private individuals, one may ask whether only attacks characterized as 'terrorist' are subject to the lowered threshold or whether the new threshold is to be applied to all cross-border attacks. This line of inquiry might indicate a certain ambiguity or arbitrariness in the law but technically there is no reason why a special, lower threshold should not apply to certain, particularly abhorred acts of cross-border violence and not to other, less castigated ones. In effect, the issue is whether the legal regime is dependent upon the designation of the private persons, on the basis of their acts, as armed bands or terrorists. Wedgwood appears to be arguing as much when she draws a distinction between 'insurgents carrying out low-level border violations' and 'terrorist attacks of the most brutal kind'.[35] This far the question remains unanswered.

---

[32] Sean Murphy 'Terrorism and the Concept of "Armed Attack" in Article 51 of the U.N. Charter' 43 *Harvard International Law Review* (2002) 41-51 at 50.
[33] Case Concerning Armed Activities on the Territory of the Congo (Democratic Republic of the Congo v. Uganda), Judgment, December 19, 2005, Separate Opinion by Judge Simma, paragraph 11.
[34] Antonio Cassese 'Terrorism is Also Disrupting Some Crucial Legal Categories of International Law' 12 *European Journal of International Law* (2001) 993-1001 at 997.
[35] Ruth Wedgwood 'Responding to Terrorism: The Strikes Against bin Laden' 24 *The Yale Journal of International Law* (1999) 559-576 at 566. Schachter, too, appears to differentiate between guerrillas

At a more general level of state responsibility, one may ask whether the rules for attributing private acts to states must be modified by the experience with terrorism and counter-terrorism operations. The International Law Commission has recently finished its review of and adopted draft articles on Responsibility of States for Internationally Wrongful Acts.[36] Chapter II addresses the question of attribution of conduct to a State and includes Article 8 on conduct directed or controlled by a State. The commentary to Article 8 states that private conduct will be attributable to a State 'only if [the state] directed or controlled the specific operation and the conduct complained about was an integral part of that operation'.[37] The Commission went on to examine both the *Nicaragua* case from the ICJ and the *Tadic* case from the ICTY but does not come out in favor of one particular finding, be it 'effective' or 'overall' control.[38] Be that as it may, the fact remains that this required level of state involvement lies beyond what the world community has found sufficient in the Afghan case.

As one example, one may consider the relationship between the Northern Alliance in Afghanistan and the US. If we assume that the US exercised neither 'effective' nor 'overall' control over the Northern Alliance, to what extent can the US be held responsible for the possible crimes that the Alliance has been accused of committing during the brief war in Afghanistan following the US attack on October 7, 2001? Interestingly, the US Defense Secretary Donald Rumsfeld was asked whether he thought Northern Alliance forces would hand over senior al-Qaeda and Taliban figures if they apprehended any. In order to explain why the US thought that the Northern Alliance would probably comply with a US request in such a situation, he outlined the relationship between the US and the Northern Alliance: 'We have a relationship with all these elements on the ground. We have provided them with food. We've provided them with ammunition. We've provided them with air support. We've provided winter clothing. We've worked with them closely. We have troops embedded in their forces and have been assisting with overhead targeting and resupply of ammunition. It's a relationship'.[39] If the level of state involvement were lowered in respect of Operation Enduring Freedom, the US would appear to become directly responsible for the actions of the Northern Alliance.

(and their cross-border actions) and terrorists, Oscar Schachter *International Law in Theory and Practice* (1991) 163.

[36] Draft articles on Responsibility of States for Internationally Wrongful Acts, adopted by the International Law Commission at its 53rd session, 2001, available at www.un.org/law, visited November 7, 2002.

[37] 104.

[38] 107.

[39] 'Department of Defense News Briefing: Secretary Rumsfeld and General Pace', November 30, 2001, available at www.defenselink.mil/news/Nov2001/t11302001_t1130sd.html, visited April 12, 2002.

10.VII. An Armed Attack

I will now turn to the question of whether the perception of what constitutes an armed attack has developed when it comes to terrorist violence. As we have just seen, the 1986 ICJ judgment considered carefully how much state support was needed in order to hold the contributing state responsible for an armed attack. The Court did not, however, develop the concept of an 'armed attack' very much, although it did claim that 'there appears now to be a general agreement on the nature of the acts which can be treated as constituting armed attacks'.[40] It made it clear that 'armed attack' is the most grave form of the use of force, as distinguished from 'less grave forms'.[41] It is clear from this that certain uses of force do not amount to an 'armed attack' but may be 'regarded as a threat or use of force, or amount to intervention in the internal or external affairs of other States' or as a 'mere frontier incident'.[42] As examples of the use of force falling below the 'armed attack' threshold, the Court mentioned the violation of an international border, reprisals and – in line with what was found above – the organization, instigation and assistance of terrorist attacks. I will now turn to the examined state practice to see how the conception of an armed attack may have evolved, particularly in regard to the 'accumulation of events' theory, which in many ways is central to responses to terrorism.

10.VII.A. An 'armed attack'

The early incidents from the 1980s were all provoked by terrorist incidents that killed a small number of people. It was clear at the time that these attacks were not 'armed attacks' in and of themselves and the incidents are better dealt with under the 'accumulation of events' theory below. An additional issue in regard to these cases is whether an attack on a civilian, i.e. non-government related, person abroad could be an armed attack. As Ghana noted in 1986: 'the fact that a national or nationals of such a State become victims of the incidents could not in our view be sufficient to trigger the use of force in the name of self-defence'.[43] This question has not been clarified by the incidents examined here.

As for the 1993 response to the alleged plot to kill the former US President, the US explicitly claimed that this was an attack on the US, which entitled the US to use force in self-defence. Reviewing the 1993 attack on Baghdad, however, one is confronted with the fact that no armed attack ever took place, since the planned

---

[40] 1986 ICJ paragraph 195.
[41] 1986 ICJ paragraph 191.
[42] 1986 ICJ paragraph 191.
[43] S/PV.2680, 32.

assassination of former President Bush had been foiled by the Kuwaiti intelligence service. Yet, even assuming that such as assassination had been carried through, it is debatable whether it would amount to an armed attack within Article 51. In this context, it is noticeable that in regard to the attempt on the life of the Israeli ambassador to London in 1982, neither the United Kingdom nor France considered this act an armed attack justifying action in self-defence. Similarly, Feder, whose whole project a mere six years before was to prove an expanded definition of an 'armed attack' in Article 51, found that the attempted assassination of the Israeli ambassador in 1982 'as a provocation was simply not serious enough to rise to the level of an armed attack'.[44] Without getting into a strict comparison, it may be suggested that an acting ambassador and a retired president are of equal stature as representatives of their country. Furthermore, as pointed out above, although relations between Egypt and Sudan deteriorated following the assassination attempt against President Mubarak, the incident was not generally perceived as an armed attack on Egypt, and the crisis was resolved, albeit slowly, through the United Nations. If nothing else, this fact belies the argument advanced by Surchin that 'the decision to respond to a threat against a nation's leader must come from the nation itself'.[45]

It remains, however, to explain and determine the legal consequences of the relatively supportive reaction to the US strike. The question is whether the reluctance to condemn the strike entails a new, broader interpretation of Article 51. This question, firstly, requires a determination that the incident with the former president is able to fit within the 'interpretative range' of Article 51: can Article 51 be interpreted to include the Bush Sr. incident or would this necessitate a more substantial normative change? It is difficult to designate a foiled assassination attempt as an armed attack. It is simply not within the reasonable meanings of the text of Article 51.[46] This indicates that we are faced with a possible normative change, which requires far greater support in order to take effect. This perspective is implicit in Kritsiotis' finding, that 'a more coherent, legal endorsement from the strike's political advocates needs to be forthcoming if this [an extended notion of self-defence] indeed is the case'[47] Based on the reactions of other states, the requisite support to effect normative change is not found. This legal analysis concludes that the specific legal significance of the 1993 is negligible although,

---

[44] Norman Menachem Feder 'Reading the U.N. Charter Connotatively: Toward a New Definition of Armed Attack' 19 *New York University Journal of International Law and Politics* (1987) 395-432 at 431.
[45] Alan D. Surchin 'Terror and the Law: The Unilateral Use of Force and the June 1993 Bombing of Baghdad' 5 *Duke Journal of Comparative and International Law* (1995) 457-496 at 470.
[46] Interestingly, whereas the US representative in the Security Council spoke of an armed attack, the US letter reporting the strike, speaks of 'the attempted attack', see S/26003, June 26 1993.
[47] Dina Kritsiotis 'The Legality of the 1993 US Missile Strike on Iraq and the Right of Self-Defence in International Law' 45 *International and Comparative Law Quarterly* (1996) 162-177, at 175.

in a larger and longer perspective, it may be seen as part of a long-term trend. If not based on legal considerations, the support for US actions must be grounded on political considerations, including the prior history between Iraq and the UN[48] and pre-2003 Iraq's status as the quintessential rogue state.

With regard to the 1998 double attack against Afghanistan and Sudan, it might be useful to separate the two, particularly since world reaction itself was somewhat differentiated: relatively more states disavowed the strike on the plant in Sudan than the attacks on the camps in Afghanistan. Various factors may be suggested to explain this difference, one being the fact that few states were convinced by the US assertion that the plant in Khartoum was indeed a chemical weapons factory. Furthemore, from a legal perspective, few states accepted the assertion that the plant was connected to bin Laden and his al-Qaeda network. On the other hand, little doubt existed as to the presence of al-Qaeda in the territory of Afghanistan. If the focus were limited to the strike against Afghanistan, the relatively positive reaction – at least in the Western hemisphere – would indicate that these states accepted that the US had been subjected to an armed attack. In this regard it is difficult to determine whether the states that were supportive of the US perceived the two bombings of the embassies as armed attacks in and of themselves or whether they recognized the accumulation of events theory, which is implicit in the US justification: 'responding to a series of armed attacks'.[49] Still, it would seem reasonable to conclude that the majority of the supportive states believe an attack on an embassy to constitute an 'armed attack' as found in Article 51.

Mention should be made of the *Diplomatic and Consular Staff* case from 1981.[50] Here, the US initiated a rescue operation on April 24, 1980 in order to rescue the diplomatic staff held hostage in the US embassy in Tehran, Iran. As is well known, the operation was aborted in Iranian territory but the US put forward the justification of self-defence. Although the Court noted the incident in its judgment, it explicitly stated that this issue was not before the Court.[51] In his dissenting opinion Judge Morozov, however, pointed out that 'there is no evidence that any armed attack had occurred against the United States'.[52] Yet, from the context it is not clear whether Judge Morozov made reference to the issue of attribution or to the definition of an 'armed attack'.

---

[48] John Quigley 'Missiles with a Message: The Legality of the United States Raid on Iraq's Intelligence Headquarters' 17 *Hastings International and Comparative Law Review* (1994) 241-274 at 270.
[49] S/1998/780, August 20, 1998.
[50] 1981 ICJ 3.
[51] 1981 ICJ 3 at 43, paragraph 94.
[52] 1981 ICJ 3 at 56-57, paragraph 8.

That the September 11 attacks reached the level of an armed attack within the meaning of Article 51 seems beyond doubt.[53] These terrorist attacks were arguably of a sufficiently grave kind and extent to qualify as an armed attack under Article 51. As one indication, one may compare the number of casualties at Pearl Harbor in 1941 (around 2400 killed) to the number on September 11 (approximately 3000 killed). In addition, the attacks took place on US territory. The main point of contention was whether the attacks could be attributed to Afghanistan, as discussed above.

The two remaining case, the Russian/Georgian and the Israeli/Syrian incidents are better evaluated under the heading of state involvement, rather than here under the question of an armed attack. Finally, one may add the ICJ judgment in the *Case Concerning Oil Platforms*.[54] Here, considering the scope of an attack, the Court, albeit as an *obiter dictum*, set out quite a modest requirement for an incident to qualify as an 'armed attack': 'the Court does not exclude the possibility that the mining of a single military vessel might' amount to an armed attack.[55]

10.VII.B. The 'Accumulation of Events' Theory

The reference to the 'accumulation of events' theory has been more or less prevalent in all the counter-terrorism attacks examined. Yet, some were more explicitly based on this theory than others – the 1980s attacks and the 2002 Israeli operation against the Palestinian territories – and they will form the focus here. In addition, recent cases from the ICJ will be considered.

In each of the cases from the 1980s, Israel and the United States made reference to a specific terrorist attack but went on to aver that that specific attack merely was one in a series. The international community, however, did not accept their claim: As is clear from the reactions in the Security Council outlined above, and as has been pointed out by various authors, third states have been reluctant to engage this line of argument and quite determinedly relate their comments to the specific incident. On this basis, several members of the Security Council found that the attempted assassination of an ambassador or the murder of three tourists, for example, did not amount to an armed attack.

---

[53] Jack M. Beard 'America's New War on Terror: The Case for Self-Defense under International Law' 25 *Harvard Journal of Law and Public Policy* (2002) 550-590 at 574.

[54] *Case Concerning Oil Platforms* (*Islamic Republic of Iran* v. *United States of America*) Judgment, 6 November 2003, General List No. 90, not yet published, all references are to the version published on the ICJ website, www.icj-cij.org, visited July 10, 2004.

[55] *Oil Platforms* case, p. 35, para. 72. For a critical comment to the Court's decision, see William H. Taft 'Self-Defense and the Oil Platforms Decision' 29 *Yale Journal of International Law* (2004) 295-306.

Without diminishing the impact of the individual terrorist attacks against Israelis, they might not amount to 'armed attacks' on an individual basis.[56] Still, considering smaller attacks, an acknowledgement of an Israeli right to react in self-defense would recognize that a series of minor attacks may accumulate into an armed attack. As mentioned above, the 'accumulation of events' approach appeared already to have been endorsed by the ICJ in the Nicaragua case when it held that incursions, 'singly or collectively', may amount to an armed attack.[57] Again, in the *Case Concerning Oil Platforms*,[58] the US asserted that the attack on the Kuwaiti tanker that had been re-flagged to the US, the *Sea Isle City,* was 'the latest in a series of such missile attacks against United States flag and other non-belligerent vessels in Kuwaiti waters in pursuit of peaceful commerce'.[59] The US similarly placed the attack on the USS *Samuel B. Roberts* in the larger context of 'offensive attacks and provocations' by the Iranians.[60] In both cases, however, the US opined that the individual attacks were in and of themselves armed attacks giving rise to the right of self-defence; the alleged pattern of Iranian use of force, the US stated, 'added to the gravity of the specific attacks, reinforced the necessity of action in self-defense, and helped to shape the appropriate response'.[61] Hence, the US did not make a claim based exclusively on the 'accumulation of events' theory. Nonetheless, the Court did address this matter:

> On the hypothesis that all the incidents complained of are to be attributed to Iran ... the question is whether that attack, either in itself or in combination with the rest of the 'series of ... attacks'

---

[56] It is, of course, possible to argue that the terrorist attack in Netanya on March 29, 2002 which killed 29, amounted to an armed attack in and of itself. If, furthermore, is it accepted that any comparison with for example the September 11 attacks must be based on some sense of population proportionality, it could be argued that that particular attack would be the equivalent of attack killing more than 1000 people, if it had taken place in the USA.

[57] 1986 ICJ 120, paragraph 231. See also Christine Gray *International Law and the Use of Force* Oxford University Press 2000 108 and 123.

[58] *Case Concerning Oil Platforms* (*Islamic Republic of Iran* v. *United States of America*) Judgment, 6 November 2003, General List No. 90, not yet published, all references are to the version published on the ICJ website, www.icj-cij.org, visited July 10, 2004.

[59] *Oil Platforms* case, *supra* note 56, p. 30, para. 62.

[60] *Ibid.*, p. 34, para. 72. In the context of the attack on the USS *Samuel B. Roberts*, the Court, however, determined that 'no attacks on United States-flagged vessels (as distinct from United States-owned vessels), additional to those cited as justification for the earlier attacks on the Reshadat platforms [i.e. the incident related to the *Sea Isle City*], have been brought to the Court's attention, other than the mining of the USS *Samuel B. Roberts* itself', *ibid.*, p. 35, para. 72. This being the case, no issue of a 'pattern of attacks' arose.

[61] *Ibid.*, p. 31, para. 62 and pp. 34–35, para. 72.

cited by the United States can be categorized as an 'armed attack' on the United States justifying self-defence.[62]

After addressing the incidents that make up the series of attacks, the Court found:

> Even taken cumulatively ... these incidents do not seem to the Court to constitute an armed attack on the United States, of the kind that the Court, in the case concerning *Military and Paramilitary Activities in and against Nicaragua*, qualified as a 'most grave' form of the use of force.[63]

Here, the Court explicitly considered whether a number of incidents 'cumulatively' amounted to an armed attack, thereby arguably implicitly accepting this approach.[64] In the case between the Democratic Republic of the Congo and Uganda, the Court again had to consider a series of attacks, and again it entertained the possibility that 'even if this series of deplorable attacks could be regarded as cumulative in character ...'.[65] This line of reasoning makes little sense unless it is presupposed that the Court has accepted the 'accumulation of events' theory.

This appreciation is of considerable interest and import since the Security Council for decades has rejected the 'accumulation of events' theory.[66] The Court's observation does leave many questions unanswered, though: One may wonder how many minor uses of force it takes to reach the level of an armed attack. Similarly, it is unclear

---

[62] *Ibid.*, p. 31, para. 64.

[63] *Ibid.*, pp. 31–32, para. 64.

[64] Ochoa-Ruiz and Salamanca-Aguado reads the Court's dictum as an indication of the opposite position of the one advocated here: 'The Court ... dismissed the argumant of the accumulation of acts giving rise to an armed attack because it evaluated each of the alleged attacks individually ...' see Natalia Ochoa-Ruiz and Esther Salamanca-Aguado 'Exploring the Limits of International Law relating to the Use of Force in Self-Defence' 16 *European Journal of International Law* 2005 499-524 at 517. Gray found that the Court 'contemplated' the issue but 'did not discuss this controversial question', Christine Gray *International Law and the Use of Force* 2nd ed. Oxford University Press 2004, 125-126. Johnstone found that the 'ICJ implicitly affirmed a version of the [accumulation of events] theory in the 2003 Iran Platforms Case, Ian Johnstone 'The Plea of "Necessity" in International Legal Discourse: Humanitarian Intervention and Counter-Terrorism' 43 *Columbia Journal of Transnational Law* 2005, 337-388 at 374.

[65] Case Concerning Armed Activities on the Territory of the Congo (Democratic Republic of the Congo v. Uganda), Judgment, December 19, 2005, paragraph 146. In that case, Judge Kooijmans opined that 'the series of attacks which were carried out ... can be said to have amounted to an armed attack in the sense of Article 51', Separate opinion by Judge Kooijmans, paragraph 32.

[66] Derek Bowett 'Reprisals Involving Recourse to Armed Force' 66 *American Journal of International Law* (1972) 1-49 at 7 and S. A. Alexandrov, *Self-Defence and Use of Force in International Law* (Kluwer Law International, 1996) 167.

whether all the minor incidents must originate from the same source[67] – for example a specific terrorist faction or organization – or is it sufficient that the attacks coming from different sources have similar motivation.

If it is accepted that the accumulation of events theory has by now been endorsed as outlined, the question remains: can it be said to be within the textual range or radius of the provision on self-defence in Article 51? Is it possible textually to fit or designate the combined effect of a series of smaller attacks as 'an armed attack'? To be sure, the traditional armed attack is an attack across the border of one state by the armed forces of another state. Different units at different points of the border would often conduct such an attack. In theory, one could imagine that the attack of a single unit would not be grave enough to constitute an armed attack but would rather be characterized as a frontier incident. Depending on the scope of the attack, no one would dismiss the assertion that the smaller attacks of the units have to be combined when the legal implications are to be considered. Of course, in this example, all the smaller attacks take place simultaneously and are obviously part of the same overall action. With regard to the accumulation of cross-border terrorist attacks, it might be justified textually – also under Article 51 – to regard their combined effect as an 'armed attack' provided that certain requirements are meet concerning the criteria that actually tie the individual attacks together, i.e. same overall strategic objective, related perpetrators etc. Indeed, Schmitt argued that the 'accumulation of events' approach 'makes particular sense in the context of terrorism'.[68] The assertion that a series of attacks may textually conceivably be accumulated to constitute an armed attack is further supported by the finding in Chapter 2 that the concept of an 'armed attack' may be thought of as a generic term in the sense that it may evolve over time.

Hence, under these conditions, it is considered that the accumulation of events theory is textually covered within the meaning of an 'armed attack' and thus that the arguments by Israel and the US have to be evaluated as a proposed interpretation of the right of self-defence, as opposed to a normative expansion of this right. Under this approach, Israel and the US have conducted material acts that they propose should be the basis of a new agreement as to the understanding of the parameters of Article 51. They also both explicitly claim to be acting under and in accordance with the underlying treaty.

As for international reaction – the final element in the analysis – it was clearly unfavorable in the cases from the 1980s. Hence, it must be concluded that the accumulation of events approach was not accepted as equivalent to an 'armed attack'.

---

[67] In the case of the 2001 Afghanistan campaign, for example, the United Kingdom claimed 'to avert the continuing threat of attacks from the same source', i.e. those behind September 11, see S/2001/947, October 7, 2001.

[68] Michael N. Schmitt 'Counter-Terrorism and the Use of Force in International Law' in 32 *Israel Yearbook on Human Rights* 2003, 53-116 at 75.

With regard to the 2002 Israeli operation, however, there was quite broad understanding for the Israeli need to react and use force in self-defence. Even if many states found the actual Israeli reaction to be excessive, and thus illegal, most accepted the self-defence claim. This is further supported by the ICJ *dictum.*

10.VII.C. Anticipatory Self-Defence

In light of this arguable acceptance by the Court of the 'accumulation of events theory', one may ask what implications this recognition has for the question of anticipatory self-defence. As mentioned in Chapter 5, the ICJ explicitly declined to address the question in the *Nicaragua* case: 'the issue of the lawfulness of a response to the imminent threat of armed attack has not been raised. Accordingly the Court expresses no view on that issue'.[69] Recently, however, the Secretary General of the UN – echoing his own High Level Panel[70] – accepted as law that states may use force in response to an imminent threat:

> Imminent threats are fully covered by Article 51, which safeguards the inherent right of sovereign States to defend themselves against armed attack. Lawyers have long recognized that this covers an imminent attack as well as one that has already happened.[71]

Even if one still has to decide on what is meant by 'imminent', one may ask: Is it a viable position to acknowledge that a series of minor uses of force may amount to an armed attack and simultaneously argue that there is no right of anticipatory self-defense?

Gray, for one, found that the reluctance of states to claim anticipatory self-defence is a clear indication of the doubtful status of this justification in international law.[72] Still, in practice, if the issue involves a number of minor incidents, likelihood is that the final incident – which breaks the camels back, so to speak – would have concluded. If this is accepted, an interesting question becomes how to determine and evaluate the additional legal criteria, i.e. immediacy/necessity. A response to a series of attacks

---

[69] 1986 ICJ 103, paragraph 194.
[70] 'A threatened State, according to long established international awl, can take military action as ong as the treatened attack is *imminent*, no other means would deflect it and the action is proportionate' A More Secure World: Our Shared Responsibility Report of the High-level Panel on Threats, Challenges and Change, A/59/565, December 2, 2004, available at www.un.org/secureworld, visited December 4, 2004, page 54, Paragraph 188.
[71] 'In larger freedom: towards development, security and human rights for all', A/59/2005, March 21, 2005, paragraph 124, available at http://www.un.org/largerfreedom/, visited August 4, 2005.
[72] Christine Gray *International Law and the Use of Force* Oxford University Press 2nd ed. 2004 130-133.

logically and legally has to be viewed in light of a future expected attack. Even if the series may be held to accumulate to an 'armed attack' any response in lieu of an expected future attack would fail the necessity test: if no future attack can be reasonably predicted, a forceful response is unnecessary. It would therefore seem that acceptance of the accumulation of events theory implicitly means an acceptance of the right to use force in anticipation of a future attack, at least in a scenario involving a series of attacks. One challenge that may be raised in this context is the fact that Article 51 used the words 'if an armed attack occurs'. Arguably, the acceptance of a right of anticipatory self-defence would entail a normative change because the textual range of Article 51 is limited in this area.[73] The practice is not entirely unequivocal as described below regarding the immediacy criteria. Yet, some of the practice is clearly premised on the existence of a right to anticipatory self-defence. With a number of eligible interpretations, as in this case, principled considerations come to the fore, as outlined in Chapter 3. Hence, in order to draw a conclusion on the permissability of anticipatory self-defence in the context of a series of terrorist attacks one has to consider developments surrounding the debates about terrorism – as outlined in Chapter 4 – and other related issues such as changing views of sovereignty and the use of force. Considering in particular the real threat posed by terrorism, a tentative conclusion would indicate that anticipatory self-defence against serious terrorist threats is now sanctioned.

10.VII.D. Forcible Counter-Measures

As noted, unnecessary and/or disproportionate uses of force – even if in self-defence – are often described as reprisals and are thus illegal. Recent comments, however, have raised the issue of possible legal forcible countermeasures in response to illegal forcible acts falling short of an 'armed attack'.[74] In the judgment in the *Oil Platforms* case,[75] the Court found that no armed attack had taken place and so no right of self-defence existed. Hence, the Court could have entertained considerations of other possible responses. It did not, however; a fact which Judge Simma found 'unfortunate' and

---

[73] Rüdiger Wolfrum 'The Attack of September 11, 2001, the Wars Against the Taliban and Iraq: Is There a Need to Reconsider International Law on the Recourse to Force and the Rules in Armed Conflict?' in 7 *Max Planck Yearbook of United Nations Law* 2003, 1-78 at 29.

[74] Johnstone has considered whether this area might be covered by 'necessity', see Ian Johnstone 'The Plea of "Necessity" in International Legal Discourse: Humanitarian Intervention and Counter-Terrorism' 43 *Columbia Journal of Transnational Law* 2005, 337-388 at 368.

[75] *Case Concerning Oil Platforms* (*Islamic Republic of Iran* v. *United States of America*) Judgment, 6 November 2003, General List No. 90, not yet published, all references are to the version published on the ICJ website, www.icj-cij.org, visited July 10, 2004.

which prompted him to outline his thoughts on the matter: He found that the Judgment might create the

> 'impression that, if offensive military actions remain below the – considerably high – threshold of Article 51 of the Charter, the victim of such actions does not have the right to resort to – strictly proportionate – defensive measures equally of a military nature. ... In my view, the permissibility of stractly defensive military action taken against attacks of the type involving, for example, the *Sea Isle City* or the *Samuel B. Roberts* cannot be denied'.[76]

Judge Simma made reference to the *Nicaragua Case* and found that in 'view of the context of the 1986 Court's dictum,[77] by such proportionate countermeasures the Court cannot have understood mere pacific reprisals ... Rather, in the circumstances of the *Nicaragua* case, the Court can only have meant what I have just referred to as defensive military action "short of" full-scale self-defence'.[78] At this point in time, however, these ideas would seem to be those of one judge and not generally accepted. Furthermore, if forcible counter-measures were to be accepted as legal under international law, this would, in the opinion of the present author, amount to a normative change in the use of force regime and would, therefore, require the qualified support in the world community, as outlined in Chapter 3.

10.VIII. Immediacy and Necessity

Turning to the issue of necessity and immediacy, this has often caused problems because the terrorist act(s) that were alleged to justify the use of force in self-defense had been completed before defensive action could be taken. In its 1986 judgment, the ICJ provided a very specific and traditional test of necessity:

> On the question of necessity, the Court observes that the United States measures taken in December 1981 (or, at the earliest, March of that year -- paragraph 93 above) cannot be said to correspond to a "necessity" justifying the United States action against Nicaragua

---

[76] Separate Opinion of Judge Simma, page 6, paragraph 12.

[77] 'While an armed attack would give rise to an entitlement to collective self-defence, a use of force of a lesser degree of gravity cannot ... produce any entitlement to take collective counter-measures involving the use of force. The acts of which Nicaragua is accused ... could only have justified proportionate counter-measures on the part of the State which had been the victim of these acts ...' 1986 ICJ, page 127, paragraph 249.

[78] Separate Opinion of Judge Simma, pages 6-7, paragraph 12.

on the basis of assistance given by Nicaragua to the armed opposition in El Salvador. First, these measures were only taken, and began to produce their effects, several months after the major offensive of the armed opposition against the Government of El Salvador had been completely repulsed (January 1981), and the actions of the opposition considerably reduced in consequence. Thus it was possible to eliminate the main danger to the Salvadorian Government without the United States embarking on activities in and against Nicaragua. Accordingly, it cannot be held that these activities were undertaken in the light of necessity.[79]

Only a few states commented in the early cases on the issues of necessity and/or immediacy – for example Qatar, stressing that 'late' responses become reprisals. In both 1993 and 1998 strikes, the issue was pertinent. The 1993 strike took place not only after the attempted assassination had been foiled but indeed several weeks later. Unless seen as part of the accumulation of events theory combined with anticipation, the 1993 response would appear to fall foul of the required immediacy and necessity. According to the US justification, however, its attack did indeed have future oriented objectives: to 'frustrate unlawful actions on the part of the Government of Iraq and discourage and preempt such activities'.[80] The 1998 attacks on the two US embassies were also arguably complete before the US responded and, hence, the questions of immediacy and necessity also arose in this case. As in the 1993 case, the US justification was in part based on anticipation of future events: the strikes took place 'to prevent and deter their [terrorist attacks] continuation'.[81]

Developments following the September 11 attacks may be viewed in two ways. One way is to see them as a further confirmation of developments already outlined. Indeed, the US described an 'ongoing threat' to the United States and stated that the actions taken were 'designed to prevent and deter further attacks on the United States'.[82] The United Kingdom also informed the Council that it had taken action in accordance with Article 51 'to avert the continuing threat of attacks from the same source', i.e. those behind September 11.[83] The fact that the US action was so widely endorsed would indicate a combined acceptance of the approach outlined here, combining the 'accumulation of events' theory with anticipatory self-defence.

---

[79] 1986 ICJ, paragraph 237.

[80] S/26003, June 26, 1993.

[81] S/1998/780, August 20, 1998.

[82] Ibid.

[83] S/2001/947, October 7, 2001. See also Alan Cowell 'Blair Depicts the Attack as Act of Self-Defense' *The New York Times* October 8, 2001.

On the other hand, these developments may be seen as a modification of the traditional concept of immediacy. The attacks were completed on September 11 and it took the US almost one month to take action against Afghanistan.[84] Yet the international community accepted this.[85] A possible reason behind this development may be found in the already noted development in the threat to the international community posed by terrorism. International terrorism has become capable of inflicting substantial damage on both persons and states so that international law has had to adapt to terrorism's modes of operation. Terrorist acts are commonly characterized by their brief duration, which does not leave the victim any chance to respond while the terrorist attack is in progress. While developments within this area appear somewhat unclear, it should be stressed that states' use of force must still be restrained by the requirements of necessity and immediacy. This means that states should not be allowed to circumvent these restraints by refering to open-ended claims such as an 'on-going war on terrorism'.

10.IX. Proportionality

In 1986, the ICJ held that

> Whether or not the assistance to the contras might meet the criterion of proportionality, the Court cannot regard the United States activities ... i.e., those relating to the mining of the Nicaraguan ports and the attacks on ports, oil installations, etc., as satisfying that criterion. Whatever uncertainty may exist as to the exact scale of the aid received by the Salvadorian armed opposition from Nicaragua, it is clear that these latter United States activities in question could not have been proportionate to that aid.[86]

Beyond this, the judgment did not develop the issue of proportionality, possibly because any findings in this regard would be *obiter dictum* due to the fact that the Court had already found the US use of force illegal.

---

[84] Kohen, for example, wrote that 'once the attack is over, the legal justification for the use of force must be different [from self-defense]' and 'the terrorist acts are finished', see Marcelo Kohen 'The use of force by the United States after the end of the Cold War and its impact on international law' i Michael Byers og Georg Nolte (ed.) *United States Hegemony and the Foundations of International Law,* Cambridge University Press, 2003, 197-23 at 209.

[85] See, for example, Cassese who notes that self-defense normally must be 'an immediate reaction' but also finds that in the Afghan case, 'states seem instead to have come to accept a *delayed response*', Antonio Cassese 'Terrorism is Also Disrupting Some Crucial Legal Categories of International Law' 12 *European Journal of International Law* (2001) 993-1001 at 998 (emphasis in original).

[86] 1986 ICJ, paragraph 237.

In spite of the fact that most states found the early Israeli actions unjustified under international law, a number of states went on to express their concerns regarding the proportionality of the actions.[87] In 1982, the United Kingdom spoke about the relationship between an assassination attempt and massive attacks on Lebanese towns and villages. Even if the accumulation of events approach was employed, Ireland found the 1982 Israeli invasion of Lebanon disproportionate. In 1985, the United Kingdom, too, spoke of arbitrary and disproportionate violence, referring to the Israeli attack on Tunisia. What is clear, from the discourse and exchanges regarding these early cases, is that the response is solely measured against the immediate preceding terrorist incident, be it the attempt on the life of an ambassador, the murder of three tourists or a bomb attack on a discothèque.

Staying with the evaluation of proportionality of a response to a single event, the ICJ recently touched upon the question of proportionality in a low-intensity conflict situation in the *Oil Platforms* case.[88] In response to two alleged Iranian attacks – a missile attacks on a Kuwaiti tanker that had been re-flagged to the US and the mining of a US naval vessel – the US attacked a number of Iranian oil installations: in response to the missile attack, on October 19, 1987, two oil platforms were attacked and destroyed;[89] in response to the mining, the US attacked the Salman and Nasr complexes on April 18, 1988.[90] In contrast to the previous attack, however, the April 1988 attack

---

[87] Indeed, Schachter found that the bombings of Tunisia and Libya 'have been condemned more for lack of proportionality than for any other reason', Oscar Schachter *International Law in Theory and Practice* (1991) 169.

[88] *Case Concerning Oil Platforms (Islamic Republic of Iran v. United States of America)* Judgment, 6 November 2003, General List No. 90, not yet published, all references are to the version published on the ICJ website, www.icj-cij.org, visited July 10, 2004.

[89] As a result of the attack, the R-7 platform was almost completely destroyed and the R-4 platform was severely damaged. While the attack was made solely on the Reshadat complex, it affected also the operation of the Resalat complex. Iran states that production from the Reshadat and Resalat complexeswas interrupted for several years, see *Case Concerning Oil Platforms (Islamic Republic of Iran v. United States of America)* Judgment, 6 November, 2003, General List No. 90, p. 25, para. 47. The text of the judgment and individual opinions is available at the ICJ website <www.icj-cij.org.> References in the following are made to the text available at the website. On the day of the attack, the US presented a letter to the Security Council justifying the attack by reference to Article 51 of the Charter: 'United States forces have exercised the inherent right of self-defence under international law by taking defensive action in response to attacks by the Islamic Republic of Iran against United States vessels in the Persian Gulf'. S/19219, October 19 1987, reprinted in the Judgment p. 26, para. 48.

[90] According to the Iranians, the attack caused severe damage to the production facilities of the platforms, and that the activities of the Salman complex were totally interrupted for four years, its regular production being resumed only in September 1992, and reaching a normal level in 1993, see *Case Concerning Oil Platforms (Islamic Republic of Iran v. United States of America)* Judgment, 6 November, 2003, General List No. 90, p. 32, para. 66. Again, on the day of the attack, the US presented a letter to the Security Council justifying the attack by reference to Article 51 of the Charter: 'United States forces have exercised their inherent right of self-defence under international law by taking defensive action in response to an attack by the Islamic Republic of Iran against a United States

'formed part of a much more extensive military action, designated 'Operation Praying Mantis', conducted by the United States against what it regarded as 'legitimate military targets'; armed force was used, and damage done to a number of targets, including the destruction of two Iranian frigates and other Iranian naval vessels and aircraft'.[91]

With regard to the 19 October 1987 attack, the Court found that it 'might . . . have been considered proportionate' if all the other conditions for invoking self-defence had been present.[92] The relative clarity and practical usefulness of this finding is undermined, however, by the Court's observations concerning the attack of 18 April 1988. In this case, the Court was concerned about the scale of "Operation Praying Mantis" of which the attacks on the Salman and Nasr platforms formed part. The Court found that it could not evaluate the part of "Operation Praying Mantis" that related to the two platforms in isolation: 'the Court cannot assess in isolation the proportionality of that action [the attacks on the Salman and Nasr] to the attack to which it was said to be a response; it cannot close its eyes to the scale of the whole operation, which involved, *inter alia*, the destruction of two Iranian frigates and a number of other naval vessels and aircraft'.[93] In spite of this statement, the Court went on to find: 'As a response to the mining, by an unidentified agency, of a single United States warship, which was severely damaged but not sunk, and without loss of life, neither "Operation Praying Mantis" as a whole, *nor even that part of it that destroyed the Salman and Nasr platforms*, can be regarded, in the circumstances of this case, as a proportionate use of force in self-defence'.[94] The formal inconsistency is not, however, the primary problem. Rather, the Court's deliberations on proportionality appear to beg the question: Assuming all other conditions were present, why might the 19 October 1987 attack, which involved two Iranian platforms, 'have been considered' proportionate to a missile attack on a tanker, whereas the April 18, 1988 attack on two platforms was not proportionate to the mining of a US naval vessel?

Overall, there are indications that the accumulation of events approach is gaining acceptance, and this development also has implications for the assessment of the proportionality of a response. Firstly, if the proportionality is to be measured against a number of preceding terrorist attacks, one response may, as argued by Ago, be more forceful than the individual terrorist acts. Secondly, if the idea of a series of attacks is adopted, the question arises as to the legitimate aims of a counter-terrorist operations and whether this will justify an added amount of force.

---

naval vessel in international waters of the Persian Gulf', S/19791, 18 April 1988, reprinted in the *Oil Platforms* case, p. 26, para. 48.
[91] *Oil Platforms* case, p. 33, para. 68.
[92] *Oil Platforms* case, p. 37, para. 77.
[93] *Oil Platforms* case, p. 37, para. 77.
[94] *Oil Platforms* case, p. 37, para. 77 (emphasis added).

In recent years, some authors have identified a growing tolerance for the use of force that goes beyond the pure defensive purposes. Thus, in 1990 Arend found that 'while states are formally unwilling to depart from the Charter paradigm, in justifying their actions they have expanded their notion of self-defense to include deterrence and even punishment'.[95] Five years later, Surchin concluded that 'developing state practice reveals that controversial military actions, including reprisals, are becoming increasingly accepted as a means of fighting terrorism'.[96] Writing in 2004, Gardam held that there is growing support for the position that it is a proportionate response to the threat of terrorism to remove a regime that is either incapable of the action necessary to deal with terrorist activity on its territory or lacks the motivation to do so'.[97]

If we observe the incidents set out in Chapters 6 through 8, all – more or less explicitly – included arguments speaking to future objectives of the use of force in self-defence. In all the letters, for example, from the US to the Security Council, deterrence has formed part of the plea of self-defence.[98] Conceptualising events as a series or pattern of attacks is clearly future oriented and this is why deterrence and prevention is appropriate. Conversely, this means that punishment, as an objective of the use of force, remains illegal because punishment is backward looking. Some have argued that deterrence requires the willingness to respond in a disproportionate way', akin to 'an eye for a tooth'.[99] That this is not acceptable to the international community became obvious in the 2002 Israeli Operation Defensive Shield, where the UN Secretary-General may reasonably be read as endorsing an Israeli right of self-defence. He went on to stress, however, that the exercise of self-defence is itself subjected to legal regulation. As Higgins noted decades ago: 'the degree of force used is a relevant factor in its own right, to be considered in any comprehensive analysis – for, if the Charter places the burden of proof on that state which resorts to force to prove that it is acting justifiably, then *a fortiori* any massive-scale measure raises a presumption of

---

[95] Anthony Clark Arend 'International Law and the recourse to Force: A Shift in Paradigms' 27 *Stanford Journal of International Law* (1990) 1-47 at 15.

[96] Alan D. Surchin 'Terror and the Law: The Unilateral Use of Force and the June 1993 Bombing of Baghdad' 5 *Duke Journal of Comparative and International Law* (1995) 457-496 at 496.

[97] Judith Gardam *Necessity, Proportionality, and the Use of Force by States* Cambridge University Press (2004) 183. See also page 167.

[98] In 1986: 'to discourage' (S/17990), in 1993: 'discourage' (S/26003), in 1998: 'to prevent and deter' (S/1998/780) and in 2001: 'to prevent and deter' (S/2001/946).

[99] Alberto R. Coll 'The Legal and Moral Adequacy of Military Responses to Terrorism' 81 *American Society of International Law Proceedings* (1987) 287-320 at 299. Taulbee and Anderson, too, that deterrence i.e. the effort to prevent recurrence, indicates 'a more indeterminate standard' for proportionality 'based on a calculation of what might be necessary to "teach a lesson"', James Larry Taulbee and John Anderson 'Reprisal *Redux*' 16 *Case Western Reserve Journal of International Law* (1984) 309-336 at 314.

unlawfulness'.[100] It was on this basis that the demands for an Israeli withdrawal were founded. As has been the case in numerous previous Israeli military operations, Operation Defensive Shield was widely perceived as disproportionate.[101] The Mexican representative, for example, stated that 'nothing justifies Israel's disproportionate and sterile use of force and its siege of the civilian population'.[102]

10.X. Use of Force and (The State of) Necessity

That a state of necessity under certain circumstances may be invoked in order to preclude wrongfulness of breaching an international obligation is undoubtedly part of contemporary international law. The justification, however, is reserved for extraordinary, extreme cases something the ILC emphasized by deliberately phrasing the provision in Article 25 of the Draft Articles on State Responsibility in the negative.

When considering whether the necessity excuse can be invoked in case of use of force against terrorists, several complications arises. The first question is whether force can be employed with reference to necessity. Ago and the ILC found, in 1980, that limited uses of force probably were not prohibited by a peremptory norm and, hence, were compatible with the necessity excuse. Indications are that today all use of force is prohibited by a *jus cogens* norm, although this is not entirely clear. The terrorist threat would next have to fulfill the cumulative conditions in Draft Article 25. One problem which has not been addressed is the balancing of interests where the interest behind the obligation breach must 'obviously be inferior to' the interest of the state invoking

---

[100] Rosalyn Higgins *The Development of International Law through the Political Organs of the United Nations* Oxford University Press (1963) 181.

[101] Higgins, for example, commented that Israel's action against Egypt in 1956 was condemned by the Security Council because the majority of states found that the invasion was 'disproportionate to the previous attack suffered, and to the imminent threat' Rosalyn Higgins *The Development of International Law through the Political Organs of the United Nations* Oxford University Press (1963) 201. Similarly, Bowett remarked how 'time and time again ... condemnations of Israel have followed when the Council has stressed the disproportionate nature of the reprisal' Derek Bowett 'Reprisals Involving Recourse to Armed Force' 66 *American Journal of International Law* (1972) 1-49 at 11. See also the exchange between the Irish and Israeli representatives in the Security Council concerning the proportionality of the 1982 Israeli invasion of Lebanon, S/PV.2377, June 8, 1982, 12 (Ireland: 'Where is the correspondence, where is the sense of proportion?' The Irish representative expressed the opinion that he was sure that Israeli losses to terrorism were 'less' that Lebanese losses) and 31(The Israeli representative called the Irish observation 'bizarre bookkeeping'). The exchange continued in S/PV.2379, June 18, 1982, 7 (Ireland) and 58-61 (Israel: 'Let us stop this silly bookkeeping. We deny his [the Irish representative] right, and indeed his constant practice, to lecture us on international law and morality'. The Irish representative, however, maintained that the invasion was 'disproportionate', Ibid. 82.

[102] S/PV.4503, March 3, 2002, 14. The British representative found that 'the deliberate use of violence and, in particular, the unproductive and unacceptable escalation in the degree of force used by the Israeli Defence Force, have got to be brought to a halt', S/PV.4506, April 3, 2002, 29.

necessity. One may argue that the essential interest under threat must be very substantial indeed in order to outweigh the use of force against another state.

However, in order for the threat to reach the required level of seriousness, one may have to anticipate systemic threats, such as a pattern of terrorist attacks as proposed by Schachter. To address a systemic problem with an ad hoc response, however, causes difficulties with both the specific conditions and more general principled considerations. Conceptually, to respond to a systemic threat with an exceptional ad hoc response, such as the necessity excuse, in many ways appears to be an oxymoron. In sum, it would seem that even if force is not excluded under the necessity excuse, conventional terrorism cannot be addressed under the state of necessity.

This leaves the issue of unconventional terrorism with a single massive attack against a large number of victims. Again assuming that the use of force in not ruled out as a given, a threatened terrorist attack employing unconventional weapons would appear to be able to fulfill the cumulative conditions for resorting to the necessity excuse. The idea of preemptive attacks as presented in the NSS document, however, would go beyond what might be excused by reference to necessity.

10.XI. Conclusion

As examplified by events at the September 2005 World Summit, it is not the diplomatic sphere that should be asked about any developments in the regulation of the use of force. It is more fruitful to examine state practice, as has been done in the present thesis. In this practice, observers have identified a 'growing support for, or at least a diminished degree of criticism of, forceful counter-terrorism operations'.[103] But what exactly does this indicate?

Initially, one may focus on the most general level and try to detect the overall development in world reaction to armed actions against terrorists. Conducting a general review of the incidents from both the 1980s and the 1990s, one may detect an increased tolerance in the international community for the use of force against terrorism. The majority of the world's states condemned all three examples from the 1980s. With regard to the two incidents from 1993 and 1998, world reaction was, if not overwhelmingly supportive, ambivalent at the very least. With regard to these episodes, a divide is discernable between Western states that are generally supportive of the use of force and non-Western states that are more hesitant or explicitly against. Turning to events since the turn of the century, much broader support has been forthcoming, exemplified primarily by the support for post-September 11 US actions. Even if September 11 and what followed may be considered unique, a shift is certainly detectable. An explanation for this relies on the developments in the general perception

---

[103] Michael N. Schmitt 'Counter-Terrorism and the Use of Force in International Law' in 32 *Israel Yearbook on Human Rights* 2003, 53-116 at 65.

of terrorism, as documented in Chapter 4. In the pre-1990s, cross-border terrorism was perceived as part and parcel of the widespread and recurring episodes of cross-border infiltration and nuisance, which included examples of national liberation struggles and superpower proxy rivalry. During the 1990s, however, with the demise of national liberation struggles and the end of the Cold War, terrorism in general has taken on a more menacing characteristic. It has not only lost the mitigating aspect of being just, but also emerged as a substantial threat in its own right. In addition, as pointed out by Schmitt, the use of force against terrorists after the end of the Cold War entails less of a risk of spillover effects.[104] Turning to the more specific components of any self-defence claim, it is suggested that the general development just outlined has effected the following realignments of or changes to the law.

State Involvement

State involvement is still a requirement. The level of state involvement, however, has been substantially modified. In 1986, the ICJ found that the state had to have 'effective control'. Only recently, in the *Tadic* judgment from the ICTY, the test was modified to one of 'overall control'. What has been induced in the present examination from state practice indicates that the state involvement is limited to tolerance of the terrorists in addition to some form of material and logistical support. This level of involvement eliminates any form of control and may be described as 'tolerance plus' or 'harbouring'. The way the trend is currently moving, mere tolerance may come to suffice sometime in the future. On a note of caution, however, one should remember that only four post-September 11 cases were investigated; and various global and regional political considerations play a part in how the cases evolved and culminated.

Armed Attack

The assault on the state resorting to self-defence must involve an armed attack. The ICJ continues to speak about the scale of the attack, but in the 2003 decision in the *Oil Platforms case* the Court declared that is was willing to accept the mining of a navy vessel as an armed attack. Considering how terrorist attacks traditionally have been limited in scope, the example with the navy vessel makes it likely that a terrorist attack may reach the required scale. More important, however, is the emerging acceptance of the accumulation of events approach. The Israeli operation in 2002, which was primarily based on the notion that the series of terrorist attacks on Israeli targets necessitated a response in self-defence, was broadly accepted. The accumulation

---

[104] Michael N. Schmitt 'Counter-Terrorism and the Use of Force in International Law' in 32 *Israel Yearbook on Human Rights* 2003, 53-116 at 102.

approach was subsequently also accepted by the ICJ in the *Oil Platforms Case*. This is a potentially huge development in the area of use of force against terrorists. Although the exact implications are still not clear. One logical inference would be the acceptance of the right of anticipatory self-defence. It should also be noted that the idea of forcible counter-measures in lieu of an armed attack remains a possibility and was recently articulated by Judge Simma in the *Oil Platforms case.*

Necessity and Proportionality

With regard to the issues of immediacy and necessity, the law appears to be relaxing the requirements. One conclusion of the case studies could be that responses in self-defence now may be delayed although broad claims of 'war on terrorism' should not be allowed to render the legal restraints meaningless. Concerning necessity, one may argue that an understanding has emerged that it may still be necessary to respond to terrorist attacks even after they have formally come to an end. The evolution observed may also be put down to the acceptance of the 'accumulation of events' theory, as outlined above. Such an acceptance has clear implications for both necessity and proportionality. The future oriented perspective of this approach will, as per proportionality, provide for the inclusion of deterrence as a legitimate aim of self-defence.

The State of Necessity

The necessity excuse was also examined. This is a somewhat controversial justification for a violation of international law. It remains unclear whether necessity may be claimed when using force. The current author believes this to be the case. Still, the excuse would be of limited use, in as much as it would not be available in the case of conventional terrorists. Only in cases of terrorists believed to contemplate deployment of weapons of mass destruction would the excuse be possible.

Based on these findings, the overall conclusion is that the law of the Charter and the corresponding customary international rules regulating the use of force have exhibited dynamism and adaptability in the face of changing threats and the resulting challenging instances of state practice. Indeed, the law has been interpreted and modified by state practice and reactions in order to remain current with the needs of the international community.

Bibliography

Abbott, Kenneth W. Modern International Relations Theory: A Prospectus in Retrospect and Prospect. Yale Journal of International Law. 2000; 25(Summer):273-276.

Abi-Saab, Georges. Some Thoughts on the Principles of Non-Intervention. Wellers, K ed. International Law: Theory and Practice. The Hague: Kluwer Law International; 1998; pp. 225-235.

Acheson, Dean. Remarks (Cuban Quarantine). American Society of International Law Proceedings. 1963; 57:13-18.

---. The Arrogance of International Lawyers. International Lawyer. 1967; 2(4):591-600.

Akehurst, Michael. Custom as a Source of International Law. British Yearbook of International Law. 1974; 47:1-53.

---. The Hierarchy of the Sources of International Law. British Yearbook of International Law. 1974; 47:273-285.

Alexander, Yonah. A Selected Bibliography on Legal Aspects of Terrorism. Israel Yearbook on Human Rights. 1989; 19:405-412.

---. Terrorism in the Twenty-First Century: Threats and Responses. DePaul Business Law Journal. 1999; 12(Fall1999/Spring2000):59-95.

Alexandrov, Stanimir A. Self-Defense Against the Use of Force in International Law. The Hague: Kluwer Law International; 1996.

Allott, Philip. State Responsibility and the Unmaking of International Law. Harvard International Law Journal. 1988; 29:1.

Almond Jr., Harry H. Using the Law to Combat Terrorism. Livingstone, Neil C. and Arnold, Terrell E. ed. Fighting Back: Winning the War against Terrorism. Lexington: Lexington Books; 1986; pp. 157-174.

Alston, Philip. The Myopia of the Handmaidens: International Lawyers and Globalization. European Journal of International Law. 1997; 8:435-448.

Amarashiha, Stafan Daya and Isenbecker, Martin. Terrorism and the Right of Asylum under the 1951 Convention. Nordic Journal of International Law. 1996; 65:223-240.

Amerasinghe, C. F. Principles of the Institutional Law of International Organizations . Cambridge University Press ; 1996.

Ansah, Tawia. War: Rhetoric and Norm-Creation in Response to Terror. Virginia Journal of International Law. 2003; 43:797-860.

Arend, Anthony Clark. International Law and the Recourse to Force: A Shift in Paradigms. Stanford Journal of International Law. 1990; 27:1.

---. Legal Rules and International Society. Oxford University Press; 1999.

Arend, Anthony Clark and Beck, Robert J. International Law and the Use of Force. London: Routledge; 1993.

Atrokhov, Wendy Turnoff. The Khasavyurt Accords: Maintaining the Rule of Law and Legitimacy of Democracy in the Russian Federation Amidst the Chechen Crisis. Cornell International Law Journal. 1999; 32:367-392.

Bibliography

Baker, Mark B. Terrorism and the Inherent Right of Self-Defense (A Call to Amend Article 51 of the United Nations Charter). Houston Journal of International Law. 1987; 10:25-49.

Baker, Stuart G. Note: Comparing the 1993 U.S. Airstrike on Iraq to the 1986 Bombing of Libya: The New Interpretation of Article 51. Georgia Journal of International and Comparartive Law. 1994; 24(Spring):99-116.

Barboza, Julio. Necessity (revisited) in International Law. Jerzy Makarczyk. Essays in International Law in Honour of Judge Manfred Lachs. Martinus Nijhoff; 1984; p. 27.

Bassiouni, M. Cherif. A Policy-Oriented Inquiry into the Different Forms and Manifestations of 'International Terrorism'. Bassiouni, M. Cherif. Legal Responses to International Terrorism: U.S. Procedural Aspects. Dordrecht: Martinus Nijhoff; 1988; p. xv-liii.

Baxter, R. R. A Skeptical Look at the Concept of Terrorism. Akron Law Review. 1974; 7(3, Spring):380-387.

Bazyler, Michael J. Capturing Terrorists in the 'Wild Blue Yonder': International Law and the Achille Lauro and Libyan Aircraft Incidents. Whittier Law Review. 1986; 8:685-709.

Beck, Robert J. and Arend, Anthony Clark. "Don't Tread on Us": International Law and Forcible State Responses to Terrorism. Wisconsin International Law Journal. 1994; 12(Spring):153-219.

Bederman, David. Revivalist Canons and Treaty Interpretation. UCLA Law Review. 1994; 41:954.

Bekker, Pieter H. F. International Decision: Land and Maritime Boundary Between Cameroon and Nigeria (Cameroon v. Nigeria, Equatorial Guinea Intervening). American Journal of International Law. 2003; 97:387-398.

Bernhardt, Rudolf. Interpretation and Implied (Tacit) Modification of Treaties. Zeitschrift FürAusländisches Öffentliches Recht Und Völkerrecht . 1967; 27:491.

Berrisch, Georg M. The Establishment of New Law through the Subsequent Practice in GATT. North Carolina Journal of International Law and Commercial Regulation. 1991; 16:497.

Beveridge, Fiona. The Lockerbie Cases. International and Comparative Law Quarterly. 1999; 48:658-663.

Bisharat, Goerge E. Peace and the Political Imparative of Legal Reform in Palestine. Case Western Reserve Journal of International Law. 1999; 31:253-291.

Bisone, Federica. Killing a Fly With a Cannon: The American Response to the Embassy Attcks. New York Law School Journal of International and Comparative Law. 2000; 20:93-115.

Blum, Yehuda Z. The Beirut Raid and the International Double Standard. American Journal of International Law. 1970; 64:73-105.

---. State Responses to Acts of Terrorism. German Yearbook of International Law. 1976; 19:223-237.

---. The Legality of State Response to Acts of Terrorism. Netanyahu, Benjamin ed. Terrorism: How the West Can Win. New York: Farrar, Straus, and Giroux; 1986; pp. 133-138.

---. Eroding the United Nations Charter . Martinus Nijhoff ; 1993.

Boed, Roman. State of Necessity as a Justification for International Wrongful Conduct. Yale Human Rights and Development Law Journal. 2000; 3:1.

Bolton, John R. Is There Really "Law" in International Affairs? Transnational Law and Contemporary Problems. 2000; 10:1-48.

Bibliography

Botha, C. J. Anticipatory Self-defence and Repirsals Re-examined. South African Attacks on ANC Bases in Neighbouring States: The 'Guns of Gaborone' or 'rAIDS Disease'? South African Yearbook of International Law. 1985; 11:138-156.

Bothe, Michael. Terrorism and the Legality of Pre-emptive Force. European Journal of International Law. 2003; 14:227-240 .

Boutros-Ghali, Boutros. The United Nations and Comprehensive Legal Measures for Combating International Terrorism. Wellens, K. ed. International Law: Theory and Practice. The Hague: Kluwer Law International; 1998; pp. 287-304.

Bowett, D. W. Estoppel before International Tribunals and its Relation to Acquiescence. British Yearbook of International Law. 1957; 33:176-202.

Bowett, Derek. Reprisals Involving Recourse to Armed Force. American Journal of International Law. 1972; 66(1):1-36.

Bowett, Derek W. International Incidents: New Genre or New Delusion? Yale Journal of International Law. 1984; 10:386-395.

Boyle, Francis A. International Law in Time of Crisis: From the Entebbe Raid to the Hostage Convention. Northwestern University Law Review. 1980; 75(5, December):769-855.

---. Military Responses to Terrorism: Remarks. American Society of International Law Proceedings. 1987; 81:288-297.

Brennan, Maureen F. Comment: Avoiding Anarchy: Bin Laden Terrorism, the U.S: Response, and the Role of Customary International Law. Louisiana Law Review. 1999; 59:1195-1223.

Brownlie, Ian. International Law and the Activities of Armed Bands. International and Comparative Law Quarterly. 1958; 7:712-735.

---. International Law and the Use of Force by States. Oxford: Oxford University Press; 1963.

---. The Relation of Law and Power. Cheng, Bin and Brown, E. D. Contemporary Problems of International Law: Esaays in honour of Goerge Schwarzenberger on his eightieth birthday. London: Stevens and Sons; 1988; pp. 19-24.

Brownlie, Ian and C. J. Apperley. Kosovo Crisis Inquiry: Memorandum on the International Law Aspects. International and Comparative Law Quarterly. 2000; 49:878.

Brunnee, Jutta and Toope, Stephen J. International Law and Constructivism: Elements of an International Theory of International Law. Columbia Journal of Transnational Law. 2000; 39:19-74.

Busuttil, James J. The Bonn Declaration on International Terrorism. International and Comparative Law Quarterly. 1982; 31:474-487.

Butler, W. E. ed. The Non-Use of Force in International Law. Dordrecht: Martinus Nijhoff; 1989.

Byers, Michael. The Shifting Foundations of International Law. European Journal of International Law. 2002.

---. Terrorism, the Use of Force and International Law after 11 September. International and Comparative Law Quarterly. 2002; 51:401-414.

Byers, Michael and Simon Chsterman. Changing the Rukes about Rules? Unilateral Humanitarian Intervention and the Future of International Law. Holzgrefe, J. L. and Robert O. Keohane. Humanitarian Intervention: Ethical, Legal and Political Dilemmas. Cambridge University Press; 2003; p. 190.

Bibliography

Campell, Leah M. Comment: Defending Against Terrorism: A Legal Analysis of the Decision to Strike Sudan and Afghanistan. Tulane Law Review. 2000; 74(February):1067-1096.

Cardona, Meliton. The European Response to Terrorism. Schmid, Alex P. and Crelinsten, Ronald D. ed. Western Responses to Terrorism. Frank Cass; 1993; pp. 245-254.

Carnahan, Burrus M. Lincoln, Lieber and the Laws of War: The Origins and Limits of the Principle of Military Necessity. American Journal of International Law. 1998; 92:213-231.

Carter, Ashton; Deitch, John, and Zelikow, Philip. Catastrophic Terrorism: Tackling the New Danger. Foreign Affairs. 1998; 77(6):80-94.

Cassese, A. ed. The Current Legal Regulation of the Use of Force. Dordrecht: Martinus Nijhoff; 1986.

Cassese, Antonio. The International Community's "Legal" Response to Terrorism. International and Comparative Law Quarterly. 1989; 38:589-608.

---. Ex injuria ius oritur: Are we Moving Towards International Legitimation of Forcible Humanitarian Countermeasures in the World Community? European Journal of International Law. 1999; 10:23-30.

---. A Follow-Up: Forcible Humanitarian Countermeasures and Opinio Necessitatis. European Journal of International Law. 1999; 10(4):791-799.

---. Terrorism is also Disrupting Some Crucial Legal Categories of International Law. European Journal of International Law . 2001; 12:993.

Chadwick, Elizabeth. Self-Determination, Terrorism and International Humanitarian Law of Armed Conflict. The Hague: Martinus Nijhoff; 1996.

Charney, Jonathan I. International Agreemenst and the Development of Customary International Law. Washington Law Review. 1986; 61:971-996.

---. Customary International Law in the Nacaragua Case Judgement on the Merits. Hague Yearbook of International Law. 1988; 16-29.

---. Universal International Law. American Journal of International Law. 1993; 87(October):529-551.

---. Anticipatory Humanitarian Intervention in Kosovo. American Journal of International Law. 1999; 93:834--841.

Charney, Jonathan I. and Danilenko, Gennady M. Consent and the Creation of International Law. Damrosch, Lori Fisler; Danilenko, Gennady M., and Müllerson, Rein eds. Beyond Confrontation: International Law for the Post-Cold War Era. Boulder: Westview; 1995; pp. 23-60.

Chayes, Abram. Remarks (Cuban Quarantine). American Society of International Law Proceedings. 1963; 57:10-13.

Cheng, Bin. General Principles of Law as Applied by International Courts and Tribunals. Grotius Publications Limited; 1987.

---. Aviation, Criminal Jurisdiction and Terrorism: The Hague Extradition/Prosecution Formula and Attacks at Airports. Cheng, Bin and Brown, E. D. Contemporary Problems of International Law: Esaays in honour of Goerge Schwarzenberger on his eightieth birthday. London: Stevens and Sons; 1988; pp. 25-52.

---. Opinio juris: a key concept in international law that is much misunderstood. Yee, Sienho and Tieya, Wang. International Law in the Post-Cold War World. London: Routledge; 2001; pp. 56-76.

Chesterman, Simon. Rethinking Panama: International Law and the US Invasion of Panama, 1989. Goodwin-Gill, Guy S. and Talmon, Stefan. The Reality of International Law: Essays in Honour of Ian Brownlie. Oxford:

Bibliography

Clarendon Press; 1999.

Chinkin, Chritine M. Kosovo: A 'Good' or 'Bad' War. American Journal of International Law. 1999; 93:841-847.

Chodosh, Hiram E. Refelctions on Reform: Considering Legal Foundations for Peace and Prosperity in the Middle East. Case Western Reserve Journal of International Law. 1999; 31:427-453.

Clapham, Andrew. Symbiosis in International Human Rights Law: The *Öcelan* Case and the Evolving Law on the Death Sentence. Journal of International Criminal Justice. 2003; 1:475-489.

Clutterbuck, Richard. International Co-operation Against International Terrorism: treaties, Conventions and Bilateral Arrangements. Sandbu, Magnus D. and Nordbeck, Peter. International Terrorism: Report from a Seminar Arranged by the European Law Students' Association in Lund, Sweden, 1-3 October 1987. Lund: Juristfoerlaget; 1987; pp. 39-55.

Colbert, Evelyn Speyer. Retaliation in International Law. New York: King's Crown Press; 1948.

Coll, Alberto R. The Limits of Global Consciousness and Legal Absolutism: Protecting International Law from Some of its Best Friends. Harvard International Law Journal. 1986; 27(2):599-620.

---. The Legal and Moral Adequacy of Military Responses to Terrorism. American Society of International Law Proceedings. 1987; 81:297-307.

Condorelli, Luigi. The Imputability to States of Acts of International Terrorism. Israel Yearbook on Human Rights. 1989; 19:233-246.

Conforti, Benedetto. The Law and Practice of the United Nations. Kluwer Law International ; 1996.

Crawford, James. The International Law Commission's Articles on State Responsibility: Introduction, Text and Commentary. Cambridge University Press; 2002.

Crawford, James Pierre Bodeau and Jacqueline Peel. The ILC's Draft Articles on State Responsibility: Toward Completion of a Second Reading. American Journal of International Law. 2000; 94:660.

D'amato, Anthony. The Concept of Custom in International Law . Cornell University Press; 1971.

D'amato, Anthony. What 'Counts' As Law? Onuf, Nicholas Greenwood. Law-Making in the Global Community. Durham: Carolina Academic Press; 1982; pp. 83-108.

---. Israel's Air Strike Upon the Iraqi Nuclear Reactor. American Journal of International Law. 1983; 77:584-588.

D'Amato, Anthony. Editorial Comment: The Imposition of Attorney Sanctions for Claims Arising from the U.S. Air Raid on Libya. American Journal of International Law. 1990; 84:705-711.

D'amato, Anthony. The Invasion of Panama was a Lawful Response to Turany. American Journal of International Law. 1990; 84:516-524.

---. International law: Process and Prospect. Transnational ; 1995.

D'Amato, Anthony. Megatrends in the Use of Force. Schmitt, Michael N. and Green, Leslie C. eds. The Law of Armed Conflict: Into the Next Millennium. Newport, Rhode Island: Naval War College; 1998; pp. 1-16.

Damrosch, Lori. Sanctions against Perpetrators of Terrorism. Houston Journal of International Law. 1999; 22(Fall):63-75.

Damrosch, Lori Fisler and and Scheffer, David J. ed. Law and Force in the New International Order. Boulder: Westview Press; 1991.

Bibliography

Danilenko, G. M. Law-Making in the International Community. Dordrecht: Martinus Nijhoff; 1993.

Davies, Peter G. G. The EC/Canadian Fisheries Dispute in the Northwest Atlantic. International and Comparative Law Quarterly. 1995; 44:917-939.

de Arechaga, E. Jimenez. General Principles of International Law Governing the Conduct of States. de Arechaga, E. Jimenez. General Course in Public International Law.

Deutch, John. Think Again: Terrorism. Foreign Policy. 1997; (Fall):10-22.

Dietl, Wilhelm. Versümnisse und Fehlschläge in der Terrismusbekämpfung: Enige Fallbeispiele. Hirschmann, Kai and Gerhard, Peter ed. Terrorismus alr weltweites Phänomen. Berlin: Arno Spitz; 2000; pp. 261-269.

Dinstein, Yoram. Comments on the Fourth Interim Report of the ILA Committee on International Terrorism (1982). Terrorism: An International Journal. 1984; 7(2):163-168.

---. The International Legal Response to Terrorism. International Law at the Time of its Codification: Essays in Honour of Roberto Ago. Milano: Multa Paucis; 1987; pp. 139-151.

---. The Right of Self-Defence Against Armed Attacks. Sandbu, Magnus D. and Peter Nordbeck (ed.). International Terrorism: Report from a Seminar Arranged by the European Law Students' Association in Lund, Sweden, 1-3 October 1987. Lund: Juridiska Foereningen i Lund; 1987; pp. 57-71.

---. Terrorism as an International Crime. Israel Yearbook on Human Rights. 1989; 19:55-73.

---. Remarks: Implementing Limitations on the Use of Force: The Doctrine of Proportionality and Necessity. American Society of International Law Proceedings. 1992; 54-58.

---. The Israeli Supreme Court and the Law of Belligerent Occupation: Article 43 of the Hague Regulations. Israel Yearbook on Human Rights. 1996; 25:1-20.

---. The International Legal Status of the West Bank and the Gaza Strip - 1998. Israel Yearbook of Human Rights. 1999; 28:37-49.

---. The Thirteenth Waldemar A. Solf Lecture in International Law. Military Law Review. 2000; 166:93-108.

---. War, Aggression and Self-defence, 3rd edition. Cambridge University Press; 2001.

---. Ius ad bellum Aspects of the _'War on Terrorism. W. P. Heere. Terrorism and the Military: International Legal Implications. Asser Press; 2003; pp. 13-22.

Doehring, Karl. The Unilateral Enforcement of International Law by Exercising Reprisals. MacDonald, Ronald St. John. Essays in Honour of Wang Tieya. Dordrecht: Martinus Nijhoff; 1994; pp. 235-242.

Dueker, Arnd. United States Bombing of Terrorist Sites in Afghanistan and the Sudan: A Sign of the Necessity of International Co-operation. International Peacekeeping. 1999; January1999-April1999:41-42.

Dugard, John. Towards the Definition of International Terrorism. American Society of International Law Proceedings. 1973; 67:94-100.

---. Terrorism and International Law. Consensus at Last? Yakpo, Emile and Boumedra, Tahar. Liber Amicorum Judge Mohammed Bedjaoui. The Hague: Kluwer Law International; 1999; pp. 159-171.

Elagab, Omer Yousif. The Place of Non-Forcible Counter-Measures in Contemporary International Law. Goodwin-Gill, Guy S. and Talmon, Stefan. The Reality of International Law: Essays in Honour of Ian Brownlie. Oxford: Clarendon Press; 1999.

Bibliography

Elias, T. O. The Modern Law of Treaties . A.W. Sijthoff ; 1974.

---. The Doctrine of Intertemporal Law. American Journal of International Law. 1980; 74:285-307.

Engel, Salo. De Facto Revision of the Charter of the United Nations. Journal of Politics . 1952; 14:132 .

---. The Changing Charter of the United Nations. The Year Book of the World Affairs. 1953; 7:71.

---. Law, State and International Legal Order: Essays in Honor of Hans Kelsen. The University of Tennessee Press; 1964.

---. "Living" International Constitutions and the World Court (The Subsequent Practice of International Organs under their Constituent Instruments). International and Comparative Law Quarterly . 1967; 16:865-910.

Erickson, Richard J. Legitimate Use of Military Force Against State-Sponsored International Terrorism . Air University Press ; 1989.

Evans, Alona E. and Murphy, John F. Legal Aspects of International Terrorism. Lexington: Lexington Books; 1978.

Evans, Gareth. When is it Right to Fight? Survival. 2004; 46:59-82.

Falk, Richard. The Validity of the Incident Genre. Yale Journal of International Law. 1987; 12:376-385.

Falk, Richard A. Remarks: McDougal's Jurisprudence: Utility, Influence, Controversy. American Society of International Law Proceedings. 280-286.

---. The Beirut Raid and the International Law of Retaliation. American Journal of International Law. 1969; 63:415-443.

---. Casting the Spell: The New Haven School of International Law. Yale Law Jourmal. 1995; 104:1991-2008.

---. Kosovo, World Order, and the Future of International Law. American Journal of International Law. 1999; 93:847-857.

Falk, Richard A.; Rosalyn C. Higgins; W. Michael Reisman, and Weston H. Burns. Myres Smith McDougal (1906-1998). American Journal of International Law. 1998; 92:729-733.

Falk, Richard A. and Weston, Burns H. The Relevance of International Law to Palestinian Rights in the West Bank and Gaza: In Legal Defense of the Intifada. Harvard International Law Journal. 1991; 32(1, Winter):129-157.

---. The Israeli-Occupied Territories, International Law, and the Boundaries of Scholarly Discourse: A Reply to Michael Curtis. Harvard International Law Journal. 1992; 33(1, Winter):191-204.

Falkenrath, Richard A. Confronting Nuclear, Biological and Chemical Terrorism. Survival. 1998; 40(3):43-65.

Farer, Tom. The Future of International Law Enforcement under Chapter VII: Is There Room for 'New Scenarios'? Delbrueck, Jost ed. The Future of International Law Enforcement: New Scenarios - New Law? Berlin: Duncker & Humbolt; 1992; pp. 39-56.

Farer, Tom J. Editorial Comment: Human Rights in Law's Empire: The Jurisprudence War. American Journal of International Law. 1991; 85:117-127.

---. The Prosepect for International Law and Order in the Wake of Iraq. American Journal of International Law . 2003; 97:621-628 .

Fassbender, Bardo. The United Nations Charter as Constitution of the International Community. Columbia Journal of

Transnational Law . 1998; 36: 529 .

Feinstein, Barry A. The Legality of the Use of Armed Force by Israel in Lebanon - June 1982. Israel Law Review. 1985; 20:362-396.

Feinstein, Lee and Anne-Marie Slaughter. A Duty to Prevent . Foreign Affairs. 2004; 136.

Feng, Gao. China and the principle of sovereign equality in the 21st century. Yee, Sienho and Tieya, Wang. International Law in the Post-Cold War World. London: Routledge; 2001; pp. 224-239.

Fenrick, William J. Attacking the Enemy Civilian as a Punishable Offense. Duke Journal of Comparative and International Law. 1997; 7:539-569.

Fidler, David P. Challenging the Classical Concept of Custom: Perspectives on the Future of Customary International Law. German Yearbook of International Law. 1996; 39:198-248.

Fields, Louis G. Contemporary Terrorism and the Rule of Law. Military Law Review. 1986; 113:1-15.

Finnemore, Martha. The Purpose of Intervention: Changing Beliefs About the Use of Force. Cornell University Press; 2003.

Finnemore, Martha and Sikkink, Kathryn. International Norm Dynamics and Political Change. International Organization. 1998; 52(4):887-917.

Fitzmaurice, Gerald. The Law and Procedure of the International Court of Justice, Vol. I and II. Cambridge University Press; 1995.

Ford, Stuart. Legal Processes of Change: Article 2(4) and the Vienna Convention on the Law of Treaties. Journal of Armed Conflict Law. 1999; 4(1):75-117.

Francioni, Francesco. Of War, Humanity and Justice: International law After Kosovo. Max Planck United Nations Yearbook. 2000; 4:107-126.

Franck, Thomas. International Legal Action Concerning Terrorism. Terrorism: An International Journal. 1978; 1(2):187-197.

---. Editorial Comment: Dulce et Decurum est: The Strategic Role of Legal Principles in the Falklands War. American Journal of International Law. 1983; 77:109-124.

---. Interpretation and Change in the Law of Humanitarian Intervention. Byers, Michael and Georg Nolte. United States Hegemony and the Foundations of International Law . Cambridge University Press; 2002.

Franck, Thomas M. Who Killed Article 2(4)? or: Changing Norms Governing the Use of Force by States. American Journal of International Law. 1970; 64:809-837.

---. The United Nations as Giarantor of International Peace and Security: Past Present and Future. Tomuschat, Christian ed. The United Nations at Fifty: A Legal Perspective. The Hague: Kluwer Law International; 1995; pp. 25-38.

---. Lessons of Kosovo. American Journal of International Law. 1999; 93:857-860.

---. Recourse to Force: Sate Action Against threats and Armed Attacks . Cambridge University Press; 2002.

Franck, Thomas M. and Lockwood Jr., Bert B. Preliminary Thoughts Towards an International Convention on Terrorism. American Journal of International Law. 1974; 68(1):69-90.

Franck, Thomas M. and Niedernayer, Deborah. Accommodating Terorism: An Offence Against the Law of Nations.

Bibliography

Israel Yearbook on Human Rights. 1989; 19:75-130.

Franck, Thomas M. and Rodley, Nigel S. After Bangladesh: The Law of Humanitarian Intervention by Military Force. American Journal of International Law. 1973; 67:275-305.

Franck, Thomas M. and Senecal, Scott C. Porfity's Proposition: Legitimacy and Terrorism. Vanderbilt Journal of Transnational Law. 1987; 20(2):195-234.

Frankowska, Maria. The Vienna Convention on the Law of Treaties before United states Courts. Virginia Journal of International Law . 1988; 21:281.

Freestone, Davis. The Principle of co-operation: Terrorism. Lowe, Vaughan and Warbrick, Colin ed. The United Nations and the Principles of International Law. London: Routledge.

Friedlander, Robert A. Retaliation as an Anti-Terrorist Weapon: The Israeli Lebanon Incursion and International Law. Israel Yearbook on Human Rights. 1978; 8:63-77.

---. Comment: Unmuzzling the Dogs of War. Terrorism: An International Journal. 1984; 7(2):169-173.

Frowein, Jochen A. The Present State of Research Carried out by the English-Speaking Section of the Centre for Studies and Research. Centre for Studies and Research in International Law and International Relations. The Legal Aspects of International Terrorism. The Hague: Hague Academy of International Law; 1988; pp. 55-96.

Garcia-Mora, Manuel R. International Responsibility for Hostile Acts of Private Persons Against Foreign States. The Hague: Martinus Nijhoff; 1962.

Gardam, Judith. Necessity, Proportionality, and the Use of Force by States . Cambridge University Press; 2004.

Gardam, Judith Gail. Proportionality and Force in International Law. American Journal of International Law. 1993; 87:391-413.

Gilbert, G. The 'Law' and 'Transnational' Terrorism. Netherlands Yearbook of International Law. 1995; 26:3-32.

Gill, T. D. Just War Doctrine in Modern Context. Gill, Terry D. and Heere, Wybo P. eds. Reflections on Principles and Practice of International Law: Essays in Honour of Leo J. Bouchez. The Hague: Martinus Nijhoff; 1995; pp. 17-64.

Gill, Terry D. The Law of Armed Attack in the Context of the Nicaragua Case. Hague Yearbook of International Law. 1988; 30-58.

---. The Eleventh of September and the Right of Self-Defense. W. P. Heere . Terrorism and the Military: International Legal Implications. Asser Press; 2003; pp. 23-37 .

Glennon, Michael J. Limits of Law, Prerogatives of Power: Interventionism after . Palgrave; 2001.

---. The UN Security Council in a Unipolar World. Virginia Journal of International Law. 2003; 44:91-112 .

---. Why the Security Council Failed. Foreign Affairs. 2003.

---. Seventeenth Waldemar A. Soft Lecture in International Law. Military Law Review. 2004; 181:143.

Goldie, L. F. E. Terrorism, Piracy and the Nyon Agreement. Dinstein, Y. International Law in a Time of Perplexity. Dordrecht: Kluwer Law International; 1989; pp. 225-248.

Goldsmith, Jack L. and Eric A. Posner. A Theory of Customary International Law. University of Chicago Law Review. 1999; 66(Fall):1113-1176.

309

Bibliography

Goldsmith, Jack L. and Posner, Eric A. Understanding the Resembleance Between Modern and Traditional Customary International Law. Virginia Journal of International Law. 2000; 40(Winter):639-672.

Goodwin-Gill, Guy S. Crimes in International Law: Obligations Erga Omnes and the Duty to Prosecute. Goodwin-Gill, Guy S. and Talmon, Stefan. The Reality of International Law: Essays in Honour of Ian Brownlie. Oxford: Clarendon Press; 1999.

Gordon, Edward. Article 2(4) in Historical Context. Yale Journal of International Law. 1984; 10:271-278.

Gray, Christine. After the Ceasefire: Iraq, the Security Council and the Use of Force. British Yearbook of International Law. 1994; 65:135-174.

---. The Principle of non-Use of Force. Lowe, V. and C. Warbrick. The United Nations and the Principles of International Law. Routledge; 1994; pp. 33-48.

---. International Law and the Use of Force . Oxford University Press; 2000.

---. From Unity to Polarization: International Law and the Use of Force against Iraq. European Journal of International Law. 2002; 13:1-21.

---. The Use and Abuse of the International Court of Justice: Cases Concerning the Use of Force after Nicaragua. European Journal of International Law. 2003; 867-905.

---. International Law and the Use of Force, 2nd ed. Oxford University Press; 2004.

260. Green, Fred. Remarks: Implementing Limitations on the Use of Force: The Doctrine of Proportionality and Necessity. American Society of International Law Proceedings. 1992; 62-67.

Green, L. C. International Law and the Control of Terrorism. The Dalhousie Law Journal. 1983; 7(2):236-256.

---. Terrorism and Armed Conflict: The Plea and the Verdict. Israel Yearbook on Human Rights. 1989; 19:131-166.

---. Terrorism and the Law of the Sea. Dinstein, Y. International Law in a Time of Perplexity. Dordrecht: Kluwer Law International; 1989.

Greenwood, Christerpher. Terrorism and Humanitarian Law - The Debate over Additional Protocol I. Israel Yearbook on Human Rights. 1989; 19:187-207.

Greenwood, Christopher. International Law and the United States' Air Operation Against Libya. West Virginia Law Review. 1987; 89:933-960.

---. Self-Defence and the Conduct of International Armed Conflict. Dinstein, Y. International Law at a Time of Perplexity. Dordrecht: Kluwer Law International; 1989; pp. 273-288.

---. Is there a Right of Humanitarian Intervention? The World Today. 1993; (February):34-40.

Gross, Emanuel. Thwarting Terrorist Acts by Attacking the Perpetrators or Other Commanders as an Act of Self-Defense: Human Rights Versus the State's Duty to Protect its Citizens. Temple International and Comparative Law Journal. 2001; 15:195-246 .

Gross, Ernest A. Revising the Charter: is it Possible? Is it wise? Foreign Affairs . 1952; 32:203.

Guernsey, Katherine N. The North Sea Continental Shelf Cases. Ohio Northern University Law Review. 2000; 27:141-160.

Guillaume, Gilbert. Terrorisme et Droit International. Recueil des Cours: Collected Courses of the Hague Academy of International Law. 1989, III ed. Dordrecht: Martinus Nijhoff; 1990.

Bibliography

Halberstam, Malvina. Terrorism on the High Seas. American Journal of International Law. 1988; 82:269-310.

Hampson, Francoise J. Proportionality and Necessity in the Gulf Conflict. American Society of International Law Proceedings. 1992; 45-54.

Handl, Gunther. The Legal Mandate of Multilateral Development Banks as Agents for Change towards Sustainable Development. American Journal of International Law. 1998; 92:642.

Hargrove, John Lawrence. The Nicaragua Judgment and the Future of the Law of Force and Self-Defense. American Journal of International Law. 1987; 81:135-143.

---. Force, a Culture of Law, and American Interests. Charney, Jonathan I.; Anton, Donald K., and O'Connell, Mary Ellen eds. Politics, Values and Functions: International Law in the 21st Century - Essays in Honor of Professor Louis Henkin. The Hague: Martinus Nijhoff; 1997; pp. 407-419.

Hart, H. L. A. The Concept of Law. Oxford University Press; 1994.

Heintze, Hans-Joachim. Völkerrecht un Terrorismus. Hirschmann, Kai and Gerhard, Peter ed. Terrorismus alr weltweites Phänomen. Berlin: Arno Spitz; 2000; pp. 217-240.

Heinze, Eric and Fitzmaurice, Malgosia ed. Land Mark Cases in International Law. The Hague: Kluwer Law International; 1998.

Henkin, Loius. The Mythology of Sovereignty. MacDonald, Ronald St. John. Essays in Honour of Wang Tieya. Dordrecht: Martinus Nijhoff; 1994; pp. 351-358.

Henkin, Louis. The Reports of the Death of Article 2(4) are Greatly Exaggerated. American Journal of International Law. 1971; 65(3):544-548.

---. Notes from the President: The missile attack on Baghdad and its justifications. ASIL Newsletter. 1993; June-August 1993:3-4.

---. International Law: Politics and Values. Dordrecht: Martinus Nijhoff; 1995.

---. Kosovo and the Law of 'Humanitarian Intervention'. American Journal of International Law. 1999; 93:824-828.

Henkin, Louis; Stanley Hoffmann; Jeane J. Kirkpatrick; Allan Gerson; William D. Rogers; David J. Scheffer, and John Temple Swing. Right v. Might - International Law and the Use of Force. New York: Council on Foreign Relations; 1991.

Herbert, Anne L. Essay: Cooperation in International Relations: A Comparison of Keohane, Haas and Franck. Berkeley Journal of International Law. 1996; 14:222-238.

Higgins, Rosalyn. The Development of International Law Through the Political Organs of the United Nations. London: Oxford University Press; 1963.

---. Policy Considerations and the International Judicial Process. International and Comparative Law Quarterly. 1968; 17(January):58-84.

---. The Place of International Law in the Settlements of Disputes by the Security Council. American Journal of International Law. 1970; 64:1-19.

---. Integration of Authority and Control: Trends in the Literature of International Law and International Relations. Reisman, W. Michael and Weston, Burns H. eds. Toward World Order and Human Dignity: Essays in Honor of Myres S. McDougal. New York: Free Press; 1988; pp. 79-94.

---. Problems and Process: International Law and How We Use It. Oxford University Press; 1994.

Bibliography

---. Some Observations on the Inter-Temporal Rule in International Law . Makarczyk, Jerzy ed. Theory of International Law at the Threshold of the 21st Century. The Hague: Kluwer Law International; 1996; pp. 173-181.

Hirschmann, Kai. Today's Terrroism: A New Challenge? Hirschmann, Kai and Gerhard, Peter ed. Terrorismus alr weltweites Phänomen. Berlin: Arno Spitz; 2000; pp. 45-56.

Hoffman, Bruce. Is Europe Soft on Terrorism? Foreign Policy. 1999; (Summer):62-76.

---. New Forms of Terrorism and The Threat of Terrorist Use of Chemical, Biological, Nuclear and Radiological Weapons. Hirschmann, Kai and Gerhard, Peter ed. Terrorismus alr weltweites Phänomen. Berlin: Arno Spitz; 2000; pp. 37-44.

Hughes, Martin. Terrorism and National Security. Philosophy. 1982; 57:5-25.

International Law Association. International Terrorism: Fourth Interim Report of the Committee. Terrorism: An International Journal. 1984; 7(2):123-146.

International Law Association (Paris Conference 1984). Committee on International Terrorism: Committee Report. Terrorism: An International Journal. 1984; 7(2):199-211.

Intoccia, Gregory F. American Bombing of Libya: An International Legal Analysis. Case Western Reserve Journal of International Law. 1987; 19(2):177-214.

Jackson, Jami Melissa. The Legality of Assassination of Independent Terrorist Leaders: An Examination of National and International Implications. North Carolina Journal of International Law and Commercial Regulation. 1999; 24(Spring):669-.

Jacobs, Francis G. Varieties of approaches to Treaty Interpretation: with Special Reference to the draft Convention on the Law of Treaties before the Vienna Diplomatic Conference. International and Comparative Law Quarterly. 1969; 18:318.

Jagota, S. P. State Responsibility: Circumstances Precluding Wrongfulness. Netherlands Yearbook of International Law. 1985; 16:249.

James, Matthew H. Comment: Keeping the Peace - British, Israeli, and Japanese Legislative Responses to Terrorism. Dickinson Journal of International Law. 1997; 15(Winter):405-450.

Jenkins, Brian M. Defense Against Terrorism. Political Science Quarterly. 1986; 101(5):773-786.

Jennings, R. Y. The Caroline and McLeod Cases. American Journal of International Law. 1947; 82-99.

---. General Course on the Principles of International Law. Recueil Des Cours Collected Courses. 1967 Feb; Tome 121.

Jennings, Robert. International Lawyers and the Progressive Development of International Law. Makarczyk, Jerzy ed. Theory of International Law at the Threshold of the 21st Century. The Hague: Kluwer Law International; 1996; pp. 413-424.

---. International Law Reform and Progressive Development. Hafner, G; G. Loibl; A. Rest; L. Sucharipa-Behrmann, and K. Zemanek (eds.). Liber Amicorum Professor Seidl-Hohenveldern - in honour of his 80th Birthsday. The Hague: Kluwer Law International; 1998; pp. 325-337.

---. Law Making and Package Deal. Jennings, Robert. Collected Writings of Sir Robert Jennings. The Hague: Kluwer Law International; 1998; pp. 760-768.

---. What is International Law and How do We Tell it when We See it. Jennings, Robert. Collected Writings of Sir Robert Jennings. The Hague: Kluwer Law International; 1998; pp. 730-759.

Bibliography

Joyner, Christerpher C. and Arend, Anthony Clark. Anticipatory Humanitarian Intervention: An Emerging Legal Norm? United States Air Force Academy Journal of Legal Studies. 1999; 10:27-51.

Joyner, Christopher C. Offshore Maritime Terrorism: International Implications and the Legal Process. Naval War College Review. 1983; 36:16-31.

Kahn, S. G. Private Armed Groups and World Order. Netherland Yearbook of International Law. 1970; 1:32-54.

Kalshoven, Frits. Remarks: Remarks: Implementing Limitations on the Use of Force: The Doctrine of Proportionality and Necessity. American Society of International Law Proceedings. 1992; 40-45.

Karl, Wolfram. Vertrag und spätere Praxis im Völkerrecht : zum Einfluß der Praxis auf Inhalt und Bestand völkerrechtlicher Verträge . Springer; 1983.

Kash, Douglas. Recent Developments: Abducting Terrorists Under PDD-39: Much Ado About Nothing New. American University International Law Review. 1997; 13:139-.

Kauppi, Mark V. Terrorism and National Security. National Security Studies Quarterly. 1998; 19-31.

Kegley, Jr. Charles W.; Raymond, Gregory A., and Hermann, Margaret G. The Rise and Fall of the Nonintervention Norm: Some Correlates and Potential Consequences. The Fletcher Forum of Wolrd Affairs Journal. 1998; 22:81-97.

Kellman, Barry. Biological Terrorism: Legal Measures for Preventing Catastrophe. Harvard Journal of Law and Public Policy. 2001; 24:417-488.

Kelsen, Hans. The Law of the United Nations, With Supplement. Praeger ; 1950.

Kenny, Kevin C. Self-Defence (120). Wolfrum, Ruediger. United Nations: Law, Policies and Practice. Munich: C.H. Beck; 1995.

Kirgis, Jr. and Frederick L. The Degrees of Saelf-Determination in the United Nations Era. American Journal of International Law. 1994; 88:304-310.

Kirgis Jr., Frederick L. Custom on a Sliding Scale. American Journal of International Law. 1987; 81:146-151.

Kirsch, Nico. Unilateral Enforcement of the Collective Will: Kosovo, Iraq and the Security Council. Max Planck United Nations Yearbook. 1999; 3(59-103).

Kittrie, Nicholas N. Comments. American Society of International Law Proceedings. 1973; 67:104-107.

Klink, Manfred. Nationale und internationale Präventions- und Bekämpfungsstrategien. Hirschmann, Kai and Gerhard, Peter ed. Terrorismus alr weltweites Phänomen. Berlin: Arno Spitz; 2000; pp. 241-260.

Knisbacher, Mitchell. The Entebbe Operation: A Legal Analysis of Israel's Rescue Action. The Journal of International Law and Economics. 1977; 12:57-83.

Koenig, Doris. Terrorism (127). Wolfrum, Ruediger. United Nations: Law, Policies and Practice. Munich: C.H. Beck; 1995; pp. 1120-1228.

Kohen, Marcelo. The use of force by the United States after the end of the Cold War and its impact on international law. Byers, Michael and Georg Nolte. United States Hegemony and the Foundations of International Law. Cambridge University Press; 2003; pp. 197-223 .

Kohen, Marcelo G. The Notion of "State Survival" in International Law. Laurence Boisson de Chazournes and Philip Sands . International Law, The International Court of Justice and Nuclear Weapons. Cambridge University Press; 1999; p. 293.

Bibliography

Kolosov, Yuri M. Limiting the Use of Force: Self-Defense, Terrorism, and Drug Trafficking. Damrosch, Lori Fisler and and Scheffer, David J. ed. Law and Force in the New International Order. Boulder: Westvire; 1991; pp. 233-236.

Kolosov, Yuri M. and Levitt, Geoffrey M. International Cooperation Against Terrorism. Damrosch, Lori Fisler; Danilenko, Gennady M., and Müllerson, Rein eds. Beyond Confrontation: International Law for the Post-Cold War Era. Boulder: Westview; 1995; pp. 141-163.

Konstantinov, Emil. International Terrorism and International Law. German Yearbook of International Law. 1988; 19:289-306.

Kontou, Nancy. The Termination and Revision of Treaties in the Light of New Customary International Law. Oxford University Press; 1994.

Kooijmans, Peter H. Some Thoughts on the Relation between Extra-Legal Agreements and the Law-Creating Process. Makarczyk, Jerzy ed. Theory of International Law at the Threshold of the 21st Century. The Hague: Kluwer Law International; 1996; pp. 425-437.

Koskenniemi, Martti. The Politics of International Law. European Journal of International Law. 1990; 1:4-32.

---. International Law in a Post-Realist Era. Australian Yearbook of International Law. 1995; 16:1-19.

---. The Effect of Rights on Political Culture. Alston, Philip ed.Oxford: Oxford University Press; 1999; pp. 99-116.

Kratochwil, Friedrich. Thrasymmachos Revisited: On the Relevance of Norms and the Study of Law for International Relations. Journal of International Affairs. 1984; 37:343-356.

Kritsiotis, Dino. The Legality of the 1993 US Missile Strike on Iraq and the Right of Self-Defence in International Law. International and Comparative Law Quarterly. 1996; 45:162-177.

---. Arguments of Mass Confusion. European Journal of International Law. 2004; 15:233-278 .

Kuijper, P. J. The Court and the Tribunal of the EC and the Vienna Convention on the Law of Treaties 1969. Legal Issues of European Integration. 1998; 25:1.

Kunz, Josef L. Individual and Collective Self-Defense in Article 51 of the Charter of the United Nations. American Journal of International Law. 1947; 41:872-879.

---. The Nature of Customary International Law. American Journal of International Law. 1953; 47:662-669.

Labor-Lederer, J. J. A Legal Approach to International Terrorism. Israel Law Review. 1974; 9(2):194-220.

Lacey, Michael. Self-Defense or Self-Denial: The Proliferation of Weapons of Mass Destruction. Indiana International and Comparative Law Review. 2000; 10:293-315.

Laqueur, Walter. Reflections on Terrorism. Foreign Affairs. 1986; 65:86-100.

Lauterpacht, Elihu. The Development of the Law of International Organizations by the Decisions of International Tribunals. Recueil Des Cours Collected Courses, The Hague Academy of International Law. 1976 Apr; Tome 152: 152.

Lauterpacht, H. Revolutionary Activities by Private Persons Against Foreign States. American Journal of International Law.

Lavalle, Roberto. The International Convention for the Suppression of the Financing of Terrorism. Zeitschrift Fur Auslandisches Offentliches Recht Und Volkerrecht. 2000; 60(2):491-510.

Bibliography

Lerner, Natan. Sanctions and Counter-Measures Short of the Use of Force Against Terrorism. Israel Yearbook on Human Rights. 1989; 19:259-270.

Levenfeld, Barry. Israel's Counter-Fedayeen Tactics in Lebanon: Self-Defense and Reprisals Under Modern International Law. Columbia Journal of Transnational Law. 1982; 21:1-48.

Levitin, Michael J. The Law of Force and the Force of Law: Grenada, the Falklands, and Humanitarian Intervention. Harvard International Law Journal. 1986; 27(2, Spring):621-657.

Levitt, Geoffrey M. Intervention to Combat Terrorism and Drig Trafficking. Damrosch, Lori Fisler and and Scheffer, David J. ed. Law and Force in the New International Order. Boulder: Westview; 1991; pp. 224-231.

Lillich, Richard B. and Paxman, John M. State Responsibility for Injuries to Allens Occasioned by Terrorist Activities. The American University Law Review. 1977; 26(2):217-313.

Lillich, Richard B. ed. Transnational Terrorism: Conventions and Commentary. Michie; 1982.

Lobel, Jules. Colloquy: The Use of Force to Respond to Terrorist Attacks: The Bombing of Sudan and Afghanistan. Yale Journal of International Law. 1999; 24(Summer):537-557.

Lord McNair. The Law of Treaties Oxford University Press . Oxford University Press ; 1961.

Lowe, Vaughan. Precluding Wrongfulness or Responsibility: A Plea for Excuses. European Journal of International Law. 1999; 10(2):405-411.

Lowe, Vaughan and Warbrick, Colin ed. The United Nations and the Principles of International Law: Essays in memory of Michael Akehurst. London: Routledge; 1994.

Lukashuk, Igor I. Customary Norms in Contemporary International Law. Makarczyk, Jerzy ed. Theory of International Law at the Threshold of the 21st Century. The Hague: Kluwer Law International; 1996; pp. 487-508.

Lumme, Pirjo Elina. The Path Towards the 1998 United Nations Convention for the Suppression of Terrorist Bombings. 1999.

Macdonald, R. St. J. The Nicaragua Case: New Answers to Old Questions? Canadian Yearbook of International Law. 1986; 127-159.

Macdonald, Ronald St. John. The Use of Force by states in International Law. Bedjaoui, Mohammed ed. International Law: Achievements and Prospects. Dordrecht: Martinus Nijhoff; 1991; pp. 717-741.

MacGibbon, I. C. Some Observations on the Part of Protest in International Law. British Yearbook of International Law. 1953; 29:293-319.

---. The Scope of Acquiescence in International Law. British Yearbook of International Law. 1954; 30:143-186.

---. Customary International Law and Acquiescence. British Yearbook of International Law. 1957; 33:115-145.

Malanczuk, P. Countermeasures and Self-Defence as Circumstances Presluding Wrongfulness in the International Law Commission's Draft Articles on State Responsibility. Zeitschrift Fur Auslaendisches Oeffentliches Recht Und Voelkerrecht. 1983; 43:705-802.

Mallison, W. T. and S.V. Mallison. The Concept of Public Purpose Terror in International Law: Doctrines and Sanctions to Reduce the Destruction of Human and Material Values. Howard Law Journal. 1973; 18:12-28.

Mallison, W. Thomas and Mallison, Sally W. The Israeli Aerial Attack on June 7, 1981, Upon the Iraqi Nuclear Reactor: Aggression or Self-Defense? Vanderbilt Journal of Transnational Law. 1982; 15(3):417-448.

Bibliography

Marston, Geoffrey. Armed Intervention in the 1956 Suez Canal Crisis: The Legal Advice Tendered to the British Government. International and Comparative Law Quarterly. 1988; 37:773.

Matheson, Michael J. The Opinions of the International Court of Justice on the Threat or Use of Nuclear Weapons. American Journal of International Law. 1997; 91:417-435.

Maxwell, Taylor. The Way to Terrorism: Typology of the Formation of Terrorist Groups. Hirschmann, Kai and Gerhard, Peter ed. Terrorismus alr weltweites Phänomen. Berlin: Arno Spitz; 2000; pp. 27-36.

McCoubrey, Hilaire and White, Nigle D. International Law and Armed Conflict. Aldershot: Dartmouth; 1992.

McCredie, Jeffrey Allen. The April 14, 1986 Bombing of Libya: Act of Self-Defense or Reprisal? Case Western Reserve Journal of International Law. 1987; 19(2):215-242.

McDougal, Myres S. The Impact of International Law Upon National Law: A Policy-Oriented Perspective. 157-236.

---. International Law, Power, and Policy: A Contemporary Conception. Recueil des Cours: Collected Courses of the Hague Academy of International Law. The Hague; 1953; pp. 133-260.

---. Some Basic Theoretical Concepts about International Law: A Policy-Oriented Framework of Inquiry. Journal of Conflict Resolution. 1960; IV(3):337-354.

---. Editorial Comment: The Soviet-Cuban Quarantine and self-Defense. American Journal of International Law. 1963; 57:597-604.

---. Agora: McDougal-Lasswell Redux: The Dorsey Comment: A Modest Retrogression. American Journal of International Law. 1988; 82:51-57.

McDougal, Myres S. and Feliciano, Florentino P. International Coercion and World Public Order: The General Principles of the Law of War. The Yale Law Journal. 1958; 67(5):771-845.

---. Legal Regulation of Resort to International Coercion: Aggression and Self-Defense in Policy Perspective. The Yale Law Journal. 1959; 68(6):1057-1165.

---. Law and Minimum World Public Order: The Legal Regulation of International Coercion. 1961.

---. The International Law of War: Transnational Coercion and World public Order. Dordrecht: Martinus Nijhoff; 1994. Notes: Orginally: Law and Minimum World Public Order: The Legal Regulation of International Coercion, New Haven, Yale University Press, 1961

McDougal, Myres S.; Lasswee, Harold D., and Reisman, W. Michael. The World Constitutive Process of Authoritative Decision. Journal of Legal Education. 1967; 19(3):253-300.

McDougal, Myres S.; Lasswell, Harold D., and Reisman, W. Michael. Theories about International Law: Prologue to a Configurative Jurisprudence. McDougal, Myres S. and Reisman, W. Michael. International Law Essays: A Supplement to International Law in Contemporary Perspective. Mineola, New York: The Foundation Press; 1981; pp. 43-141.

McDougal, Myres S and Reisman, W. Michael. The Prescribing Function in the World Constitutive Process: How international Law is Made. 355-380.

McDougal, Myres S. Harold D. Lasswell and James C. Miller. The Interpretation of Agreements and World Public Order: Principles of Content and Procedure. Yale University Press ; 1967.

McDougal, Myres S. Reisman W. Michael. International Law in Policy-Oriented Perspective. Macdonald, R. St. J. and Johnston, Douglas M. The Structure and Process of International Law: Essays in Legal Philosophý, Doctrine and Theory. The Hague: Martinus Nijhoff; 1983; pp. 103-129.

Bibliography

McGinley, Ferald P. Practice as a Guide to Treaty Interpretation. The Fletcher Forum . 1985; 9:211-230.

McWhinney, Edward. International Terrorism: United Nations Projects for Legal Control. Terrorism: An International Journal. 1984; 7(2):175-184.

Meijers, H. How is International Law Made? Netherlands Yearbook of International Law. 1978; 9:3-26.

Meron, Theodor. When do Acts of Terrorism Violate Human Rights? Israel Yearbook on Human Rights. 1989; 19:271-279.

Merrills, J. G. Land and Maritime Boundary Between Cameroon and Nigeria (Cameroon v. Nigeria, Equatorial Guinea Intervening), Merits, Judgment of October 10, 2002. International and Comparative Law Quarterly. 2003; 52:788-797.

Mertus, Julie. 'Terrorism' as Ideology: Implications for Intervention. American Society of International Law Proceedings. 1999; 78-79.

Micco, Richard T. Putting the Terrorist-Sponsoring State in the Dock: Recent Changes in the Foreign Sovereign Immunities Act and the Individual's Recourse against Foreign Powers. Temple International and Comparative Law Journal. 2000; 14(1):109-147.

Moore, John Norton. Prolegomenon to the Jurisprudence of Myres McDougal and Harold Lasswell. Virginia Law Review. 1968; 54:662-688.

---. Toward Legal Restraints on International Terrorism. ASIL Procedings. 1973; 67:88-94.

---. The Secret War in Central America and the Future of World Order. American Journal of International Law. 1986; 80:43-127.

---. Deception and Deterrence in "Wars of National Liberation," State-Sponsored Terrorism and Other Forms of Secret Warfare. Carolina Academic Press; 1997.

Morison, William L. Myres S. McDougal and Twentieth-Century Jurisprudence: A Comparative Essay. Reisman, W. Michael and Weston, Burns H. eds. Toward World Order and Human Dignity: Essays in Honor of Myres S. McDougal. New York: Free Press; pp. 3-78.

Mrazek, Josef. Prohibition of the Use and Threat of Force: Self-Defense and Self-Help in International Law. Canadian Yearbook of International Law. 1989; XXVII :81.

Muellerson, Rein. The Interplay of Objective and Subjective Elements in Customary Law. Wellens, K. ed. International Law: Theory and Practice. The Hague: Kluwer Law International; 1998; pp. 161-178.

---. The Use of Force Between its Past and Future. International Peacekeeping. 1999; 5:115-128.

---. The ABM Treaty: Changed Circumstances, Extraordinary Events, Supreme Interests and International Law. International and Comparative Law Quarterly. 2001; 50(July):509-539.

Müllerson, Rein. Ordering Anarchy: International Law in International Society. Dordrecht: Martinus Nijhoff; 2000.

---. *Jus ad bellum* and International Terrorism. Israel Yearbook of International Law . 2003; 32:1-52.

Müllerson, Rein and Scheffer, David J. Legal Regulation of the Use of Force. Damrosch, Lori Fisler; Danilenko, Gennady M., and Müllerson, Rein eds. Beyond Confrontation: International Law for the Post-Cold War Era. Boulder: Westview; 1995; pp. 93-139.

Murohy, John F. Comments on the Fourth Interim Report of the ILA Committee on International Terrorism (1982). Terrorism: An International Journal. 1984; 7(2):193-197.

Bibliography

Murphy, John F. Introduction. Terrorism: An International Journal. 1984; 7(2):119-122.

---. Punishing International Terrorists: The Legal Framework for Policy Initiatives. New Jersey: Rowman and Allanheld; 1985.

---. The Future of Multilateralism and Efforts to Combat International Terrorism. Columbia Journal of Transnational Law. 1986; 25:35-99.

---. Military Responses to Terrorism: Remarks. American Society of International Law Proceedings. 1987; 81:318-319.

---. State Support of International Terrorism: Legal, Political, and Economic Dimentions. Boulder: Westview; 1989.

---. The Use of Armed Force. Murphy, John F. State Support of International Terrorism: Legal, Political, and Economic Dimentions. Boulder: Westview Press; 1989; pp. 85-111.

---. Commentary on Intervention to Combat Terrorism and Drug Trafficking. Damrosch, Lori Fisler and and Scheffer, David J. ed. Law and Force in the New International Order. Boulder: Westview Press; 1991; pp. 241-243.

---. The Control of International Terrorism. Moore, John Norton; Tipson, Frederick S., and Turner, Robert F. National Security Law. Carolina Academic Press; 1996.

Murphy, Sean. Terrorism and the Concept of "Armed Attack" in Article 51 of the U.N. Charter. Harvard International Law Review. 2002; 43:41-51.

Myjer, Eric P. J. and Nigel D. White. The Twin Towers Attack: An Unlimited Right to Self-Defence? Journal of Conflict and Security Law. 2002; 7:5.

Netanyahu, Benjamin ed. Terrorism: How the West Can Win. New York: Farrar, Straus, and Giroux; 1986.

Nicolas, Stephanie R. Negotiating in the Shadow of Outlaws. Journal of Transnational Law and Policy. 2000; 9(Spring):385-418.

Nobel, Peter. Terrorism and Human Rights. Sandbu, Magnus D. and Nordbeck, Peter. International Terrorism: Report from a Seminar Arranged by the European Law Students' Association in Lund, Sweden, 1-3 October 1987. Lund: Juristfoerlaget; 1987; pp. 103-109.

Nordquist, Myron H. and Wachenfeld, Margaret G. Legal Aspects of Reflagging Kuwaiti Tankers and Laying of Mines in the Persian Gulf. German Yearbook of International Law. 1988; 31:138-164.

Nydell, Matt S. Tensions Between International Law and Strategic Security: Implications of Israel's Preemptive Raid on Iraq's Nuclear Reactor. Virginian Journal of International Law. 1984; 24(2):459-492.

O'Brien, William V. Reprisals, Deterrence and Self-Defense in Counterterror Operations. Virginian Journal of International Law. 1990; 30:421-478.

O'Connell, D. P. The Influence of Law on Sea Power. Manchester: Manchester University Press; 1975.

O'Connell, Mary Ellen. Regulating the Use of Force in the 21st Century: The Continuing Importance of State Autonomy. Columbia Journal of Transnational Law. 1997; 36:473-492.

Okowa, Phoebe N. Case Concerning the Gabcíkovo-Nagymaros Project (Hungary/Slovakia). International and Comparative Law Quarterly . 1998; 47:688-697.

Onuf, N. G. and Peterson, V. Spike. Human Rights from an International Regime Perspective. Journal of International Affairs. 1984; 37:329-342.

Bibliography

Onuf, Nicholas Greenwood. Reprisals: Rituals, Rules, Rationales. Wodrow Wilson School of Public and International Affairs: Princeton University; 1974 Jul.

---. Global Law-Making and Legal Thought. Onuf, Nicholas Greenwood. Law-Making in the Global Community. Durham: Carolina Academic Press; 1982; pp. 1-83.

Paasche, Franz W. Note: The Use of Force in Combatting Terrorism. Columbia Journal of Transnational Law. 1987; 25:377-402.

Parks, Hays. The Protection of Civilians from Air Warfare. Israel Yearbook on Human Rights. 1997; 27:65-111.

Partan, Daniel G. Military Responses to Terrorism: Remarks. American Society of International Law Proceedings. 1987; 81:288.

Paust, Jordan J. Response to President's Notes on Missile Attack on Baghdad. American Society of International Law Newslatter. 1993 Sep.

Pauwelyn, Joost. Conflict of Norms in Public International Law: How WTO Law Relates to other Rules of International Law. Cambridge University Press; 2003.

Pease, Kelly Kate and Forsythe, David P. Human Rights, Humanitarian Intervention, and World Politics. Human Rights Quarterly. 1993; 15:290-314.

Pedersen, Fred C. Comment: Controlling International Terrorism: An Analysis of Unilateral Force and Proposals for Multilateral Cooperation. Toledo Law Review. 1976; 8(Fall):209-250.

Peters, Anne. There is Nothing More Practical than a Good Theory: An Overview of Contemporary Approaches to International Law. German Yearbook of International Law . 2001; 44:25-38.

Plant, Glen. The Convention for the Suppression of Unlawful Acts Against the Safety of Maritime Navigation. International and Comparative Law Quarterly. 1990; 39:27-56.

Polat, Necati. International Law, the Inherent Instability of the International System, and International Violence. Oxford Journal of Legal Studies. 1999; 19(Spring):51-70.

Pugh, Michael. Legal Aspects of the Rainbow Warrior Affair. International and Comparative Law Quarterly. 1987; 36:655-669.

Quigley, John. Israel's Forty-Five Year Emergency: Are There Time Limits to Derogations from Human Rights Obligations? Michigan Journal of International Law. 1994; 15(Winter):491-518.

---. The Rule of Non-Inquiry and Human Rights Treaties. Catholic University Law Review. 1996; 45(Summer):1213-1248.

---. The Role of Law in a Palestinian-Israeli Accommodation. Case Western Reserve Journal of International Law. 1999; 31(Spring/Summer):351-380.

Raby, Jean. The State of Necessity and the Use of Force to Protect Nationals. Canadian Yeabook of International Law. 1988; XXVI:253.

Rapoport, David C. Terrorism and Weapons of the Apocalypse. National Security Studies Quarterly. 1999; Summer:49-67.

Ratner, Steven R. Jus ad bellum and jus in bello after September 11. American Journal of I Nternational Law. 2002; 96:905-921.

Rauch, Elmar. The Protocol Additonal to the Geneva Convention for the Protection of Victims of International Armed

Conflict and the United Nations Convention on the Law of the Sea: Repercussions on the Law of Naval Warfare. Berlin: Duncker & Humbolt; 1984.

Reisman, W. Michael. Unilateral Action and the Transformation of the World Constitutive Process: The Special Problem of Humanitarian Intervention.

---. The Regime of Straits and National Security: An Appraisal of International Lawmaking. American Journal of International Law. 1980; 74:48-76.

---. International Law Making: A Process of Communication. American Society of International Law Proceedings. 1981; 101-120.

---. Editorial Comment: Coercion and Self-Determination: Construing Charter Article 2(4). American Journal of International Law. 1984; 78:642-645.

---. International Incidents: Introduction to a New Genre in the Study of International Law. The Yale Journal of International Law. 1984; 10(1):1-20.

---. Remarks: McDougal's Jurisprudence: Utility, Influence, Controversy. American Society of International Law Proceedings. 1985; 273-280.

---. Old Wine in New Bottles: The Reagan and Brezhnev Doctrines in Contemporary Internartional Law and Practice. Yale Journal of International Law. 1988; 13:171-198.

---. No Man's Land: International Legal Regulation of Coercive Responses to Protracted and Low Level Conflict. Houston Journal of International Law. 1989; 11:317-330.

---. Editorial Comment: International Law after the Cold War. American Journal of International Law. 1990; 84:859-866.

---. Sovereignty and Human Rights in Contemporary International Law. American Journal of International Law. 1990; 84:866-876.

---. Allocating Competences to Use Coercion in the Post-Cold War World: Practices, Conditions, and Prospects. Damrosch, Lori Fisler and Scheffer, David J. ed. Law and Force in the New International Order. Boulder: Westview Press; 1991; pp. 26-48.

---. New Scenarios of Threats to International Peace and Security: Developing Legal Capacities for Adequate Responses. Delbrueck, Jost ed. The Future of International Law Enforcement: New Scenarios - New Law? Berlin: Duncker & Humbolt; 1992; pp. 13-38.

---. Forum: The Baghdad Bombing: Self-Defence or Reprisals?: The Raid on Baghdad: Some Reflections on its Lawfulness and Implications. European Journal of International Law. 1994; 5:120-133.

---. Designing and Managing the Future of the State. European Journal of International Law. 1997; 8:409-420.

---. The Lessons of Qana. Yale Journal of International Law. 1997; 22:381-399.

---. International Legal Responses to Terrorism. Houston Journal of International Law. 1999; 22(Fall):3-61.

---. Kosovo's Antinomies. American Journal of International Law. 1999; 93:860-862.

Ress, Georg. Die Bedeutung der nachfolgenden Praxis für die Vertragsinterpretation nach der Wiener Vertragsrechtskonvention (WVRK). Bieder, Roland and Georg Ress. Die Dynamik des Europäischen Gemeinschaftsrechts/The Dynamics of EC-Law. Nomos; 1987.

Reuter, Paul. Introduction to the Law of Treaties. Kegan Paul International ; 1995.

Bibliography

Reynolds, James S. Expansion of Territorial Jurisdiction: A Response to the Rise in Terrorism. Journal of National Security Law. 1997; 1(1):105-110.

Richardson III, Henry J. 'Failed States', Self-Determination and Preventive Diplomacy: Colonialist Nostalgia and Democratic Expectations. Temple International and Comparative Law Journal. 1996; 10(Spring):1-78.

Roberts, Anthea Elizabeth. Traditional and Modern Approaches to Customary International Law: A Reconciliation. American Journal of International Law. 2001; 95:757-791.

Roberts, Guy. Military Responses to Terrorism: Remarks. American Society of International Law Proceedings. 1987; 81:318.

Roberts, Guy B. Self-Help In Combatting State-Sponsored Terrorism: Self-Defense and Paecetime Reprisals. Case Western Reserve Journal of International Law. 1987; 19(2):243-293.

---. The Counterproliferation Self-Help Paradigm: A Legal Regime for Enforcing the Norm Prohibiting the Proliferation of Weapons of Mass Destruction. Denver Journal of International Law and Policy. 1999; 27(Summer):483-539.

Robinson, Glenn E. The Growing Authoritarianism of the Arafat Regime. Survival. 1997; 39(2):42-56.

Rodick, Burleigh Cushing. The Doctrine of Necessity in International Law. Columbia University Press; 1928.

Rodley, Nigel S. Can Armed Opposition Groups Violate Human Rights? Mahoney, K. E. and Mahoney, P. Human Rights in the Twenty-first Century. Dordrecht: Kluwer Law International; 1993; pp. 297-318.

Rogers, John M. Prosecuting Terrorists: When Does Apprehension in Violation of International Law Preclude Trial? University of Miami Law Review. 1987; 42:447-465.

Romano, John-Alex. Note: Combatting Terrorism and Weapons of Mass Destruction: Reviving the Doctrine of a State of Necessity. Georgetown Law Journal. 1999; 87(April):1023-1057.

Ronzitti, Natalino. Rescuing Nationals Abroad Through Military Coercion and Intervention on the Grounds of Humanity. Dordrecht: Martinus Nijhoff; 1985.

---. Use of Force, Jus Cogens and State Consent. Cassese, Antonio. The Current Legal Regulationof the Use of Force. Matinus Nijhoff; 1986; p. 147.

---. Passage Through International Starits in Time of International Armed Conflict. International Law at the Time of its Codification: Essays in Honour of Roberto Ago. Milano: Multa Paucis; 1987; pp. 363-383.

---. Lessons of International Law from NATO's Armed Intervention Against the Federal Republic of Yugoslavia. The International Spectator. 1999; XXXIV:45-54.

---. The Legality of Covert Operations Against Terrorism in Foreign States. Bianchi, A. Enforcing International Law Norms Against Terrorism. 2004; pp. 17-24.

Rosenstock, Robert. The Declaration of Principles of International Law Concerning Friendly Relations: A Survey. American Journal of International Law. 1971; 65:713-735.

Rostow, Eugene. Overcoming Denial. Netanyahu, Benjamin ed. Terrorism: How the West Can Win. New York: Farrar, Straus, and Giroux; 1986; pp. 146-148.

Rostow, Nicholas. The International Use of Force Aftre the Cold War. Harvard International Law Journal. 1991; 32(2, Spring):411-421.

Roth, Brad R. Bending the Law, Breaking it, or Developing it? The United States and its Humanitarian Use of Force in the Post-Cold War Era. Byers, Michael and Georg Nolte. United States Hegemony and the Foundations of International Law. Cambridge University Press; 2003; pp. 232-263 .

Rowe, Peter. Kosovo 1999: The Air Campaign: Have the Provisions of Additional Protocal I Withstood the Test? International Review of the Red Cross. 2000; 82(837):147-164.

Rowles, James P. Military Responses to Terrorism: Substantive and Procedural Constraints in International Law. American Society of International Law Proceedings. 1987; 81:307-317.

Rubin, Alfred P. Current Legal Approaches to International Terrorism. Terrorism: An International Journal. 1984; 7(2):147-161.

Rubin, Benjamin. PLO Violence and Legitimate Combatancy: A Response to Professor Green. Israel Yearbook on Human Rights. 1989; 19:167-185.

Saddy, Fehmy. International Terrorism, Human Rights, and World Order. Terrorism: An International Journal. 1982; 5(4):325-351.

Sadurska, Romana. Threats of Force. American Journal of International Law. 1988; 82:239-268.

Sandbu, Magnus D. and Nordbeck, Peter. Introduction. Sandbu, Magnus D. and Nordbeck, Peter. International Terrorism: Report from a Seminar Arranged by the European Law Students' Association in Lund, Sweden, 1-3 October 1987. Lund: Juristfoerlaget; 1987; pp. 11-19.

Sato, Tetsuo. Evolving Constitutions of International Organizations . Kluwer Law International ; 1996.

Scales Jr., Robert H. Russia's Clash in Chechnya: Implications for Future War. National Security Studies Quarterly. 2000; Spring:49-57.

Schachter, Oscar. Towards a Theory of International Obligation. Virginia Journal of International Law. 1968; 8(2):300-322.

---. The Invisible College of International Lawyers. Northwestern University Law Review. 1977; 72(2):217-226.

---. The Legality of Pro-Democratic Invasion. American Journal of International Law. 1984; 78:645-650.

---. The Right of States to Use Armed Force. Michigan Law Review. 1984; 82(April/May):1620-1646.

---. Self-Help in International Law: U.S. Action in the Iranian Hostage Crisis. Journal of International Affairs. 1984; 37:231-246.

---. Remarks: McDougal's Jurisprudence: Utility, Influence, Controversy. American Society of International Law Proceedings. 1985; 266-273.

---. In Defense of International Rules on the Use of Force. University of Chicago Law Review. 1986; 53:113-146.

---. Introduction: Self-Judging Self-Defense. Case Western Reserve Journal of International Law. 1987; 19(2):121-128.

---. The Extraterritorial Use of Force Against Terrorist Bases. Houston Journal of International Law. 1989; 11:309-316.

---. Just War and Human Rights. Pace University School of Law Yearbook of International Law. 1989; 1(1):1-19.

---. The Lawful Use of Force by a State Against Terrorists in Another Country. Israel Yearbook on Human Rights. 1989; 19:209-231.
  Notes: Also in Han, Henry H. (ed.); Terrorism and Political Violence: Limits and Possibilities of Legal Control, Oceanea Publications, New York, 1993, 243-266

Bibliography

---. International Law in Theory and Practice. Dordrecht: Marinus Nijhoff; 1991.

---. United Nations Law in the Gulf Conflict. American Journal of International Law. 1991; 85:452-473.

---. Remarks: Implementing Limitations on the Use of Force: The Doctrine of Proportionality and Necessity. American Society of International Law Proceedings. 1992; 39-40.

---. Sovereignty - Then and Now. MacDonald, Ronald St. John. Essays in Honour of Wang Tieya. Dordrecht: Martinus Nijhoff; 1994; pp. 671-687.

---. New Custom: Power, *Opinio Juris* and Contrary Practice. Makarczyk, Jerzy ed. Theory of International Law at the Threshold of the 21st Century. The Hague: Kluwer Law International; 1996; pp. 531-540.

---. The Decline of the Nation-state and its Implications for International Law. Charney, Jonathan I.; Anton, Donald K., and O'Connell, Mary Ellen eds. Politics, Values and Functions: International Law in the 21st Century - Essays in Honor of Professor Louis Henkin. The Hague: Martinus Nijhoff; 1997; pp. 13-28.

---. The Role of Power in International Law. American Society of International Law Proceedings. 1999; 200-205.

Schaefer, Andrew. 1995 Canada-Spain Fishing Dispute (the Turbot War). Georgetown International Environmental Law Review. 1996; 8:437-449 .

Scheideman, Sara N. Note: Standards of Proof in Forcible Responses to Terrorism. Syracuse Law Review. 2000; 50:249-284.

Schmitt, Michael N. Counter-Terrorism and the Use of Force in International Law. Israel Yearbook on Human Rights. 2003; 32:53-116.

Schneider, Jan. The Forst ICJ Chamber Experiment: The Gulf of Maine Case: The Nature of Equitable Result. American Journal of International Law. 1985; 79:539-577.

Schreiber, Ross E. Note: Ascertaining Opinio Juris of States Concerning Norms Involving the Prevention of International Terrorism: A Focus on the U.N. Process. Boston University International Law Journal. 1998; 16(Spring):309-330.

Schwabach, Aaron. Yugoslavia v. NATO, Security Council Resolution 1244, and the Law of Humanitarian Intervention. Syracuse Journal of International Law and Commerce. 2000; 27:77-101.

Schwebel, S. M. Aggression, Intervention and Self-Defence in Modern International Law. RC.

Schwebel, Stephen M. Indirect Aggression in the International Court. Damrosch, Lori Fisler and and Scheffer, David J. ed. Law and Force in the New International Order. Boulder: Westview Press; 1991; pp. 298-303.

Schwelb, Egon. Amendments to Articles 23, 27 and 61 of the Charter of the United Nations. American Journal of International Law. 1965; 59:834.

Shaikh, Ayaz R. A Theoretic Approach to Transnational Terrorism. Georgetown Law Journal. 1992; 80:2131-2174.

Shamgar, Meir. An International Convention Against Terrorism. Netanyahu, Benjamin ed. Terrorism: How the West Can Win. New York: Farrar, Straus, and Giroux; 1986; pp. 157-161.

Shannon, Vaughn P. Norms are What States Make of Them: The Political Psychology of Norm Violation. International Studies Quarterly. 2000; 44:293-316.

Shapira, Amos. The Six-Day War and the Right of Self-Defence. Israel Law Review. 1971; 6:65-80.

Shapiro, Howard M. Terrorism in a Democratic Society. Journal of National Security Law. 1997; 1(1):95-104.

Bibliography

Sharp Sr., Walter Gary. The Use of Armed Force Against Terrorism: American Hegomony or Impotence? Chicago Journal of International Law. 2000; 1(1):37-47.

Sheehan, Jeffrey A. The Entebbe Raid: The Principle of Self-Help in International Law as Justification for State Use of Armed Force. The Fletcher Forum. 1977; 1(Spring):135-153.

Shen, Jianming. Terrorism and International Responses: Toward More Effective Suppression, Prevention and Elimination of Terrorism and Other Forms of Violence. American Society of International Law Proceedings. 1999; 80.

Shubber, Sami. Is Hijacking of Aircraft Piracy in International Law? British Yearbook of International Law. 1968; 43:193-204.

Simma, Bruno. The Charter of the United Nations: A Commentary. Oxford University Pres; 1994.

---. NATO, the UN and the use of force: legal aspects. European Journal of International Law. 1999; 10:1-22.

Simma, Bruno and Andreas Paulus. The Responsibility of Individuals for Human Rights Abuses in Internal Conflict: A Positivist View. American Journal of International Law . 1999; 93:302-316 .

Sinclair, Ian. The Vienna Convention on the Law of Treaties. Manchester: Manchester University Press; 1984.

---. The International Law Commission. Cambridge: Grotius, Cambridge University Press; 1987.

Singh, J. N. Use of Force Under International Law. New Delhi: Harnam ; 1984.

Skubiszewski, K. Use of Force by States. Collective Security. Law of War and Neutrality. Soerensen, Max ed. Manual of Public International Law. New York: St. Martin's Press; 1968.

Slaughter, Anne-Marie and Steven R. Ratner. Symposium on Method in International Law: The Method is the Message. American Journal of International Law . 1999; 93:410-423.

Slaughter, Anne-Marie and William Burk-White. An International Constitutional Moment. Harvard International Law Journal . 2002; 43:1-21.

Sofaer, Abraham D. Fighting Terrorism Through Law. Department of State Bulletin. 1985; 85(2103):38-42.

---. Terrorism and the Law. Foreign Affair. 1986; 64:901-922.

---. Terrorism, The Law, and the National Defense. Military Law Review. 1989; 126(Fall):89-123.

Sohn, Louis B. Enhancing the Role of the General Assembly of the United Nations in Crystallizing International Law. Makarczyk, Jerzy ed. Theory of International Law at the Threshold of the 21st Century. The Hague: Kluwer Law International; 1996; pp. 549-561.

Sornarajah, Muthu-Cumaraswamy. 'Terrorism' NOT Useful for Analysing Random Violence. American Society of International Law Proceedings. 1999; 79-80.

Sprinzak, Ehud. The Great Superterrorism Scare. Foreign Policy. 1998; (Fall):110-124.

Stavropoulos, Constantin A. The Practice of Voluntary Abstentions by Permanent Members of the Security Council under Articel 27, Paragraph 3, of the Charter of the United Nations. American Journal of International Law. 1967; 61:737-752.

Stein, Torstein. How Much Humanity Do Terrorists Deserve? Delissen, Astrid J. M. and Tanja, Gerard J. Humanitarian Law of Armed Conflict: Challenges Ahead: Eassays in Honour of Frits Kalshoven. Dordrecht: Martinus Nijhoff; 1991; pp. 567-581.

Bibliography

Stein, Torsten. International Measures Against Terrorism and Sanctions By and Against Third States. Archiv Des Völkerrechts. 1992; 30:38-54.

Stephan III, Paul B. Prevention and Control of International Terrorism. Stephan III, Paul B. and Klimenko, Boris M. International Law and International Security: Military And political Dimensions, A US-Soviet Dialogue. New York: M.E. Sharpe; 1991; pp. 321-354.

Stern, Brigitte. Custom at the Heart of International Law. Duke Journal of Comparative & International Law. 2001; 11:89-108.

Stone, Julius. Hopes and Loopholes in the 1974 Definition of Aggression. American Journal of International Law. 1977; 71:224-246.

Strawson, John. Palestine's Basic Law: Constituting New Identities Through Liberating Legal Culture. Loyola Los Angeles International and Comparative Law Journal. 1998; 20(March):411-432.

Stromseth, Jane E. Commentary on the Use of Force Against Terrorism and Drug Trafficking. Damrosch, Lori Fisler and and Scheffer, David J. ed. Law and Force in the New International Order. Boulder: Westview Press; 1991; pp. 237-240.

Stuesser, Lee. Active Defense: State Military Response to International Terrorism. California Western International Law Journal. 1987; 17(1):1-42.

---. Active Defense: State Military Response to International Terrorism. California Western International Law Journal. 1987; 17(1):1-42.

Sucharitkul, Sompong. Terrorism as an International Crime: Questions of Responsibility and Complicity. Israel Yearbook on Human Rights. 1989; 19:247-258.

Sundberg, Jacob W. F. Comments on the Fourth Interim Report of the Committe on International Terrorism. Terrorism: An International Journal. 1984; 7(2):185-192.

---. Introduction to International Terrorism - The Tactics and Strategy of International Terrorism. Sandbu, Magnus D. and Nordbeck, Peter. International Terrorism: Report from a Seminar Arranged by the European Law Students' Association in Lund, Sweden, 1-3 October 1987. Lund: Juristfoerlaget; 1987; pp. 21-38.

Surchin, Alan D. Note: Terror and the Law: The Unilateral Use of Force and the June 1993 Bombing of Baghdad. Duke Journal of Comparative and International Law. 1995; 5(Spring):457-496.

Suzuki, Eisuke. The New Haven School of International Law: An Invitation to a Policy-Oriented Jurisprudence. Yale Studies in World Public Orden. 1974; 1:1-48.

Talmon, Stefan. The Cyprus Question before the European Court of Justice. European Journal of International Law . 2001; 12:727-750.

Tan, Dawn. International Law and the Use of Force: The Force of United Nations Norms and Processes in the Arab-Israeli Conflict. Singpore Law Review. 1997; 18:404-454.

Tanca, Antonio. Foreign Armed Intervention in Internal Conflict. Dordrecht: Martinus Nijhoff; 1993.

Taulbee, J. L. Retaliation and Irregular Warfare in Contemporary International Law. International Lawyer. 1973; 7(1):195-204.

Taulbee, James Larry and Anderson, John. Reprisal Redux. Case Western Reserve Jurnal of International Law. 1984; 16:309-336.

Teichman, Jenny. How to Define Terrorism. Philosophy. 1989; 64:505-517.

Bibliography

Teplitz, Robert F. Taking Assassination Attempts Seriously: Did the United States Violate International Law in Forcefully Responding to the Iraqi Plot to Kill George Bush? Cornell International Law Journal. 1995; 28:569-618.

Terry, James P. State Terrorism: A Juridical Examination in Terms of Existing International Law. Journal for Palestine Studies. 1980; 10:94-117.

---. Countering State-Sponsored Terrorism: A Law-Policy Analysis. Naval Law Review. 1986; 36:159-186.

Thirlway, H. W. A. International Customary Law and Codification. Leiden: A.W. Sijthoff; 1972.

Thirlway, Hugh. The Law and Procedure of the International Court of Justice 1960-1989, Part Three. British Yearbook of International Law. 1991; 62:56.

Thornberry, Patrick. Internmational Law and its Discontents: The U.S. Raid on Libya. Liverpool Law Review. 1986; 8(1):53-64.

Thürer, Daniel. The "Failed State" and International Law. International Review of the Red Cross. 1999; (No. 836):731-761.

Tipson, Frederick Samson. The Lasswell-McDougal Enterprise: Roward a World Public Order of human Dignity. Virginia Journal of International Law. 1974; 14(3):535-585.

Toefer, Charles. Recent Books on International Law: Book Review: Limits of Law, Prerogatives of Power: Intervention after Kosovo. By Michael J. Glennon. American Journal Of International Law. 2002; 96:489-493 .

Toensing, Victoria. The Legal Case for Using Force. Livingstone, Neil C. and Arnold, Terrell E. ed. Fighting Back: Winning the War against Terrorism. Lexington: Lexington Books; 1986; pp. 145-156.

Tomuschat, von Christian. Gewalt und Gewaltverbot als Bestimmungsfaktoren der Weltordnung. Europa Archiv. 1981; 11:325-334.

Travalio, Gregory M. Terrorism, International Law, and the Use of Military Force. Wisconsin International Law Journal. 2000; 18(1):145-191.

Trimble, Philip R. A Revisionist View of Customary International Law. UCLA Law Review. 1986; 33:665-732.

---. Review Essay: International Law World Order and Critical Legal Studies. Stanford Law Rev. 1990; 42:811-845.

Tucker, Robert W. Reprisals and Self-Defense: The Customary Law. American Journal of International Law. 1972; 66:586-596.

Vamvoukos, Athanassios. Termination of Treaties in International Law: The Doctrines of Rebus Sic Stantibus and Desuetude. Clarendon Press; 1985.

Verwey, W. D. Humanitarian Intervention under International Law. Netherlands International Law Review. 1985; 32:357.

Veway, Wil D. The International Hostages Convention and National Liberation Movements. American Journal of International Law. 1981; 75:69-92.

Villiger, Mark E. Customary International Law and Treaties. Kluwer Law International; 1997.

Waldmann, Peter. Terrorismus als weltweites Phänomen: Eine Einführung. Hirschmann, Kai and Gerhard, Peter ed. Terrorismus alr weltweites Phänomen. Berlin: Arno Spitz; 2000; pp. 11-26.

Waldock, C. H. M. The Regulation of the Use of Force by Individual States in International Law. Recueil Des Cours:

Bibliography

Collected Courses of the Hague Academy of International Law. 1952.

Wedgwood, Ruth. NATO's Campaign in Yugoslavia.

---. Unilateral Action in the U.N. System.

---. Proportionality and Necessity in American National Security Decision Making. American Society of International Law Proceedings. 1992; 58-62.

---. The Enforcement of Security Council Resolution 687: The Threat of Force Against Iraq's Weapons of Mass Destruction. American Journal of International Law. 1998; 92:724-728.

---. NATO's Campaign in Yugoslavia. American Journal of International Law. 1999; 93:828-834.

---. Responding to terrorism: The Strikes Against bin Laden. Yale Journal of International Law. 1999; 24(Summer):559-.

Weil, Prosper. Towards Relative Normativity in International Law. American Journal of International Law. 1983; 77:413-442.

Weisburd, A. Mark. Use of Force: The Practice of States since World War II . Penn State Press; 1997.

---. The War in Iraq and the Dilemma of Controlling the International Use of Force. Texas International Law Journal . 2004; 39:521-560 .

Weller, Marc. The US, Iraq and the Use of Force in a Unipolar World. Survival. 1999; 41(4):81-100.

Weston, Burn H. Remarks: McDougal's Jurisprudence: Utility, Influence, Controversy. American Society of International Law Proceedings. 1985; 266.

White, N. D. The Legality of Bombing in the Name of Humanity. Journal of Conflict and Security Law. 2000; 5:27-43.

Wilkinson, Paul. The Strategic Implications of Terrorism.

Williams, Sharon A. International Law and Terrorism: Age-Old Problems, Different Targets. Canadian Yearbook of International Law. 1988; 87-117.

Willson, Carolyn L. Changing the Charter: The United Nations Prepares for the Twenty-First Century. American Journal of International Law. 1996; 90:115-126.

Wing, Adrien Katherine. The Palestinian Basic Law: Embryonic Constitutionalism. Case Western Reserve Journal of International Law. 1999; 31(Spring/Summer):383-426.

Witten, Samuel M. The International Convention for the Suppression of Terrorist Bombings. American Journal of International Law. 1998; 92:774-781.

Wolfke, Karol. Custom in Present International Law. Martinus Nijhoff; 1993.

---. Some Reflections on Kinds of Rules and International Law-Making by Practice. Makarczyk, Jerzy ed. Theory of International Law at the Threshold of the 21st Century. The Hague: Kluwer Law International; 1996; pp. 587-595.

---. Treaties and Custom: Aspects of Interrelation. Klabbers, J. and Lefeber, R. ed. Essays on the Law of Treaties. Kluwer Law International; 1998.

Wolfrum, Rüdiger. The Attack of September 11, 2001, the Wars Against the Taliban and Iraq: Is There a Need to Reconsider International Law on the Recourse to Force and the Rules in Armed Conflict? Max Planck

Bibliography

Yearbook of United Nations Law . 2003; 7:1-78.

Wright, Quincy. The Cuban Quarantine. American Society of International Law Proceedings. 1963; 57:9-10.

Wu, Edieth Y. Saddam Hussein as Hostes Humani Generis? Should the U.S. Intervene? Syracuse Journal of International Law and Commerce. 1998; 26:55-94.

Yee, Sienho. The News the *Opinio Juris* "Is Not a Necessary Element of Customary [International] Law" Is Greatly Exaggerated. German Yearbook of International Law. 2000; 43:227-238.

Yoder, Amos. The Effectiveness of UN Action Against International Terrorism: Conclusions and Comments. Terrorism: An International Journal. 1983; 6(4):587-592.

---. United Nations Resolutions against International Terrorism. Terrorism: An International Journal. 1983; 6(4):503-517.

Zacklin, Ralph. The Amendment of the Constitutive Instruments of the United Nations and Specialized Agencies. A.W. Sijthoff; 1968.

Zedalis, Rex J. Preliminary Thoughts on Some Unresolved Questions Involving the Law of Anticipatory Self-Defense. Case Western Reserve Journal of International Law. 1987; 19(2):129-170.

Zemanek, Karl. What is "State Prectice" and Who Makes It? Beyerlin, Ulrich; Bothe, Michael; Hofmann, Rainer, and Petersmann, Ernst-Ulrich. Recht zwischen Umbruch und Bewahrung: Festschrift für Rudolf Bernhardt. Berlin; 1995; pp. 289-306.

---. Unilateral Legal Acts Revisited. Wellens, K. ed. International Law: Theory and Practice. The Hague: Kluwer Law International; 1998; pp. 209-221.

---. New Trends in the Enforcemnet of erga omnes Obligations. Max Planck Yearbook of United Nations Law. 2000; 4:1.

Zimmer, Gerhard. Terrorismus udn Völkerrecht: Militärische Zwangsanwendung, Selbstverteidigung und Schutz der internationalen Sicherheit. Aachen: Shaker; 1998.

Zoller, Elisabeth. The "Corporate Will" of the United Nations and the Rights of the Minority. American Journal of International Law. 1987; 81:610-634.

Zubel, Eric. The Lockerbie Controversy: Tension Between the International Court of Justice and the Security Council. Annual Survey of International and Comparative Law. 1999; 5(Spring):259-285.

Zuckerman, Adrian A. S. Coercion and the Judicial Ascertainmant of Truth. Israel Law Review. 1989; 23(No. 2-3):357-374.

Index

Index